Whither Socialism?

The Wicksell Lectures

A Search-Equilibrium Approach to the Micro Foundations of Macroeconomics, Peter A. Diamond, 1982

The Informational Role of Prices, Sanford J. Grossman, 1989

Whither Socialism? Joseph E. Stiglitz, 1994

Whither Socialism?

Joseph E. Stiglitz

The MIT Press
Cambridge, Massachusetts
London, England

Third printing, 1996

© 1994 Massachusetts Institute of Technology

This book was set in Palatino by Asco Trade Typesetting Ltd., Hong Kong and was printed and bound in the United States of America.

Library of Congress Cataloging-in-Publication Data

Stiglitz, Joseph E.
  Whither socialism / Joseph E. Stiglitz.
    p.   cm. — (The Wicksell lectures ; 1990)
  Expanded on the Wicksell Lectures presented at the Stockholm School of
  Economics in April 1990.
  Includes bibliographical references and index.
  ISBN 0-262-19340-X (h), 0-262-69182-5 (p)
  1. Mixed economy—Mathematical models. 2. Capitalism—Mathematical models.
3. Neoclassical school of economics. I. Title. II. Series.
HB90.S78   1994
330.12'6—dc20   93-43188
                                                                    CIP

The Wicksell Lectures

In 1958 The Wicksell Lecture Society, in cooperation with the Social Science Institute of Stockholm University, the Stockholm School of Economics, and the Swedish Economic Association, inaugurated a series of lectures to honor the memory of Knut Wicksell (1851–1926). Until 1975 lectures were given each year. After a period of dormancy the series was reinaugurated in 1979 by the Swedish Economic Association. Starting with the 1982 lectures, a set of lectures has been offered every two years.

Contents

mkt failure + govt failure

13 Asking the Right Questions: Theory and Evidence   231

14 Five Myths about Markets and Market Socialism   249

15 Some Tentative Recommendations   255

16 Philosophical Speculations   269

17 Conclusions   279

Preface

This book expands on the Wicksell Lectures I presented at the Stockholm School of Economics in April 1990. I had originally planned to present an overview of the current state of the economics of information, the focus of much of my research during the past two decades. But the events in Eastern Europe—the collapse of socialism at a wholly unanticipated rate—raised new policy questions and revived old theoretical issues: How was the transition to a market economy to be effected? What did these experiences have to say about the long-standing debate concerning the choice of alternative economic systems?

These questions were related to a third: What did conventional economic models have to say about such fundamental economic issues? The conclusion that I reached went beyond the critique that the standard models had little to say about these questions. It seemed to me that the standard models were partly to blame for the disastrous situation in which so many Eastern European countries found themselves. In an oft-quoted passage, Keynes wrote

The ideas of economists and political philosophers, both when they are right and when they are wrong, are more powerful than is commonly understood. Indeed the world is ruled by little else. Practical men, who believe themselves to be quite exempt from any intellectual influence, are usually the slaves of some defunct economist. Madmen in authority, who hear voices in the air, are distilling their frenzy from some academic scribbler of a few years back. I am sure that the power of vested interests is vastly exaggerated compared with the gradual encroachment of ideas.

A strong case could be made for the proposition that ideas about economics had led close to half the world's population to untold suffering.

Neoclassical economics often set itself up in contradistinction to Marxian economics. But neoclassical economics, at least in the version that became popular within the Anglo-American community, did not really provide a viable alternative. It provided a model of the economy that seemed too distant from the underlying forces which generated support for Marxian economics in its hypotheses, its descriptions, and its concerns. By arguing that we were seemingly in the best of all possible worlds, it did not speak adequately to the needs of those who saw economic misery all around them. Worse still, while showing the power of markets, it seemed to argue that socialism could work: Market socialism could make use of markets, and yet the economy be spared the worst features of capitalism.

That this conclusion was wrong seems by now apparent. But why it is wrong is instructive. It tells us something about both the economy and the models we have used to study capitalism. A major objective of these lectures is telling that story.

It will come as no surprise to those who have followed my work that I see the critical failing in the standard neoclassical model to be in its assumptions concerning information. In my earlier work on the economics of information, I had shown that slight perturbations in the standard information assumptions drastically changed all the major results of standard neoclassical theory: The theory was simply not robust at all.

It is my hope that these lectures go beyond the by now familiar carping with the standard model, to show how the new information theoretic paradigm can provide new insights into the theoretical issues of how the economy functions—for instance, the role of competition and decentralization—and into the policy prescriptions for the practical issues facing the economies in transition. I should emphasize, however, that while it is the informational assumptions underlying the standard theory which are perhaps its Achilles heel, its failures go well beyond that: The assumptions concerning completeness of markets, competitiveness of markets, and the absence of innovation are three that I stress.

The construction of a new paradigm is a slow process. What I have called the standard theory has been repeatedly refined over the years. The theory can now be stated with great mathematical generality. Yet that greater generality does not help the relevance of the theory. The question of whether the underlying theory has anything to say about our economy does not rely at all on differentiability of the relevant functions. That so much of our profession's resources should have been devoted to refining a model that has so little to say about the economy suggests an inefficiency in the market place of ideas, which is at least as great as the inefficiency in the markets for capital and labor.

Formal mathematical models capturing some aspect of the ideas discussed in the following pages—for instance, the role of competition in providing information, the role of decentralization in organizations where each individual has limited information, or the role of government intervention in economies with incomplete markets and imperfect information —have been developed. But it is not my intention here to review or extend those models: The interested reader can turn to the references. Rather, it has seemed to me that the function of a lecture series such as this is to put into perspective a set of ideas. If I have succeeded in raising doubts about the reigning paradigm, if I have persuaded the reader that there is an alternative paradigm worth pursuing, and if, on that account, there is a slight reallocation of our profession's intellectual resources, then I will have accomplished my purpose. If the lectures prove helpful to those in the process of transition, if not in providing answers, at least in helping to frame the discussion, then I will be even more pleased.

I owe a great debt to my students, colleagues, and, in particular, coauthors with whom I have discussed many of the ideas in this book over the past two decades. The influences of Richard Arnott, Avi Braverman, Partha Dasgupta, Bruce Greenwald, Michael Rothschild, Barry Nalebuff, Steve Salop, David Sappington, Carl Shapiro, and Andrew Weiss should be particularly evident. Research assistance was provided by Joshua Gans and Michael Smart. Their insightful comments have greatly improved the final manuscript. Jean Koentop and Linda Handelman did their usual excellent secretarial jobs, editing the manuscript as they typed.

I have benefited too from the many comments of colleagues who attended the lectures in Stockholm and colleagues who participated in seminars in Budapest, Prague, and Rome, at which versions of various chapters were presented. My interest in the problems of socialism goes back to graduate student days, when I made an expedition to the Central School of Statistics in Warsaw to talk with Lange and Kalecki and their disciples. I gained many insights into the theory and practice of socialism, and I greatly appreciated their gracious hospitality. My interest in the problems of transition was first piqued in 1981, at a meeting sponsored by the National Academy of Sciences and the Chinese Academy of Social Sciences in Wingspreads, Wisconsin (at which I presented an early version of one of the chapters of this book), and a return visit in Beijing the following summer. Since then, I have had the good fortune to make several visits to Hungary, Czechoslovakia, Romania, Russia, and China, but I cannot claim, on the basis of these quick glimpses, to be an expert on the host of problems that these countries face. I hope, and believe, that the theoretical insights may be of some value.

I would like to acknowledge the assistance of several organizations that have provided financial support and facilitated the research that lies behind these lectures: the National Science Foundation, the Sloan Foundation, the Hoover Institution at Stanford University, the Government of Romania, the Institute for Policy Reform, the Ministry of Finance of the People's Republic of China, and the World Bank. Most important, I would like to acknowledge the support of Stanford University, which has created an atmosphere in which active discussion of the most fundamental ideas is carried out in an open and vigorous manner and which has provided me with colleagues and students from whom I learn so much every day.

Whither Socialism?

1   The Theory of Socialism and the Power of Economic Ideas

We have come to learn in this century of the power of economic ideas. It is not just in the debating halls of academe that rival views of how society should organize itself have been contested but on the battlefields of Korea, Vietnam, Afghanistan, and Central America. To be sure, in each case, more than just economic ideologies were at stake. The guerrillas in Vietnam or Honduras would not have cared about, even if they had understood, the debates over the labor theory of value or other tenets of Marxian economics. Still *beliefs* in an alternative economic system that held promise of a better life in this world held sway over their actions no less than beliefs in alternative religious systems—as holding out the promise of eternal salvation in the next world—held sway over those who fought so fiercely in the religious battles in the aftermath of the Reformation. Those beliefs have been dealt a hard blow by the events in Eastern Europe during the past couple of years, particularly with the collapse of the Soviet government within the last year.

But if we were to seek a date at which socialism ceased to be viewed as a viable alternative to capitalism, we have to look before the emancipation of the Eastern European countries in 1989. Besides, their rejection of socialism was as much a political statement, a rejection of an economic system that had been forced upon them by an occupier, as it was a statement about the virtues of that ideology. We must look, I think, to the privatizations within France beginning in the early 1980s, by an avowedly socialist government, reversing a pattern of nationalization which that government had instituted but a few short years before. There were inklings that the faith in the socialist ideology may have been crumbling in the years before: Greek Prime Minister Andreas Papandreou, another avowed socialist, took as one of the main goals of his government the "socialization of the nationalized enterprises," recognizing explicitly that the older view, that nationalizing an enterprise would ensure that the goals of the enterprise would be coincident with "national interest," however that was defined, had no basis in reality, at least in the context of Greece. The collapse of socialism as an economic ideology was as remarkable in many ways as the almost contemporaneous collapse of the Soviet bloc, representing the culmination of an economic experiment of a half-century's duration. It was an experiment that was conducted with considerable forethought, based as it was on an ideology of more than a century's standing. The ideology had withstood the scrutiny of time. Its premises and conclusions had been widely debated, and it included among its adherents some of the greatest minds over a period of more than a hundred years. Even today the Marxist ideas and ideals that underlay the economic ideology remain alive, not only within the third world but in other disciplines. A full and coherent account of the rise, persistence, and partial fall of this set of beliefs would be fascinating but would take me beyond the scope of these lectures. But one of the themes that I do hope to develop is that, indirectly and unintentionally, neoclassical models of the economy played a central role in promulgating and perpetuating a belief in market socialism—one of the central variants of the socialist model—as an alternative to capitalism. I argue in these lectures that if the neoclassical model (or its precursors) had provided a correct description of the economy, then market socialism would indeed have had a running chance of success. Thus the failure of market socialism serves as much as a refutation of the standard neoclassical model as it does of the market socialist ideal. In these lectures I attempt to explain more precisely what is wrong with that model and to provide the basic ingredients of an alternative paradigm.

By most accounts the results of the experiment with socialism are unambiguous: The experiment was a failure. Like most social experiments it was not a controlled experiment, so there is controversy about exactly what inferences are to be made—to what extent were the basic ideas (if not the ideals) of socialism at fault and to what extent were the failures attributable to the manner in which the ideas were implemented, to what may be referred to as "specific design features"?[1]

The repressive political system that accompanied the socialist experiment is also sometimes blamed: *Democratic* market socialism has never really been tried. But a case can also be made that the social experiment was more successful than it would have been in the absence of Communist oppression: for, at least to some extent, the repressive political system provided a substitute—the stick—for the absence of the carrot of economic incentives. There is a corresponding issue of whether there is a causal link between the oppressive political system and the socialist economic system. If not the inevitable consequence of giving the state a monopoly in the ownership of the means of production, there may still be a "tendency" for the concentration of power in one sphere to lead to a concentration of power in the other.

While academicians may speculate about these matters, most of the countries involved seem resolved to move toward a market economy. They see the prosperity of the countries of Western Europe, North America, and East Asia, and they hope that by emulating their economic system, they too will experience similar prosperity. They face a difficult transition problem—how to go from where they are today to where they want to be. While there is considerable conviction that they want the fruits of a market economy, there may not be the same conviction that they want either the cost—the extremes of poverty that characterize most of the poorer of the market economies, among which many of these countries surely must be counted[2]—or that they are willing to bear the costs of transition. Finally, market economies come in a variety of hues and shades. The socialist economies face a difficult set of problems in deciding which form they wish to take. Indeed not all of the former socialist countries are fully committed to having market economies. Some are discussing a third way, but critics dismiss it as impossible—as the matter is commonly put, you can't be a little bit pregnant.

For economic theorists the problems facing the socialist economies represent a challenge. Here we have a set of countries embarking on the choice of an economic system. Surely economic theory should provide considerable guidance. Regrettably economic science—at least until recently—has had very little to say about these fundamental matters, and even less to say about the important issues of transition. The typical advice of the visiting consultant making a hurried trip to one of the economies embarking on a transition path is to emphasize repeatedly the importance of markets, a lesson seemingly by now well learned (though market advocates would say that it is a lesson that cannot be repeated too often and, as simple as it may seem, the full import of which seems difficult to absorb—even in economies long accustomed to markets). Indeed there seems to be a certain instant attraction between the old ideologues of the left and the ideologues of the right. Both are driven by religious fervor, not rational analysis. As many of the ideologues have rejected the Marxian ideology, they have adopted the ideology of free markets. There is a joke that Milton Friedman is the most widely respected economist within the Soviet Union—though his books and articles have yet to be read. He is a symbol of an ideology, and it is an alternative belief system that they seek.

Of course there is much in the way of anecdotal evidence—the fact that market economies have done well is constantly recited. Anecdotal evidence—while surely better than no evidence—is a weak reed upon which to base a choice of an economic system. Anecdotal evidence of fifteen years ago led many textbook writers (including Paul Samuelson) to suggest that there might be a trade-off between freedom and growth—that the socialist economies were in fact growing faster than market economies. Popular discussions of the time suggested that democracy and freedom might be luxuries that only the rich could afford: Those that were committed to growing rapidly might have to choose the socialist path, even if there seemed to be a correlation (necessary or not) between that and the loss of freedom. Even countries that did not adopt the full rigors of the Soviet model were persuaded that certain of its features—central planning, heavy industrialization, public ownership of the basic means of production, high rates of forced savings—were important ingredients in any successful development program. Today—in historical perspective a scant few years later—all of these empirical judgments are being questioned. (Of course there are a number of economists who never wavered in their belief in markets, who are now saying "I told you so." But some of these may be more akin to security market analysts who are always predicting bear markets or bull markets. Their day in the sun eventually comes, but this should not be attributed either to their acumen or the rigorousness of their analysis.) Moreover the anecdotal evidence is far from unambiguous concerning what course of action these countries should take: One commonly held interpretation of the Asian miracle—the rapid growth of Japan, Korea, Singapore, and Taiwan—is that government played a crucial role in "governing the market."[3]

When I ask, "Does economic science have much to contribute to these discussions?" I mean more than the recitation of anecdotal evidence and the repetition of economists' faith in markets: Are there "theorems" that tell us that market economies will necessarily do better than socialist economies, or that privatization will improve the efficiency of state enterprises? Are there analytical results that tell us something about the appropriate balance and role of government and the private sector—for virtually all of the success stories involve mixed economies with large governments. Transforming to a market economy does not entail a withering away of the state but a redefinition of its role. What guidance does economic science have to offer on these matters?

For the past half-century a simple paradigm has dominated the economics profession—variously referred to as the *competitive paradigm*, or the neoclassical or Walrasian model. The most precise statement of that paradigm is provided by the model of Arrow and Debreu (1954; see also Arrow 1951b; Debreu 1959). It postulates large numbers of profit- (or value-) maximizing firms interacting with rational, utility-maximizing consumers in an economy in which there is a complete set of perfectly competitive markets—for all goods, in all periods, in all states of nature (for all risks), at all locations. Most who claim that the model has much to say about the real world believe that its conclusions are robust to weakening the precise assumptions employed by Arrow and Debreu (e.g., with respect to the completeness of markets).

I want to argue in these lectures that the competitive paradigm not only did not provide much guidance on the vital question of the choice of economic systems but what "advice" it did provide was often misguided. The conceptions of the market that underlay that analysis mischaracterized it; the standard analyses underestimated the strengths—and weaknesses—of market economies, and accordingly provided wrong signals for the potential success of alternatives and for how the market might be improved upon. By the same token, that paradigm cannot be relied upon to provide guidance to the former socialist economies as they seek to build new economic systems.

The fundamental problem with the neoclassical model and the corresponding model underlying market socialism[4] is that they fail to take into account a variety of problems that arise from the absence of perfect information and the costs of acquiring information, as well as the absence or imperfections in certain key risk and capital markets. The absence or imperfections of these markets can, in turn, to a large extent be explained by problems of information. During the past fifteen years, a new paradigm, sometimes referred to as the information-theoretic approach to economics (or, for short, *information paradigm*),[5] has developed. This paradigm is explicitly concerned with these issues.[6] This paradigm has already provided us insights into development economics[7] and macroeconomics.[8] It has provided us a *new new welfare economics*,[9] a *new theory of the firm*,[10] and a new understanding of the role and functioning of financial markets. It has provided us new insights concerning traditional questions, such as the design of incentive structures.

These information-theoretic concerns have not only enriched and changed the answers to traditional economic questions; they have led to new questions being posed. To the classical three questions of economics —what should be produced, how should it be produced, and for whom should it be produced—we now add a fourth—how should these

decisions be made, and who should make them. In the economy of Joan
Robinson (or Arrow and Debreu), decision makers, and the structure of
decision making, play no role. Joan Robinson described the job of the
manager of a firm as simply looking up in the book of blueprints the
appropriate page corresponding to current (and future) factor prices. That
page would show what technology minimized costs at those factor prices.
Were life so simple! Of course, if life were so simple, being a manager
would be a truly boring job, worthy of the disdain cast by the traditional
British academic, and the lack of concern of Lange, Lerner, and Taylor for
managerial incentives would be of little moment: They could essentially be
replaced by automata.

In summary, in this book I want to show how the perspectives of the
new information paradigm can provide at least some limited insights into
the basic issues facing the former socialist economies. Beyond that I want
to address some basic, long-standing issues in the theory of economic
organization: I want to argue that much of the older debate about the
desirability of market socialism was misguided; it was based on an incorrect
understanding of how competitive markets work, a misunderstanding to
which the Walrasian model may have contributed in no small measure.
(The Austrians, I believe, sensed this, and they strove to create an alternative vision of the market economy. But they never succeeded in articulat-
ing and formalizing their views in a way that was entirely satisfactory as
a coherent alternative to the Walrasian paradigm, and accordingly, apart
from occasional footnote references, they have remained outside the mainstream, at least the American/Western European mainstream. I will have
more to say about the relationship between the ideas presented here and
the Austrian tradition later in this book.[11])

After explaining the limitations of the earlier theories and debates, I will
attempt to articulate what I see as the basic issues, the insights that can
be gleaned from what we have learned in the past fifteen years, and the
questions that remain to be resolved. I will close this book with some
remarks attempting to apply the lessons learned to the problems of transition facing the Eastern European countries.[12]

The Traditional Results on Comparative Economic Systems

As of perhaps ten or fifteen years ago economic science has had three sets
of results to guide those wishing to choose among alternative economic
systems.

The Fundamental Theorems of Welfare Economics and Adam Smith's
Invisible Hand

First, there were the fundamental theorems of welfare economics (Arrow
1951b; Debreu 1959), the formalization of Adam Smith's famous invisible
hand argument. Smith argued that not only are individuals led through the
pursuit of their self-interest by an invisible hand to pursue the nation's
interest, but this pursuit of self-interest is a far more reliable way to ensure
that the public interest will be served than any alternative—surely better
than relying on some government leader, as well-intentioned as that leader
might be. Smith's argument provides the basis for the reliance on market
economies.

The fundamental theorems of welfare economics made precise the sense
in which and the conditions under which markets are efficient. What is
generally referred to as the first fundamental theorem of welfare economics
shows that under certain conditions every competitive equilibrium is Pareto
efficient—that is, no one can be made better off without making someone
worse off. What is generally referred to as the second fundamental theorem
of welfare economics provides conditions under which any Pareto-efficient
allocation of resources can be obtained through market mechanisms. The
fundamental theorems of welfare economics form the basis of the "market
failures" approach to government intervention.[13] Markets do not work
perfectly when there are important externalities, and hence the rationale for
pollution taxes. Markets cannot provide public goods, and hence the rationale for public expenditures on roads, defense, and other public works. The
market distribution of income might not be socially desirable, and hence
the rationale for government redistribution programs.

The market failures approach argues that there is indeed a role for government, but it is a limited role: Government simply needs to correct the
well-defined market failures, which it can do with simple tools having
minimal effects on the mode of operation of the market economy. For
instance, problems of externalities can be addressed through corrective
(Pigouvian) taxes. Even when the government is uncertain of the tax rate
that will achieve particular pollution control objectives, market mechanisms
can be employed: The government can issue marketable pollution permits.[14] To be sure, the government has further, limited responsibilities: It
has to provide public goods and to levy taxes to finance them. It might also
have to take actions to ensure that markets are actually competitive. The
second fundamental theorem of welfare economics further delineated the

limited role of government: Even if the distribution of income was unsatisfactory, only limited government intervention was called for. "All" the government had to do was redistribute initial endowments (wealth) in a lump-sum (nondistortionary) manner.

Behind both theorems was the notion that the price system provided a powerful instrument for allocating resources. Textbook expositions of the power of the price system often went beyond the ideas reflected in the fundamental theorems of welfare economics, to talk about the "informational efficiency" of the market economy and the price system. No one has to know fully the preferences of individuals, the technologies of production, and the availability of resources. No one even needs to know how to make as simple a commodity as a pencil. Prices convey information about the scarcity of resources. They convey information from households to firms concerning what consumers want, and from firms to households about the resource costs associated with consuming each commodity. The price system ensures that the economy produces the commodities that individuals want.

While advocates of the market economy often waxed poetic about its beauties and powers, the theorems that underlay the rhetoric actually had little to say about "information." The theorems did not, for instance, discuss how well the economy processed new information—indeed, in their models, there was not a flow of new information—nor whether it was efficient in its allocation of resources to the acquisition of information that was relevant to the allocation of resources. It did not even recognize the conflict between the efficiency with which the economy transmits information and knowledge and the incentives that are present for the acquiring of information and knowledge: If, say, stock market prices perfectly and instantaneously transmitted information, then no investor would ever have any incentive to acquire information. Stock markets must be characterized by imperfect information, so long as information is costly. There is, as Grossman and Stiglitz (1976, 1980a) put it, "an equilibrium amount of disequilibrium." But the fundamental theorems of welfare economics have absolutely nothing to say about whether that equilibrium amount of disequilibrium is in any sense efficient. Are, for instance, the expenditures on information acquisition and dissemination too little, too much, or just right?

By the same token, for inventors or innovators to obtain a return on their inventive activities, there cannot be a free dissemination of technological knowledge. As my discussion below will emphasize, the informational problems that the competitive market economy handles efficiently are extremely limited.

The Lange-Lerner-Taylor Theorem

The second set of results is sometimes referred to as the Lange-Lerner-Taylor theorem. It is concerned with establishing the equivalence between two alternative institutional arrangements for the economy; it asserts the equivalence between market economies and "market socialism."

Market socialism refers to a form of economic organization where the government owns the means of production (as under any socialist system) but uses prices in much the same way that market economies do to allocate resources. Under market socialism managers are instructed to maximize profits, just as managers under capitalism maximize profits. Prices are set so that demands are equal to supplies.

The principal differences between market economies and market socialism are the mechanisms by which prices are set and the ownership of capital. For price setting under market socialism, a government planning agency replaces the to-and-fro of the market place or the mythical Walrasian auctioneer.[15] The fact that capital is owned by the government means that rather than shareholders receiving dividend checks (representing the "profits" of the firm), the dividends are sent to the government.

A corollary of government ownership of capital is that the government has to assume responsibility for allocating capital. In most renditions of market socialism the government does not do this by a balancing of supply and demand (in the manner in which other goods are allocated) but rather by a more direct allocative mechanism.[16] But if the government allocates capital in exactly the same way that private firms would allocate it, then the resource allocations emerging from the two systems would be identical.

The idea of market socialism was a powerful one. It suggested that it was possible to have all the advantages of market economies without the disadvantages attendant to private property and the frequently associated large concentrations of wealth. Market socialism, it was thought, could at the same time avoid the major pitfalls facing Soviet-type socialism. This required that essentially all of the information about technology[17] had to be communicated to the central planner, who had to make millions of decisions concerning what goods were to be produced and how they were to be produced. The central planner would have to decide what goods each factory should produce, whence it should receive its inputs, and where it should ship its output. Hayek had rightly criticized this view, arguing that the central planner could never have the requisite information. Market socialism seemed to suggest that the central planner does not need to have all of the detailed information—apart from his or her role in allocating investment, the central planner does nothing more than the Walrasian auctioneer, an important actor in conventional expositions of competitive economies. The fundamental theorems of welfare economics enhanced the power of market socialism: The second fundamental theorem assures us that the government can, through market socialism, attain any Pareto-efficient outcome.

During the past decade Hungary and a number of other countries have tried to follow a path of market socialism (or at least what they view as an adaptation of that model) with quite limited success.[18] The seeming failures of that approach led to two reactions. Among some, at least for a while, there was a desire to return to nonmarket systems; among the majority, a desire to travel farther along the road to markets. Among almost all, there are growing doubts about the viability of the kind of third road represented by market socialism.

To what should we attribute the failure of market socialism? The Lange-Lerner-Taylor theorem, when combined with the fundamental theorems of welfare economics, suggests that the economy should be able to obtain any Pareto-efficient outcome. What more could one want out of life, or at least out of the economy?

On Centrally Planned Economies and the Neoclassical Paradigm

Though in this book I will concentrate on the comparison between markets and market socialism, rather than, for instance, the comparison between markets and centrally planned economies, it should be clear that many of the issues that I raise here apply to that comparison as well. One of my arguments will be that if the neoclassical model of the economy were correct, market socialism would have been a success; by the same token, if the neoclassical model of the economy were correct, centrally planned socialism would have run into far fewer problems than it had encountered. Samuelson described the economy as the solution to a maximization problem; the fundamental theorem of welfare economics showed that under strong assumptions his insight was correct.[19] In addition mathematical techniques, like linear programming, combined with high-speed computers, suggest that it is possible to "solve" directly for the efficient allocations of resources. As I noted above, the Arrow-Debreu model suggests that competitive markets are an efficient algorithm for "solving" the economy's resource allocation problem, but these new techniques and technologies suggested that we could dispense with that algorithm—thereby dispensing with all the problems associated with the market mechanism—and still obtain solutions to the problem of how society's resources should be efficiently allocated.[20]

(It is perhaps worth noting that while earlier work on algorithms for solving complicated maximization problems suggests that those that involved "prices" [using duality] and "decentralization"—seeming analogues to the way that markets solve the resource allocation problem—were efficient, more recent work has produced more efficient algorithms that do not seem to have any direct market analogue. This supports my view that what is at issue in the analysis of how the economy allocates its resources is more than just the solution to a complicated maximization problem: economics is far more complicated, and more interesting, than the engineering approach that prevailed in the decades following Samuelson's *Foundations of Economic Analysis*.)[21]

Coase's Theorem (or Conjecture)

The final set of ideas is commonly referred to as Coase's theorem (though it was never stated in a precise enough form really to merit that appellation). Coase emphasized the importance of property rights. According to Coase, if property rights are assigned clearly, individuals have an incentive to work out efficient economic arrangements. It does not matter so much who gets the property rights (this affected, of course, the distribution of welfare) as that someone does. Inefficiencies such as the "Tragedy of the Commons"—the excessive grazing on common land, excessively rapid drilling of common oil pools, excessive fishing in international waters—are the result of failure to assign property rights. Other inefficiencies arise out of circumscribing property rights: The failure to allow water rights to be sold led to misallocation of water in the western part of the United States.

Socialist economies thought of themselves as destroying many private property rights, and many of the failures of socialism are attributed to that: The residents of apartments did not have the incentive to maintain their apartments, because they could not appropriate any returns from those activities by selling their apartments (just as cities with rent control face similar problems).[22] Managers of state-owned enterprises have inadequate incentives to enhance the value of the enterprises under their charge; unlike the owners of enterprises, they cannot reap the full benefits of their efforts.

From our current perspective the socialist economies were less successful in abolishing private property rights than they might have thought; for managers had considerable discretion in allocating the (often underpriced) output (often in return for similar favors from other managers). Jobs from which an individual cannot be fired can similarly be viewed as "property rights." Of course these were restricted property rights: The worker, for instance, could not sell his job to another worker. And because property rights were restricted, a variety of distortions arose. The Coase perspective has a clear prescription: Market socialism, like any other form of socialism, is doomed, simply because ownership rights in property are not well defined. When property is owned by everyone, it is in fact owned by no one; no one has the appropriate incentives. In this perspective, then, the first task in the transition to the market economy is privatization of the state property.

While the argument that the absence of well-defined private property rights, or restrictions on property rights, frequently gives rise to distortions is correct, the other fundamental conclusions are not. First, the clear assignment of property rights does not necessarily lead to efficiency. Public good problems, for instance,[23] are not resolved by Coase's theorem. While Coase and his followers paid passing attention to the possibility that transactions costs might impede parties "bargaining" to an efficient outcome, in the presence of imperfect information (giving rise to what may be viewed as transactions costs), inefficient outcomes frequently arise; indeed mutually beneficial deals simply may not occur, as one party tries to convince the other that the value of the relationship to him is small, in an attempt to appropriate a larger fraction of the surplus that accrues from the relationship (see, e.g., Farrell 1987).[24]

Second, the absence of well-defined private property rights need not give rise to problems. There is a large and growing literature showing how, in varying contexts, local communities have avoided the Tragedy of the Commons by a variety of regulatory devices.

More generally, there is some question about whether the absence of well-defined property rights is the *central* problem. There are two pieces of evidence in support of this. The first is that most large firms are not run by owners but by hired managers. The question of whether it makes much difference whether the manager works for a disparate set of shareholders, or for the state, is one to which I will return later. The second is the rapid growth in the South of China: the absence of well-defined property rights has not prevented double-digit growth rates.

Not only is it the case that the absence of private property rights may not be the central problem; it is not even clear that with privatization the government can accomplish its objectives as effectively as it can if it directly controls the enterprise. The question of whether privatization dominates public control is one of the central issues to which I will turn in chapter 9. The fundamental privatization theorem discussed there suggests that it does not.

The Central Themes of These Lectures

I have now set the stage so that I can state more fully the six central themes of this book:

1. The standard neoclassical model—the formal articulation of Adam Smith's invisible hand, the contention that market economies will ensure economic efficiency—provides little guidance for the choice of economic systems, since once information imperfections (and the fact that markets are incomplete) are brought into the analysis, as surely they must be, there is no presumption that markets are efficient.

2. The Lange-Lerner-Taylor theorem, asserting the equivalence of market and market socialist economies, is based on a misguided view of the market, of the central problems of resource allocation, and (not surprisingly, given the first two failures) of how the market addresses those basic problems.

3. The neoclassical paradigm, through its incorrect characterization of the market economies and the central problems of resource allocation, provides a false sense of belief in the ability of market socialism to solve those resource allocation problems. To put it another way, if the neoclassical paradigm had provided a good description of the resource allocation problem and the market mechanism, then market socialism might well have been a success. The very criticisms of market socialism are themselves, to a large extent, criticisms of the neoclassical paradigm.

4. The central economic issues go beyond the traditional three questions posed at the beginning of every introductory text: What is to be produced? How is it to be produced? And for whom is it to be produced? Among the broader set of questions are: How should these resource allocation decisions be made? Who should make these decisions? How can those who are responsible for making these decisions be induced to make the right decisions? How are they to know what and how much information to acquire before making the decisions? How can the separate decisions of the millions of actors—decision makers—in the economy be coordinated?

5. At the core of the success of market economies are *competition, markets,* and *decentralization.* It is possible to have these, and for the government to

still play a large role in the economy; indeed it may be necessary for the government to play a large role if competition is to be preserved.

There has recently been extensive confusion over to what to attribute the East Asian miracle, the amazingly rapid growth in countries of this region during the past decade or two. Countries like Korea did make use of markets; they were very export oriented. And because markets played such an important role, some observers concluded that their success was convincing evidence of the power of markets *alone*. Yet in almost every case, government played a major role in these economies. While Wade may have put it too strongly when he entitled his book on the Taiwan success *Governing the Market*, there is little doubt that government intervened in the economy *through* the market.

6. At the core of the failure of the socialist experiment is not just the lack of property rights. Equally important were the problems arising from lack of incentives and competition, not only in the sphere of economics but also in politics. Even more important perhaps were problems of information. Hayek was right, of course, in emphasizing that the information problems facing a central planner were overwhelming. I am not sure that Hayek fully appreciated the range of information problems. *If* they were limited to the kinds of information problems that are at the center of the Arrow-Debreu model—consumers conveying their preferences to firms, and scarcity values being communicated both to firms and consumers—then market socialism would have worked. Lange would have been correct that by using prices, the socialist economy could "solve" the information problem just as well as the market could. But problems of information are broader.

2   The Debate over Market Socialism: A First Approach

The debate over socialism in general, and market socialism in particular, has had a long and noble history, with notable contributions in the 1930s by Lange, Lerner, and Taylor, on the one side, and Hayek, on the other. There were many strands to this debate. Some have been lost in more recent discussions, while others have received greater stress.

For instance, modern discussions emphasize the unrealism of market socialism arising from its failure to take into account the political economy problems: Do bureaucrats have the incentives to carry out the prescriptions provided by the advocates of market socialism? Thus critics of market socialism argue that the relevant comparison is not between the idealized government postulated by the socialists and the market economy, but between how the economy would perform under actual government control and the market economy. But older discussions emphasized the unrealism of the competitive model of the economy: Given the pervasiveness of increasing returns, the relevant comparison was not between market socialism and competitive markets, but between market socialism and monopoly capitalism.

Much has happened in the world—and in economic theory—in the more than fifty years since those great debates occurred. Not only has the vocabulary economists use been changed, but there have, I believe, been marked advances in economic science that allow us to reexamine these old questions from new perspectives. Looking at these questions from the perspective of the new information paradigm is, as I have said, the central objective of this book. But before embarking on a detailed development of my arguments, I want to provide a broader sketch of how recent advances in economics enter into the old debates. Ironically some of these advances have breathed new life into the argument for market socialism—just as the economies that had been trying market socialism are in the process of abandoning it. At the same time some of these advances have raised new questions concerning both the necessity and viability of market socialism.

Why Modern Theory Might Suggest a Greater Plausibility for Market Socialism[1]

At least two of the central results of modern economic theory should, if anything, have reinforced the belief in market socialism.

Absence of Futures Markets and the Role of Government in Allocating Investment

It should be obvious that if market economies are to function in the way its advocates claim, markets in which goods and services can be traded must exist. One of the underlying assumptions in the by now standard model of (competitive) market economies—the model that seemingly provides the intellectual foundations of whatever belief one has in the market economy—is that there is a complete set of markets. This is a stronger assumption than might appear at first glance. To be sure, there are "markets" for steel, for labor, for land, for stocks, for wheat; while these markets may not be "perfect"—there may not be the large number of buyers and sellers in each of these markets envisaged by the competitive model—and most of these markets may not be organized in the way envisaged by the standard theory, with an auctioneer calling out prices until the market-clearing level is attained, still there is a general consensus that the economists' basic market model provides a good approximation at least for many of these goods and services.

But the assumption that there is a *complete* set of markets goes beyond this. There must exist markets on which not only today's goods and services are traded but on which future goods and services are traded.[2] There are of course some future markets: One can buy corn or wheat for delivery three or six months hence. But for most goods and services (beyond a few agricultural commodities, for a few months into the future) there do not exist markets where one can trade today for future delivery.

These futures markets are essential for making the correct investment allocations. Concern about the market economy's ability to allocate and coordinate investment in a socially productive way of course underlay many of the calls for socialism in both this and the previous century. Without the requisite markets there are no prices to perform the coordinating/information roles that are essential if a market economy is to be efficient. Each firm must form expectations concerning what prices in the future are going to be, and those expectations are based, in part, on its beliefs about what other firms are doing. Other firms go to great efforts to keep that information secret. Thus, rather than there being a mechanism for coordinating investment decisions, market economies seem to provide incentives that provide obstacles to coordination. There are many real-world manifestations of this failure: At times there may be excessive entry into an industry, at other times shortages develop. Indeed even government attempts at limited intervention to provide the requisite information through indicative planning[3] (as in France) seem to have failed, as firms seem to have lacked the necessary incentives to reveal truthfully their plans (and in many cases may have had strategic incentives to provide other than truthful information).

There must exist markets not only for periods in the immediate future but for *all* periods extending *infinitely* far into the future. Without a complete set of futures markets extending infinitely far into the future, the economy can set off on a path that is locally intertemporally efficient—it looks exactly like an ordinary rational expectations path, with the real returns (capital gains plus rents) on all assets being equal—and only in the distant future does it become evident that the economy is inefficient. There appear to be no private incentives to correct this potential for seeming long-run inefficiency. The intuition behind this result is simple. Consider a firm, in 1990, contemplating building a factory, which it plans to use for twenty years, and then sell to some other firm. To make its decision, it must form an estimate of the value of the building at the end of twenty years, that is, in the year 2010. But the value of that building at the end of twenty years will depend, in part, on the supply of other buildings constructed between now and twenty years hence. Even those decisions will depend on expectations concerning what will happen still further in the future. Consider, for instance, a building being considered for construction ten years hence, that is, in the year 2000. Its owners will want to know what they can sell their building for, say, twenty years after construction, that is, in the year 2020. The value of a building in the year 2020 will depend on the supply of buildings at that date, which in turn will depend on the levels of construction between now and the year 2020. Now consider a building being contemplated for construction in the year 2010. Its owners will want to know the value of buildings in the year 2030, and so on. Thus decisions today are inextricably linked to what goes on in a web of interconnections extending onward forever. In practice firms do not go through this complicated process of reasoning. Business managers base their decisions on hunches and guesses. The point of the theoretical argument is just this: Even under the best of conditions, with business managers engaging in the most rational analyses, in the absence of markets extending infinitely far

into the future, there is no assurance that markets lead to efficient outcomes. Surely, if business managers short-circuit this, by engaging in less
sophisticated, calculations, our confidence in the efficiency of the market
outcome should be even further weakened.

Long-Run Dynamics: A Technical Digression

It has long been recognized that the dynamics of optimization models
generates saddle point paths (e.g., Samuelson and Solow 1953); that is, with
"well-behaved" problems, there is a unique path, starting from any set of
initial conditions, satisfying the intertemporal efficiency conditions that
converge to the steady state. All other paths satisfying the intertemporal
efficiency conditions diverge. Still this was not a serious economic problem;
there was always a further condition, the transversality condition, which
had to be satisfied along an optimal path, and this transversality condition
ensured convergence to the steady state. Hahn (1966) showed that similar
problems arise if there are more than one capital good in a *descriptive* model
of the economy. But, he argued, there is, in the absence of futures markets
extending infinitely far into the future, no way to ensure that market
economies converge to the steady state. The subsequent literature (Shell
and Stiglitz 1967) showed that the instability of the economy can be
eliminated if the assumption of perfect foresight (rational expectations) is
replaced with other assumptions concerning expectations, such as adaptive
expectations, with sufficiently slow speeds of adaptation. It was also shown
that other specifications of the economy can result in the equilibrium being
a stable node; for instance, in a model of money and growth, Shell et al.
(1969) showed that from any initial value of the capital stock and nominal
money supply, there are many paths that converge to the same steady
state. Other studies (Stiglitz 1973a) showed that there are rational expectations equilibria that, while they do not converge to a unique steady state,
also did not "explode." Indeed he showed that there can be a multiplicity
of nonconvergent paths consistent with rational expectations.

It is curious how the same analytical results can be interpreted in different ways. The early workers in this field (Samuelson 1967; Hahn 1966;
Shell, Sidrauski, and Stiglitz 1969) thought that the saddle point equilibria
present a problem for the capitalist economy, for in the absence of futures
markets extending infinitely far into the future, there is no way to ensure
that the economy will choose the unique path converging to the steady
state. To be sure, the existence of a multiplicity of equilibria (illustrated by
the case where many paths converge to the steady state) presents a prob-

lem: First, the economist may not be able to predict which of the paths the economy will choose; and second, some of these paths may be "better," in some sense, than others, and there is no assurance that the economy will pick out the better one. But these economists were more concerned with the problem of economic instability, and the obvious inefficiency that may result (and may be very large), than with the perhaps small differences in welfare associated with the choice of one rather than another of the convergent paths.

By contrast, in the recent rational expectations literature, saddle points are viewed as good, and nodes as bad. Those in the rational expectations school wanted to show that the market economy is efficient. By showing that there is a unique path satisfying the rational expectations conditions —if they could establish that (1) that unique path is the "socially optimal" path, and (2) the economy always behaves consistently with rational expectations—then they claim to have established that the market economy is efficient. In contrast, with nodes, there are many paths starting from any initial condition. How can one tell which path the economy will follow? And since not all of these paths will be Pareto efficient, nodes raise the possibility that the economy will follow an inefficient trajectory.

It is noteworthy that each of the hypotheses underlying the rational expectations analysis is questionable. Thus not only may there not be a unique rational expectations equilibrium but, except under strong conditions, the rational expectations equilibrium may not be Pareto efficient, as I will show in the next chapter. But most important for our current purposes, there is no reason to believe that without futures markets extending infinitely far into the future, even if there is a unique path converging to the steady state, the market economy will "choose" that path. The contention by those attempting to claim that the market economy (with rational expectations) is efficient, and will accordingly move along the (unique) path converging to the steady state, is *not* based on a resolution of the problems that Hahn and others had raised. These problems were simply ignored. It was *assumed* that the economy acted as if there were a single individual maximizing his or her utility over an infinite lifetime. The individual would ensure that the transversality condition would be satisfied—and so too, it was *asserted*, would the economy. The fact that futures markets extending infinitely far into the future were required was simply ignored.

In short, whether for the obvious reason that in the absence of futures markets the price system cannot perform its essential coordinating role with respect to future-oriented activities, such as investments, or for the more subtle reasons just discussed, that in the absence of futures markets, *extending infinitely far into the future,* the market economy is likely to exhibit dynamic instabilities—there is no reason to believe that *even with rational expectations* it will converge to the steady state; there is no presumption that markets, left to themselves, will be efficient. For advocates of market socialism, the implication of this analysis seems clear: There is a need for the kind of government control of the allocation of investment envisaged in market socialism.

The Principal-Agent Problem and the Separation of Ownership and Control

The earlier discussions of market socialism paid scant attention to problems of incentives. Managers maximized profits, at the prices given to them by the pricing bureau, because they were told to do so, and they did what they were told to do. This failure to consider managerial incentives has been one of the strongest criticisms of market socialism. Even before the market socialist debate of the 1930s, observers of modern capitalism had noted that there was a separation of ownership and control (Knight 1921; Berle 1926; Berle and Means 1932). If there was a separation of ownership and control, did it make much difference whether the shares were owned by millions of individuals directly or by "all" of the people through the state? Advocates of market socialism suggested that it did not.

The analysis of the consequences of the separation of ownership and control has been one of the major subjects of research in the economics of information. The branch of the literature[4] which goes under the rubric of "principal-agent theory" can be thought of as providing rigorous underpinnings for the literature of the 1950s stressing managerial discretion (e.g., by March and Simon 1958; Marris 1964). It establishes that with costly information, shareholders can only exercise limited control over managers. Contemporaneous and subsequent theoretical literature on takeovers and other control mechanisms further reinforced the conclusion concerning (at least limited) managerial autonomy. These theoretical observations have, if anything, been confirmed by the subsequent developments during the merger and takeover mania of the late 1970s and 1980s. For large firms there is no "single owner" maximizing the expected present discounted value of profits, or even long-run market value.[5] Does ownership really matter? Is BP any less efficient than Texaco?[6] Canadian National Railways than Canadian Pacific?[7] Has there been any rape of the public interest greater than that by Ross Johnson and his cronies of the shareholders of RJR?[8]

Why Modern Theory Might Suggest Market Socialism Is Less Necessary Than Previously Thought

Modern theory has been, however, somewhat more evenhanded in weighing in on the debate over market socialism than the previous discussion might have suggested. Two further results of modern theory have more ambiguous implications.

Competition

As I noted earlier, at least some of the advocates of market socialism believed that the relevant choice was not between competitive markets and market socialism but between monopoly capitalism and market socialism.[9] They believed that in large sectors of the economy, competition was not viable. An essential assumption in the analysis establishing the efficiency of market economies is that every firm be a price taker; the firm must act as if it believes that it has no effect on the prices it receives for the goods it sells or the prices it pays for the factors it buys. The growth of large enterprises in the early part of the twentieth century led many economists to extrapolate the trend and to envisage a market economy in which each of the major sectors—steel, oil, automobiles, aluminum, and so on—was dominated by one, or at most a few, firms. Economic theory bolstered these predictions: The technologies involved large fixed costs. New organizational techniques, such as introduced by Alfred Sloan at General Motors, meant that the increasing costs associated with larger-scale enterprises, arising from lack of organizational control, could be limited. The establishment of national markets, and national media to advertise in those national markets, provided further bases for returns to scale. With no major source of decreasing returns to the firm, and some major sources of increasing returns, one would expect each industry to be dominated by one, or at most a few, firms.[10]

Thus the choice facing economies was (1) to allow monopoly capitalism to take hold, with the distortions in resource allocations (and almost inevitably the concentration of political power) that arise; (2) to have direct government control of these sectors; or (3) to attempt to regulate and control the exercise of monopoly power, either by breaking up the monopolies (with the possible resulting loss of efficiency from failing to exploit economies of scale) or by controlling anticompetitive practices. Few democratic governments found the first acceptable. The United States was perhaps most aggressive in pursuing the third strategy. But by midcentury, more than fifty years after the passage of the landmark antitrust legislation, many of the core American industries remained highly concentrated; even successes, like the breaking up of Standard Oil, had ambiguous effects, as there was widespread belief that the Seven Sisters acted much like a cartel, with tacit collusion and an understanding of common interests in limiting competition replacing outright collusion. The antitrust laws had lead to greater subtlety in noncompetitive behavior! These events simply reinforced belief in the second strategy—government ownership and control.[11]

Countervailing this intellectual trend, which one might have thought would have provided greater support for market socialism, is the internationalization of the world economy. Competition is limited by the scale of the market, and as the scale of the market has changed, so has the effectiveness of competition. Thus, while through the 1960s, GM, Ford, and Chrysler dominated the American automobile market, today their market power has eroded, as they face effective competition in all segments of the market from Japanese and European producers. While the American market may have been large enough only to sustain three large producers, the world economy is large enough to sustain many more.

Keynesian Economics

Of all the market failures the one whose impact in eroding public confidence in market processes was the greatest was the Great Depression, the worst example of the periodic slumps that had plagued market economies throughout the centuries of capitalism. The existence and persistence of unemployment can be viewed as providing a convincing refutation of the neoclassical model: for in that model, all markets, including the market for labor, clear.

Curiously the debate on market socialism did not focus on the relative macroeconomic merits of the alternative systems, and the historical evidence is of limited value: Though the socialist economies "solved" the unemployment problem, their solution *may* have been to make it disguised rather than open. The socialist economies did seem to exhibit fluctuations in growth rates, evidence of fluctuations in economic activity.

Still there are theoretical reasons to think that market socialism would alleviate the underlying problem. One of the central themes in recent macroeconomic work has traced economic slumps to "coordination failures." To put the matter baldly, there are no jobs because there is no demand for the output of firms, and there is no demand for the output of firms because people do not have jobs. *If* the economy was well described by the Arrow-

Debreu model, *if* there were, for instance, a complete set of markets, then these coordination failures presumably would not occur. Advocates of market socialism argue that it can overcome the coordination failure problem, and thus avoid the huge loss of economic efficiency associated with the periodic downturns that have characterized market economies.

Another recent theme has seen economic downturns as a consequence of capital market imperfections, which inhibit the economy's ability to spread and diversify risks.[12] Thus, if firms perceive an increase in risk, they will reduce the level of their investment. Reductions in cash flow may force a reduction in investment, if firms face credit rationing and if there are impediments to their raising capital in other forms (e.g., through equity). Again, market socialism, with its direct control of investment, would seem to alleviate these problems: It would presumably set investment at the level required to sustain full employment.

During the 1970s and early 1980s there was another strand of work in macroeconomics which suggested that these macroeconomic concerns were not of much importance. Market economies quickly adjusted to disturbances. The tendency in American universities not to include economic history as part of the study of economics has reinforced a shortness of memory, leading many American academic economists to conclude that recessions were a problem of the past—if they were a problem then. But unfortunately, the major recession of the early 1980s, the recession of the early 1990s, and the persistence of high unemployment rates in Europe provided a rude awakening to those who believed that cyclical unemployment was a thing of the past. These experiences should have sent one message: Something was fundamentally wrong with the Arrow-Debreu model. If that model were correct, unemployment would not exist, and it would be hard to explain the volatility of the economy, given the role of prices in absorbing shocks and given the role of inventories, savings, and insurance markets in buffering both individual firms and households from the impact of shocks.

But while Keynes as well as the subsequent research in new Keynesian economics has provided an explanation for both unemployment and economic volatility—while it has attempted to identify precisely what is wrong with the Arrow-Debreu model that can account for these observations—there was another message of Keynes that was clearly heard: The macroeconomic ills of capitalism were curable. One didn't need to institute fundamental reforms in the economic system. One only needed selective government intervention. It is in this sense that Keynesian economics greatly weakened the case for market socialism.

As important as these issues are, a fuller treatment would take me be-yond the scope of this book.

Doubts on the Relevance of the Lange-Lerner-Taylor Theorem: Some Preliminary Thoughts

On balance, I suspect that the developments in modern economic theory which I briefly reviewed—the recognition of the importance of (the ab-sence in market economies of a complete set of) futures and risk markets, the separation of ownership and control, the imperfections of competition, and the recurrence of economic fluctuations and unemployment—should have led to greater doubts concerning the effectiveness of market processes.

Yet most economists would today reflect greater, not less, confidence in market processes than they would have fifty years ago. They would, in particular, cast doubt on the *relevance* of the Lange-Lerner-Taylor theorem. Casual observation would suggest that market socialist economies are not identical to capitalist economies, not even remotely so. The model of mar-ket socialism underlying that theorem is seriously flawed.

But our contention is that it is equally important to observe that the model of the market economy—underlying not only that theorem but also the fundamental theorems of welfare economics—is seriously flawed. With a bad model of the market economy and a bad model of the socialist economy, no wonder that any semblance of the equivalence of the two could, at most, be a matter of chance!

Hayek versus Stiglitz

Most of the next chapter is concerned with explaining why the standard neoclassical welfare theorems have little to say to those embarking on a choice among alternative economic systems. This conclusion, and even my stress on the reason for this conclusion, the imperfections of information, may seem familiar to many readers versed in the Austrian tradition. Hayek argued forcefully that the perfect information model simply could not capture the central role of prices and markets in transmitting and aggregat-ing information.

My disagreement is not with this assertion, nor with *many* of his other conclusions, such as the importance of the planning undertaken by firms. My concerns are two-fold: First, because Hayek (and his followers) failed to develop formal models of the market process, it is not possible to assess claims concerning the efficiency of that process, and second (and relatedly), in the absence of such modeling, it is not possible to address the central issues of concern here, the *mix* and *design* of public and private activities, including alternative forms of regulations (alternative "rules of the game" that the government might establish) and the advantages of alternative policies toward decentralization-centralization. As Sanford Grossman and I wrote some fifteen years ago,

Although this earlier [the Lange-Lerner-Taylor-Hayek] debate was presumably about the informational efficiency of alternative organizational structures, models in which the systems had to adjust to new information were not formulated; rather it was argued that if the information were to be the same, the allocation would be the same, and thus, a comparison of alternative organizations came down to issues like a comparison of cost differentials arising from different patterns of information flows, or different speeds of convergence. (Grossman and Stiglitz 1976, 252)

To be sure, any simple model cannot capture the complexity of the information problems confronting the economy. No simple model can capture the processes by which institutions adapt to changing circumstances. We run the risk that in formulating a simple model, with a simple set of informational problems to be overcome, the market process might appear to perform quite well when in reality, with a more realistic set of informational problems, its performance would be much poorer. (The converse is also possible, though it seems less likely: The market does poorly on simple problems but performs well in the more complex problems for which it was adapted.)

Advocates of the Austrian tradition often defend the lack of formal modeling—and the corresponding absence of formal efficiency theorems: The market economy is an organic process, too complicated to be reduced to the simplistic formal models. The job of the economists is to describe this organic process and to see the kinds of impediments that the absence of a legal structure, on the one hand, or excessive government intervention, on the other, might impose for it. But while they may not resort to, or even like, the standard welfare criterion of Pareto optimality, there are strong normative overtones in their discussions. Darwin may have thought that he was simply describing the evolutionary process when he asserted that it resulted in the survival of the fittest, but such statements require a definition of the "fittest" and an analysis of the general equilibrium, dynamic properties of the system. Today we recognize that evolutionary processes, under a wide variety of circumstances, may not possess "efficiency" properties.[13]

And the fact that the world is more complicated than any model which we might construct does not absolve us of the need for testing our ideas out using simple and understandable models. If markets do not work efficiently under these idealized circumstances, how can we be confident that they would work efficiently under more complicated circumstances? Only by an act of (and indeed a leap of) faith!

The research program in which I have been engaged over the past two decades has set out to construct a number of such simple models, evaluating how market processes work in gathering, transmitting, and processing a variety of different kinds of information, in a variety of different market contexts. In the next five chapters, I describe some of the results of that research.

3   Critique of the First Fundamental Theorem of Welfare Economics

In this and the next chapter I return to the fundamental theorems of welfare economics. In this chapter I argue that the first fundamental theorem of welfare economics—asserting the efficiency of competitive economies—is fundamentally flawed. Quite contrary to that theorem, competitive economies are almost never efficient (in a precise sense to be defined below). The next chapter presents a similar critical analysis of the second fundamental theorem of welfare economics. In both chapters I focus on the problems that arise from the assumptions of perfect information and a complete set of markets. Other problems, such as those associated with other assumptions of these theorems like the absence of endogenous technological change, are taken up in later chapters.

The first fundamental theorem asserted that every competitive economy was Pareto efficient. This is the modern rendition of Adam Smith's invisible hand conjecture:

Man has almost constant occasion for the help of his brethren, and it is in vain for him to expect it from their benevolence only. He will be more likely to prevail if he can interest their self-love in his favor, and show them that it is for their own advantage to do for him what he requires of them.... It is not from the benevolence of the butcher, the brewer, or the baker that we expect our dinner, but from their regard to their own interest. We address ourselves, not to their humanity but to their self-love, and never talk to them of our own necessities but of their advantages.

Smith went on to describe how self-interest led to social good:

He intends only his own gain, and he is in this as in many other cases, led by an invisible hand to promote an end which was no part of his intention. Nor is it always the worse for society that it was no part of it. By pursuing his own interest he frequently promotes that of the society more effectually than when he really intends to promote it.[1]

It is the first welfare theorem that provides the intellectual foundations of our belief in market economies. Like any theorem, its conclusions depend on the validity of the assumptions. A closer look at those assumptions, however, suggests that the theorem is of limited relevance to modern industrial economies.

The Greenwald-Stiglitz Theorems on the Efficiency of Competitive Markets[2]

It is often interesting to note which assumptions an author highlights, by labeling them "assumption A.1 ... A.10" and which assumptions are hidden, whether deliberately or not: the unspoken assumptions that go into every model, the assumptions that are made in passing, as if they were no more than a reminder of conventional usage, or the assumptions that are embedded in certain basic definitions. The notion that market equilibrium should be characterized by demand equaling supply is, for instance, presented as part of the definition of equilibrium in the standard competitive model. It is implied that it should be obvious that if demand were not equal to supply, there would be forces for change, so that the situation would not be an equilibrium.[3] More recent work in economies with imperfect information has shown that that conclusion is not correct; competitive[4] market equilibrium may be characterized by demand exceeding supply (as in the Stiglitz-Weiss 1981 models of credit rationing) or by supply exceeding demand (as in the Shapiro-Stiglitz 1984 model of unemployment with efficiency wages).[5] Similarly the standard competitive model begins with the implicit assumption of a linear price system (a fixed price per unit purchased), while we now know that competitive markets with imperfect information may be characterized by nonlinear price systems, where there may, for instance, be quantity discounts.[6] The standard assumption that competitive equilibrium drives profits to zero can also be shown not to be valid in models with imperfect information.[7]

The Importance of Informational Assumptions

The fact that so many of the standard results do not remain valid when the extreme assumptions of perfect information are dropped serves to emphasize the general—and until recently, insufficiently recognized—importance of informational assumptions in competitive equilibrium analysis. The concerns about unspoken assumptions are of equal importance to the question at hand—the evaluation of alternative ways of organizing the economy. The first fundamental theorem of welfare economics is based on the assumption that there is perfect information, or more accurately, that information is fixed—and in particular unaffected by any action taken by any individual, any price, or any variable affected by the collective action of individuals in the market—and that there is a complete set of risk markets. Whenever these conditions are not satisfied the market is not *constrained* Pareto efficient; that is, there are interventions by the government that could be unambiguously welfare improving. These interventions respect the same limitations on markets and costs of information (and marketing) that affect the private economy. Indeed government intervention can be shown to be desirable, even if the government is extremely limited in its instruments, for instance, if the government is limited to simple (linear) price and uniform lump-sum[8] interventions. Beyond that, the nature (and even the magnitudes) of the desirable interventions can be related to observable market parameters, such as how different groups in the population respond to changes in wages and prices.[9]

In a sense Debreu and Arrow's great achievement was to find that almost singular set of assumptions under which Adam Smith's invisible hand conjecture was correct.[10] There are, to be sure, a few other singular cases in which the market might be constrained Pareto efficient. For instance, the absence of risk markets would have no consequences if everyone were identical and faced identical shocks, so that even if there were risk markets, there would be no trading in them;[11] or if the quantities of all goods consumed by all individuals were observable, then economies in which there were moral hazard would be constrained Pareto efficient.[12] (The welfare economics of economies with moral hazard is explored in greater detail by Prescott and Townsend 1980. The differences in conclusions between Greenwald and Stiglitz and Prescott and Townsend is attributable to the fact that the latter focus on this special case which Arnott and Stiglitz 1985 as well as Greenwald and Stiglitz had shown to be efficient.)

Externality Effects in the Presence of Imperfect Information and Incomplete Markets

The essential insight of Greenwald and Stiglitz was that when markets are incomplete and information is imperfect, the actions of individuals have externality-like effects on others, which they fail to take into account. (The externalities are generally like "atmospheric" externalities in that their level depends on the actions of all individuals together.) Some examples may help illustrate what is at issue:

1. *Incomplete risk markets.* Suppose that there are many states of nature, but only one risky asset, apple trees. The number of apple trees planted determines (stochastically) the number of apples produced next year, and this in turn determines the price and profitability, in each state of nature, of owning an apple tree. As individuals plant more apple trees, the probability distribution of the returns from planting apple trees changes, and since apple trees are, by definition, the only risky investment, it is as if one asset (the old probability distribution) is replaced by a new one. Each investor of course takes the probability distribution of returns as given, even though it changes as more trees are planted. The effect of each individual's action on that probability distribution can thus be viewed as an externality.[13]

2. *Variable labor quality (adverse selection).* Consider the problem of imperfect information about the quality of laborers. Firms may know the average quality of labor being offered in a union hiring hall. They may even know how that quality is affected by the wage paid.[14] Their demand for labor, at each wage, will depend on this quality variable. On the other hand, each worker, whether of high or low quality, does not take into account the effect of his or her decisions concerning the amount of labor to supply on the average quality of labor (and accordingly on the demand for labor). In effect, if low-quality laborers were to decide to supply more labor, at any given wage, it would lower the profits of the firm. Their actions would have an externality effect on firms. By the same token, it is easy for the government to affect the quality mix, for instance, by taxing or subsidizing commodities that have a differential effect on the labor supply of low and high-ability individuals.[15]

3. *Incentive (moral hazard) problems.* Individuals buy insurance because they are risk averse. But insurance means that they do not have to bear the full consequences of their actions: Their incentives to avoid the insured-against event are attenuated. Each individual takes the insurance premium as given. Of course, if all take less care, the insured event will occur more frequently, and premiums will rise.

This example also shows how the government can effect a Pareto improvement. By taxing and subsidizing various commodities, the government can encourage individuals to take greater care. Suppose that the insured-against event is damage from fire, and one of the major causes of fires is smoking in bed. Smoking in bed is particularly dangerous if the individual also drinks too much. One might imagine, in principle, an insurance contract requiring that the individual not smoke in bed after drinking, but this would be hard to enforce. (The insurance company could install TV monitors in every bedroom, but some might view this as an intrusion on privacy.) But by taxing cigarettes and alcohol, the government can discourage smoking and drinking in general, and as a by-product, smoking in bed after drinking would be discouraged as well. For at least small taxes, the welfare gains from the reduced "moral hazard" would more than offset the welfare losses from the distortions (deadweight loss) in consumption patterns induced by the taxes.[16] It should be clear that taxes and subsidies should be set so as to encourage care, for instance, by subsidizing goods that are complements to taking care, and taxing substitutes. The optimal tax rates are set so that at the margin, one balances the benefits of induced care with the marginal deadweight loss. Both of these can be related to empirically observable magnitudes (e.g., the compensated [own and cross] price elasticities of demand and the elasticities of "care" with respect to various prices). Thus, while government and private insurers lack the information necessary to prevent moral hazard—they cannot directly control actions—the government has the instruments with which to alleviate the effects of moral hazard and the information required to use those instruments.[17]

Powers of the Government

This example also serves to illustrate the powers that the government may have that the private sector does not. There is a "folk theorem"[18] (or what would be a folk theorem, were it true) that says that anything that the government can do, the private sector can do as well or better: Alleged advantages of the government only arise from "unfair" comparisons, for instance, a government with costless information can improve on market allocations when markets face costly information. It was to avoid this criticism that I focused on the concept of *constrained* Pareto efficiency.

But the question still needs to be addressed: How does the government differ from other economic organizations? Why can it do things that others cannot? This is the question I addressed in my book *The Economic Role of the State*, where I argued that the government's power of compulsion (associated with its property of universal membership) gave it distinct advantages (and concern about abuses of those powers gave rise to constraints that resulted in distinct disadvantages). Thus the government can prohibit the manufacture of cigarettes—no private individual or group of individuals can do this. (Of course, to enforce this prohibition, the government must have the power to observe the production of cigarettes. If there were no economies of scale in production, then it might be difficult for the government to enforce this prohibition. But with significant economies of scale, if the government could not enforce the prohibition, it could at least increase the costs of cigarettes significantly.) By the same token, the government can impose a tax on the production of all cigarettes. It may be possible to observe, and hence to tax, the production of cigarettes even if it is not possible to observe individual consumption levels (it is impossible to monitor secondary trades). No private insurance firm or collection of insurance firms could "force" all cigarette companies to pay a tax on their production. Suppose that they bribed them, by offering them a payment conditional on their increasing the price. Then a new company could come along, charge a slightly lower price, take away all of their customers, and make a profit. This is just an illustration of the fact that the government does have powers that the private sector does not have, powers that in certain instances (if well used) could result in a Pareto improvement. (For other examples, see Stiglitz 1989f, 1991c.)

Some Cautionary Notes on the Interpretation of the Greenwald-Stiglitz Theorems

The Greenwald-Stiglitz and related theorems have three interpretations: First, as we have seen, in certain cases they provide well-identified forms of welfare-enhancing government intervention. Second, they suggest that it may not be possible to decentralize efficiently, in the manner suggested by the fundamental theorems of welfare economics. I will return to this theme later in the chapter. Third, and perhaps most important, they remove the widespread presumption that markets are necessarily the most efficient way of allocating resources. There is, to repeat, no general theorem on which one can base that conclusion. (There may of course be other bases for reaching that conclusion, a point to which I will come shortly.)

In this perspective the Greenwald-Stiglitz theorems should not primarily be taken as a basis of a prescription for government intervention. One of the reasons that they do not provide a basis for prescription is that doing so would require a more detailed and formal model of the government. When the central theorem of economics asserted that no government—no matter how benevolent, no matter how rational—could do any better than the market, we had little need for a theory of the government: It could only make matters worse. But the Greenwald-Stiglitz theorems assert that there is a *potential* role for government. Whether and how the government should intervene is a question to which I will return later. (Presumably, since governments are political institutions, the answer will depend in part on the form that those institutions do or can take. The theorems do tell us, if the government decides to intervene through, say, taxes and subsidies, the critical parameters on which the rates of those taxes and subsidies should depend.)

Other Reasons Why Market Economies with Imperfect Information May Not Be Pareto Efficient

While the Greenwald-Stiglitz theorems provide the most forceful refutation of the first fundamental theorem of welfare economics, several other results of the information paradigm provide equally fundamental criticisms. I want to draw attention to but three, two of which have to do with how information-theoretic considerations lead to the conclusion that *other* assumptions of the standard competitive model (which underlie the fundamental theorem of welfare economics) will not be satisfied. The list below is not meant to be exhaustive. I have tried to focus on what I see as the central *economic* assumptions.[19]

Incompleteness of Markets

We emphasized in chapter 2 the importance in the standard competitive paradigm—and the unrealism—of the assumption that there be a complete set of markets, including a complete set of risk and futures markets.

Transactions Costs

The incompleteness of market can itself be explained by transactions costs, an important component of which is information costs. There are costs associated with establishing a market. If there were markets for each of the millions of commodities, each of the billions of contingencies, each of the infinity of future dates, then so much of societies' resources would be absorbed in organizing these transactions that there would be little left over to be bought and sold on each of these markets!

Once we recognize the myriad events that affect us, we recognize the impossibility of having even a complete set of risk markets (insurance against all contingencies). Each firm is affected not only by the events that affect the industry but by idiosyncratic events—the illness of its president, a breakdown in one of its machines, the departure of a key salesperson. The firm itself can buy insurance for many of the risks it faces, such as that its trucks get into accidents or that its factories burn down, but most of the risks it faces cannot be insured against. The notion that there be markets for each of these risks is mind-boggling.

Inconsistency between Assumptions of "Complete Markets" and "Competitive Markets"

Just as the high dimensionality of the "states of nature" makes it obvious that a complete set of securities simply cannot exist, so too the high dimensionality of the product space makes it obvious that a complete set of markets for commodities cannot exist once we remember that products are defined by a complete specification of their characteristics: Products of different quality are treated as different commodities, and products de-livered at different dates and location are treated as different commodities. Arrow and Debreu's idea of treating commodities at different dates and in different states of nature as different commodities seemed like a nice mathe-matical trick, enabling the extension of the standard model to a new, much wider range of problems, but upon closer examination the underlying spirit of the model was vitiated: Either there simply could not exist a complete set of markets (there would have to be a *perfectly competitive* market for the delivery of a machine of a particular specification to a factory at a particular date at a particular time) or, if there did exist a complete set of markets, it is hard to conceive of each of those markets as being "perfectly" competitive (i.e., that there be so many traders on both sides of the market that each trader believes it has a negligible effect on price). Of necessity, the markets would have to be thin and imperfectly competitive.[20] Consider, for instance, the market for labor. Each individual is different, in myriad ways. A complete set of markets would entail there being a different market for each type of labor—a market for Joe Stiglitz's labor, which is different from the market for Paul Samuelson's labor, which in turn is different from the market for plumbers, which in turn is different from the market for unskilled labor, and so on. If we are careful in defining markets for homogeneous commodities (Joe Stiglitz's labor delivered at a particular date, in a particular state, at a particular location), then there is only one trader on one side of the market (Joe Stiglitz). If we expand the markets to embrace all theoretical economists, then it is obviously more competitive. But we have had to drop the assumptions that commodities are homogeneous and that the set of markets is incomplete; there is not a *separate* market for each homogeneous commodity.

Asymmetric Information and Complete Markets

Imperfect information obviously serves to ensure that the set of securities cannot be complete, since individuals can only trade in commonly observed states.[21] If I promise to deliver to you something in a particular set of states, it has to be observable to both of us that the state has occurred; to use the legal system to enforce such a contract, it has to be verifiable to an outside, third party. The inability to do so clearly limits the set of securities.

But beyond that, asymmetries of information greatly limit the opportunities to trade, a notion captured in the familiar maxim: I wouldn't want to buy something from someone who is willing to sell it to me. Of course the old principles concerning differences in preferences and comparative advantage providing motives for trade still remain valid, but there is another motive for trading, which can be put baldly as "cheating." While in traditional exchanges both parties are winners, if I can get you to pay more for something than it is worth—to buy a used car that is a lemon—I win and you lose. Farmers have a strong incentive to sell their crops on futures markets, but most do not avail themselves much of this opportunity, and for good reason. Those markets are dominated by five large trading companies, who have every incentive to be more informed than the small farmer. The differential information means the farmer is at a disadvantage; the trading companies can make a profit off of the farmer's relative ignorance. Knowing this, a choice is made to bear the risk rather than pay the price.

Asymmetries of information give rise to market imperfections in many markets, other than the insurance market, futures markets, and the market for used cars. Consider, for instance, the market for "used labor," workers who already have a job. Their present employer normally has more information concerning their abilities than do prospective employers. A prospective employer knows that if it makes an offer to attract an employee from another firm, the other firm will match it, if the worker is worth it, and will not if the worker is not. Thus, again, the prospective employer is in a heads you win, tails I lose situation: It is only successful in hiring the new employee if it has offered higher wages than the current (well informed) employer thinks the worker is worth. To be sure, there are instances when the prospective employee's productivity at the new firm will be higher than at the old job—the employee is better matched for the job—or where there are other (nonpecuniary) reasons why the individual may wish to move (to be near relatives, or get away from them). As a result there is *some* trade in the used labor market, but apart from younger workers who are trying to get well matched with a firm, these markets tend to be thin.

Similarly equity provides more effective risk distribution between entrepreneurs and suppliers of capital than does credit; providers of equity share the risk, while with credit (bank loans and bonds) the residual risk is borne by the entrepreneur or the firms' original shareholders.[22] Yet equity markets are notoriously imperfect; only a small fraction of new investment is provided by equity.[23] One of the reasons for this is asymmetries of information: The sellers of equity are better informed than potential buyers; they are most anxious to sell shares in their company when the market has overpriced their shares. Buyers know this. Thus the willingness of firms to issue shares sends a signal to the market, that the sellers think that the shares are overpriced. The market responds, and the price of shares falls.

There are, to be sure, *other* reasons—besides a firm's shares being overpriced—for a firm to issue shares. The owners of a firm may be risk averse, and, as we have noted, equity provides a more effective method of sharing risk than do other methods of raising capital. (In some sectors, like insurance, regulations require that firms raise capital via equity.) Outsiders ("the market") cannot, however, tell whether the reason the firm is selling shares is that its shares are overpriced, that its bankers refuse to lend it money, or that the firm's owners recognize that equity is a more effective way of distributing risk. In fact, when firms issue shares, on average, the price falls (on average, the decline in the value of existing shares equals about 30 percent of the amount raised;[24] in some cases the decline is far greater than the amount raised): The market assigns some probability to the chance that the firm is issuing shares because they are overpriced. From the perspective of the firm this makes issuing shares very costly. And it is this which (at least partly) explains the relatively little reliance on equity as a means of raising new capital.

Moral Hazard

Asymmetries of information give rise to two problems, referred to as the (adverse) selection[25] and the incentive or moral hazard problems.[26] Both are seen most clearly in the context of insurance markets, but they arise in a variety of other contexts as well. The first problem results in firms being unable to obtain insurance on their profits: clearly the firm is more informed about its prospects than any insurance firm could be, and the insurance firm worries that if the firm is willing to pay the premium, it is getting too good of a deal. That is, there is a high probability that the insurance firm will have to pay off on the policy.

Moral hazard also leads to limited insurance. The more complete the insurance coverage, the less incentive individuals or firms have to take actions that ensure that the insured-against event does not occur. Because the actions that would be required to reduce the likelihood of the insured-against event occurring are often not observable (and/or it cannot be verified that the insured took the requisite action), the payment of the insurance cannot be made contingent on the individual or firm taking those actions. Thus health insurance firms would like those they insure not to smoke or to be in places where they suffer the consequences of "second-hand smoke," that is, smoking by others. But insurance firms cannot observe these actions, and hence cannot require those they insure not to smoke.[27]

The provision of *complete* insurance would greatly attenuate incentives, so much so in many cases that for the insurance firm to break even would require charging such a high premium that the policy would be unattractive. Thus, in general, whenever there is moral hazard, there will be incomplete insurance.[28] Analogous incentive issues arise in many other markets. In most firms pay is not just paid on performance. Input (effort) is not easily monitorable. It may be possible to monitor output, but if pay is based solely on output, compensation would be highly variable, since there are many determinants of output, besides effort. In effect, by making pay depend only partially on performance, firms are providing some insurance to their workers, though incomplete insurance. If pay did not depend at all on performance, workers would have no incentive to provide any effort at all.[29] Thus both moral hazard and adverse selection provide reasons for markets to be *thin*; in some cases the market might actually be closed. When combined with other transactions costs, they reinforce the conclusion that we expect markets to be incomplete.

Inconsistency between Assumptions of Perfect Information and Complete Markets

Somewhat more subtly, the number of markets that exist affects the information structure of traders; that is, prices in different markets convey information. If the futures price of wheat is very high, one can infer that informed individuals in the market either believe that demand in the future will be high or supply low. Uninformed traders can thus glean some information from informed traders by looking at prices; and just how much information they can glean depends on what markets exist. In some cases uninformed traders can glean all of the information from informed traders. (The discussions of academic economists sometimes seem to recall the religious debates of the Middle Ages on how many angels could dance on the head of a pin: There was a long discussion of whether one could infer from market prices the state of nature of the economy.[30] If, for instance, there were a single random variable affecting the return to a particular security, and if there were some informed individuals who knew the value of that random variable, then the price would fully reveal that random variable. If that were true for *every* risky security, prices would fully reveal the state of nature. But the "event" space is so much larger than the price space—there are hundreds of variables that affect the profitability of a firm —that it seems absurd to hope that anyone by looking at prices could infer the state of nature.)

It should be clear of course that for traders to have incentives to gather information required that information not be perfectly disseminated in the market. If, simply by looking at market prices, those who do not spend money to acquire information can glean all the information that the informed traders who have spent money to acquire information have, then the informed traders will not have any informational advantage; they will not be able to obtain any return to their expenditures on information acquisition. Accordingly, *if there were a complete set of markets, information would be so well conveyed that investors would have no incentives to gather information.* (Of course with all participants having the same [zero] information, incentives to trade would be greatly reduced.) To put the matter differently, the assumptions of "informed" markets[31] and "a complete set of markets" may be mutually exclusive.[32]

Conceptual Impossibility of a Complete Set of Markets

The problems with the assumption of a complete set of markets run deeper. Later in these lectures I will emphasize the importance of innovation, but it is hard to conceive of there being markets for contingencies (states) that have not yet been conceived of: Surely an event such as the discovery of the principles underlying atomic energy and the subsequent development of commercial atomic power is an event of immense *economic* importance, in particular for owners of other energy resources. Yet how could markets in these risks—or in the risks associated with lasers or transistors—have existed before the underlying concepts had been developed? This is a fundamental incoherence between the ideas of a complete set of markets and notions of innovation.[33]

I have detailed several of the fundamental reasons why markets are likely to be incomplete. For many purposes it does not matter why they are incomplete. It only matters that they are incomplete.

Absence of Competition

Another critique of the fundamental theorem of welfare economics is that it *assumes* that there is perfect competition, that every firm is a price taker. Most markets are in fact not perfectly competitive. One reason is that when information is imperfect and costly, markets will normally not be perfectly competitive. Imperfect information confers on firms a degree of market power. Though there is competition, it is not the perfect competition of textbook economics, with price-taking firms; it is *more* akin to monopolistic competition, of the kind discussed a half-century ago by Chamberlin.[34] (I will return to this point later; for now I simply want to emphasize that the welfare results are strongly dependent on firms being price takers, that is, on there being *perfect* competition.) Because of imperfect information, if a firm raises its price, not all the firm's customers will immediately be able to find a firm that charges a lower price for the same commodity; indeed customers may well infer that other firms have raised their prices as well. By the same token, if it lowers its price, it does not instantly garner for itself all the customers from the higher-priced stores. Search is costly, and so those in the market rarely know the prices being charged by all the firms selling every good in which they are interested.

The imperfections of competition arise not only, however, from imperfect information but also from fixed costs, many of which are information-related costs. There are fixed costs that arise directly in production—the overhead costs of running a firm—and fixed costs associated with acquiring information about how to produce. This means that there is unlikely to be a very large number of firms producing every quality of every good at every location at every date in every state of nature. As we noted before, with even small fixed costs, many of these "markets" will have relatively few suppliers.

For these and other reasons, firms face downward-sloping demand curves. Markets may be highly competitive—but not perfectly competitive. Each of the deviations from perfect competition may be small, but when added up, they may amount to something—a myriad of small deviations leads to a picture of the economy that is markedly different from that of the standard paradigm. In particular, only under highly stringent conditions is the economy (constrained) Pareto efficient.[35]

The reason for this can be put simply. With downward-sloping demand curves, price—which measures consumers' marginal benefit or willingness to pay—exceeds the marginal cost. Lerner (1944) pointed out that if all firms faced the same elasticity of demand, were produced by labor alone, and the elasticity of supply of labor were zero, then even with monopolies the economy could be Pareto efficient. But this is a singular case. In general, the supply of labor is not inelastic, so monopoly in the goods market affects real wages and, in turn, the supply of labor; likewise the degree of monopoly (the elasticity of demand) differs across products.

Lerner (and other early writers) focused on the relative quantities of different goods that would be produced under imperfect competition. It is also that case that the set of goods that is produced may not be the most desirable set. A firm produces a product if the revenues it attains exceed the costs. In making its decision, the firm does not care to what extent its profits are garnered at the expense of other firms. If it produces a new commodity, it will shift the demand curve of other firms to the left as in figure 3.1. It may shift some firm's demand curve to the left enough that it no longer is profitable for it to produce. There is a loss of consumer surplus (the shaded area ABC). The consumer surplus lost may exceed the consumer surplus gained from the production of the new commodity.

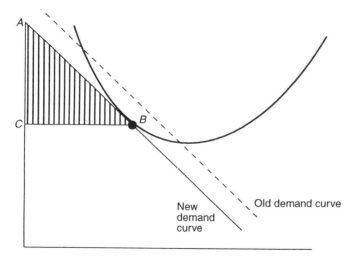

Figure 3.1
Introducing a new commodity may not increase social welfare. The new commodity shifts the demand curve to the left, making it no longer profitable to produce. The loss in consumer surplus (the shaded area ABC) may be greater than the consumer surplus associated with the new product.

Markets Create Noise

Finally, we think of one of the great virtues of market economies is its ability to "solve" information problems efficiently. Yet when information is costly, firms act to take advantage of that. In doing so, they may *create* noise[36]—they create, some times deliberately, information problems for consumers.

Temporary price reductions ("sales"), though we normally do not view them from this perspective, create price dispersion. Costly search gives firms good reason to charge different prices, or to temporarily reduce prices. Low-priced firms can gather for themselves a larger customer base, but the high-priced firms can still survive, serving only those who have high search costs and who have not had the good fortune to find a low-priced firm. The high-priced firms compensate for the smaller scale of their sales with a higher profit (price) per sale. Figure 3.2 shows a case where the only equilibrium must entail price dispersion. Suppose that all firms were to charge the same price. Each firm contemplates what would happen should it lower (or raise) its price. If it raises its price, it loses customers to other firms. If it lowers its price, it "steals" customers away from other firms. It

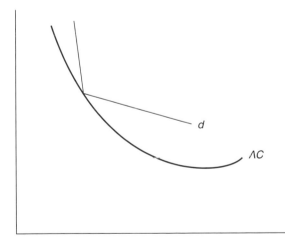

Figure 3.2
The unique equilibrium may entail price dispersion. With costly search, the increase in sales from lowering prices may be greater than the loss in sales from increasing prices. If all firms charged the same price, there would be a kink in the demand curve at that price. There cannot then exist a single-price, zero-profit equilibrium: At the point of tangency between the demand curve and the average cost curve, it pays the firm either to increase or decrease the price charged.

steals those who have easiest access to information (low-cost searchers). There may be relatively few of these (for a small decrease in the price) at any firm, but there are many firms from which it can steal customers. The total percentage increase in its sales from a 1 percent decrease in its price may be either smaller or larger than the decrease in its sales from a 1 percent increase in its price, depending on the number of other firms from which it can steal customers, and the number it steals from each firm (which in turn depends on how many low-search-cost individuals there are). Figure 3.2 depicts the case where the percentage increase in sales from a decrease in price is quite large, relative to the percentage decrease in sales from an increase in price: The demand curve has a kink. But it is clear that if this were the case, there could not exist a zero-profit, single-price equilibrium. We have drawn the average cost curve through the posited single price—the point where there is the kink in the demand curve. It clearly pays the firm either to increase or decrease its price. Either way, it makes a profit.

Thus, while price dispersion gives rise to search and other activities directed at reducing the "noise" of the market, and search limits the extent to which prices may differ in the market, the fact of the matter is that the existence of imperfect information—costly search—is what creates the price dispersion in the first place. The price dispersion itself arises, in part, not in response to *exogenous* changes in economic circumstances, or the differences in economic circumstances facing different firms, but endogenously, as part of the market equilibrium where each firm recognizes the consequences of the fact that search is costly. (That is, while Grossman and Stiglitz 1976 and Lucas 1972 emphasized the role of costly information in limiting the extent of arbitrage, reducing the differential impact of exogenous shocks, it is actually the case that markets create noise.)

The New and the Old Market Failures

These results, combined with the Greenwald-Stiglitz theorem, reduce the confidence we have in the presumption that markets are efficient. There are two important differences between the new market failures, based on imperfect and costly information and incomplete markets, and the older market failures associated with, for instance, public goods and pollution externalities: The older market failures were, for the most part, easily identified and limited in scope, requiring well-defined government interventions. Because virtually all markets are incomplete and information is always imperfect—moral hazard and adverse selection problems are endemic to all market situations—the market failures are pervasive in the economy. The Greenwald-Stiglitz analysis of these market failures is designed not only to identify the existence of the market failure but also to show the kinds of government interventions that will be Pareto improvements. Their analysis goes beyond this to identify the behavioral parameters (e.g., supply and demand elasticities) that determine the optimal corrective tax rates. Yet a full corrective policy would entail taxes and subsidies on virtually all commodities, based on estimated demand and supply elasticities for all commodities (including all cross elasticities). The *practical* information required to implement the corrective taxation is well beyond that available at the present time, and the costs of administering such corrective taxation (which were ignored in the Greenwald-Stiglitz analysis) might well exceed the benefits when the markets' distortion is small. Thus it seems reasonable that the government should focus its attention on those instances where there are large and important market failures—say, in the major insurance markets (for health care, perhaps even automobile insurance), risks associated with job security, and imperfections of capital markets. I will return to these practical considerations later in this book. For now I simply want to emphasize the essential difference between the new and the old market failures: the pervasiveness of the problems posed by imperfect information and incomplete markets.

Information, Prices, and the Efficiency of Market Economies

To some readers the claim that market economies are inefficient in the presence of imperfect information may seem curious, and quite at odds with the Austrian tradition. One of the claims frequently made of the price system is its informational efficiency. As we tell students in the basic introductory courses, no firm has to know even how to make a pencil; no firm need know the scarcity of any of the inputs that go into pencils, or the preferences of consumers. All that each person needs to know is the price received for outputs and the price paid for inputs. The great insight of the first fundamental theorem of welfare economics, of Adam Smith's invisible hand, is that even with access to this extremely limited information, markets can produce Pareto-efficient outcomes.

To be sure, there is great informational efficiency: Under the idealized conditions of the Arrow-Debreu model, prices do convey information efficiently from producers to consumers, and vice versa. Yet this is an extremely limited information problem. When a heavier informational burden is placed on markets—when it must sort among workers of different ability or securities of different qualities, when it must provide incentives to workers in the presence of imperfect monitoring, when it must obtain and process new information about an ever changing environment—markets do not perform so well, even in terms of our limited welfare criterion of constrained Pareto efficiency.

Market Socialism and Market Failures

This chapter has explained the importance of imperfect information and incomplete markets as an explanation of why market economies fail to be (constrained) Pareto efficient, why they fail to attain the standards of economic efficiency predicted by the neoclassical paradigm. Socialism, and market socialism, was intended to achieve greater economic efficiency without the attendant social costs of capitalism. But market socialism, in assigning to the government the responsibility for running "markets" (or "as if" markets), when such markets did not function well in the private sector, did not resolve these problems: The theory of market socialism, for the most part, was not based on an analysis of these market failures, and of the reasons why government might be able to resolve them, but rather on the naive comparison of the actual performance of market economies and the hypothesized performance of a market socialist economy with an idealized view of government. This idealization not only failed to take into account the political realities, but more important from the perspective of this chapter, failed to take into account essential economic realities.

The new information paradigm has revealed that "market failures" are indeed pervasive in the economy. They appear in virtually every transaction among private parties in the economy, and while they may be small in each case, cumulatively they are important. Moreover the market failures are not like those concerning air pollution, for which a well-defined and effective government policy can often easily be designed. This pervasiveness of failures, while it reduces our confidence in the efficiency of market solutions, also reduces our confidence in the ability of the government to correct them. Most important from our perspective, neither the theory nor the practice of socialism paid any attention to these problems.[37]

4   A Critique of the Second
Fundamental Theorem

The first welfare theorem was important because it said that in using markets, we ensure the efficiency of the economy. The Greenwald-Stiglitz theorem (and the other developments cited earlier) has removed any theoretical grounds for the presumption for the correctness of that view. By the same token, the second welfare economics proposition asserted that every Pareto-efficient allocation could be attained through the use of market mechanisms. "All" that is needed is to have the government engage in some initial lump-sum redistributions.

This theorem is widely interpreted as meaning that we can divorce the issue of efficiency from distribution. It is not an argument against markets that the resulting distribution of income is undesirable. If society does not like the distribution of income, the government's distribution branch (to use Musgrave's terminology) just alters the initial endowment of resources, through lump-sum redistributions.

The New New Welfare Economics: The Consequences of the Absence of Lump-Sum Taxes

But governments do not engage in lump-sum redistributions—and for good reasons. They do not have the information required to implement such taxes in an equitable manner. Governments clearly believe that different individuals should pay different taxes. As a basis of taxation, they inevitably rely on observable variables, like income or wealth, variables that are alterable. Hence the taxes are distortionary.

Once we recognize that redistributions are inevitably distortionary, we must also recognize that changing the distribution of endowments has an effect on the overall efficiency of the economy. This is illustrated in figure 4.1 in which is drawn the utility possibilities curve for a simple economy with two individuals; this gives the maximum level of utility attainable by

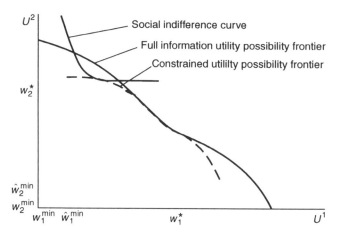

Figure 4.1
With information constraints, the utilities possibilities curve lies inside the curve where lump-sum taxes are allowed.

one (group of) individual(s), given the level of utility of the other. The solid line gives the utility possibilities schedule, given that the government has perfect information about who belongs to which group so that it can effect a lump-sum transfer. The dashed line shows how information constraints move the utilities possibilities curve inward.[1] Now suppose that we could express society's attitudes toward equality by a social indifference curve, as depicted in the figure. We see that given the indifference curve depicted, it is optimal to have distortionary taxes. Efficiency and equity considerations cannot be separated. Had the economy had a different initial endowment of resources, the magnitude of redistributive taxation required might have been less, and accordingly society's welfare (both group's) could have been higher.

The fact that redistributive taxation is, in general, distortionary has given rise to the "new new welfare economics."[2] The "old new welfare economics" emphasized that interpersonal utility comparisons were impossible: All that economists could do was to characterize the set of Pareto-efficient resource allocation. But the "old new welfare economics" assumed that lump-sum redistributions were possible. The "new new welfare economics" recognizes the limitations on the government's information. It focuses on the concept[3] of "Pareto-efficient taxation"—enabling us to define the maximum level of utility that one group can attain given the level of utility of other groups, *given the limitations on information that the government can employ in the process of redistribution*. Thus the new new welfare economics recognizes that the opportunity set facing the government is not the solid line in figure 4.1, but the dashed line that lies below it; how much it lies below it at any particular point depends on the initial distribution of wealth.

Economic Efficiency and Distribution

The previous section explained one of the reasons that distribution and efficiency concerns cannot be separated: The extent of inequality in initial endowments determines the extent to which government must rely on distortionary redistributive taxation to attain any given desired final distribution of welfare. But the extent of inequality as well as the nature of information problems affect the exact relationship between inequality and economic efficiency. In some cases high degrees of inequality may reduce economic efficiency (in a natural sense, as will be clear from the discussion that follows), while in other cases some inequality may enhance economic efficiency. We now take a closer look at the relationship between efficiency and distribution.

Incentive Problems

Issues of incentive are at the core of economics: Some economists have gone so far as to suggest that they are *the* economic problem. Incentive issues are intimately connected with issues of distribution. Sharecropping illustrates one aspect of the relationship. In many agrarian economies there is a great deal of inequality in wealth, resulting in a divergence between the ownership of land and labor. A prevalent contractual arrangement in less developed countries entails landlords and tenants sharing the proceeds. This sharecropping arrangement has been widely criticized, at least since Marshall, on the ground that workers' incentives are attenuated. If the landlord gets 50 percent of the output, it has the same enervating effect on labor effort that a 50 percent tax would have. More recent literature has viewed sharecropping contracts more positively; they reflect the market's trade-off between incentives and risk bearing, as illustrated in figure 4.2.[4] A pure rental contract (where the tenant rents the land for a fixed payment) would provide the worker with good[5] incentive, since the worker gets to keep all of the extra output that any additional effort on his or her part might yield; still the worker would have to bear all the risks. A pure wage contract would shift the risk to the landlord—the worker's income would not depend, for instance, on the vagaries of the weather—who would

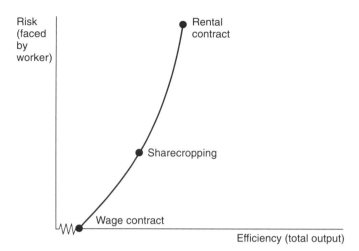

Figure 4.2
In trade-offs between risk and incentives, a pure rent contract provides strong incentives (so output is high), but the worker has to bear all the risk. A pure wage contract provides weak incentives, but the worker bears no risk. Sharecropping contracts represent a compromise.

generally be able to bear that risk more easily (because of the landlord's greater wealth), but the worker would then have no incentive other than that provided by direct (and costly) supervision. The sharecropping contract represents a compromise. Many readers were misled by my early (1974) formulation of equilibrium in a sharecropping economy (as the solution to the problem of maximizing the welfare of, say, the landlord given the expected utility of the tenant and given the information constraint) to the belief that such economies are Pareto efficient and that there was no loss in output from sharecropping, contrary to Marshall's dictum. That is an incorrect interpretation. I only characterized the equilibrium as having contract efficiency, a form of local efficiency. General equilibrium efficiency requires much more, and a direct implication of the Greenwald-Stiglitz theorems, referred to earlier, is that sharecropping economies with more than one good are, in general, not constrained Pareto efficient. But more relevant for our purposes here is the observation that even were the sharecropping contract constrained Pareto efficient, output may still be substantially lower than in the absence of sharecropping: A redistribution of land can have an enormous effect on national output. The effect would be the same as that of reducing a 50 percent wage tax to zero: Most observers would suggest that such a change could potentially have enormous effects.[6]

Why Excessive Inequality May Be a Problem

The intuitive reason why issues of distribution and efficiency cannot be separated can be easily seen. In economies with costly monitoring, and a separation of "capital" from "labor," the owners of capital must provide workers with incentives. These incentives are necessarily imperfect and costly.[7] If each farmer owned the land he or she worked, or if each worker owned the capital goods with which he or she worked, there would be no incentive problem.

More generally, the distribution of initial wealth has effects on the nature and magnitude of the incentive problems facing society.[8] One way, for instance, that incentive problems can be ameliorated is for workers to post bonds. Guarantees are useful in providing employers with assurances not only concerning work performance but also labor turnover; with adequate assurances employers will have greater incentives to provide training, and this will enhance economic efficiency. The potential of workers to put up bonds for good performance is affected by their initial wealth. Borrowing is no substitute. As we noted in our discussion of sharecropping (see note 5 above), borrowing to pay the rent is not different from paying the rent at the end of the period; in both cases incentive (moral hazard) problems arise from the possibility of default: The borrower may have insufficient incentives to avoid bankruptcy, and to maximize the returns (which will accrue to the lender) in those circumstances where bankruptcy does occur.

Problems from Insufficient Concentration of Wealth

Greater equality of course does not necessarily reduce all incentive problems. Efficient production may require large-scale enterprises, entailing large amounts of capital. The problems of the separation of ownership and control, to which I referred earlier and to which I will return later, then arise because of "too little" inequality: Indeed there is some evidence that firms in which there is concentration of ownership (even if those with large ownership interests do not directly manage the firm) behave more "rationally." In the next section I will discuss two examples of this—in takeover activity and in taxation. But as I indicate below, the solution to these problems which the Eastern European countries are likely to seek will not entail increases in inequality and concentration of ownership, but rather the development of alternative control processes.

I stress the results on the link between issues of distribution and issues of efficiency, because some of the recent discussions of reform within

Eastern Europe have stressed efficiency concerns, with limited regard to the consequences for distribution. Years from now this lack of concern for distribution, I will argue later, may come to haunt these economies, not just in the form of social unrest, but more narrowly in terms of long-run economic efficiency. At the very least, there is no intellectual foundation for the separation of efficiency and distributional concerns.

The Fundamental Nondecentralizability Theorems

One interpretation of the second welfare theorem is that it establishes the viability of decentralization: *Any* Pareto-efficient resource allocation can be obtained via a decentralized price mechanism, with *extremely* limited government intervention. In particular, the government does not have to intervene in the basic processes of resource allocation. While the issue of decentralization is very much at the fore of debates on alternative economic systems, the concept of decentralization has many alternative meanings. My use of that term within this book will reflect the variety of uses current in economics, as well as the ambiguities associated with those uses.

Virtually all concepts of decentralization involve decision making occurring at a multitude of different units within the economy. Questions in the definition of decentralization arise from the multitude of forms which "interventions" from higher authorities can take. The ambiguity in the concept of decentralization is illustrated by considering the possibility of nonlinear taxes. Nonlinear taxes can be designed to give the firm or individual no "choice" other than to take the action desired by the central planner. The individual or firm in a sense does make a choice, but the central authorities have so circumscribed those choices, by defining sufficiently unattractive payoffs for choices other than that desired by the central authority, that there is *really* no choice. Most interventions constrain choices to some degree. There is no simple way of "ranking" interventions by the amount of "true" discretionary powers left to the separate units.[9]

Several recent results in the economics of information have cast doubt on the validity of the decentralizability result: There are strong limits to the extent that the economy can be decentralized through the price mechanism. The following sections take up five aspects of this.

The Greenwald-Stiglitz Theorem and Decentralization

The Greenwald-Stiglitz theorems establish that constrained Pareto-efficient allocations cannot generally be obtained without *some* form of government intervention, though in some cases that intervention may be limited to the imposition of a set of linear excise taxes (taxes at a fixed rate per unit purchased, consumed, or produced). Because decentralization is not, in general, a viable way of obtaining Pareto-efficient outcomes, I sometimes refer to the Greenwald-Stiglitz theorem as the "fundamental nondecentraliz-ability theorem."

If the only feasible interventions of the government were linear taxes, and/or if the government could always implement any constrained Pareto-efficient allocation through the use of linear taxes, then the "spirit" of the older decentralization results will still be satisfied. Government intervention would be required to redistribute wealth, though, as I noted in the first section of this chapter, the redistribution would in general be distortionary. There would still be some government intervention required beyond this, but the intervention is still limited: "All" the government has to do is to impose a set of taxes/subsidies on various commodities.

But the problems of decentralizing Pareto-efficient resource allocations are actually far worse than the Greenwald-Stiglitz theorem would suggest, and for four reasons: cross-subsidization, the pervasiveness of nonconvexities, externalities, and nonlinearities.

Cross-subsidization

One of the central results (though one not often commented upon) of the Arrow-Debreu model is that Pareto efficiency is obtained in that model without any *cross-subsidization*. To use perhaps an Americanism, every firm can stand on its own bottom. This is not true in the presence of imperfect information—even in the seeming absence of any increasing returns.[10] Arnott and I (1989) have analyzed in detail the economics of moral hazard —problems that arise, for instance, in insurance markets where the provision of insurance affects the incentives of the insured to take actions that reduce the likelihood of an accident. We show that competitive equilibrium, in which insurance companies covering each risk "stand on their own bottom" are not (constrained) Pareto efficient; welfare can be improved, say, by tax-ing some (possibly insurance) industry to provide a subsidy to one or more of the (other) insurance industries. (We refer to the inefficiency that results when such cross-subsidizations do not occur as the *cross-subsidization mar-ket failure.*) The intuition behind this result is that small taxes on industries in which moral hazard problems are not important have second-order effects (the deadweight loss increases with the square of the tax rate). On the other hand, the loss in welfare from moral hazard/incentive problems is first order; or more to the point, the increased effort resulting from a subsidy to complements to effort can be first order and have first-order effects on welfare.

The Pervasiveness of Nonconvexities

Another problem in decentralization occurs when there are nonconvexities in the economy. This was brought out clearly in early discussions of the second fundamental theorem, where it was recognized that for natural monopolies some form of government intervention was required. But I am not concerned here with this relatively well-understood problem with decentralization. Rather, I am concerned with the *pervasive nonconvexities* associated with imperfect information.

At an intuitive level, the fact that there are nonconvexities associated with information should be clear: Information can be considered a fixed cost (see chapter 2). It is a cost incurred regardless of what is done with it, and fixed costs give rise to nonconvexities. Similarly the value to a firm of discovering a better way of making a widget depends on the number of widgets made. The total and marginal return to expenditure on R&D increase with the scale of production.

Radner and Stiglitz (1984) have shown, in the context of statistical decision theory, that the value of information is never globally concave (see figure 4.3.) The return to a little bit of information is always zero, and if that information has a positive cost, then the net return is negative. "If ignorance is not bliss, at least it is a local optimum."[11]

But nonconvexities are even more pervasive than the results discussed thus far would suggest: Whenever there are moral hazard problems, incentive problems, or selection problems (involving incentive compatibility constraints or self-selection constraints) there are (in the relevant space) nonconvexities, no matter how seemingly well behaved the problem is.[12] (An intuitive interpretation of this is that the incentive constraints can be thought of as involving the first-order conditions of the individual's or firm's maximization problem. Thus the concavity of the entire maximand, including the embedded incentive constraints, involves third derivatives of the utility or profit function, and there are no natural economic constraints on those derivatives.) Arnott and Stiglitz (1988a) show in the simplest of moral hazard models that the indifference curves between benefits and costs are essentially never quasi-concave and that the set of policies, described by their benefits and premiums, generating nonnegative profits is never convex. This is illustrated in figure 4.4 for the case where the

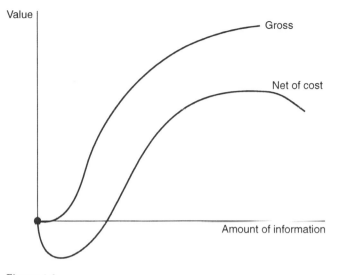

Value |

Gross

Net of cost

Amount of information

Figure 4.3
Nonconcavity is characteristic of the value of information. "If ignorance is not bliss, at least it is a local optimum."

individual has a choice between two activities, smoking and nonsmoking. The probability of a fire increases with the proportion of time the individual spends smoking. With no insurance, the individual will not smoke; with complete and free insurance, where he or she bears none of the consequences of smoking, the individual will smoke. For any given premium, there is a particular level of benefit for which the individual is indifferent between smoking and not smoking; at higher levels of benefit, the individual smokes, at lower levels of benefits he or she does not. And as the premium increases, the benefit at which the individual is indifferent between smoking and not smoking decreases. The locus of {benefit, premium} combinations for which the individual is indiffferent between smoking and not smoking is downward sloping and is referred to as the "switching line." There are thus two regimes, below the switching line, where individuals do not smoke, and above it, where they do. In each regime individuals have different indifference curves, one representing the trade-off between benefit and premium when the individual smokes the other when he or she does not. Obviously in each regime the indifference curve is positively sloped: As benefits increase, the premiums individuals are willing to pay increase. The indifference curves get flatter as benefits increase, since the extra premium individuals are willing to pay for a given increase in benefits decreases. At the switch line, however, the

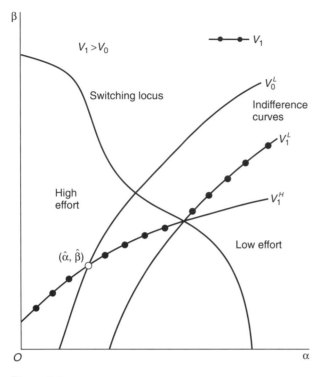

Figure 4.4
With moral hazard, even the simplest models give rise to nonconvex indifference curves. Here the individual has two activities, smoking or not smoking. The switching locus is the combination of {benefits, premiums} that leaves the individual indifferent between the two. The indifference curve {benefits, premiums} has the scalloped shape depicted. The axis labeled α denotes the benefit and β the premium (paid only in the event that no accident occurs.) Superscript L denotes the "low effort—high accident probability—activity," H the "high effort—low accident probability—activity," so V^L is the indifference curve of the individual who undertakes the low accident activity. Through any point, there are two indifference curves, one representing the low accident activity and the other the high accident activity. Since the individual is indifferent between the two along the switching locus, it is clear that at point $(\hat{\alpha}, \hat{\beta})$ the individual prefers the high effort (low accident) to the low effort (high accident). (Utility increases with lower premiums and higher benefits.)

indifference curve becomes abruptly steeper, as depicted; in the smoking regime (above the switching line) the value of an increase in benefits is much greater, since the likelihood of a fire is higher. Thus the true indifference curve, representing the change in action as well as marginal valuations as benefits increase, is scallop shaped, as depicted: There is a fundamental nonconvexity in indifference curves.

There is a corresponding fundamental nonconvexity in the feasibility set, the set of {benefit, premium} policies that at least break even. Below the switching locus, when individuals do not smoke, there is a low probability of a fire. To just cover benefits, premia must increase linearly with benefits, as depicted in figure 4.5. Similarly, if individuals smoke, premiums must increase with benefits, but the requisite premium must be much higher, to compensate for the higher probability of a fire. The feasibility set must take into account that below the switching line, individuals do not smoke, and above it, they do: the shaded area depicted in figure 4.5. It is clearly nonconvex. This example illustrates how, with the simplest of assumptions, with seemingly well-behaved utility functions, nonconvexities naturally arise in the presence of moral hazard/incentive problems. In more realistic settings, in which individuals have a wider range of choices of actions, both the feasibility set and the indifference curves may appear to be even more irregular.

Some of the potential consequences of these nonconvexities had been recognized earlier (e.g., the possible desirability of random policies).[13] For our purposes, what is important is the *nondecentralizability* of the constrained Pareto-efficient resource allocations. Not only is government intervention required, but "linear" interventions will not suffice.[14] The intuitive reason why nonconvexities lead to problems is illustrated in figure 4.6 where we have drawn a nonconvex production possibilities schedule; the optimal allocation, the tangency between the "representative individual's" indifference curve and the production possibilities curve, is at an interior point E. If firms maximize profits, given the relative prices (marginal rates of substitution) at E, they will choose a corner point such as A. By the same token, in our insurance model with moral hazard, with nonconvex indifference curves the optimum may be at point E in figure 4.7. At that set of relative prices individuals will choose to purchase more insurance than E (they go to E'). When they do so, however, the level of care decreases, and as a result E is not feasible.

I stress these results for several reasons. The underlying mathematical structure of economics, as it developed from Samuelson's *Foundations of Economic Analysis* to Debreu's *Theory of Value* stressed the importance of

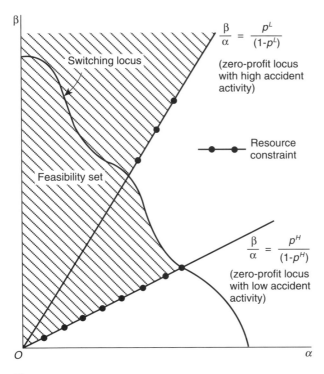

Figure 4.5
The set of policies that at least breaks even is also not convex. p^L is the probability of an accident if the individual exerts low effort (undertakes the high accident activity). Thus profits are zero if the individual undertakes a low level of effort, and $\alpha p^L = \beta(1 - p^L)$; similarly for the high level of effort. In the region where the individual undertakes the high level of effort, profits are positive about the zero-profit locus $\alpha p^H = \beta(1 - p^H)$; similarly in the region where the individual undertakes the low level of effort, profits are positive above the zero-profit locus $\alpha p^L = \beta(1 - p^L)$. The total feasibility set is thus the shaded area depicted.

convexity, for the fundamental existence results, for the welfare results of competitive markets (in particular, for the second fundamental theorem of welfare economics), and for the derivation of comparative statics. Beyond that, it was well understood that with sufficient nonconvexities markets would not be competitive. There were plausible arguments that "normally" these convexity assumptions would be satisfied by consumers and producers, the exceptions being limited and requiring government intervention. Normally we expected the law of diminishing returns and diminishing marginal rates of substitution to prevail.

Once the imperfections and costs of information are taken into account, the assumption of convexity is no longer plausible; the nonconvexities are

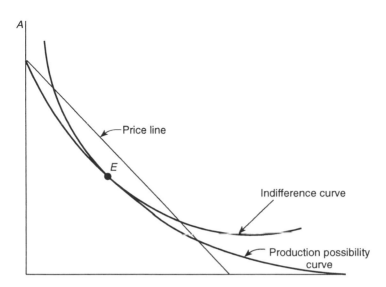

Figure 4.6
With nonconvex production sets, the Pareto-efficient equilibrium may not be able to be sustained through a price system.

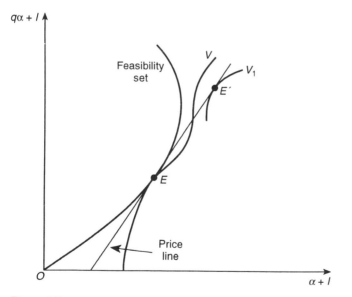

Figure 4.7
Given the nonconvexity of indifference curves arising where there is moral hazard, it may not be able to sustain the efficient equilibrium through a price system.

pervasive. With the pervasive nonconvexities the government interventions required to attain Pareto-efficient allocations can no longer be as limited as the second fundamental theorem suggested. Not only are lump-sum interventions not feasible, they are not sufficient, and not even *linear* interventions will suffice.

Externalities

The main insight of the Greenwald-Stiglitz analysis was to show that whenever markets were incomplete and information was imperfect, actions that individuals or firms took generated "externalitylike" effects. The unproductive worker, in deciding to work more hours, lowered the mean quality of those offering themselves in the labor market and thus exerted a negative externality on others. The smokers, in deciding to smoke more, increased the average probability of a fire, and the necessary offsetting increase in premiums acted as a negative externality on all those buying fire insurance. These were externalities that, under certain circumstances, could be offset by appropriately designed excise taxes, thus preserving the "spirit" of decentralization.

But there may be many classes of externalities that are not so easily offset. Consider the tenant-landlord relationship, where issues of incentives and risk sharing lead to an optimal sharecropping contract. Then any action that the tenant takes that affects the output of the farm has an externalitylike effect on the landlord. The landlord benefits from the tenant's use of fertilizer, not only directly, through the increased direct yield, but also indirectly if the fertilizer increases the marginal product of the tenant, and accordingly the tenant works harder. The landlord thus has an incentive to subsidize the use of fertilizer. The "input market" (fertilizer), the land market, and the labor market thus become interlinked. Government interventions (e.g., a generalized subsidy on fertilizer) may not suffice, since the magnitude of the supply responses (e.g., the effort response of the worker to the increased fertilizer utilization, which in turn may depend on the magnitude of the increment in the marginal productivity of labor resulting from the increased supply of fertilizer) may not be uniform across all farms; the landlord may be in a better position (because of detailed information concerning both the land and the tenant) to provide the "correct" level of subsidy, which is likely to vary considerably from farm to farm. Thus the argument in favor of decentralization—that relevant information is localized—itself helps to explain why full decentralization (with land, labor, and fertilizer markets being run independently, with only limited central government intervention) will not work. At the same time partial decentralization, with interlinked markets, may not suffice to ensure economic efficiency without government intervention, particularly if secondary sales of, for instance, fertilizer cannot be prevented.

The example, illustrating the advantages of "interlinked markets" with complex relations among participants, applies far more generally. The web of relations observed in product markets (e.g., by producers and those who market their goods) and in credit markets (firms often provide credit both to suppliers and customers) are other examples that come easily to mind.

Nonlinear Payment Schedules

The final problem with the simple kind of decentralization envisaged by market socialism and reflected in the standard competitive paradigm has to do with nonlinearities. As we noted earlier, the Greenwald-Stiglitz theorem says that the decentralized market economy does not, in general, yield constrained Pareto-efficient outcomes. It showed the existence of simple taxes and subsidies that could make everyone better off. But these were simple interventions. If the government intervened in this way only, the spirit of decentralization would, as I have emphasized, be preserved. A market socialist economy could run itself much as Lange and Lerner might have envisaged, with the primary difference being that the "planner" would have had to call out different prices for producers and consumers. (This is the framework envisaged in Stiglitz and Dasgupta 1971.)

But more recent work in optimal incentives/optimal taxation has established that such simple interventions will suffice in restoring the economy to (constrained) Pareto efficiency only under somewhat restrictive mathematical conditions. For instance, the literature on Pareto-efficient tax structures referred to earlier suggests that, in general, governments need to impose taxes that depend on the level of consumption of each and every commodity in quite complicated ways; for example, the amount of tax imposed on the consumption of commodity A may depend on the level of consumption of commodity B.

Precisely parallel problems arise in the context of firms, workers, and creditors within the market. Universities allow their workers to consult outside for, say, one day a week. This can be viewed as a simple nonlinear tax (pay schedule): No tax is imposed on the first eight hours, a prohibitive tax on work in excess of eight hours. A beer company says to its distributor that it may sell so much of other companies' beer, but if it sells too much of these other companies' beers, it will lose its franchise.

Thus optimal interventions by the government in the market, as well as optimal contractual arrangements among parties within the market, often are highly complex, reflecting information-induced externalities, nonlinearities and quantitative constraints, and employ cross-market constraints and information. These results have profound implications, both for economic theory and for the feasibility of the kind of decentralization envisaged in the standard neoclassical (Arrow-Debreu) model.

Efficiency requires not the complete decentralization suggested by the neoclassical paradigm but partial decentralization—what we observe, in our economy consisting of many large firms which experience only limited decentralization. The interactions and information-induced business relations (or agglomerations) may interfere with the effectiveness of competition—at least the simplistic form of competition envisaged in standard models. In some cases all that is affected is the "unit" over which competition occurs; for example, if the landlord provides the fertilizer, the relevant unit of competition is the landlord-cum-fertilizer seller. In some cases the web of interconnections (externalities) is so complex that the externalities are not effectively addressed in this manner (e.g., see Arnott and Stiglitz 1985). In still other cases, where there are important intertemporal interlinkages and ex ante competition (competition for individuals or firms to sign contracts), competition may be very limited once the contracts are signed. With imperfect foresight and imperfect insurance markets, ex ante competition is far from a full substitute for ex post competition.[15] In still other cases the fact that so many firms and individuals are tied together in a nexus of ongoing relations serves to provide an important impediment to competitive entry and to the overall competitiveness of the market.[16]

Government interventions may require far more information than in those cases where all the government needs to do is to impose a linear tax or subsidy, and hence the kind of decentralization envisaged by Lange and Lerner, and by the other market socialists, simply will not work. It was the belief in the *simple* (linear) price system that underlay their theories, and it is this belief that these modern information-based theories have questioned.

But, again, we observe the seeming paradox: While these modern theories have questioned the viability of market socialism, they have, at the same time, weakened our confidence in (at least our simplistic view of) competitive economies, and the models we have constructed to describe them. On the one hand, these theories do correctly predict many of the complex forms of business relations we observe. On the other hand, they suggest that we should observe more complex relations more frequently. For instance, only under highly restricted conditions should piece rate contracts or sharecropping contracts be linear. The simple forms of such contractual arrangements observed in practice are not those that most of the information-theoretic models would have predicted, except under assumptions that themselves can be refuted on other grounds.[17]

While there are "explanations" of the prevalence of "excessively simple" (from the theoretical perspective) contracts—they are easy to understand; employees do not think that the employer is trying to "game them" by introducing a contractual arrangement that the employer understands but the full implications of which the employee only faintly grasps[18]—still the point remains that the standard paradigm leaves unexplained essential aspects of economic relations, raising questions about the validity of the model in general and its central conclusion, the decentralizability through the price system. Accordingly the suggestion that market socialism would do as well as the market economy by imitating, not the market economy, but the model of the market economy—the decentralized model using the price system to communicate all the relevant information—is, to say the least, suspect.

Summary

This and the previous chapter have reviewed some of the recent developments in welfare economics. The previous chapter focused on the first fundamental theorem of welfare economics, asserting the efficiency of competitive market economies. These recent developments have reduced our confidence in the presumption that markets are efficient. They have provided an increased *potential* role for government intervention, and in doing so, they have, indirectly, buttressed the argument for market socialism.

This chapter has focused on the second fundamental theorem of welfare economics, which has been given three alternative interpretations. Each of these has been called into question. The first focuses on the limited role for government: All the government needs to do to attain any Pareto-efficient resource allocation is to engage in lump-sum redistributions; the market will take care of the rest. I have argued, in contrast, that in the presence of imperfect information, lump-sum distributions of the kind envisaged in the traditional model simply are not feasible. The costs of government interventions required to correct the inadequacies of the market's distribution of wealth are greater than envisaged by the traditional theory.

The second fundamental theorem of welfare economics implies that issues of economic efficiency and distribution can be neatly separated. This separation has proved extremely useful for economists who would like to focus on the concept of "economic efficiency," putting issues of distribution to the side. I have pointed out in this chapter that in the presence of imperfect information, issues of efficiency and distribution cannot be so easily separated. For instance, whether the economy is or is not Pareto efficient may itself depend on the distribution of income.

Finally, the second fundamental theorem of welfare economics is often presented as establishing the decentralizability of the economy. By contrast, I have pointed out that there are five fundamental results in the economics of information showing the strong limitations on the extent to which the economy can be decentralized through the price mechanism:

1. The Greenwald-Stiglitz theorem can be thought of as establishing the nondecentralizability of the economy, for it shows that markets, left to themselves, essentially never result in a constrained Pareto optimum when markets are incomplete or information is imperfect.

2. In economies in which markets are incomplete and information is imperfect, externalitylike effects arise and are pervasive.

3. The Arnott-Stiglitz theorem establishes that, in general, it is desirable to have cross-subsidization (even in the absence of direct externality effects).

4. The ability to decentralize using the price system requires that there be no nonconvexities, but nonconvexities are pervasive.

5. Optimal incentive structures, in the presence of imperfect information, almost always entail nonlinear payment schedules.

I have shown that the argument for decentralization based on the second fundamental theorem of welfare economics is fundamentally flawed. But this should not be interpreted as implying that I am arguing against the conclusion that the economy can be, or should be, run in a decentralized manner. In chapter 9, I return to the issue of decentralization and provide some alternative perspectives.

Market socialism implicitly employed the second fundamental theorem of welfare economics as the organizational basis of the economy. It avoided the criticism that the informational requirements of socialism using a central planner were so burdensome as to make socialism not feasible. It argued that socialism could make use of the same kind of decentralization of information that the market economy employed; prices could just as effectively convey information under socialism as they could under the market economy, and information about technology, for instance, could continue to reside in the individual firms.

The arguments that I have presented show the limitations of the second fundamental theorem, but they also suggest that this perspective is flawed. But it is not only that prices do not convey all of the relevant information required for a decentralized economy to be run efficiently. As I will argue in later chapters, the set of informational problems that the economy must address are far richer than those envisaged by either the standard models of the market economy or the models of market socialism. While market economies may solve these problems imperfectly, under market socialism these problems were not even addressed.

One of the critical distinctions between markets and market socialism is the ownership, and allocation, of capital. The extent of intervention required to ensure that capital will be allocated in an efficient way in a market economy is far larger than envisaged in the traditional theory. The socially acceptable (or desirable) distributions of wealth almost inevitably entail a separation of ownership and control, leading to the same kinds of incentive problems for market economies as are associated with nonmarket economies. These are issues we will take up in greater detail in the following chapters.

5   Criticisms of the
Lange-Lerner-Taylor
Theorem: Incentives

In the previous two chapters we asked to what extent do the fundamental theorems of welfare economics help inform us about the choice among alternative economic systems, in particular the choice between markets and government. The answer was negative: We have no general theorems ensuring the efficiency (even the constrained efficiency) of market economies; we have general theorems stating that, in principle, there are welfare-enhancing government interventions.

We noted too that to a large extent these theorems do not address the central issues of concern—for instance, the efficiency of the market in processing information or in choosing the right workers, the right managers, or the right investments. When we looked more closely into those issues, the market did not improve its score: We identified several key problems with how market economies perform those functions. But I should emphasize that these discussions leave out many of the central attributes of market economies. The most important issues concerning innovation or decision making under uncertainty are not adequately addressed. The evolutionary mechanisms of market economies are not touched upon. And the view of competition—price-taking behavior—does not even come close to capturing some of the most important virtues of the competitive process. We will turn to these issues later. For now I want only to caution against prejudging the question with which I am ultimately concerned here, the role of the market, on the basis of the negative results obtained so far.

I now want to turn my attention to the second cornerstone of the traditional comparison of alternative systems, the Lange-Lerner-Taylor theorem on the equivalence of (competitive) market economies and market socialism. As I suggested earlier, the result is clearly wrong: It is based on an incomplete or inaccurate model of market socialism, and an incomplete or inaccurate model of markets. As we will see, the two failures are closely intertwined.

As in most of this book, I want to abstract from problems of political economy. This is, undoubtedly, a mistake: In trying to determine the balance between the public and the private sector, political economy questions can become of central importance. But there is enough to say about the more narrow concerns of economics.

In this book I argue that the model of market socialism (and the Arrow-Debreu model of the competitive economy, on which it is based) made five crucial mistakes. Market socialism

1. underestimated the significance of the incentive problem,

2. underestimated the difficulty of making a "full-pricing" system work, and correspondingly underestimated the role of nonprice allocation mechanisms within the economy,

3. underestimated the difficulty of allocating capital,

4. misjudged the role and function of decentralization and competition,

5. simply ignored the role of innovation in the economy.

In these errors market socialism was not alone, as I have emphasized: Each of these charges could be leveled—in my judgment, fairly so—against the standard neoclassical model of the economy, the twin brother of the market socialist model. This chapter is devoted to the first error, with the following chapters taking up the remaining problems in turn.

Incentive Problems

Perhaps the most important failure of market socialism was its underestimate of the significance of incentives. In market socialism managers (much like other workers in the economy) simply did what they were supposed to. Of course, in the model of the economy which was formulated, managers had a fairly trivial job; they were—with no insult meant—little more than low-grade engineers. They performed some maximization problems, subject to some constraints. There were none of the elements of judgments and creative solution of problems upon which managers pride themselves.

As we noted earlier, the very criticisms of market socialism are themselves, to a large extent, criticisms of the neoclassical paradigm. This is true here too: Incentives (except in a very limited sense to be explained below) play no role in the standard neoclassical theory. A worker gets paid for doing the job contracted to do; if he does not do the job, he does not get paid. There is no problem of monitoring, of ascertaining whether the worker has or has not done the job. Accordingly employers have no concern about motivating the worker: There is a price for a job, and that ends the matter. To be sure, we talk about prices and profits providing firms with incentives to produce, but the broader class of incentive problems—of firms having an incentive to maintain a reputation, to produce high-quality goods and to satisfy their customers—do not arise. There is a price for each quality of good. The price shows the firm how the market values each quality; buyers have no problem ascertaining quality, and firms produce the quality that they have agreed to produce.

It is clear that this paradigm misses out on many of the most important and interesting economic issues. Firms need to motivate their workers. Lenders worry about borrowers repaying. Owners worry about managers taking the right actions. What is of concern is not only levels of effort but appropriate risk taking. Owners worry whether managers are taking too little or too much risk; lenders worry about whether those to whom they have lent money are undertaking too much risk, thus making it less likely that they will repay their loans. The importance of the latter should be particularly stressed: For in many cases it is no more difficult to make one decision than another. What is at stake is not "effort" but "risk," and the difficulties of monitoring whether appropriate risks are being taken are far more formidable even than monitoring effort.

The standard paradigm goes astray at three distinct points. First, it assumes that the variables of interest are costly and perfectly observable. The employer can costlessly ascertain the level of effort and make its payment contingent on the employee providing the contracted for level of effort.

Second, decision making plays no role in the standard paradigm. The employee can be given instructions: Do this in contingency A, do that in contingency B, and the employer can monitor whether contingency A has occurred, and whether the employee has conformed to the contract. By contrast, in reality the employee has information that the employer does not have, information which is important for determining what action should be taken, and it is often difficult for the employer to know whether the employee has acted "correctly."

Third, it is often costly to enforce contracts. People who borrow money may not pay it back. One firm may make investments, on the basis of a commitment of another firm to buy its products, and the second firm may attempt to renege on its commitments.

Each of these "problems" gives rise to incentive issues. Individuals have discretion in the level of effort that they undertake, in the actions they take in different contingencies, in whether they "live up" to the terms of an agreement. The problem of economic incentives is how to design monitoring and reward structures that "align" incentives. This is an issue which was never even addressed within the Arrow-Debreu framework but which has become a central concern of the new information economics. The difficulties of monitoring directly, the difficulties of designing compensation schemes based on what is observable, and the difficulties of designing contracts that are self-enforcing or can be enforced through legal systems at a reasonable cost, have all been a central concern of this literature.

The failure to provide incentives is generally viewed as a central reason for the failure of the Soviet system, and a fundamental flaw in the idea of market socialism. This has led many commentators to suggest that all that is required is to restore the market system, with private property; this will instantly restore incentives, and restore the economy to health. I believe this reasoning is fundamentally flawed: It overestimates the role of financial incentives, and it underestimates the problems of control of large enterprises, which are shared by both public and private enterprises.

To be sure, state enterprises face incentive problems at both the organizational level (in the form of soft budget constraints) and at the individual level (in the form of constraints, dictated by concerns about equity, on admissible compensation schemes as well as on job security) which are different from those facing private firms. Still, *at the managerial level*—at the level at which most decisions get made, and which would seem to be crucial in determining organizational performance—the incentive problems that arise in large enterprises and the solutions (e.g., incentive pay) would seem to differ little between those that are privately or publicly owned.

The remainder of the chapter is divided into five subsections: The first section argues that shareholders have limited control over their managers, so managers have considerable autonomy. The second argues that financial incentives play a much more limited role than conventional theory suggests. The third argues that many aspects of corporate behavior can best be understood as a consequence of limited control by shareholders of those who manage the firms that shareholders supposedly "own." The fourth argues that banks may play a much more active role in governance than conventional theory suggests. The fifth attempts to set out some of the implications for reform in the former socialist countries.

Managerial Discretion and Control

Earlier, in chapter 2, I referred to the importance of the consequences of the separation of ownership and control associated with the modern corporation. The early literature on managerial capitalism, which grew out of the earlier work of Knight (1921) and Berle and Means (1932) (see also Marris 1964; Baumol 1959; March and Simon 1958), was dismissed as being without theoretical foundations: If firms did not maximize stock market value, they would simply be taken over by someone who did. As we noted earlier, the recognition in the early 1970s that information was costly, and that the costs of information gave managers considerable discretion, provided the beginnings of the missing theoretical foundations. We now understand better why each of the alleged control mechanisms works so imperfectly:[1]

1. *Management as a public good.* The management of any enterprise is like a public good. All holders of a class of securities benefit if the return to that security increases. Thus there is no incentive for small equity owners to monitor the firm's executives. Even large shareholders in a typical firm own but a small fraction of the shares, and thus have *insufficient* incentives—though if their stake is large enough, the difference between the "optimal" level of monitoring and the actual level of monitoring may be relatively small.

2. *Voting as a public good.* Voting mechanisms, by the same token, suffer from the usual free-riding problems (the "voting paradox"): Not only does it not pay any small shareholder to become informed, it does not pay for them to vote (on issues that are subject to proxy vote), if there is any cost to voting. While we resolve this voting paradox in national elections by trying to inculcate in our children a "moral responsibility" to vote, so far at least, little attention has been place on the "moral responsibility" in voting in elections for members of the board.

3. *Inadequacy of the takeover mechanism.* Most striking perhaps are the results on the inadequacy of takeover mechanism. On the one hand, investors appear to have limited incentives to become informed about mismanaged firms, to take them over: In practice, the firms taking over other firms have not gained from doing so (see, e.g., Jarrell, Brickley, and Netter 1988), and in competitive takeover markets we would not expect to see them gain.[2] If there is more than one bidder, the price should be bid up to the "full" market value. There may be large costs to finding undervalued firms, but

once it is ascertained that a firm is undervalued, determining the extent to which it is undervalued may be relatively costless. If making a bid reveals the fact that the bidder knows the firm is undervalued, then anyone spending any money searching for undervalued firms would obtain no return on that investment. This is an extreme case, yet it illustrates the general principle that the private return to investing in information of this kind may be much lower than the social return.[3]

On the other side, minority shareholders of an undervalued (perhaps mismanaged) firm have no incentive to sell it to someone who, they believe, will enhance its value: By holding on to their shares, they will participate as well in the gain in value. The only reason they have to sell is if they believe the firm taking over will decrease its market value (perhaps at the same time as it increases its efficiency, since it diverts the taken-over firm's wealth into their own pockets). This is just another manifestation of the free-rider problem to which I referred earlier (see Grossman and Hart 1980, 1988).[4]

Weak Role of Traditional Incentives

If "owners" cannot or do not monitor their executives, the natural alternative is to provide them financial compensation designed to make their interests coincide. Some of the recent theoretical literature describes ways by which "high-powered" incentives can be provided to employees, by letting them receive the *entire* value of the output of the firm, with the managers paying at the same time a large fixed fee.[5] In effect the executives become the owners in that they receive all the residual income. There are strong assumptions underlying these analyses, such as that each individual be risk neutral[6] and have sufficient capital to finance this fixed fee.[7] With risk aversion, optimal contracts may entail fairly low-powered incentives, depending on the magnitude of the risk (see, e.g., Stiglitz 1975b).

Most workers' pay is not highly dependent on performance. A relatively small portion of workers receive a significant fraction of their income as a result of piece rates. There is a variety of reasons for this: Costs of measuring effort and output, difficulties in ascertaining quality of output and effort, the stochastic elements in the relationship between effort and output (so that even were output perfectly measurable, it would provide an imperfect indicator of the level of effort), and the difficulties of adjusting piece rates to changes in technology. Moreover the multiplicity of objectives or outputs (e.g., workers train and monitor other workers), and the fact that piece rate pay diverts attention toward the rewarded activities but away from the other activities, imply that piece rates may not be effective in ensuring that workers behave in a way that maximizes firm profits.[8]

My concern, however, is more with managerial decision making than with workers. In practice financial incentives of management in large enterprises appear very weak: Management typically receives less than 0.3% of each increment in profits that its actions garner for the firm (Jensen and Murphy 1990). This may seem surprising, given the important role the stock options seem to play as part of managerial compensation. Stock options are justified as providing strong incentives: If the firm does well, the manager will be rewarded. But while stock options are intended to reward management for good performance, typically when the firm goes through a bad period, other forms of compensation are increased, so that total compensation remains relatively insensitive to firm performance.

There are other reasons to suspect claims that options are designed to provide management with incentives. Stock options are dominated as a means of rewarding executives: There are alternative methods that have decided tax and risk advantages. In a meeting a few years ago of personnel officers of major corporations at which the design of executive compensation schemes was discussed, I asked whether they employed stock options because (1) they were unaware of the tax disadvantages—a strong implicit condemnation of their competence; or (2) they were attempting to hoodwink shareholders, who thought that giving out shares was much like printing money (it cost the company nothing): Shareholders were unaware of the consequences of dilution. While the latter has a certain semblance of dishonesty, a better face can be put on it: Management sees their responsibility as maximizing share value, and if the market reflects the ignorance of the typical shareholder,[9] then management sees its responsibility as exploiting the market's ignorance. The answer I received was (with one exception): (1) they were indeed unaware of the tax consequences, (2) but even now that they were aware of these adverse tax consequences, they would not change their compensation scheme, since they believed it was still desirable to exploit the uninformed shareholders.[10]

Explanations of the Weak Role of Traditional Incentives

Among the list of explanations for the failure to rely on "traditional" incentive schemes cited above, there is one that I want to emphasize—the difficulty of ascertaining both an individual's input and output. Such is particularly true of managers and of others involved in decision making. Important decision making is done collectively, for obvious reasons: Each individual has limited information, and the errors of the organization are likely to be reduced if more than one individual is involved in important decisions (see chapter 9). When decision making is done collectively, it becomes very difficult, if not impossible, to assign responsibility for failures, or successes for that matter. Indeed many, if not most, individuals go to great trouble to make it difficult to assign blame. They make sure that others have been appropriately consulted, and they are careful about what they put down on paper. Oral communication is much more subject to reinterpretation—to claiming that if one's advice turns out to be wrong, the advice was not correctly understood or fully followed. When individuals put pen to paper, to leave, as the expression goes, a paper trail, they are careful that it reads like a Delphic oracle.

Incentives in the Arrow-Debreu Model and the General Theory of Incentives

In the Arrow-Debreu model individuals are all on a piece rate, they get a fixed amount of pay for each unit they produce. The theory of incentives suggests that only under highly restrictive conditions will this be the optimal form of incentive. Compensation schemes are generally more complicated, entailing, for instance, nonlinear bonuses. The standard paradigm provides no explanation of this, while the new information paradigm does.

Beyond the relationship between pay and performance, employment contracts often involve other quite complicated provisions. There are, for instance, frequently restrictions on the employee undertaking outside employment. If what individuals received for each unit of output were equal to the (marginal) value of output, firms would not care how much output any individual produced. Firms would therefore not impose such restrictions, just as they would have no reason to be concerned with individuals' effort, and accordingly would be unconcerned with motivating them.

These observations have two implications: (1) Individuals do not, at the margin, seem to receive a marginal return commensurate with the marginal value of their contribution. (2) The "control systems" employed by the economy are more complicated than just price systems, and certainly more complicated than "linear" price systems.[11] They involve quantitative restrictions, used as indirect control mechanisms when direct control mechanisms or direct incentive mechanisms are costly or difficult to implement.[12] There are other examples of what may be viewed as quantitative restrictions: Consider a situation where, because of economies of scope, individuals have multiple tasks to perform, but the noise associated with measuring performance in the different tasks differs. The general theory of incentives argues that with risk-averse workers, stronger incentives should be given for the performance of those tasks that are more accurately measured. But the consequence is that workers will divert their attention toward these tasks. As a result it may be desirable to restrict the tasks assigned to each individual—forgoing the gains to be had from the economies of scope.[13]

Incentives and Competition

In some sense the Arrow-Debreu model and the Lange-Lerner-Taylor theorem not only do not address the central incentive issues facing the economy, they give the wrong impression about the relationship between competition (at least the peculiar form of competition which goes by the rubric of "perfect competition") and incentives, a point to which I will return in chapter 7. Competition, in the form of contests—in which rewards depend on relative performance—can and does play an important role in providing incentives, but this is a quite different perspective on competition than that provided by the traditional paradigm.

Evidence for and Consequences of Managerial Autonomy

The fact that takeovers and the other "control mechanisms" such as shareholder voting provide only limited control over managers presents a problem because, as we now understand, managers' interests and shareholder interests can diverge—for instance, managers may devote their energies and the firms' resources into entrenching themselves and into promoting their own careers and interests[14] (see, e.g., Hannaway 1989; Milgrom and Roberts 1988; Shleifer and Vishny 1989; Edlin and Stiglitz 1992). As I have shown, these divergences cannot and are not easily or ever fully corrected by means of compensation schemes.

There are a variety of consequences of this divergence. The fact that managers appropriate a small fraction of the returns to their effort suggests that they will exert too little effort.[15] But, as I noted earlier, perhaps far more important are the distortions in decision making. In some circumstances managers may have an incentive to undertake too much risk, in undertaking some quite new endeavor. After all, they are gambling with someone else's money. If they succeed, they may be given credit, and the specialized knowledge thus acquired will provide them an opportunity to bargain for higher pay. If the endeavor fails, at least the financial costs are borne largely by others. In other circumstances (and there is a general view that this is the more prevalent case) managers have an incentive to undertake too little risk. While shareholders may be widely diversified, and thus are risk neutral, managers have a large stake in the firm. Even if the "official" compensation schedule provides a large bonus for extraordinary performance—a nonlinearity in the payment schedule which, if large enough, would induce risk-taking behavior—managers worry that if the project fails, their career with the firm will be jeopardized, and their attractiveness to outsiders will be reduced. This worry more than offsets the promise of higher pay if the project is highly successful.

In many cases it may be difficult to ascertain whether a manager is doing the job well or not. Outsiders are likely to look at *relative performance* (as we noted earlier). If a firm does badly, but all other firms in the same industry are also doing badly, the manager will not be blamed. This provides a strong incentive for firms to undertake similar actions: Doing what others are doing ensures that one cannot do much worse than others.[16] A concrete example of this was provided by the banking industry in the 1970s and 1980s. During the 1970s many banks lent large amounts to Latin America, more than would seem prudent (based on theories of diversification, and historical experiences concerning defaults on sovereign debt). When in the early 1980s the consequences became evident—as many of the large debtor countries found themselves unable to repay the loans—few, if any, bank managers were "punished." The fact that each was not alone in making these bad portfolio allocations made it seem like a "reasonable" mistake, and therefore a mistake that should not be punished.

While these distortions seem perhaps obvious, there is a wider range of more subtle distortions.[17] Managers' pay depends in part on their bargaining position vis-à-vis the owners: How easily they can be replaced (e.g., by the board of directors).[18] That depends on both the extent to which specific knowledge is required to run the company and the extent to which there may exist differences in information about the company between current managers and outsiders. The greater the specific knowledge required, and the greater the informational asymmetries, the more entrenched the management and the stronger its bargaining position. But these are largely variables under the control of management. They provide, for instance, a motive for the firm to undertake projects (investments) whose value is hard for outsiders to judge. Consequently, by their very nature, it is hard to quantify the extent to which investment decisions get distorted.

The theoretical arguments that firms with widely held ownership should not be well managed—or at least managed in the interests of shareholders—are buttressed by some empirical evidence, though in the case of some of the distortions discussed in the previous paragraph, obtaining detailed evidence would appear to be particularly difficult. There are two categories of behavior in which, however, the discrepancy seems well documented.

Takeovers

I have already noted the observations of managerial indiscretions associated with the takeover frenzy of the 1980s, Ross Johnson of RJR-Nabisco providing perhaps the classic example. The evidence goes beyond these anecdotes: The takeover movement itself seems somewhat of a puzzle, since the firms taking over seem to gain little if anything, for they have to compete with others, and the auction process drives prices up to "full value." The study of Morck, Shleifer, and Vishny (1989), showing that the likelihood of takeovers is greater, the larger the picture of the manager in the firm's annual report, supports the hubris theory: It is not business judgment but managerial ego that drives much of the takeover activity. It appears that the likelihood of value-decreasing takeovers decreases as the share of the firm owned by management and larger controlling interests increases.

Tax Paradoxes

In recent years tax economists have provided further evidence of the consequences of the separation of ownership and control, of inefficiencies associated with managerial autonomy: They have identified a large number of tax paradoxes, instances in which firms pay far more in taxes than they need to. What is important about tax paradoxes is that taxation is one of the few arenas in which we lowly economists can assess the efficiency of the market economy. Few of us have the technical abilities to know whether GM is truly efficient in the production of cars. To be sure, its relative performance, say, compared to Toyota and Nissan, suggests that it is not. Yet the executives of GM will cite differences in labor and capital between their firm and the Japanese firms, arguing that, given the environment in which they are operating, they are indeed fully as efficient as they can be. But the tax structure is reasonably easy for any of us to understand: It is a "technology" contained in perhaps less than a hundred volumes of laws, rules, and regulations. The principles are even easier to grasp. We can explain even to undergraduates why, until 1986, in the United States, it never paid firms to distribute funds to their shareholders in the form of dividends; it was always better to buy back shares or to engage in some other set of operations that resulted in shareholders receiving money from the corporation in the form of capital gains. The fact that firms continue to pay dividends came to be called the dividend paradox (Stiglitz 1973b), and while numerous papers have been written trying to explain away the tax paradox, none of them is satisfactory. Indeed the point I want to emphasize here is that at least in discussions with officials in closely held corporations, it appears that there was a recognition of the disadvantages of dividend distributions, and they relied far less heavily on them. The publicly held corporations were more concerned with the perceptions of soundness that regular dividend payments seem to provide, than the more fundamental issue of minimizing tax liabilities. Markets are not totally stupid: They learn gradually, and, as Shoven and Bagwell (1989) point out, there was a marked increase in the fraction of funds distributed from the corporate sector to the household sector in tax-favored ways during the fifteen years after the dividend paradox came to be recognized.

Other tax anomalies support the view that publicly held firms often put form—the appearance of profits—over substance: The use of FIFO over LIFO accounting, while it increases the present discounted value of tax liabilities, increases the short-term reported cash income of the firm. Thus many publicly held firms continue to use this accounting convention, even when the costs of doing so increased enormously as the rate of inflation increased.

For the same reason, presumably, many publicly held firms failed to use accelerated depreciation, which would have decreased the present discounted value of tax liabilities, even as it decreased reported earnings in the short run. What is remarkable about some of these anomalies is that the firm could have "come clean"—it could have reported to its shareholders what its "true" profits would have been under the alternative accounting methodologies, explaining that it was using the particular accounting practice only to reduce its tax liabilities.

Still another example is provided by the use of stock options for rewarding executives. As we have noted, firms claim they use these stock options because they provide good incentives: If the executive succeeds in increasing the value of the firm, the executive participates in the gain. Yet these schemes are not well designed. What the firm wants to do is to reward executives for doing better than the market. To the extent that the gain simply reflects a boom in the stock market, the executive should not be rewarded. By the same token these schemes impose risk on the executive: When the stock market goes down, executives are punished, even though the downturn in the market was beyond their control. Executives should be rewarded on the basis of relative performance.[19]

Popular discussions often cited the tax advantage of stock options, since the gain was taxed under the more favorable terms of capital gains. Yet such analyses failed to take into account the tax liability of the corporation.

One can obtain the incentive effects of stock options (or better still, the incentive effects of relative gains in stock values) by linking pay to (relative) performance, without explicitly using stock options, at the same time saving on taxes, on the combination of individual plus corporate taxes.[20] The widespread failure to recognize this in publicly held corporations reflects the separation of ownership and control. Managers in widely held firms can, evidently, hoodwink shareholders into thinking that stock options are "cheaper": Issuing shares seems almost as costless as printing money. Only gradually have shareholders come to understand the large costs from the dilution of their stake in the firm.

It appears that the tax inefficiencies, whatever their form, are more likely to occur when there is separation of ownership and control.

Alternative Control Mechanisms

The preceding three subsections have argued that managers have considerable autonomy, that compensation schemes provide only a partially effective instrument for aligning incentives, and that as a result firms often do not seem to act in the interests of shareholders. There are in fact alternative "governance" structures—besides those emphasized in the traditional literature—that limit the scope of managerial autonomy and make it more likely that managers act reasonably efficiently, and there are alternative mechanisms for inducing workers to behave in the interests of the firm.

Banks and Corporative Governance

While the traditional mechanisms for ensuring that managers do not simply act in their own interest have limited efficacy, an alternative control mechanism—banks—may be effective. This perspective may seem surprising. After all, banks have no "nominal" control. In the United States they are even precluded from having representatives on boards of directors, and if they take too active a role in firms, they may lose some of their senior status in the event of a bankruptcy. But banks have one power that share-holders do not have: They have the power to demand their money back (at the end of the loan period), and if the firm fails to comply, they have (limited) rights to take over the firm.

Because of the bank's limited risk, there is less diversification—while a firm may have millions of shareholders, it has a limited number of lenders. These relatively few major lenders act cooperatively. They "take turns" being the lead banker and taking charge of monitoring the loan. The fact that there are few lenders to any single firm means that the free-rider problem is attenuated, and the fact that the same, limited number of lenders interact repeatedly in lending operations means that cooperative arrange-ments (one might say collusive behavior) can be sustained, further reducing the significance of the free-rider problem in monitoring (Stiglitz 1985b).

(The fact that several large banks, with widely diversified ownership, lend to the same firm may at first seem paradoxical. There should be little to be gained from this diversification, and something to be lost—from the attenuated incentives to monitor, with some of the benefits of monitoring by any one lender accruing to the other lenders. But, given the cooperative behavior, this loss would be limited. One possible explanation is provided by the theory of peer monitoring [Arnott and Stiglitz 1991; Stiglitz 1990c]. A standard question in the theory of monitoring is who monitors the monitors. One obvious solution is peer monitoring: Supervisors or workers or lenders, for instance, monitor each other. Peers often have more informa-tion, simply as a by-product of their other activities; just as learning can be a relatively costless joint product with production, so too can monitoring be. But for peer monitoring to be effective, peers must have an incentive to monitor. When several banks have an "exposure" to a lending risk, even while one bank is the lead bank, the others have sufficient interest to "monitor the monitor.")

This perspective—the importance of banks as a control mechanism—was originally discussed by Berle (1926). It was revived, within the infor-mation-theoretic context, by Stiglitz (1985b) and has received increasing attention as economists look more to the success of Japan where banks seem to play a particularly visible role.

Going beyond Financial Incentives

The fact that direct economic incentives seem to be so limited for most executives has led Simon (1991) and Akerlof (1991) to suggest that one has to look beyond economic incentives to understand managerial behavior, that the success of firms requires the "identification" of the individual with the firm's objectives, that individuals adopt the firm's success as their goal.

How important are these noneconomic motives remains a question of debate. In the early days of the Soviet Revolution, it was perhaps the case that these noneconomic incentives played an important role. In some cases they appear to have been so strong that they could essentially substitute for economic incentives. Similarly, in war times, noneconomic motives play an important role in calling forth extraordinary levels of effort. But in the longer run, noneconomic motives do not, by themselves, seem to suffice. Yet this should not lead us to conclude that they cannot play an important role in motivating workers, as a complement, rather than a substitute, to financial incentives.

Implications for the Former Socialist Economies

The importance of these "control" problems has become central to discussions in the former socialist economies of how to organize their financial systems: Should they follow the Japanese, German, or American models? And how should they go about privatizing? The absence of concentrations of wealth implies that the problem of "management as a public good" is likely to arise no matter how these countries proceed in their privatizations. But some of the proposals (discussed in a later chapter) involve "people's capitalism"—widespread ownership of shares, within which the problems of control are likely to be particularly acute. While one could presumably "solve" the problem with a random lottery, awarding each large firm to a single individual, such a "solution" would hardly be politically palatable. Given the inevitability of the separation of ownership and control, the question that needs to be addressed is, How can the "control" problem be addressed? Here the design of the financial system is likely to be important (see chapter 12).

The success during the past twelve years of China, and particularly the southern provinces, suggests both that ownership (private property) is less important, and that there are other governance structures that may be effective, at least in the short run. Growth has been based on enterprises that are owned by villages, townships, other government enterprises, a variety of state agencies, and so on. There is *shared* governance. Managers are given wide latitude, and oversight is provided by the various stakeholders, not only the nominal "owners" (who themselves are mostly public organizations) but by industry ministries and local finance bureaus who depend on the success of these enterprises for their revenues.

Differences between Public and Private Enterprises

We have, in this chapter, come full circle: We began by arguing that one of the key reasons for the failure of market socialism was that it underestimated the importance of incentives. We then pointed out that so too did the Arrow-Debreu model. But then we went on and argued that perhaps, after all, incentives were *less* important as a critique of market socialism than popular discussions would suggest for two reasons: First, under capitalism, at the managerial level, incentive structures are weak. Second, public enterprises could provide to their managers the same incentives that capitalist enterprises with widely held stock ownership provide to their managers.

Both systems may face problems. But do incentives provide insights into the *crucial* differences? The debate on this issue has remained at a relatively unsatisfactory level. Discussions focus on two issues:

First is the question of the *ability* of market socialism to emulate a market economy. There are some who emphasize the role of the stock market in providing incentives. It is not (as I have explained) that managers have to be paid stock options but rather that the stock market provides information not otherwise available for evaluating managerial performance. The market is forward-looking and provides the best assessment of changes in the expected present discounted value of the firm. I find this argument completely unpersuasive for three reasons. First, there is simply too much noise in the stock market. Stock market prices are affected by a host of considerations, only some of which are directly related to the actions of the manager. And why should we believe that the judgments of the uninformed investors (the dentist in Peoria, Illinois, or the retired car salesman in Florida) are the most reliable judgments concerning the firms' future prospects?[21] The evidence concerning the relatively low actual reliance by capitalist firms on stock market values cited earlier, and their failure to attempt to design compensation schemes that extract more of the "information" about the managers' contributions (by looking at relative performance), suggests that in market economies this information is not really at the center of the design of compensation schemes. Second, most companies are not listed on the stock market, and there is no evidence that these companies suffer (with respect to the design of managerial incentive schemes) a great deal as a result. Third, at most, stock information can be relevant for the pay of the top executives in large corporations. Most managers manage subunits, whose value is not provided by the stock market. There are other, more reliable, ways of assessing the contribution of managers.

The second question focuses on the *incentive* of those who control the firm to implement incentive structures. Here it is sometimes argued that those who run public enterprises simply do not have an incentive to be concerned with economic efficiency and thus do not have an incentive to design, or implement, appropriate incentive structures. Again, I find this argument unpersuasive. The incentive—and willingness—of the president of Petrofina, of BP, or of Texaco to implement good incentive structures does not appear to differ markedly. Part of the reason is that these firms are in a competitive environment where the efficiency of the enterprise can be relatively easily assessed. It is not so much ownership that is crucial but the existence of competition.

There is, to be sure, a relationship between the two: Many of the state enterprises are in areas where competition is limited. Consider natural monopolies like telecommunications. There is evidence here that competition promotes efficiency. Opening up competition in certain parts of the U.S. telephone industry has, it is widely believed, had significant effects on the industries' efficiency, reaffirming the assertion that what may be important is not so much ownership but competition.

State enterprises *may* face different economic environments than do private enterprises. Later I will discuss the consequences of "soft budget constraints." State enterprises may be under pressure to pursue noneconomic goals, such as regional employment. State enterprises may be subjected to civil service constraints in their employment policies. All of these may adversely affect the efficiency of state enterprises. It may be hard for the government to commit itself to allow state-owned enterprises to act as if they were private; that is, it may be hard to commit itself to allowing competition, to hardening budget constraints, not to subjecting the enterprise to political pressure, and not to subjecting it to civil service requirements. These commitment problem—which may be viewed as "political economy problems" or "public sector incentive problems"—appear to be closer to the core of the distinction between markets and market socialism than do differences in managerial incentives.

There is a certain irony in this recent debate. The central message of the Lange-Lerner-Taylor theorem was that ownership did not matter: One could have the advantages of the price system without the disadvantages associated with private ownership. The critics of market socialism, in pointing out the failure of market socialism to recognize the importance of incentives, failed to recognize this basic insight. Incentives are important. Designing incentive structures is difficult. But the question remains, does ownership matter for the design of incentive structures?

6

Market Rationing and
Nonprice Allocations
within Market Economies

Just as the market socialism model underestimated the importance of incentive problems, it overestimated the role of prices and it underestimated the difficulties of making the price system work. It is of course not surprising that Lange, Lerner, and Taylor would also choose to stress the role of prices in allocating resources. They based their analyses on the traditional paradigm, which argued for the primacy of the role of prices in allocating resources, with prices determined to equate demands and supplies. They differed from the traditional model only in their view of the processes by which prices were to be determined. Rather than relying on market forces, or a mythical Walrasian auctioneer, to equate demands to supply, they wanted to rely on the visible hand of government. But the prices in the two theories were performing exactly the same role.

The chapter is divided into five sections. In the first, I explain why prices not only do not but *cannot* function in the way presumed by the standard model. I then proceed to argue that in fact prices do more (and less) than is envisaged in the traditional paradigm; that is, the standard model both overestimated the role of prices in providing signals concerning economic scarcity and underestimated the role of prices in performing some other vital functions that arise when there is imperfect information. This leads to an extensive discussion of the role of nonprice mechanisms in resource allocation. The problems associated with the allocation of capital provide an excellent opportunity to understand the causes and consequences of the limitations of the price mechanism, and the role of alternative mechanisms for resource allocation. So in the last half of the chapter I turn to a detailed discussion of the capital market. I conclude by returning to my central theme: the implications of these lessons for market socialism.

Why Prices Cannot Function in the Way Presumed by the Standard Model

The underlying problems with the "price" model arises from the complexity of the commodity space and the costs of observing the myriad differences among commodities.

Complexity of the Commodity Space

In the examples we teach our students, we talk about apples, oranges, and wheat. But any farmer can tell you that there is no such thing as a price for an apple. The price depends on the kind of apple, its freshness (and a variety of other quality characteristics), its location, and the time of the year. Industrial commodities are even more complicated, having a larger number of relevant attributes.[1]

An example of the complexity of the product space was recently provided by the U.S. Defense Department, when it put up for bidding a standard, white T-shirt, the kind of commodity that can be purchased in any clothing store for a few dollars. The specifications were thirty small-print pages. Even then I suspect that the product was incompletely specified. Of course most consumers do not have to articulate completely what it is that they are buying when they buy a T-shirt—suggesting that there is a fundamental difference between the way actual markets work and how they are envisaged to work in the market socialist model.

The Impossibility of Planners Setting a Complete Set of Prices
The complexity of the commodity space has two fundamental implications. First, it makes it virtually impossible for a central planner to set prices, or to set prices in a way that adequately reflects this diversity of characteristics and that results in products of the right characteristics being produced. For instance, there would have to be prices for *each* quality level (a continuum) and each quality level would have to be precisely specified. Since every commodity has many dimensions, even if there were a limited number of specifications in each direction, the full dimensionality of the product space is enormous. (Think of a commodity with ten characteristics, such as color, durability, length, and width. If each dimension could take on ten values, then the dimension of the price space for this single commodity would be ten billion!)

The Consequences of Not Fully Specifying Commodities

Market socialist economies (and government procurement agencies in market economies) learned the hard way what happens when the product is incompletely specified. If a price is specified for "nails," short nails made out of any cheap material will be produced. If the length is specified, but not the thickness, then excessively thin nails will be made. If length and thickness is specified, the producer may still make nails out of a cheap material, which may be excessively brittle. For more complex commodities, almost no matter how many characteristics are specified, there remains scope for discretion, and in particular, cost cutting that adversely affects how well the commodity performs the task for which it is intended.

The Costs of Fully Specifying Commodities

But the problems go beyond the fact that it is extremely costly to provide complete specifications of very complex commodities, as the T-shirt anecdote above illustrates. If all the inputs (materials, etc.) are fully specified— for instance, the material of which the nail is to be composed—it forecloses opportunities for finding alternative materials that meet the user's needs as well or better but are less expensive. If only the characteristics of the nail were specified, it may become a matter of judgment about whether those "characteristics" have been satisfied. Even then there remains the question of trade-offs: Some material might exceed the original standard in some characteristic, and fall short in another. What price should the producer receive for such a commodity? Market socialism provides no answer, other than requiring the planner to provide a complete set of prices (an impossible task).

The market socialist model—and the neoclassical model—both fail to recognize the importance of the interface between producers and those who use the products being produced. The central message of those models, that communication between producers and consumers could be limited to price signals, is fundamentally wrong.

The process of production is often more one of "negotiation" than of "price taking." Firms negotiate delivery times, product characteristics, as well as price. Information (about the needs of the buyers, the technological capabilities of the sellers) is transmitted in the process. Prices do play an important role in this interaction. The qualitative statement, "it would be hard to make a nail that will do what you want it to do," becomes a quantitative statement, "I can do it, but the cost of the nail will be $1.23 per nail."

Imperfect Competition

Another important consequence of the richness and complexity of the product space to which I called attention in earlier chapters is that markets are frequently—perhaps I should say usually—imperfectly competitive. The products produced by one firm usually differ slightly, in one or more of the many characteristics, from those produced by others. There is, to be sure, competition: The buyer will check with other producers, to see if they make a product that better meets his or her needs at a lower cost. But this is not perfect competition; it is not the kind of competition described by the Arrow-Debreu model or its extensions.[2]

Imperfect and Costly Information

The complexity of the commodity space, which by itself would be sufficient to explain why the price model is inappropriate, is not the only reason for its failure. A second explanation[3] has to do with the costs of observing differences in the commodities; that is, even if we could costlessly *specify* all the relevant characteristics, ascertaining whether a particular item does or does not have those characteristics is expensive. In such a situation prices may affect the average quality of what one in fact obtains in a market transaction. Elsewhere I have explained at length the causes and consequences of the dependence of quality on price (Stiglitz 1987b).

The Repeal of the Law of Supply and Demand

Perhaps the most important consequence is "the repeal of the law of supply and demand." When the quality of labor depends on the wage rate paid, or the "quality of a loan" (the likelihood that the loan will be repaid) depends on the interest rate charged, or the quality of a product depends on the price charged, the (competitive) market equilibrium may be characterized by rationing—demand not equaling supply. This may provide part of the explanation of the widespread phenomena of unemployment in the labor market and credit rationing in the capital market. Even though there is an excess supply of labor, firms do not cut the wage they pay, since doing so may reduce the quality of labor, with a resulting reduction in profits. By the same token, there may be credit rationing when lenders do not raise the interest rate charged despite an excess demand for credit, since doing so would adversely affect the probability of a default.

The Role of Prices

In the previous section I explained why prices cannot function in the way presumed by the standard model, why there cannot, in fact, be the complete set of prices envisaged by the Arrow-Debreu model. But in doing so, I showed that prices do more—and less—than is envisaged by the traditional paradigm. There are four aspects of this that require emphasis:

First, there are an important set of economic functions, *screening and providing incentives*, that were almost totally omitted from the traditional paradigm.

Second, when markets do not clear, or more generally, when there are selection, incentive, and other incomplete information problems, nonprice mechanisms are generally employed to help allocate resources.

Third, when markets do not clear, prices do not necessarily convey the kinds of signals concerning scarcity, which was presumably the major insight of the Arrow-Debreu model (and the market socialist model which was based on the same set of concepts). With wages set by efficiency wage considerations (e.g., to make sure that workers do not shirk), wages may well be above the opportunity cost of labor. Information about scarcity may be conveyed in ways other than through prices; firms respond, for instance, to signals such as "orders" and "changes in inventories."

Fourth, while prices (wages, interest rates) no longer perform (at least perfectly) their role in conveying information about scarcity, they perform other economic functions: They affect the quality of what is traded on the market.

It should be emphasized that a "social planner" setting prices optimally would not, in general, set them so as to equate demand to supply but would take cognizance of the effect on quality—of both the selection and incentive effects of prices. This means of course that the information requirements imposed on the central planner are far larger than in the standard market socialist paradigm, where communication between the planner, firms, and consumers can be quite limited: The firms simply communicate how much they are willing to produce at each price the planner calls out, and consumers communicate how much they wish to purchase at each price. Now, the planner has to gather information about the qualities of the objects being produced/sold at different prices and about consumers' evaluations of those qualities. The planner might, in general, set prices at other than market-clearing levels, though not at the level at which they would be set in a market economy.

Nonpricing Mechanisms in Resource Allocation

The importance of the nonpricing mechanisms in resource allocation can be seen in two different ways.

First, a large fraction of all production occurs *within* firms, within a context in which there is only limited reliance on pricing. GM is larger than many countries. While a full discussion of what determines the boundary of firms, what production takes place within firms, would take me beyond the scope of this book, the important point I want to stress is that much economic activity is not governed, except indirectly, by price relations.

The allocation of capital provides the second important example. Capital is not allocated by an auction market, with those who are willing to bid the highest getting the capital. The reason is obvious: The bid is a promise to pay back a certain amount in the future, and that promise may be broken. In allocating capital, it is important to know not only what the user "promises" but what is actually likely to be repaid. A wide array of financial institutions has arisen to do just that. Banks "allocate" capital, but they do not simply rely on the price mechanism. Those who say they are willing to pay the highest interest rate may not in fact be those for whom the expected return—taking into account the probability that the promise is broken—is highest.

Contracts and Reputations

The fact that the price system is limited implies that economic relations are frequently governed by both *contracts* and *reputations*, factors that are totally ignored in both the Arrow-Debreu model and the models of market socialism, both of which focus exclusively on prices. The importance of contracts and reputations can be seen in almost every market to which we turn. Consumers, for instance, rely heavily on reputations in choosing products. In our earlier example of the consumer buying a T-shirt, we noted that the typical consumer does not have to articulate completely what it is that is being bought. If the product is disliked—if it is not as durable as the seller claims—the product is simply not bought again. The buyer (and the producer) rely on reputations. By the same token, lenders rely heavily on the reputation of the borrower.

Contracts almost always involve nonprice terms. Credit contracts, for instance, often have provisions for collateral. They often have provisions that restrict the amount that the borrower can borrow from other sources.

Not only do they typically have restrictions on the uses to which the funds can be put, but they also may have restrictions on other activities that the firm can undertake. The earliest principal agent literature (my discussion of sharecropping) stressed the importance of nonprice terms, such as the amount of land that a landlord would provide a tenant, and the provisions of other inputs. Insurance and employment contracts often have "exclusivity" provisions: The insured agrees to report the purchase of any other insurance for the same risk from other insurance firms; the worker agrees not to work for other employers. Insurance contracts often have other "quantity" provisions: The insured agrees to install fire extinguishers.

Contracts are required because there simply are not "markets" for all the possible commodities (where we differentiate among commodities at different locations, dates, states of nature, qualities, etc.) in the world, and reputations are required simply because we cannot write down all the desired characteristics; even if we could, it would be impossible (and/or expensive) to adjudicate through a legal system all the possible disputes that might arise.[4]

And both the Arrow-Debreu model, and the model of market socialism, simply do not take either of these forms of economic interactions into account.

Rents and the Reputation Mechanism

It is not only true that the Arrow-Debreu model and the models of market socialism do not describe those sectors of the economy in which reputation mechanisms are important—as they so frequently are—but it is also the case that the reputation mechanism requires a modification of how we view the pricing system as working.

In particular, if the maintenance of reputation is to provide an incentive, there must be a cost to losing one's reputation. This means that at the margin, sellers cannot be indifferent as to whether they do or do not sell the commodity (workers cannot be indifferent as to whether they do or do not work.) Economic relations *must* entail rents, payments in excess of the minimum necessary to induce an individual to be willing to engage in the transaction. Profits, in the conventional sense, cannot be driven to zero; price cannot equal marginal costs. The basic pricing relations underlying the "theory of value" are, in that sense wrong, and the corresponding model of market socialism, based on the standard theory of value, must on that account also be incorrect.[5]

Underestimation of the Difficulties of Allocating Capital

In the traditional view of market socialism, markets were used to allocate goods—given the capital stock—but capital was not allocated by a market system. The failure of markets to allocate capital efficiently, including its failure to coordinate investment decisions, provided part of the rationale for the turn to market socialism.

Market socialists were correct here in identifying a market failure: While, as I pointed out in the previous section, they did not fully grasp the problems that arose from the absence of a complete set of prices, they thought they understood the consequences of the more obvious absence of a complete set of futures and risk markets. They thought that it proved their point that government had to take responsibility for allocating capital.

We argue that the failure of the Arrow-Debreu model was not just that it assumed that there was a full set of futures and risk markets. Its failure was more profound: It failed to recognize the inherent information problems associated with the allocation of capital.

But while (by definition) the Arrow-Debreu model simply ignored the problems that arose from the lack of futures and risk markets, the market socialists were naive in believing that the government could easily remedy this market failure. They did not inquire deeply into its source. More generally, the very reasons—largely information—that lead markets to have problems with allocating capital (which I will discuss below) have posed serious problems for alternative allocative mechanisms.

The Consequences of the Absence of Futures Markets

Consider, for instance, the absence of futures markets, which means that firms have to make estimates of future prices, both of what they sell and of the inputs that they purchase. But the government also must make estimates of the shadow prices of goods and services. There are two key issues, the capacity to make the correct forecasts and the incentive to do so.

Capacity to Solve Coordination Problems
Traditional discussions of market socialism focus on the lack of a coordinating mechanism (in the absence of futures markets). With futures markets, each producer knows the prices that will prevail, say, for steel ten years from now, and adjusts his production accordingly. Equilibrium requires that his planned production equal the demand at the prices that will be prevailing ten years from now. This is of course a fantasy, and critics of markets

cite the excess capacity that arises in some industries at some times and the shortages that arise in others as evidence that this is not even a good "as if" story. Without a complete set of markets, there can be massive coordination failures. Underlying this coordination failure is an information problem: Each producer of steel not only has no incentive to share information about his production plans with other producers; he has incentives to hide information, or even to provide misleading information. One firm may gain from the mistakes made by others.

Since the government owns all firms under market socialism, there is no such incentive. Indeed, since the government is making all investment decisions, it has all the requisite information to ensure that these coordination failures do not occur.

But critics of market socialism argue that the failures of the market are not so great, and that market socialism does not really provide a remedy. While there may be coordination failures, in most cases, the social losses are minimal. Even if too many pizza parlors open up, so there is excess capacity, leading some to leave, the social loss is only the sunk costs, which cannot be recovered, and these are frequently but a small fraction of the total costs. Adjustments can occur fairly rapidly. Only in the case of heavy industries, like steel and chemicals, do significant coordination problems arise.

Critics of market socialism argue that governments have neither the capacity nor the incentive to solve well the coordination problems. Recall the basic argument for market socialism: It was based on the premise that no central planner could gather, process, and disseminate the information required to control effectively the economy. Market socialism emphasized that a central planner needed only to have limited information, the information contained in prices. The decentralization that this allowed was what made socialism work. But here, advocates of market socialism seem to be claiming that a central set of markets, those entailing investment (and, implicitly, markets for goods and services at all future dates), can be dispensed with and that the government can indeed gather, process, and disseminate all the relevant information. To critics of market socialism, the inefficiencies in the allocation of investment that arose under all varieties of socialism were not mere accidents but an inevitable consequence of the lack of capacity of any organization, no matter how well intentioned, to solve these massive information problems.

To be sure, the model of market economies—based on a complete set of markets—does not provide us with any theoretical justification for the belief that markets perform well. Indeed there is evidence that markets often do not perform those functions well: not only the kind of microevidence cited earlier, but the macroevidence, of periods of massive excess capacity, often attributed to coordination failures.[6] And the Greenwald-Stiglitz theorem assures us that in general, market allocations will not be constrained Pareto efficient.

Moreover there are large firms, like General Motors and Exxon, which manage annual investment flows that exceed those of many small countries. If private firms have the capacity to do this, why shouldn't governments of at least smaller economies? Indeed even in larger economies, such as Germany and Britain, there are only three or four large banks, which directly or indirectly control a substantial fraction of the entire flow of investment.

The advocates of market socialism made, however, a critical mistake, in not paying sufficient attention to the institutions (e.g., banks) which have arisen under capitalism to solve the problems created by absent markets. They are not a perfect substitute. But they may result in an allocation of investment that is better than it otherwise would be—and better than it is under market socialism. (As I indicate in chapter 12, under socialism, banks did not perform the central informational roles that they do under capitalism.)

Perhaps the central reason that markets (including the institutions that have developed in response to the absence of futures markets) do a better job of allocating investment has to do with incentives.

Incentives to Solve Coordination Problems
What are the incentives provided that the government's estimates of shadow prices be accurate, that all relevant factors be taken into account? In the market those who make a mistake are (in theory) disciplined, and they bear a large part of the costs of those mistakes. This is not so in the case of publicly owned enterprises, particularly if they face soft budget constraints.

The Stock Market and the Price Discovery Function[7]

Though there is not a complete set of futures/risk markets in any capitalist economy, critics of market socialism argue that there are *more* markets under capitalism than under market socialism. In particular, there are stock markets. By definition, when firms are owned entirely by the government, there is no market on which their value can be assessed.

The information conveyed by stock market values is considered to be of importance for at least two reasons: It provides information that can be made the basis of incentive contracts, and it provides information relevant for the allocation of investment. The contention is that the market provides the best estimate of the future present discounted value of the stream of returns generated by the firm. Accordingly it is argued, for instance, that the signals that are available in the case of firms that make bad investment decisions—the market value of the firm—are not available in the case of publicly owned enterprises, and therefore it is more difficult for publicly owned enterprises to "punish" bad investment decisions.

I contend that while the stock market does provide *some* information, the information that it provides is of limited value, either as a basis of the allocation of investment or for the design of an incentive structure. Quite to the contrary of the contention of the market paradigm, reliance on the stock market may actually result in a distortion of the allocation of resources. I argue that much of the expenditure on information collected in connection with the stock market has little social return. Finally, I will argue that even if there were significant advantages associated with the information revealed by the stock market, those advantages do not necessitate the complete privatization of the nationalized enterprises, a point that is of considerable relevance for the former socialist economies as they go about the process of reform.

Limited Value of Stock Market Information
There are several reasons that the information revealed by the stock market is of limited value either in the design of incentive structures or in the allocation of investment.

The first is that the information is too "coarse" for the allocation of investment. It does a steel firm little good to know that the "market" thinks that steel will be doing well in the future. The steel firm needs to know what kind of steel to produce, with what kind of process. The stock market simply cannot provide that information. The steel firm to make its investment decision must undertake a detailed project evaluation. By the time the firm has undertaken such an evaluation, the information contained in the stock market price is essentially redundant.[8]

Moreover one of the principal tasks of the firm's managers is to obtain the specialized information required to make such investment decisions. It seems implausible that those who speculate in the stock market would have much to add to the information of the firm's managers. Indeed decisions within the divisions of a firm—both incentive and investments—occur without the aid of the information provided by the stock market.

The Discrepancy between Social and Private Returns to Information
Much of the information collected on the stock market is not related to the long-term performance of the enterprise but is an attempt to predict short-term movements in the stock prices. Keynes's analogy between the stock market and a beauty contest is apposite: The question was not to guess who was the most beautiful person but who the other judges will judge to be the most beautiful. Thus resources are allocated to obtaining information not about the fundamentals, but about perceptions.

More generally, much of the expenditure on information collected on the stock market has little, if any, social value. For stocks that are already traded, there is a zero-sum game: The gains of one party are at the expense of the other. The quest is to find information that will affect market price slightly before others do. If I know about some event—such as the failure of a harvest in Russia—that will affect the price of wheat, slightly before others do, I can buy wheat futures (or stocks whose price increase when the price of wheat increases) and make a capital gain. Knowing that information a few minutes, hours, or days earlier than that information otherwise would have been known may have little, if any, allocative effect; it does not increase the economy's efficiency. Its primary consequence is to give private rents to those who get the information early. *Information acquisition activities related to the stock market are basically rent-seeking activities.*[9]

An analogy (based on a suggestion by Larry Summers) may make the argument clearer.[10] Assume that one were in a room, listening to a lecture, such as this one, and hundred dollar bills fall to the ground, like manna from heaven, one by the foot of each person in the room. There are two ways of proceeding: Each person could immediately bend down and pick up a $100 bill, interrupting the important learning activity that is going on. Alternatively, each could wait until the lecture is over, and then each could bend down. Clearly the latter is more socially efficient: There is no interruption to the important activity that is going on, and the slight delay of thirty minutes in picking up the $100 has almost no consequence. Though socially efficient, this is not a Nash equilibrium: Each individual, seeing that the others are delaying, would have an incentive to bend down and pick up as many $100 bills as may be possible. The only Nash equilibrium entails everyone spending resources trying to grab as many bills as they can, as fast as they can. In the situation where everyone is symmetric, they each get one bill, as they would have if they waited. In the situation where some are faster than others, the gains of the faster ones are at the expense of the slower ones: There are private rents, but no social returns.

Much of the activity in the stock market cannot really be explained by any rational behavior.[11] It is what I have referred to elsewhere as the "rich man's horse track," or the middle class gambling casino. Since trading on the stock market is essentially a zero-sum game, it increases risk without, on average, increasing mean returns. Rational individuals would do better simply by holding the market as a whole—and increasingly this is exactly what they are doing.

This is true even if some individuals are better informed than others (without actually spending money to acquire the information). The less informed, if they are rational, would realize that they are less informed. They would realize that the informed would only be buying shares from them if they thought those shares were going to rise in value more than the market (adjusting for risk), and they would only be selling shares if they thought those shares were going to rise in value less than the market. They thus would not be willing to trade.

The only circumstance in which they would be willing to trade is if the trade is motivated by changes in circumstances that differentially affect different groups. Thus, if individuals chose their stock market portfolio to insure against human capital risks (e.g., miners sell short shares in mines, as a way of insuring against those events that may put their jobs at risk), then shocks to human capital would result in a desire to reallocate stock market portfolios. But there is little evidence that most individuals choose their stock market portfolios to insure against human capital risks. By the same token, if there were large differences in risk aversion between older individuals, who are selling off their portfolios, and younger individuals, who are investing, then there would be a life cycle motive for portfolio adjustment. Again this does not seem to describe well what goes on in the stock market.

The Distorting Role of the Stock Market

The fact that the information collected is often not that which is of greatest social value means that to the extent that firms are concerned about the prices of their shares, their behavior may be distorted. Thus, if firms' managers' pay is based on the short-run movements in stock prices, firms are likely to take actions that are likely to increase their stock market value in the short run. Evidence of this kind of myopic behavior abounds. Though much of this evidence is anecdotal, a close look at behavior with respect to taxes provides some hard evidence: Firms take actions that appear to increase after-tax earnings even when those actions at the same time increase the present discounted value of tax liabilities. Thus for years firms used FIFO accounting when a switch to LIFO would have decreased reported earnings and reduced the present discounted value of tax liabilities; many firms did not use accelerated depreciation for the same reason.[12] There are a wider range of distortions that may arise: Managers try to paper over negative results, in the hope that information about those results become public after they cash in their stock options. (They may in such circumstances try to create noise, making it difficult for the market to interpret what is going on.[13] They may, for instance, buy a firm with a strong current cash flow to obscure losses in other parts of the business.) To be sure, this kind of behavior might be expected to some extent regardless of the design of the compensation structure. But less reliance on stock markets might induce boards of directors to place more reliance on direct observation, on comparisons with how other firms in the industry are doing (e.g., how GM is faring in comparison with Toyota).

Privatization not Needed
Finally, we need to note that whatever information is made available by a stock market can be obtained without full privatization. The government can sell *some* shares in a publicly owned firms. The difficulty is that market valuations may reflect as much judgments concerning future government subsidies as they do those concerning the value of existing assets. This is also true for the market value of any firm whose profits depend on government actions, including regulated firms and those partially protected by tariffs and quotas. (Later I will explain why a strong argument can be made that it is far preferable for the government to retain large ownership shares rather than distributing all shares through voucher schemes.)

Nonprice versus Price Allocations in Capital Markets

Earlier I pointed out that capital markets cannot be well described as auction markets. Capital is not simply given to the highest bidder. There is what may be viewed as a *direct* allocative mechanism at work. Banks *screen* loan applicants, just as a central planner would, in principle, screen project applicants.

There is another implication of informational imperfections in the capital market to which I referred earlier: Lenders employ a variety of nonprice provisions in the loan contract in an attempt both to sort among loan applicants better and to provide better incentives. Loan contracts are not described simply by the interest rate; there is a whole variety of terms, including collateral, and provisions relating to default, that has important consequences for both parties to the contract.

Differences between Markets and Market Socialism

The fact that both markets and market socialism engage in direct allocative mechanisms does not mean, of course, that they are identical. The incentives of banks and planners may differ. Critics of market socialism emphasize the failure of incentives to ensure an efficient allocation of investment, particularly in the presence of soft budget constraints. But as the recent savings and loan debacle in the United States illustrates, there may be marked discrepancies between private incentives and social returns in market economies as well. The S&L's squandered a considerable fraction of America's entire savings for one year.[14] To be sure, the blame may be put on government programs. But the more general observation of the potential inefficiency of market allocations of investment (see chapter 2) remains valid.

Risk Assessment

The allocation of capital requires estimates not only of expected returns associated with alternative investments but also of risk. The capital asset model has forcefully emphasized that the appropriate measure of risk is "correlation with the market." But it is not clear that the absence of a complete set of risk markets, that is what firms in capitalist economies focus upon.

There are several pieces of evidence in support of this conclusion. When a firm asks its managers to assess the desirability of an investment, they typically include a risk assessment, and by risk assessment they do not mean a statement of the correlation of the returns of the project (e.g., a newly designed airplane) with the stock market. Rather, they mean the variability of own return.[15]

The firm cannot of course obtain insurance against the bad outcomes, even the idiosyncratic ones. The standard capital asset pricing models assume that shareholders can fully diversify against idiosyncratic risks. Thus, even if the firm cannot buy insurance, shareholders with widely diversified shareholdings act risk-neutrally with respect to idiosyncratic risks. The conclusion is that firms—acting in the interests of those shareholders—should act in a risk-neutral manner. But these models have several fatal flaws.

First, they ignore the principal-agent problem: Firms are not run directly by shareholders but by managers. Managers have to be provided with incentives to perform well. Their incentives have to be based on the actual performance of the firm. In general, for these incentives to have significant effects, they must represent a substantial fraction of the managers' income/wealth. But then the manager is likely to act in a risk-averse manner: If the firm goes bankrupt, for instance, the manager is likely to lose his or her job, and the bankruptcy of the firm is likely to serve as a negative signal, adversely affecting future job prospects.[16]

Second, they ignore the fact that there is often incomplete diversification among shareholders: Often the principal shareholders, the companies' founders, have a significant fraction of their wealth tied up with that firm. There is a good reason for this. The amount of shares original shareholders are willing to retain provides a signal concerning those shareholders' view of the firm's future prospects. If they think the firm is not likely going to do well—if they think the market has overpriced their shares—then they are more anxious to sell their shares. A commitment by the original shareholders to retain substantial shareholdings thus is likely to enhance the market value of the firm's shares. With incompletely diversified portfolios, these controlling shareholders (effective control may be exerted even if they own substantially less than 50 percent of the shares) are likely to wish the firm to act in a risk-averse manner—and they will look not at just correlation with the stock market in assessing risk but at own variance.

There are a variety of other theories that explain why, despite the risk-sharing advantages of equity, firms seem to make limited use of equities. (Greenwald and I refer to this as equity rationing, though, as I will shortly explain, it is not so much that they cannot issue equities, as that the cost of doing so is so high that firms find it unattractive to issue equities.) There is by now quite strong evidence that equity markets account for a relatively small fraction of new capital raised in almost all countries (see table 6.1). Recent empirical evidence suggests why—when firms issue new equities—there are marked declines in share prices. On average, the total value of the decrease in outstanding share prices for seasoned firms is around a third of the amount of capital raised (Asquith and Mullins 1986), and in the case of small firms, with a less well-established reputation, the price declines are often much larger. The information-theoretic research has provided explanations, based on incentive and selection effects, for why these price declines are quite expected.[17] For instance, we explained earlier why the original shareholders are more likely to sell their shares if they think that the market has overpriced them. The market knows this. Thus

Table 6.1
Net sources of finance, 1970–89 (weighted average, undepreciated, revalued)

	France	Germany	Japan	Britain	United States
Internal	66.3	80.6	71.7	98.0	91.3
Bank finance	51.5	11.0	28.0	19.8	16.6
Bonds	0.7	−0.6	4.0	2.0	17.1
Equity	−0.4	0.9	2.7	−8.0	−8.8
Trade credit	−0.7	−1.9	−7.8	−1.6	−3.7
Capital transfers	2.6	8.5		2.1	
Other	−14.9	1.5	1.3	−4.1	−3.8
Statistical adjustment	−5.1	0.0	0.1	−8.2	−8.7
Notes	1970–85	1970–89	1970–87	1970–89	1970–89

Source: Unpublished flow of funds figures from the CEPR International Study of the Financing of Industry. Data courtesy of Tim Jenkinson and Colin Mayer.

the act of selling shares conveys information—the fact that those who control the firm, who almost always have a substantial share in the firm and therefore have much to gain if they sell overvalued shares, are willing to do so leads the market to conclude that the shares are likely to be overpriced. The price falls as a result.

Indeed in some cases the effect I have just described can be so strong as to completely shut down the market. I illustrate this principle to my students by holding an auction of the money in my wallet in my back pocket. I know the amount in the wallet. I auction off 1 percent shares. I reserve the right to bid, or equivalently, not to sell my shares. What is the "equilibrium" price? Eventually the students catch on to the game: They figure out that I will only sell a 1 percent share if the amount they offer me is more than the value of a 1 percent share. If I have $100 in my pocket, if they offer me less than a $1, I will not sell, and if they offer me more than a dollar, I will. They are in a tails they lose, heads I win situation. The only equilibrium price is zero.[18]

This analogy would suggest that there is no equity market, but it ignores the basic reasons for trade in the first place: If I am risk averse, and I do not know how much money is in my wallet (or, more aptly, I do not know how much oil is in the oil well that is located in my backyard), then I would like to divest myself of that risk. The market of course cannot tell whether the reason I want to sell shares is because I am risk averse—a good reason—or because the market has overvalued my shares. *On average*, those who are most interested in selling shares are those who know that their shares are overvalued, and the market takes this into account. But the market still exists because there are *some* who are willing to sell their shares even when the shares are underpriced (relative to expected values), simply to divest themselves of risk.

There is an alternative theory that emphasizes the effect of capital structure (debt–equity ratios) on managerial incentives. This is looked at from two perspectives. With most finance coming in the form of debt, the original shareholders, including management, are likely to own a larger fraction of the equity; accordingly they appropriate a larger fraction of the returns from their efforts.[19] The second perspective emphasizes the discipline provided by debt, with its fixed obligations. My colleague Robert Hall sometimes refers to this as the "backs-to-the-wall theory of corporate finance." With sufficiently high debt managers must work hard, simply to meet their debt obligations and to avoid bankruptcy. The converse is that if managers have excess cash (as the oil companies did after the sharp increase in oil prices in the 1970s), then they are more likely to squander it, or at least not spend it wisely: The experience of the oil companies is certainly consistent with this observation.[20]

The limitation on equity markets is important not only because it means that there is limited risk diversification but also because it implies that firms must raise capital through borrowing. In borrowing, there is a chance that the firm will not be able to meet its obligations and that it will go bankrupt. The fact that earlier discussions ignored the costs of bankruptcy represents the third important mistake made by the literature, which measures risk by covariance with the market as a whole. There has been considerable controversy over exactly how important bankruptcy costs are. At one level the central point is that bankruptcy costs have adverse effects on managers, and since managers are the ones who make decisions, they will act to avoid bankruptcy and thus will act in a risk-averse manner.

Those who argue that bankruptcy is not that important point out that resources do not disappear in the event of bankruptcy; control over assets simply gets reassigned. Though it is true that much of the popular press ignores this point, it is nevertheless the case that there may be significant real costs associated with bankruptcy. These include the loss of organization capital resulting from corporate reorganizations. Moreover typically bankruptcy interferes with contractual arrangements. While the bankruptcy is being worked out, the firm may find both suppliers looking for alternative customers, and customers looking for alternative suppliers. Other firms are reluctant to enter into new contractual arrangements, and the firm is likely to find it difficult to recruit new employees. Reputation mechanisms are likely to be impeded, since those mechanisms imply that the firm has a future. Under bankruptcy the future of the firm is at best extremely clouded. With reputation mechanisms unable to provide effective incentives to enforce contracts (e.g., to ensure quality), more costly alternative incentive mechanisms may have to be employed.[21]

I have argued in this subsection that markets' assessment of risks is likely to differ from the "social" assessment—the market is likely to be more focused on own variance. *Ideally* social planners, in making their investment decisions, would focus on social risks. But experience suggests matters are not so simple. On the one hand, those making planning decisions generally do not bear the costs of the mistakes that they make. They may, however, get credit for any great achievements under their direction. This may lead to a bias for excessive risk taking. Thus governments are more likely to undertake grandiose projects, like SST projects. The difference between the government and the private sector's willingness to do so has less to do with the failure of the market to recognize spillovers, or some excess weighting of own-variance, but rather with the fact that those who are making the decisions are not putting up their own money.

To counteract this, in principle, one could provide those involved in investment decision making with the same kinds of incentive structures that capitalist corporations provide their managers. Managers could be punished for mistakes. In some branches of government, managers do seem to act in an excessively risk-averse way. Because it is hard to evaluate whether, given the information that was available at the time, a "good" decision was made, high reliance is placed on procedures, giving rise to the bureaucratic red tape that so often characterizes the public sector.

Though I do not propose here to set forth a general theory ascertaining when managers within the public sector pay too little or too much attention to risk (to own-variance), it is important to recognize that it is not apparent that market socialism provides an easy remedy for the failures in risk assessment within capitalist economies.

The Risk from Uncoordinated Investment Decisions
But there may be an additional element of risk in market economies: In the absence of futures markets there is no price system to coordinate investment decisions. This leads, at times, to excessive investment in some sectors (or even aggregate excess investment) and shortfalls at other times in other sectors. Again, *in principle*, under market socialism coordination is much easier. To be sure, if there were a *complete* set of futures and risk markets, they would perform this coordination role. But those markets do not exist (and "expectations" are but an imperfect substitute).

France attempted to address these investment coordination problems through the use of indicative planning. But firms did not have any incentive to reveal truthfully their plans. On the contrary, they had some incentives to try to mislead their rivals, such as by indicating that they would invest heavily, discouraging others from expanding their capacity. With government ownership under market socialism, even if investment were done in a decentralized manner, the incentives not to reveal correctly investment plans would presumably be attenuated.

How important these coordination problems are, however, remains moot, as I noted earlier. They are likely to be relatively unimportant if the plant size is small and if the gestation period for a plant is small. Every year several new plants are being constructed, so the presence of excess capacity can readily be detected and mistakes corrected. There are probably only a few industries (e.g., large-scale chemicals) where the investment coordination problem is very important. For these, there remains the problem of international coordination, which is not resolved by market socialism within a country.

Markets, Market Socialism, and Models of the Market Economy

This chapter has looked at some of the central aspects of how the standard Arrow-Debreu (neoclassical) model looks at the economy. The Arrow-Debreu model, while it makes the strong assumption that there is a complete set of markets,[22] stresses the role of prices in allocating resources. Market socialism borrows that idea, but recognizes the absence of the Walrasian auctioneer ensuring that the markets are set at their market-clearing levels and the absence of futures/risk markets for coordinating investment decisions. Accordingly, it uses prices as the key mechanism for allocating resources *given* the stock of capital, but uses direct allocative mechanisms for investment.

I have stressed that *both* views are wrong concerning the role of prices: Prices (and markets) play a more limited role in resource allocation, and nonprice mechanisms a more important role. While market socialism was correct in identifying the existence of problems of the standard paradigm (and actual markets) in allocating investment, it did not correctly identify what the nature and source of those problems were. Therefore it could not adequately address the question of whether a change in ownership—to public ownership—would redress the observed deficiencies. Many of the information problems that are inadequately dealt with by the market would represent problems for which market socialism would not provide an obvious remedy.

I have noted, for instance, that the neoclassical model paid insufficient attention to the problems of allocating capital: The auction model provides an inadequate description of what actually goes on (or should go on). But the problems of allocating capital, including those of risk assessment, are likely to be no less difficult for the public sector than for the private. Similarly *neither* the traditional market model nor the model of market socialism really paid adequate attention to incentives: I have shown that the price system deals with only a limited subset of the incentive problems facing real economies. The *central* problem of incentives usually discussed in connection with market socialism, incentives of managers, appears no less of a problem under capitalism. The standard neoclassical model never even attempts to come to terms with this fact. The standard market solution that "firm managers maximize market values" is off the mark in much the same way as the market socialist prescription that managers will be told to maximize market values. I have discussed not only the fact that there is a separation of ownership and control but also the limitations of all the control mechanisms and incentive devices designed to bring managerial actions into accord with shareholder interests. The managerial incentive problem remains a quandary for capitalist economies—a quandary with which the Eastern European countries will have to deal as they proceed in the process of transition to market economies.

The competitive market paradigm has exercised an enormous influence over how we think about how the economy functions. Some of the insights it provides are critical to understanding economic behavior: the importance of competition, the role of prices, the interdependence of markets, the potential for decentralization. But most of these insights are incomplete, as I have shown and will show throughout this book: Though competition is important, it is not well described by the kind of price competition of the Arrow-Debreu model. Prices are only one part of the market resource allocation mechanism. The interdependence of markets operates not only through prices but also through credit markets, and decentralization is limited.

Review of Major Findings

This chapter is the second of five in which I challenge the Lange-Lerner-Taylor theorem, which provides the intellectual basis of market socialism.

It may be useful at this juncture to recapitulate where we have gone, and where we will be going. My central message should by now be familiar: the standard neoclassical (Arrow-Debreu) model does not provide an adequate description of how the market economy operates, and therefore a socialist economy built on a model that simply imitates the *model* of the market economy, altering only who "owns" the firms, could not have been expected to fare well. To be fair, my criticisms of the market socialist model is more balanced: for some of the *alleged* criticisms are no less criticisms of the market economy, and to the extent that that is true, the market socialist economies might fare no worse than market economies.

This was the case, for instance, of the issue of managerial incentives, one of the central criticisms of the market socialist model. In the last chapter, I agreed with the popular perception that incentives are important. But they represent no more a problem for the market socialist economy than they do for many large corporations.

This chapter, however, goes to the heart of the market socialist model: its imitation of the market economy in using the price system as the central way of controlling and coordinating economic activity, other than investment. My contention has been that the actual price system is far more complex, that the actual "control/information" system of market economies embraces far more than the Arrow-Debreu model suggests, and that market socialism went seriously astray by focusing on only one aspect of economic relations—the price mechanism as characterized by the Arrow-Debreu/Walrasian model.

Arrow and Debreu had the critical insight to realize that for the competitive economy to work in the way that classical economists had envisaged, there would have to be a full set of markets, extending infinitely far into the future and covering all risks. They did not explore either the reasonableness of that assumption or the consequences of its failure. That is the task that has fallen to us. I have provided a variety of reasons why there cannot be a full set of markets, equally applicable to market and market socialist economies. Among the consequences I cited were the following:

1. The quality of what is traded is affected by the price of the good in that price conveys information.

2. Where information is conveyed by nonprice mechanisms, the direct interface between producer and consumer becomes important, and inventories and order backlogs take on critical information roles.

3. Contracts and reputation become a central part of economic relations; nonprice terms in contracts are often as important as the price terms.

4. Direct screening takes on an important role: Funds are allocated not just to the highest bidder; capital markets are not conducted as auction markets.

These *descriptions* of how markets operate help illuminate the failures of the market socialist model, which did not seek to employ this richer set of mechanisms involved in economic relations. Among the more important direct implications for the standard conclusions of the neoclassical model (beyond the overembracing one I emphasized in chapters 3 and 4, that the fundamental theorems of welfare economics no longer apply) are the following three:

1. Competitive equilibrium may not be characterized by supply equaling demand, markets may not clear; there may be unemployment (hardly news to the millions of unemployed workers throughout the world), and there may be credit rationing.

2. Since competition tends to be imperfect, models of imperfect competition in the spirit of Chamberlin may provide a better description of the economy than the perfectly competitive models.

3. Prices are not driven down to marginal costs; rents must persist if reputation mechanisms are to work.

Market socialism did recognize the limitations of the market price mechanism in allocating capital, but here, it failed to recognize the reasons for this, the alternatives that were in fact employed by markets, and their advantages (and perhaps disadvantages). However, as in my discussion of incentives, I must emphasize that there are common problems in both approaches.

Advocates of the virtues of the market tend to dismiss Arrow and Debreu's fundamental insights concerning the necessity of a complete set of markets by saying a good stock market—of the kind we have—is all we need.[23] In this chapter I have tried to debunk that myth, by showing that while the stock market does provide some information, it does not provide the information required to make rational investment decisions, and while some of the information that is acquired in the stock market may have private value, much of it has little social value. The stock market has only a limited role in guiding investment in market economies, and indeed it may have more of a distorting role than a constructive role. Even if stock markets did have a largely constructive informational role, market socialist economies could avail themselves of this information while retaining control of most of the shares of the corporation.

Having denigrated the central role of the stock market, I am still left with the more difficult question of comparing how markets and market socialist systems allocate investment. Here again, my arguments served primarily to question the naive views of the advocates of each system. The most problematic issue concerns risk: Would managers in one or the other system be more concerned with nonsystematic (sometimes referred to as firm-specific) risks? In principle, both markets and government ownership can provide effective spreading of such risks over the entire economy, so decisions should be made in a risk-neutral way. I have questioned whether in either system, this is the way decisions are in fact made, since decisions are made by managers and managers are not risk neutral with respect to the outcomes. In principle, governments could perform a more effective role in coordinating large-scale investments, avoiding the problems of excess capacity which sometimes is evidenced in market economies, though I question the importance of this in the modern international setting.

The crucial difference appears to lie not so much at the level of managerial decision making but of organizational accountability: Who bears the cost when a project like the SST fails? How these differences get translated into incentives for managers is a question to which I will return later.

Robustness of the Competitive Paradigm

I have thus completed the first part of my argument against the Lange-Lerner-Taylor equivalency theorem. I have argued that the model underlying views about both markets and market socialism provides an inaccurate description of either how markets work or how a market socialist economy might work. (In the following three chapters I will continue my discussion of the basic ingredients underlying the standard market paradigm, including the role of competition and decentralization.)

The relevance of the fundamental welfare theorems, as well as of the Lange-Lerner-Taylor equivalency theorem depends, as I have said, in part at least on whether the implied model of the market economy is even approximately correct. Theorems are of course simply a matter of deductive logic: Either the conclusions follow from the assumptions or they do not. The question with which I am concerned is, however, more judgmental: I am asking whether a particular set of assumptions provides the basis of a "good" description of the economy. These are, to a large extent, empirical matters—though I would argue that judgments concerning the relevance of the standard model hardly require a high degree of subtlety.

Still, theorems or analytic propositions can be useful, in several ways. First, we can ask, is the model robust? Do slight changes in the assumptions—particularly the assumptions about which we may have limited confidence—result in marked changes in the conclusions? The explorations within the economics of information over the past fifteen years have, I believe, provided a quite resounding answer: The competitive paradigm is not robust. Not only are the basic welfare theorems extremely sensitive to the assumption of imperfect information,[24] so too are the existence and characterization theorems. With a slight amount of imperfect information, equilibrium may not exist, prices may not be at the competitive level, competitive market equilibrium may be characterized by positive profits, markets may not clear.

Second, we can ask, are there modifications of the model (possibly quite significant) that would be required to make the model more reasonable, to incorporate features of the economy that are clearly of first-order importance, that would necessitate a major change in either the structure of the model or in its conclusions?

In the first question, I was concerned only with minor perturbations around the "received" model, for instance, what would happen if there were only slight costs of search, or only slight differences among workers, unobservable to the employer. The second question is concerned with more fundamental perturbations, such as the possibility of innovation (which was completely precluded from the standard model). It is to this question that I turn in chapter 8.

7   Competition[1]

At least since the time of Adam Smith, competition has played a central role in economics. It is because of competition that individuals and firms, pursuing their own self-interest, are led, as if by an invisible hand, to do what is the common good. Yet, though almost all economists applaud competition, the concept of competition has many different meanings. The enthusiasm of economists for competition is not moreover shared so universally. People in business talk about destructive competition. And naturally, when a competitor appears to be losing in competition, his assertion is that the competition is unfair. Likewise industries losing the competitive battle from foreign firms seek protection, always claiming that their rivals have some unfair advantage.

When we stress the importance of competition to our students, we tend to make reference to a number of associated ideas: to markets, incentives, and decentralization. Markets work partly because of competition and partly because of the advantages that result from decentralization. Competition is important because it provides incentives. While the concepts are closely tied together, they are not inextricably linked: A monopolist can organize production in a decentralized way, there can be competition even when there are relatively few firms, and there are a variety of ways of providing incentives.

We need to understand more clearly the distinct roles played by each of these concepts, and this and succeeding chapters are devoted to these issues. I am concerned both with the roles that competition and decentralization do and can play in the economy, as well as with the models that we use to study competition and decentralization and that help shape our thinking—and our policy recommendations. Here I am concerned that the standard neoclassical model—the model of competition reflected in the *perfect competition* paradigm—does not reflect adequately the nature of competition and the role it performs in our economy. More broadly, I want to argue three propositions:

1. While competition has a variety of meanings, the common sense meanings are quite different from those captured in the "perfect competition" model of neoclassical theory.

2. Competition plays a vital role, but a rather different one than that reflected by the standard Arrow-Debreu model.

3. When information is imperfect—or in sectors of the economy where innovation is important—markets will essentially always be imperfectly competitive. (We will postpone until the next chapter the discussion of innovation and its implications for the market/market socialism debate.)

I conclude the chapter with a discussion of the implications of the analysis for the debate over market socialism and for competition policy, particularly within the former socialist economies. I will argue, on the one hand, that market socialism is not the only, or the best, remedy for the problems posed by imperfect competition and, on the other, that the former socialist economies must work hard to establish appropriate competition policies.

Concepts and Roles of Competition

In their attempt to understand the conditions under which Adam Smith's invisible hand conjecture was correct, economists have evolved a precise notion of competition—perfect competition—the essential feature of which (for our purposes) is that all firms face a horizontal demand schedule. There are so many firms that each firm believes that, should it increase its price by even a small amount, it would lose all of its customers.

It is ironic that in this limiting case of competition, upon which economists have lavished so much of their attention over the past half-century, most of the features of competition—as they appear in ordinary usage of the term—are absent. In the Arrow-Debreu model (the model that formalizes the notion of perfect competition)[2] there is no competition to produce goods more cheaply or to produce better products. There is no strategic corporate policy to outwit rivals. To be sure, profits are maximized if firms minimize their costs of production. But to get customers—as many as the firm could possibly want—all the firm needs to do is charge ever so slightly less than the "market price."

Few markets are perfectly competitive. In almost all markets firms perceive themselves as facing downward-sloping demand curves. To be sure, there is usually some competition. There are relatively few markets in which there is a single firm, a monopoly, or in which the firms collude perfectly (a cartel). Thus most markets are characterized by imperfect competition, which takes on a variety of forms: oligopoly, Schumpeterian competition—emphasizing competition for new products and for R&D more broadly—and monopolistic competition. Each of these forms in turn can take on a variety of shapes. Monopolistic competition, for instance, can arise from ordinary product differentiation (e.g., resulting from differences in location) or from imperfect information and costly search.

Theory of Contests

A use of the concept of competition which is much closer to the ordinary usage of the term is reflected in the recently developed theory of contests. The theory of contests emphasizes that in many economic situations, rewards are based on relative, not absolute, performance.[3] The most obvious example of a contest is a patent race, where the first firm to discover the product gets the patent. But there are many other examples: Salespeople are often rewarded on the basis of how well they do relative to others; there is often an implicit contest among the vice presidents of a firm as to who will be chosen to be president. Persistent performance below the average is often rewarded by being fired. Indeed Bertrand competition for commodities that are perfect substitutes has the profits per unit of the firm depending on the difference between the marginal cost of production of the most efficient producer and the second most efficient producer.

Contests and Incentives
Competition of this form serves an important economic role. It can be shown to be an efficient way of providing incentives: The marginal returns to effort may be very high, yet the amount of risk borne may be limited.[4] (More generally, contests enable the design of incentive schemes that allow for the separation between incentives and residual returns—and in that sense, between incentives and risk bearing.)

Contests When Information Is Limited
Contests can be particularly important in situations where information is limited, and where accordingly the firm finds it difficult to adjust incentives in the appropriate way. When a task is easy, one should reduce the rewards for performing the task commensurately, but the employer often

lacks information on the difficulty of the task. Consider what happens in a simple contest with two players if it suddenly becomes easier to make widgets or to sell some item. If one player kept a constant effort, the other would realize that, at little cost, he or she could do more, and increase the chance of winning the contest. Thus that player strives harder. The rival recognizes this and also strives harder. In equilibrium they both strive harder. Their behavior has adjusted appropriately to the changed economic circumstances.[5]

Without contests we often do not know whether a firm is performing well or not. It was the evidence that Japanese car companies could produce cars (of comparable quality) in the United States at substantially lower costs that finally convinced shareholders of GM that the management of that company was doing something wrong. It was the evidence that MCI could produce long-distance telephone services at a lower price than AT&T was charging that led to a reassessment of phone services in the United States. The information provided by competition provides vital information in judging how well a firm is doing. This information is useful not only for outsiders, but for the firm itself. Should the firm be trying harder? Is it doing as well as it could be? A standard of comparison is necessary to answer these questions. Finally, contests provide a basis for selection, for ascertaining who is "better," and therefore who should be chosen for promotion or to get more resources.

Thus contests facilitate two of the central economic functions—selection and incentives. While perfect competition can only arise in markets in which there are a very large number of firms, contests can arise in markets in which there are many or a few participants. Contests more closely capture the spirit of rivalry that occurs in markets that we traditionally classify as imperfectly competitive. Often in markets with only two or three firms, they compete vigorously. But the competition does not take the form of price competition, stressed by the standard economic theory. Rather it takes the form of competition for technological change and quality, producing new and better products, and accompanying the products with new and better services.

Contests and Economic Efficiency
While there is a widespread consensus among economists that competition of this form promotes economic efficiency, at the present time the analytical base is not as firm as in the case of perfect competition. We know that there are marked inefficiencies associated with monopoly. But there are no simple results for imperfect competition. Under some circumstances, for

instance, patent races may result in excessive expenditures on R&D; firms may race *too* fast to get the prize. The social return is simply the *increase* in the present discounted value of the surplus generated by having the invention earlier than otherwise; the private return from increased expenditure is the increased probability of winning the patent race, times the entire value of the patent.

Other Roles for Competition

In recent years arguments for competition have been extended beyond the realm of conventional commodities to new areas, most forcefully to education. There is a growing view that competition between private and public schools would produce a higher-quality education at a lower cost. Public schools would benefit, as they strive to compete with the private schools. In this usage the concept of competition has moved a long way from that associated with the "perfect competition" model. The standard assumptions required for that model are not well satisfied by education. The standard model, for instance, assume consumers who are perfectly informed about the commodity they are purchasing. With education, parents are making the decisions on behalf of their children, and the parents typically have only limited information. There are seldom a large number of producers (schools) within a given locale—certainly not enough to justify a "price"-taking assumption. Product differentiation is key—different schools emphasize different things. Yet there is a broader set of arguments that suggests that competition may be important precisely because markets do *not* work perfectly. There are many dimensions to this, and I can only touch on some of the more important. Albert Hirschman (1970) has emphasized the role of exit, voice, and loyalty as "control" mechanisms—ways by which consumers can communicate with producers. Competition makes exit a viable alternative, an effective way of communicating dissatisfaction. When individuals choose a school, they feel more committed to it, and this makes them more likely to participate—to exercise the "voice" option. They are more likely to provide the public goods associated with monitoring. (There is a public good aspect of the management of any publicly provided service.)

This brings me to the boundary of the noneconomic aspects of competition. Here competition has both a positive and a negative side. Competition often plays a positive role in enhancing group identification. Group identification has positive incentive effects and facilitates cooperation among members of the group. The importance of these basic aspects of competition are one of the reasons we encourage our youth to participate in team sports, and why firms often organize production activities around competing teams.

Negative Effects of Competition

But competition sometimes takes a destructive turn.

Raising Rivals' Costs

One broad category are situations where one party does better by making the other party do worse. This is called "raising rivals' costs." The classic example are the law school students who rip out the critical pages of the library books to impede their rivals from studying. In imperfectly competitive environments firms often engage in practices that raise rivals' costs: Profits may be enhanced more by doing so than by lowering their own costs.[6]

Rent Dissipation

There are other contexts in which competition does not serve social goals: Resources get dissipated in the competition for rents. Though there has been much discussion of rent seeking in the public sector, as special interest groups compete to get the benefits of public largesse, either through direct expenditures or, more hidden, through protection from competition, competition for rents also occurs in the private sector. There is often an ambiguity, for instance, concerning the extent to which competition among managers is directed at making the firm a more effective organization, or at enhancing the manager's chances of sharing in the rents that often accrue to top executives (particularly in large American corporations).

Conflict between Competition and Cooperation

Finally, there is often a conflict between competition and cooperation. Of course the distinction between cooperation and collusion may often be subtle: Collusion is nothing more than cooperation to pursue the joint interests of the members of an industry at the expense of others. When there are spillovers (externalities) among the activities of firms within an industry, there is the potential for true social and private gains from cooperation. This is most evident, for instance, in joint research ventures (which will be discussed briefly later). Since the benefits of research are seldom fully appropriated by the discoverer, there are frequently positive benefits that accrue to other firms in the industry from a discovery made by one firm. In the absence of cooperative research, there may be insufficient ex-penditures. Yet programs and policies that facilitate this cooperative behavior always risk the danger of facilitating less constructive collusive behavior at the same time.

On Changing Perceptions of the Role of Competition

As I noted in the beginning of this chapter, economists have long emphasized the importance of competition in the economy. The analysis of the previous section agreed with that traditional conclusion: Competition does play a number of important roles in the economy. But my discussion suggested not only that the ordinary usage of the term competition is not well reflected in the traditional economics paradigm of "perfect competition" but that the traditional perfect competition model may give us only limited insights into the roles that competition plays. It is important to understand the role and nature of competition in modern economies, both in order to develop appropriate government policies toward competition and to ascertain the prospects of market socialism. One of the motivations behind market socialism was the belief that, in modern industrial economies, nothing approaching the perfect competition ideal was possible. A market socialist economy could *emulate* the behavior of an idealized perfect competition economy—something not achievable under capitalism. Understanding whether this is achievable, and more broadly, whether achieving this would suffice to attain the virtues of a competitive market economy, depends on a thorough understanding of the nature and role of competition in the economy.

The subject of the role of competition has been one of considerable debate during the past twenty years. In this part of the chapter, I briefly review this debate, which I divide into three stages.

The Early Economic Rationale for Competition Policy

The first stage can be thought of as beginning with Adam Smith, who argued that competition ensured that each firm and individual, pursuing private interests, was actually promoting the public good. It took almost two centuries for the economics profession to translate Adam Smith's insight into a rigorous theorem. That theorem, the first fundamental theorem of welfare economics upon which we focused in chapter 3, shows that under *perfectly competitive* markets, the economy is Pareto efficient—that is, no one can be made better off without making someone else worse off.

Economic efficiency (in the sense of Pareto) required more than a loose sense of competition: It required that there be so many firms that each believed it had *no* effect on market prices—it faced a horizontal demand curve for its product.[7] Here then was a rationale for government intervention: If for one reason or another, markets failed to be competitive, the government needed to intervene to ensure that they were. Without such intervention, there was a "market failure." The economic role of government was to correct market failures.

The theory provided one set of circumstances under which we might not expect to see competition: when there were economies of scale, of sufficient magnitude, that the market equilibrium entailed a limited number of firms. In the circumstances in which competition was limited by these economies of scale, competition policy was not the way to achieve economic efficiency. There was no way both to have competition and to take full advantage of the economies of scale. Thus some other form of intervention was required, such as government regulation or ownership (as under market socialism).

In a sense, while the market failures theory provided a rationale for government intervention—to maintain competition—the only circumstances under which the theory suggested that there would be imperfect competition were those in which competition policy was not an adequate remedy. This line of reasoning seemed to be a fatal blow to the market failure rationale for competition policy but did seem to strengthen the case for government ownership, as under market socialism.

Why Competition Policy Is Unnecessary

The intellectual rationale for competition policy received a further setback in the second stage of the debate, which at the same time undermined the argument for market socialism based on the *failure* of competition as a rationale for market socialism. In the second stage of the debate, two claims were made: First, the losses from monopoly were much smaller than had previously been thought, and second, actual competition was not required to attain competitive outcomes.

Harberger Triangles
The first point was argued forcefully by Arnold Harberger, who attempted to quantify the welfare loss from the higher prices that monopoly brought. He showed that most of the effects of the exercise of monopoly power were simply income transfers: The monopolist gained at the expense of

consumers. The economic *inefficiency* (measured by the deadweight loss, the so-called Harberger triangle)[8] amount to no more than a few percent of GNP, at most. The implication is clear: If essentially *all* that is at stake is a matter of redistribution, then there are other ways of dealing with the problem. One didn't need competition policy, and one certainly didn't need the massive reorganization of the economy that market socialism entailed.

Contestable Markets
The second line of attack suggested that Harberger himself may have overestimated the losses from monopoly. Monopolists might not be able to raise the price over the competitive level—they might not be able to enjoy monopoly profits; if they attempted to do so, some other firm would enter to try to grab the profits away. What was relevant in this view was not the level of actual competition but the presence of potential competition. These ideas, which became popularized in the late 1970s and early 1980s under what is referred to as the "contestability doctrine,"[9] can be traced at least back to Demsetz (1968) and the Chicago school.

Their analysis was based on the premise that there were no real "barriers to entry." In the absence of any such barriers, competition, either actual or potential, ensured that profits were driven to zero, even if there were only one firm in the market. Proponents of the contestability doctrine argued that equilibrium would occur at the intersection of the demand curve and the average cost curve, the lowest price at which the output could be produced without government subsidies. Any firm that tried to charge a higher price would be undercut by a new entrant, who could charge a lower price, steal all the customers, and make a profit.[10] If this contention had been correct, then it would have meant that we could stop worrying about monopoly capitalism. There may be monopolies, but potential competition ensures that these monopolies cannot exercise monopoly power! With "contestable markets" (as markets where potential competition served to discipline firms were called) competition policy was simply unnecessary. Evidently the populist concerns that had originally given rise to the demand for competition policies represented a misunderstanding of the workings of market economies: Standard Oil simply could not have raised its price above average cost, without attracting sufficient entry to force its price back down. Both concerns about the distributive and efficiency consequences of economic power, in the form of monopolies, were misguided. The best face that can be put on the populist measures was that they reflected an excessively high rate of impatience: Market forces do not act instantaneously. This means that the monopolist might have been able to exercise monopoly power temporarily, but not for long, and that presumably the present discounted value of the efficiency losses (or even the distributive effects) must be negligible.

Conduct

Competition policies in the United States have focused on both structure and conduct, on both the number of firms (or potential firms) and specific practices designed for, or which might have the effect of, reducing competition. Thus practices such as price fixing, predatory pricing, exclusive dealing, exclusive territories, and other vertical restraints were looked at askance, if not outright forbidden.

But the theories stressing the strength of the forces of competition within the economy argued that restrictive practices would only be employed if there were resulting efficiency gains. In the absence of such efficiency gains, some other firm, not employing these inefficient practices, would enter the market and drive out the inefficient arrangements. In court cases it became standard practice for defense attorneys and their hired economists to cite, and look for, these efficiency gains.

For instance, Anheuser Busch (the brewer of Budweiser beer) defended its practice of employing what were, in effect, exclusive territories for distributors by citing the benefits that such a system yielded in terms of freshness of canned beer. If two distributors supplied Budweiser beer to the same retailer, neither would have the incentive to provide fresh beer. Presumably the retailer who was sold stale beer would not be able to tell which distributor had sold it stale beer. Moreover, when there is a sole distributor of beer to a retailer, that distributor has an incentive to monitor closely the retailer, to ensure that beer is rotated on the shelf in such a way that no customer ever gets stale beer. A single distributor knows that if customers get stale beer, they will buy less of it, and sales will go down. Retailers have an insufficient incentive, for if a customer were to get stale beer, some of the costs of lost sales would be borne by the distributor.[11] But with two distributors, they "share" the costs, and neither has full incentives. In short, there is a public good problem that can be avoided, or at least reduced, if there is a single distributor.

Is staleness important in *canned* beer? Blind tastings show no evidence that consumers can taste the difference. But Anheuser Busch argued that blind tastings were not a true test. Surely, if freshness is important (as it is in milk, or even in photographic film), there are easy ways to ensure freshness: Simply stamp each can with the date. But Anheuser Busch argued that this would simply confuse the customer.

These arguments may seem farfetched, but they are advanced, and courts have found them convincing, giving deference to the firms' "business judgment." I do not want to dwell on the plausibility or implausibility of such arguments; rather, I simply want to emphasize that the competitive market hypothesis argues that if we see such practices persist, they *must* reflect some form of efficiency gain.

Viewed from this perspective, competition policy—whether aimed at structure or conduct—is unnecessary. If the arguments were correct that even in the presence of nonconvexities where only one firm produces in a market, potential competition ensures efficient outcomes, and if those arguments could be extended to the particular kinds of nonconvexities associated with technological change (see below), then we would at last have an intellectual foundation for the belief in the efficiency of capitalist industrial economies (at least if we ignored imperfect information).

But critics of competition policies go farther: Such policies are not benign, for concerns that they will be (wrongfully) subjected to antitrust prosecution may inhibit firms from taking full advantage of economies of scale or scope or even from employing efficiency-enhancing practices that might be interpreted as restrictive. The stochastic nature of court decisions opens up opportunities for rent-seeking activity by smaller firms (or their lawyers), claiming (falsely) that they were injured by the anticompetitive practices of their larger rivals. Thus competition policy is worse than unnecessary—it is not benign; rather, it is actually harmful.[12]

This has led some experts (e.g., Judge Posner) to argue for a per se rule rather than a rule of reason in assessing restrictive practices. That is, such practices should, per se, be legal.

Fundamental Implications
The conclusion of this second stage of the debate over competition in the market economy was striking: Not only were the competition policies to which the lack of competition had given rise unnecessary, but so too was the kind of fundamental restructuring of the economy envisioned by market socialists.

The New View

During the past decade, a new view has emerged. This new view not only provides a critique of the contestability doctrine (or more broadly, of the "Chicago" school)[13] but for the first time provides a coherent rationale for antitrust policy. This view directly attacked both its conclusions and its arguments. As Partha Dasgupta and I put it in an earlier paper (1988a), alluding to the strong support that such theories received from those who would like to be free of the restraints imposed by the antitrust laws,

The hope that a theory of potential competition would at least enable the extension of welfare economics to modern industrial economies, while it may have been well funded, was not well founded. (p. 570)

Basic Premises
The new view is based on three premises:

1. There are a variety of market imperfections that give rise to barriers to entry and limited competition.

2. In imperfectly competitive environments firms engage in a variety of practices that either facilitate collusion or restrict competition; such practices not only result in higher prices, but also distort the economy and lead to economic inefficiencies.

3. The welfare losses associated with monopoly may be much greater than suggested by the Harberger welfare triangles.

This view argues that not only was Adam Smith correct, when he wrote that "People of the same trade seldom meet together, even for merriment and diversion, but the conversation ends in a conspiracy against the public, or in some contrivance to raise price,"[14] but also that these anticompetitive attempts have real effects—they are not simply undone by actual or potential competition.

Limited Competition: Evidence
The new view begins with the observation that competition in the industrial sector is imperfect. The pieces of evidence to support this contention go well beyond simply citing the extent of industrial concentration in particular sectors of the economy. Robert Hall (1988), for instance, provides econometric evidence that in recessions, price is significantly in excess of marginal cost, a situation that could not persist if competition was perfect.

Most firms clearly perceive themselves as facing downward-sloping demand curves. They do not believe that were they to lower their price by an arbitrarily small amount, they would face an unlimited demand for their product. This criticism is particularly telling, since it is the belief that they face horizontal demand curves that is at the center of economists' arguments that competitive markets result in economic efficiency.

Limitations on Competition: Theory
It is no surprise, given what we have learned from recent advances in economic theory, that markets are far from perfectly competitive.

Natural Oligopolies   I noted that earlier discussions focused on "natural monopolies," industries in which either fixed costs loomed so large that at the relevant levels of production, average costs were still declining, or industries in which even variable costs might be falling with scale. Attention was focused on utilities, such as electricity.

But we now realize that fixed costs—nonconvexities—are far more pervasive. As my discussion of the next chapter will emphasize, R&D expenditures are essentially fixed (sunk) costs, and accordingly, industries in which R&D expenditures loom large may be close to natural monopolies. So too learning by doing—where marginal costs of production fall as production increases—gives rise to nonconvexities.

These and other nonconvexities need not give rise to natural monopolies—to industrial structures where there is a single firm—but to natural oligopolies, where there are relatively few firms, sufficiently few that the assumption of "perfect competition" simply cannot be taken seriously.

Monopolistic Competition   Competition will also be imperfect whenever individuals value variety (or different individuals value different attributes of a commodity differently), so that the market as a whole values variety, and when producing variety has a cost, because of the fixed costs associated with producing each variety. There will then be at least some products, perhaps many products, that are produced by one or at most a few firms. There will be of course close substitutes but not perfect substitutes; the firm will face a downward-sloping demand curve for its products. It will have some market power. Once we take into account differences in location, in delivery times, in services, there are few sectors in a modern industrial economy where such product differentiation is *not* important, where each firm does not perceive itself as facing a downward-sloping demand curve. *At best*, there is monopolistic competition, not perfect competition.[15]

Imperfect Information
The horizontal demand schedule facing any firm is based on the hypothesis that if the firm raises its price, it loses all of its customers, and if it lowers its price, it grabs the entire market. But that in turn requires that those purchasing from other firms know that it has lowered its price, or that the

firm's customers can instantly find the other firms that are selling the commodity for a lower price. As a result of imperfect information, firms can raise their prices without losing all of their customers and can lower their prices without grabbing the entire market.

What is relevant of course is not only imperfections of information concerning price but also quality. If a firm lowers its price, customers at other stores may worry that the product is not really just the same product; it may (in some way that is not obvious) be of a lower quality.

It is sometimes suggested that all that is required to ensure competitive pricing is that there be some consumers or workers with low search costs who can arbitrage the market. This argument is false: So long as there are enough uninformed consumers, there are some stores that will charge high prices, with the higher prices offsetting the smaller customer base.[16] The low search cost individuals do not ensure that the high search cost individuals are not "overcharged," though, to be sure, the more low search cost individuals there are, the lower the average price that the high search cost individuals must pay. By the same token, however, the more high search cost individuals there are, the more the low search cost individuals must search in order to find the low price stores.

Analyses of the consequences of limited information and small consumer transactions costs have shown that even small search (transaction) costs may give rise to what appears as large monopoly power. Diamond (1971), for instance, has shown that even arbitrarily small search costs may result in the market equilibrium being the monopoly price. Even though there may be many firms in the market, these small search costs have consequences all out of proportion to their magnitude. The argument is simple: Assume that all firms are charging the same price, lower than the monopoly price. If any firm raises its price just slightly—by an amount less than the search costs, the cost of going to another store—it will not lose any customers. It thus pays the store to raise its price by that amount. But this implies that it pays all stores to raise their prices. The process continues until the monopoly price is reached.[17]

In many markets, such as loan markets, information costs serve to fragment the market, to make the effective number of competitors far fewer than they might seem. Borrowers differ from one another in the likelihood that they will repay. An essential function of financial institutions is to assess the likelihood of repayment, and to charge interest rates reflecting that information. Making such judgments requires information, which is costly and time-consuming to acquire. Given that, not surprisingly, borrowers tend to have banking relationships with one, or at most a few, lending institutions; when a borrower is turned down by his bank, he cannot simply go out to any one of the other banks in the market. To these other banks, the borrower is an "unknown," and will be treated as such, being charged a higher interest rate to reflect the greater risk which they have to bear. Thus, from the borrower's perspective, the number of banks that are effectively competing for him may be very limited.

There is thus a certain similarity between transportation costs—which have provided part of the basis of the traditional theory of monopolistic competition—and information costs. While transportation costs may be relevant for determining the extent to which different banks compete in providing depository services to, say, a given commercial customer—any bank is willing to accept any individual's deposits and to sell those services at a particular price—it is information costs that are relevant for determining competition in loan markets.

Limitations on Potential Competition

In the previous paragraphs I have argued that there is both theory and evidence in support of the hypothesis that firms, in general, face down-ward-sloping demand curves. As my earlier discussion indicated, if markets were really contestable, then the fact that any firm faced a downward-sloping demand curve would be irrelevant—both for the firm and for the analyst assessing its policy implications. What keeps a firm from raising its price is not the demand curve for its product but the certain knowledge that were it to raise its price above average costs, there would be entry that would virtually instantaneously bid away its customers and ensure that it would not realize any profits. To put it another way, potential competition does ensure that any firm faces a horizontal demand curve, at least to the "left" of where it is producing in equilibrium, at the point where price equals average cost.

The fact that firms often seem to believe (or act as if they believe) that they can raise prices without losing all of their customers suggests that potential competition, if present at all, has only limited effects. Limitations on competition are only the beginning of the analysis: We need to know why competition is limited, if we are to make a judgment about whether competition policy can improve matters. To put it another way, we need to know why firms face downward-sloping demand curves and why there exist barriers to entry (which limit the ability of potential competition to discipline the existing firms in the market) to ensure that they do not charge prices in excess of average costs and that they are efficient.

Barriers to Entry

Bain (1956) provided a taxonomy of the barriers to entry; many of the advances of the new view can be seen as providing interpretations, in terms of recent developments in economic theory, of these barriers. I have time here only to highlight two or three of the more important barriers.

Sunk Costs   One of the major insights of modern strategic theory emphasized that what was relevant for decisions concerning entry into a market was not the existence of profits in the market today but what would happen after the firm entered.[18] Potential entrants were smart enough to know that incumbent firms would not keep prices unchanged should they enter. Entrants had to make a forecast of what would happen. There was necessarily considerable uncertainty about such forecasts.

An important aspect of firm decisions concerning entry is, What happens if the incumbent firm lowers its price to the point where there no longer are profits for me? Can I leave and recover my costs?

If there are sunk costs, then (by definition) the firm will not recover its costs. Sunk costs thus serve to deter entry (Salop 1979). There is an even stronger result: If competition *after* entry is very fierce (e.g., there is Bertrand competition under which price is driven to the marginal cost of the second most efficient firm), then even arbitrarily small sunk costs can serve as a perfect entry barrier.[19] An incumbent firm can charge the monopoly price and be perfectly immune from the threat of entry. The reasoning is simple: If firms face, say, a constant-returns-to-scale technology beyond the sunk cost, then the entrant knows that, after entry, price will be driven down to marginal cost (which equals average variable costs). While the firm continues to produce, it will not be able to earn a return on its sunk investment, and if the firm leaves, it will not be able to recover these costs. Hence the potential entrant knows that the existence of large profits is a mirage: If the firm enters the market, the large profits will disappear.

Proponents of the contestability doctrine had always cited airlines as the paradigm. If any firm should charge higher than average costs on a particular route, other airlines could quickly divert their planes to the new route, undercutting the existing airline. If the incumbent responded, the entering firm had nothing to lose. It could simply fly its plane back to where it was originally. This argument concerning contestability of the airlines industry provided a central part of the rationale for airline deregulation in the late 1970s. The world has not turned out the way that these advocates of the contestability doctrine had forecast. It is not only that competition was limited—after an initial spate of entry, there has been a shakeout, to the point where in the United States there are now only three major airlines that are not in bankruptcy or that have not recently gone through bankruptcy, and competition on many routes is very limited, with some routes' prices much higher than can be accounted for by average costs. Even small sunk costs seem to matter a great deal. To enter a market, customers need to know that you have entered. There are, for instance, sunk costs associated with advertising. And the computer reservation systems have ensured that ex post competition can be very effective; any price cut is instantaneously matched. Thus the general maxim that stronger ex post competition results in weaker ex ante (potential) competition seems to have been borne out.

Sunk costs are important. A central aspect of firms in most industrial sectors is research and development. Such expenditures are, for the most part, sunk. They are not like the purchase of a building. Even a partially completed building has a well-defined market value. A firm could, at any stage, sell the building and recover most of what it has spent. Only the idiosyncratic expenditures (e.g., the company logo painted on the walls of every room) are truly sunk. In contrast, a half-completed research project represents sunk costs that the firm could not recover should it exit. It can be shown that such costs can give rise to strong entry barriers in patent races, ensuring that a firm that has a small head start will not face significant competitive threats (Dasgupta and Stiglitz 1988a).

Strategic Barriers to Entry   Both technology and firm behavior can give rise to entry barriers. Firms can, and do, for instance, engage in predatory pricing, both to deter potential entrants from actually entering and to drive out those who are so foolish as to enter.

Even in the absence of strategic policies, an incumbent monopolist has an advantage over new entrants. Schumpeter had a vision of a succession of short-term monopolies. Each temporary monopolist would be challenged by a successive new entrant. In a succession of papers written in the late 1970s and early 1980s, this view has been successfully challenged.[20] Consider the simple problem of installing new capacity in an industry with "lumpy" investment. The threat of potential competition does force the monopolist to install new capacity faster than it might otherwise. But it pays the monopolist to install the new capacity sufficiently early that it would not pay any entrant to beat the monopolist to the draw. Thus there are innate forces leading to monopoly power, once established, to persist.[21]

These arguments show that the monopolist has an incentive to preempt potential entrants. In the late 1980s this argument was strengthened by showing that to preempt potential rivals, in some circumstances the incumbent monopolist need take only a small action.[22] This is referred to as ε-preemption. Consider a patent race. If the incumbent firm has a slight head start over its rivals, and has made a credible commitment to win the race, then rivals will be deterred from entering. They know that any expenditures they make can and will be more than matched by the incumbent. Thus, once the incumbent has established this small head start, it can relax and proceed at its own pace, as if immune from potential competition.

These arguments perhaps exaggerate the limitations on the effectiveness of competition. There are many stories of firms resting on their laurels and being surpassed. IBM perhaps provides the most recent striking example. There are stories of innovations coming from unexpected sources, or taking advantage of skill bases that differ from those of the incumbent monopolist, to produce a competing product. The success of Canon copiers against the established leader, Xerox, exemplifies this. But in the design of competition policy, the issue is not so much whether competition sometimes, or often, works, but rather, are there circumstances in which it does not, and in which government intervention may be called for? The theories of preemption and ε-preemption serve to remind us that even without such strategic policies as predatory prices, obviously aimed at deterring entry, entry may be limited and potential competition may provide only limited discipline.

Competition Policy

During the past century there have been marked changes both in the policies by which governments regulate and promote competition and in the arguments they use to justify those policies. In recent years economists have had an enormous influence in the evolution of those policies. We may not have Plato's philosopher-king, but we do have the economist-lawyer: In the United States, at least, individuals such as Judge (Professor) Posner have had an enormous influence in the evolution of current competition policy. While as academics we can hardly fault the attempt to bring rationality into any area of public discourse, problems arise from the unsettled nature of economic theory. All too often the lags in the dissemination of ideas are such that they get applied just as they are being discredited, or at least doubt is being cast on their general validity.

This is true in competition policy: Many of the economic principles that underlie some of the recent changes or proposed changes in competition policy are based on economic assumptions or models of dubious relevance to the markets in question. The contestability/potential competition doctrines have been gaining strength in the courts, just as they have been losing credence within the academic arena.

The objective of this part of the chapter is to summarize (at a theoretical level) some of the central issues of the current debates over competition policy within the United States. I hope, and believe, that these perspectives will have relevance to other countries that are in the process of reassessing their competition policies. I have found it useful to frame the discussion historically. It is not only that the current debates reflect the historical evolution of competition policy, but such a review also serves to highlight some of the contrasting perspectives on competition policy.

Populist Roots

It was images of robber barons—Rockefellers and Morgans—that gave rise to antitrust policies in the United States in the late nineteenth century. Monopolies were being formed in important industries, such as oil and steel. A few people were becoming immensely wealthy. But the concern was with more than the inequality of wealth: There was concern about the consequences of the agglomeration of economic power. No doubt the concern was as much about the political implications—and the broader implications for the nature of society—than about narrower economic concerns. To be sure, there was the widespread suspicion that those who formed these monopolies had more in mind than the simple "rationalization" of industry: It was unlikely that economic power, once formed, would not be exercised. Prices would be raised.

It was to be more than three-quarters of century before Arnold Harberger was to do his pioneering work quantifying the welfare loss from such price increases. Had his analysis, suggesting that the welfare losses of monopoly were limited, somehow been known to those debating the Sherman Antitrust Act, the original act instituting competition policy in the United States, would this have changed matters? I think not. What was at stake was more than a calculus of efficiency losses: It was a vision of how the economy functioned, some notion (to use modern terms) of a level playing field and a fair game. Small players were simply at a disadvantage playing against the big bullies.[23]

The Economic Debate

The economists entered the scene later, but with considerable influence. We have seen in the previous sections the vacillations in economists' thought—from the early market failures view, emphasizing the necessity of *perfect* competition if economies are to be efficient, but focusing attention only on natural monopolies; to the view that the welfare losses even from monopoly are limited, and that what is required is not actual competition but potential competition; to the *new view*, showing that limitations on competition are likely to be far more pervasive than the early market failures theory suggested. At a minimum the new view provides a powerful critique of the contestability doctrine, with its implicit view that competition policy is unnecessary. The new view has shown that markets may not be efficient and that profits may not be zero. There is *potential* scope for competition policy both to limit profits and to increase efficiency.

The new view stresses the importance of *imperfect* competition, as opposed to monopoly, the center of concern in the older market failures approach. It argues not only that in most markets in modern industrialized countries, competition is limited but that the welfare losses from limited competition may be much greater than had previously been thought to be the case—and may be significantly different from those associated with monopoly.

Welfare Losses from Limited Competition

The new view has shown that the *economic* welfare losses associated with imperfections of competition may be far greater than the Harberger triangle measurements would suggest.

It is not *just* that prices are raised relative to marginal costs of production. Costs of production themselves may be adversely affected, as when firms engage in activities to raise rivals' costs or to deter entry.[24] Indeed in some cases the main effect may be on costs of production rather than profits.[25]

We can distinguish two kinds of effects, those that affect the behavior of firms directly and those that affect the behavior of firms' managers (and thus the behavior of firms, though indirectly). In traditional models, firms increase their profits by producing new products that consumers like and by producing existing products at lower costs. They sustain their profits by keeping ahead of their competitors, continually bringing out better products and lowering their costs of production. In theories of imperfect competition, firms can increase and sustain their profits in four additional ways: by rent seeking, deterring entry, reducing the degree of competition, and raising rivals' costs.

Rent Seeking

When there are profits or rents, there may be competition to get those profits or rents. Firms may spend an amount equal to those profits to obtain them. The resulting welfare loss (a waste of resources) will typically be much greater than the welfare loss associated with an increase in prices (much of the effect of which is a transfer of resources, from consumers to producers).

The concept of rent seeking was first developed in the context of political economy models, where the profits (or rents) arose from government-imposed barriers to entry. Thus firms might spend considerable resources to induce the government to raise a tariff or impose a quota. The principle of rent seeking applies, however, equally well when there are other sources of limitations to competition. Thus research directed at getting around an existing patent can be thought of as rent seeking.

Entry Deterrence

Earlier in the chapter, I described strategic barriers to entry: Firms can engage in practices that deter other firms from entering the market, enabling the incumbent firm to sustain its profits. Many of these practices are wasteful. Firms may, for instance, construct excess capacity, demonstrating a willingness and capacity to respond to entry by lowering prices and increasing production. (In cases where the excess capacity has no effect on the marginal cost of production, prices charged consumers are unaffected by the excess capacity; the entry-deterring expenditures are purely dissipative.) Research activity may be directed at obtaining patents designed to block the development of a rival product.

Actions Directed at Altering the Degree of Competition

There is a fundamental difference between markets in which there is a single firm (i.e., no competition) or in which there is perfect competition, and those in which there is imperfect competition. In the former cases the extent of competition is, by definition, fixed, while under imperfect competition firms' actions may affect the degree or extent of competition. The practice of exclusive territories provides an example of a restrictive action that can affect the degree of competition. Suppose that there are two firms in the industry. One can show that when producers sign such exclusive territorial contracts with distributors, the elasticity of the demand curve facing each firm for its products will be lower. Accordingly, at each price charged by the firm's rival, it is optimal for the firm to charge a higher price. The net effect is obvious: The equilibrium price will be higher. Indeed the equilibrium price may be so much higher that profits of the producers are higher, even if they are able to capture little, if any, of the profits of the distributors. (In the presence of perfect competition among distributors, distributors' profits are zero.)

This is an example of a practice that restricts competition in order to raise prices. In imperfectly competitive environments firms always face the conflict of whether to compete or to collude. They may increase their profits by trying to undercut rivals and steal their customers, or they may increase their profits by persuading their competitors to collude with them, to raise prices. In the United States explicit collusive price fixing is illegal. But there may exist practices that facilitate tacit collusion, or that have collusionlike effects. The most notorious of such practices, and perhaps the most striking, is the "meeting the competition" policy. A firm announces that it will "not be undersold." It will match any price cut of any rival. Sounds like a paradigm of competitive behavior? Wrong: It is actually a practice that results in higher consumer prices. Every rival knows that it does not pay to lower its price. Price competition simply cannot be used to get customers. This policy allows an equilibrium in which the cartel (monopoly) price can be sustained.

Raising Rivals' Costs
In imperfectly competitive environments, a firm's profit depends on its costs *relative* to that of others. For instance, with Bertrand competition the profits of a firm per unit are equal simply to the difference between its marginal costs and that of its rivals. A firm can raise its profit thus either by lowering its costs, or by raising its rival costs. It is apparent that there can be destructive competition—where each firm tries to raises its rival costs —as well as constructive competition.[26]

Managerial Slack
Standard theory holds that firms, whether in competitive markets or monopolies, produce whatever output they produce at the lowest possible price. They have full incentives to reduce those costs, balancing expenditures today on cost reduction with the benefits to be received. (To be sure, if output is lower under monopoly, there will be less incentive to reduce costs, since the total savings from reducing unit costs of production will be

smaller.) Yet there is a widespread perception that firms that are freed from the discipline of the marketplace often are inefficient. In the older literature (Leibenstein 1966) this was referred to as X-inefficiency. Recent theoretical literature has contributed to our understanding of this phenomena in two ways.

First, because of imperfect information it is often difficult for shareholders to tell whether a firm is being efficient, except by way of comparison. In the first section of this chapter, we showed how the information provided by relative performance is thus of vital importance, in judging how well a firm's management is doing; such information can and does play a constructive role in the design of incentive systems as well as in selecting managers for promotion and in allocating resources among competing units. Under monopoly, with a single producer, this information is absent, with predictable consequences.

While information economics has thus explained the importance of competition in providing a basis of designing incentive structures and, more broadly, evaluating managerial performance, it has also provided an explanation for why such control mechanisms are so important, as we saw in earlier chapters. There we noted the growing recognition of the limitations on the degree of control imposed, either by shareholder voting or by the takeover mechanism, on managerial behavior. The real possibilities for managerial malfeasance—incompetence, or worse—have been well documented. These imperfections in the managerial control systems make competition in the product market all the more important. A competitive product market imposes a discipline on management in large, publicly held corporations that is not provided in any other way.

Defining the Relevant Market

It should by now be clear that the new view provides markedly different perspectives on competition policy than that provided by older views. As an illustration, consider the question of the definition of the relevant market.

It has become standard practice to begin the assessment of the effectiveness of competition by an analysis of the "relevant" product and geographical market. What firms are producing close substitutes to the product being produced? If transportation costs are high, then a producer at a distant location is not in the same geographical market and does not pose much effective competition. Lowering of transportation costs for many products has resulted in a larger geographical market. Within a wider geographical market there are more producers, and hence the market is more likely to be competitive. This has led some observers to conclude that in the new global environment antitrust policy is really unnecessary. There may be only three producers of cars in the United States, but there are many more major producers in the world. Many of them do compete in the U.S. market, and all of them presumably could. Thus the car market is competitive.

There is some truth in this view, or to put it more accurately: Opening up international markets, reducing barriers to trade, is one of the most important instruments in competition policy. But while there are some, perhaps many, products for which international competition suffices, there are many products for which this is not true.

Markets may be "localized" not only because of transportation costs, but also because of information and marketing barriers. The transportation costs of cars to the United States from Europe were relatively low thirty or forty years ago. Yet European cars provided only limited competition, partly because of the lack of an adequate dealership system (and the system of exclusive dealings undoubtedly made it more difficult for a European car firm to establish a nationwide dealership system) and partly because of limited information about these cars by American consumers.

Within localized markets, returns to scale may appear and serve as an effective entry barrier. Distribution routes have the same economies of scale and scope that we associate with local telephones and other utilities. The marginal cost of delivering a good to a store B located between A and C may be small, and the marginal cost of delivering a second brand of beer to any store may be small. Thus in many areas there are only two or three beer distributors. The locus of imperfections of competition in the beer industry may not be so much in the production of beer (for which the economies of scale appear to be more limited) as in its distribution.

Competition Policy and Its Limitations

While the new view has emphasized the important scope for competition policy, it has also recognized that competition policy can have deleterious effects. Four concerns have been raised. First, in some cases competition policy has been used as an instrument to limit competition. One firm, worried about the competitive threat of another, charges it with an unfair trade practice. Lower prices are attacked as predatory pricing. And distinguishing predatory pricing from good, old fashioned, competitive pricing is not an easy task. The old view held that prices below marginal costs were predatory. But once we take into account learning by doing, the relevant marginal cost is not the current marginal cost. The firm must take into account the reduction in marginal costs resulting from its extra production today. (In the absence of discounting, this has the effect of lowering the current effective marginal cost to the firm's long-run marginal cost.) But "long-run" marginal costs—taking into account the reductions in the marginal cost of production as a result of learning in the future—are merely expectational. A firm may claim that it is charging a low price because it believes that it will give it a strategic advantage, simply as a result of learning. Its rival claims the firm is engaged in predation. In practice, the two may be effectively indistinguishable.

Second, antitrust policies interfere with cooperative efforts to engage in R&D. This concern has led to legislation allowing some cooperative R&D efforts. Some advocate further exemptions, while others are concerned that under the guise of R&D cooperation, a broader range of collusive activities will be undertaken.

Third, antitrust policies put American firms at a disadvantage relative to foreign firms, many of whom are not subjected to as stringent antitrust regulations.

It is hard to know what to make of this claim that "bigness" is necessary for international competitiveness. In many cases no evidence of important economies of scale or scope are presented, and in the absence of such evidence, the contention seems more a self-serving argument for the aggrandizement of economic power. When there is evidence of economies of scale, the government faces a real quandary: a trade-off between efficiencies of scale and the potential exercise of market power. Only in the cases where there is sufficient international competition to limit the exercise of market power is it clear how that conflict should be resolved.

The final concern with antitrust policy is with its costs. Litigation costs have soared. Economists have been a major beneficiary, but this is hardly the basis for recommending it.

There is no easy answer to the question of how to design a competition policy that is "fair" and promotes economic efficiency, but for which the costs of implementation are reasonable.

The new view provides us with some tentative suggestions. We should perhaps make more extensive use of *per se* rules. The rough justice (or rough efficiency) that such rules provide may be no rougher, and far less costly, than provided by the kind of judicial process currently employed. Thus, despite the long use of "efficiency" defenses for restrictive practices, few instances where they were important seem to have been documented.

Restrictive practices like exclusive dealings and exclusive territories should perhaps simply be made illegal.

Competition and the Problems of Transition

The issue of competition poses a particular set of problems for the Eastern European countries that are currently in the process of making a transition to a market economy. A central issue in the transition process is the speed of privatization (see chapter 6).[27]

Advocates of rapid privatization have a mythologized view of market processes. In their view, markets quickly lead to assets being used by those who can deploy them most effectively. Eliminating trade barriers and other barriers to entry rapidly leads to the release of pent-up entrepreneurial energies. I have participated in discussions where concerns about the lack of adequate transport to bring farmers' products to markets, the lack of middle people to purchase farmers' goods (to distribute them either directly to markets or to processing plants) and to provide farmers with inputs, such as seed and fertilizer, the lack of credit to finance the purchase of inputs—all of these and other market deficiencies, it was argued, would be met "within a matter of weeks" by a quickly grown crop of new entrepreneurs, supplemented, where necessary, by an invasion of foreign entrepreneurs. Concerns about lack of competition and market-created entry barriers—of the kind that have preoccupied the industrial organization literature during the past ten years—are dismissed out of hand: One does not need antitrust laws, so long as the government itself does not create barriers. Adam Smith simply had it wrong when he wrote, "People of the same trade seldom meet together, even for merriment and diversion, but the conversation ends in a conspiracy against the public, or in some contrivance to raise prices."

I have argued that much more than "unfettered competition" is required to make markets work effectively: There must, for instance, be well-functioning financial markets, and there must be a legal framework that provides for bankruptcy and the enforceability of contracts. Among the "other ingredients" for success is a set of laws to ensure the viability of competition. Making competition work may be particularly problematic in some of these countries in transition. Making the government's commitment to competition credible may be equally problematic; without such a commitment, governments in these countries will be besieged with attempts to obtain protection.

Strong Competition and Free Trade Policies

Indeed, in all countries, there are strong political pressures for protection from competition (as Adam Smith emphasized)—both from competition from abroad and competition within. I suspect that this is more likely to be true in Eastern European countries that have not experienced competition before. Some of the disadvantages of competition—such as failing businesses—will become apparent before some of the long-run advantages manifest themselves. Moreover the ideologies under which many of the business and political leaders were brought up, stressing the advantages of coordination within state monopolies and the disadvantages of disorganized markets, are supplemented by popular views of the importance of bigness—these countries, it will be alleged, will need big companies to compete with the big companies of Western Europe, Japan, and the United States. Finally, the infant-industry arguments for protection will be used to justify "temporary" protection from foreign competition as these countries adapt to the different standards required for trading with non-Communist countries.

The forces for noncompetition will be further enhanced because of the close personal working relationships that may have been established in the days when the entire industry was within a single state monopoly. There will be a natural inclination of some of these individuals, who were socialized into cooperative behavior, now that the parts of the industry for which they are responsible are supposed to compete against each other, to try to organize "more orderly" markets and to undertake "joint ventures of mutual interest"—cover names for collusive behavior. Given the limited check that potential competition and, in the short run, at least in many industries, international competition is likely to play, such collusive behavior may be profit maximizing. As Willig (1992) has emphasized, strong antitrust laws are required, and it is much easier to implement these laws before the privatization process begins. Once it starts, strong vested interests will arise to try to limit the scope for competition.

The consequences of the lack of competition are evident in the case of food processing. Farmers producing perishables are dependent on local processors (particularly given the limitations on the transportation system), and these can exercise monopsony powers to limit the prices paid to farmers. Monopsony rents, rather than going to the government, accrue to the owners of the food-processing plants: Farmers see little gain from privatization; it is just a change of who receives the rents.

Commitments to Competition

There are several things that the Eastern European countries can do to make their commitment to competition more credible, beyond just passing strong antitrust laws and *not* imposing barriers to trade. One of the most effective commitments would be joining the Common Market—and the acceptance of the Eastern European countries within the Common Market may be one of the most important forms of help that Western Europe can extend to the East, not so much (in the short run) because of the potential gains from trade but more because of the potential gains from the *commitment* to competition and trade. It eliminates (or at least discourages) a whole range of rent-seeking activities. Finally, opening up the privatization process to foreign firms may have a benefit beyond the additional source of capital and entrepreneurship—in enhanced competition.

Government as a Source of Monopoly Power

While this chapter has been concerned with what the government can and should do to facilitate competition in the private sector, we need to bear in mind that government is often the source of monopoly power and sometimes facilitates collusion. Stigler's regulatory capture hypothesis (1971), while it may not have the generality that he supposed,[28] certainly alerts us to the possibility that regulators may help ensure that collusive behavior is maintained, when competitive forces would make it difficult to sustain. (The alcoholic beverages industry in the United States probably provides an example of this.[29])

In preferring to be freed from the discipline of competition, government is no different from other institutions in our society, and it is no less agile in coming up with arguments for why competition in its sphere is inappropriate. Public schools do not want to compete on equal financial terms with private schools. The post office does not want to compete with other deliverers of first class mail.

During the past decade there have been privatizations, converting government enterprises into private ones. More important in many cases than changing the "ownership" is changing the market structure—subjecting these enterprises to competition. The challenge is to devise mechanisms for introducing more competition into the provision of public services. Though political competition provides some check, it is a blunt instrument, with only limited effectiveness. Decentralization in the provision of public services to local communities is one way to enhance competition in this arena, discussed briefly in chapter 9.

Excessive Concern about Monopoly

Although I have emphasized in this chapter the importance of effective competition policies for the economies in transition, there is another danger whose specter has become all too evident during the last couple of years. In the transition process there will be many opportunities for "arbitrage" profits. Markets will not adjust instantaneously to eliminate these profits. For decades people within the former socialist economies have been indoctrinated in the view that profits are evil, and they will be—and have been—tempted to label profits as evidence of the exercise of monopoly power. There will be pressures to construct, in the name of preventing monopoly capitalism, a regulatory regime that closely replicates many of the features of the socialist regimes. The fear of the exercise of monopoly power will lead people to take actions that will reduce competition.

Market Socialism and Competition

We have argued in this chapter that real competition was essentially absent from the standard Arrow-Debreu model—a fact that the market socialists failed to grasp.[30] Market socialism could preserve the essential property of competitive markets: Households and firms were told to be price takers.[31] The market socialists thought that by ordering managers to maximize profits, taking prices as given, they could achieve Pareto efficiency—what an idealized *competitive* market economy could have achieved, but what an actual market economy cannot achieve. Thus, while the market socialists showed how one could do as well with market socialism as one could do within the *model* of the perfectly competitive economy, the failure of the socialist economies to embrace competition accounts for the lack of success of market socialism no less than the other deficiencies noted in previous chapters.

To return to our basic theme: Had the neoclassical model provided a good description of the market economy, market socialism would have had a much better running chance of success. But price-taking behavior is a pale reflection of the true meaning of competition in a market economy. It is perhaps ironic that this should turn out to be one of the key sources of failure of market socialism. After all, as we noted in chapter 1, it was the worry about monopoly capitalism that provided much of the original motivation for market socialism—the belief that competition would not survive in modern industrial economies. Both events and developments in economic theory have confirmed the lack of viability of *perfect* competition, but the worries concerning *monopoly* capitalism have, by the same token, been proved unfounded.

Conclusions

Competition is important. It is important as a source of information—to know whether firms are in fact being efficient. It is important in promoting innovation, as we will see in the next chapter. The form of competition— price-taking behavior—captured in the Arrow-Debreu model reflects neither of these concerns. Actual markets economies are not competitive in the sense of the Arrow-Debreu model. Market socialists were misled by the Arrow-Debreu model into thinking that they could get all of the advantages of the market economy simply by using the price system. Indeed they thought they could do better than *actual* market economies because they recognized that in actual market economies large industrial firms did not exhibit price-taking behavior. Had the Arrow-Debreu model captured the essence of market economies, they might well have been correct: Perfect competition is not viable in modern industrial economies, not only because of the prevalence of conventional increasing returns (the factor upon which the earlier discussions focused) but also because of the importance of product diversity, imperfect information, and innovation.

But competition is vital for different reasons than those envisaged by the Arrow-Debreu model, and it is the failure to take cognizance of these vital roles that played an important role in the failure of socialism in all of its variants. It is imperative that the Eastern European countries take cognizance of the importance of sustained competition as they design their programs of transition.

In chapter 3 we emphasized one central assumption in this analysis: that of perfect information. There we narrowly focused on how, in the absence of perfect information, competitive markets (with price-taking behavior) are not, in general, (constrained) Pareto efficient. In this chapter we have seen two further consequences of imperfect information: First, it means that in general markets are not perfectly competitive; and second, it provides a new role for real competition, the kind of competition we actually see.

Imperfect information is, however, not the only important limitation of the traditional paradigm: It also assumes that there is no technological change. Technological change is the hallmark of modern industrial economies, and it is accordingly surprising—one might say shocking—that a theory that ignored technological change should have had, for so long, the central place that it has occupied. Technological change, like imperfect information, alters both the prospects for perfect competition and the role played by actual competition. This is the subject of the next chapter.

8   Innovation

The past century has been marked by unparalleled increases in worker productivity and standards of living. Innovations, such as the automobile, the transistor, the computer, the airplane, have transformed all of our lives. The success of the capitalist market economy is in no small measure due to its success in promoting innovation, and the failure of the Soviet economies is in no small measure due to their inability to sustain innovation, outside a quite limited area, mainly surrounding the military.

Innovation played no role in the markets/market socialism debate, just as innovation plays no role in the neoclassical paradigm. To be sure, there are references in popular discussions to how market economies promote innovation, but the Arrow-Debreu model, which, as I have repeatedly noted, provides the most well-articulated summary of the neoclassical paradigm and which provides the basis of the widespread belief in the efficiency of competitive markets, explicitly assumes that technology is given. There is no scope for innovation.

The fact that innovation was ignored by the standard paradigm led those who turned their attention to alternative economic systems to ignore innovation as well. In the long run this was perhaps the most damming criticism of all the versions of socialism, including market socialism. As I have demonstrated throughout this lecture, by focusing on why market socialism failed, we have obtained a lens through which to see the deficiencies of the standard neoclassical models of the economy.

A major recent development in economic theory has been the recognition of the importance of technological change for modern industrial economies,[1] not that its importance had not been recognized earlier. As Schumpeter complained (1942), these concerns had not been brought into the mainstream of economic theory. Schumpeter's complaints were well justified—even today most graduate curricula do not include any but the most superficial discussions of technological change in the core courses. Of course it is not only that technologies change that is important but that firm make decisions that affect the pace of innovation; decisions about production are affected by how those production decisions affect learning (learning by doing).[2] How firms allocate resources to research and development is a central concern of modern industrial enterprises.

My criticism of the standard model goes beyond, however, the complaint that the model provides us no insight into these questions of how firms make decisions concerning, for instance, how much to spend on R&D. Rather, it is that the *standard Arrow-Debreu model (the competitive paradigm) not only does not include (endogenous) changes in technology but its framework is fundamentally inconsistent with incorporating technological change.* What is more, it is not just that competition is imperfect—that firms are not price takers—but that the form and nature of competition—competition to develop new and different products—is simply not well captured by the standard Arrow-Debreu model.

Innovation and Competition

Advocates of the standard paradigm might well have argued (two decades ago) that it was a reasonable research strategy to explore first models without technological change; we should understand them well before moving on to the harder questions associated with technological change. We now know enough about technological progress that it seems quite convincing that it will not be possible to extend (in any straightforward way) the standard paradigm, which ignores technological change, to analyze modern industrial economies, where it is central.

Imperfect Competition and the Appropriation of Returns

The principal reason is simple (and one well understood by Schumpeter): Firms engage in R&D in order to obtain a return on their investment; to obtain a return on their investment, there must be imperfect competition. To see this, assume that a firm discovered a way of producing a product at (constant) marginal cost but that information about the new technology was freely available. Then with fierce (Bertrand) competition, prices would be driven down to this level (price equals marginal cost). Yet, since marginal cost equals average variable cost, the firm doing the innovating would be unable to obtain any return on its investment in reducing costs.

Governments have long recognized this, and accordingly they grant firms patents, which provide them temporary monopoly rights. There may be competition for R&D, but the nature of this competition is not well described by the competitive price-taking model.[3]

Fixed Costs

It is not only the case that competition must be imperfect, if there is to be any innovation. Technological change entails the kinds of "nonconvexities" (fixed, sunk costs, increasing returns to scale) that naturally give rise to imperfect competition.[4] If the firm develops a cheaper way of making widgets, for instance, then the total cost saving is greater the greater the level of production.

Formally, if the production function is of the form $Q = A F(K, L)$, where K and L are inputs into the production process and A is the state of technology, and if F has constant (or not sharply decreasing) returns to scale and A can be increased by increasing inputs (inputs devoted to research), then the production process as a whole exhibits increasing returns to all factors.

Learning by Doing

If there is learning by doing, then the firm that produces more (today) has lower costs (in the future), just as with standard decreasing cost functions. In a sense, unless there are offsetting decreasing returns to scale (e.g., from organizational diseconomies), sectors in which R&D or learning by doing is important are natural monopolies. Viewed from this perspective, natural monopolies are not just limited to utilities, like gas, water, telephone, and electricity, but they are pervasive within industrial economies.

Natural Oligopolies

Even when there is not a natural monopoly, there may be a natural oligopoly: In many sectors there appear to be high fixed costs associated with innovation, sufficiently high costs that the number of firms that can actively compete is limited. This is true, for instance, of the chemical industry and the airplane manufacturing industry. In the latter it appears that without government subsidies, there might have been only one or two manufacturers of large jet passenger planes in the entire world.

To be sure, there are both economies and diseconomies of scale: It is often hard to manage R&D in large-scale enterprises, and as a result there is some evidence that a disproportionate share of innovations has occurred in small firms. While IBM was able to maintain a dominant share of the computer market for a long time, with the advent of PCs smaller firms have not only been able to enter the market but to thrive. As concentration in this segment of the computer market has declined, concentration in other segments such as software (or at least operating system software) has actually increased.

Will Potential Competition Suffice?

In the previous chapter I considered the argument that even if there were a limited number of firms, the economy still might behave competitively: What was critical was not the actual level of competition but the level of potential competition. When I discussed this issue in the last chapter, the problem was whether, in the presence of nonconvexities, the threat of entry ensured (1) that profits would be driven down to zero and (2) that economic efficiency would be attained.

The existence of profits does not necessarily attract entry: What firms care about is what profits will be like *after* entry. If entrants believe that there will be fierce competition, then they may fear that prices will be driven down to, or close to, marginal costs. When there are sunk costs (costs that cannot be retrieved if the firm exits the industry), then entry will be deterred. The firm knows that in the event of such fierce competition, it cannot simply exit and recover its costs.

The expenditures on R&D are not only fixed (do not vary with the scale of production), but they are sunk costs; once the money is spent, it cannot be recovered. These high, fixed, sunk costs act as a natural barrier to entry, limiting both the level of actual competition and the scope of potential competition.

Monopolies and the Pace of Innovation

So far I have established that industries in which innovation is important are likely to be, at best, imperfectly competitive. The next question is, What is the effect of the degree of competition on the pace of innovation? The evolution of our understanding of these issues has had a curious history, which merits brief discussion.

A First View: Monopoly Discourages Innovation

Early discussions of monopoly capitalism suggested that innovation under monopolies would be low. Firms would recognize that new innovations would destroy the value of their previously constructed capital, and this would dampen their enthusiasm for engaging in research.[5]

Some thirty years ago Arrow (1962b) provided a different argument that monopolies would engage in too little research. His argument was based on the *assumption* that the monopolist failed to capture the consumer surplus associated with lowering prices and that the monopolist produced less than competitors, so cost savings was lower. (Total cost savings are proportional to the scale of production.) Both of these assumptions may be questioned. If monopolists can engage in nonlinear pricing, then they can obtain at least some of the consumer surplus. If *all* sectors of the economy are characterized by imperfect competition, then the scale of production within any sector may be greater or less than it would be under competition, depending on the elasticity of the supply of labor and the elasticity of demand for the particular product, relative to that in other sectors.

The statement that there is "too little research" under monopoly implies, of course, a comparison. There are questions about what the relevant comparison should be. *Given* the level of output under monopoly, the level of R&D is efficient. If there is a lower level of output in some sector as a result of monopoly, then it pays to do less research. (The value of a reduction in costs by a given amount is proportional to the level of a output.) This is of course just a reflection of the general result that even when there are monopolies (of final goods), the economy is productively efficient.

An alternative comparison is with a competitive market, in which the government finances R&D. (If, after the innovation, the market remains competitive, then R&D must receive government support.) But then we need to ask how the government is to raise the revenue. If the government has to levy distortionary taxes, then those taxes may result in lower output levels (in the same circumstances that monopoly pricing results in lower output levels) and correspondingly lower levels of expenditure on R&D.

The patent system can be viewed as a benefit tax, with those purchasing the commodity paying, through higher prices, the cost of the associated R&D. In the presence of imperfect information concerning who benefits from particular innovations (so that lump-sum taxes on the beneficiaries cannot be imposed), such benefit taxation may be desirable.[6]

A Second View: Excessive Entry under Competition

While the previous arguments suggested (at least before they were qualified) that with monopoly there was too little R&D, they do not provide an assessment of whether with competition there was too much or too little

R&D. Obviously, without a patent system, researchers could not obtain any return to their innovation, and therefore there would be too little research. But what happens if there is an infinite-lived patent so that the innovator can appropriate the full return to the innovation.

There was concern that competition for patents might lead to *excessive* expenditures on R&D. The profits appropriated by firms when they obtained a patent did not reflect the social marginal return—obtaining the innovation somewhat earlier than it otherwise would have been developed.[7] The consequence of a new firm entering the patent race might be that the invention occurred only a short time earlier than it otherwise would have occurred, yet the firm's return is equal to the value of the innovation.

Of course entry into the patent race is determined by the *expected* returns: The firm must take into account the fact that there is less than a probability of one of winning the patent race. If all firms were identical, the expected, or average, return is just the value of the patent divided by the number of entrants. Entry occurs until this expected, or average, return is equal to the cost of entering the race. The problem is similar to that of a common pool: fishing boats enter a common pool, until the value of the average catch of each ship equals the cost of the ship. But, if the aggregate size of the catch increases less than proportionately with the number of ships, the marginal catch of an additional ship is less than the average, and accordingly, with free entry, there will be excessive entry. So too the expected (presented discounted) value of the patent increases far more slowly than proportionately with the increase in the number of those entering the patent race. (Doubling the number of those in the patent race is not likely to so speed the expected time of discovery that the expected present discounted value of the innovation is doubled!) Thus the social marginal return to an additional entrant is far less than the private return: With free entry there is excessive entry.

A Third View: Schumpeterian Competition

As I noted earlier, Schumpeter recognized that with technological change competition was important, though imperfect. He thought of the economy as characterized by a succession of monopolists; innovation was like a process of creative destruction, as one innovation made obsolete the previous one. The threat of entry was what kept firms on their toes. The incumbent could not rest on its laurels—competitive pressure forced it to keep engaging in research. Thus markets were characterized by a succession of temporary monopolies.

Similarly, in my discussion above of free entry I assumed that firms were symmetrical and that entry would occur until expected (average) returns equaled the cost of the R&D: There would be zero profits in the R&D sector, just as there would be zero profits in other competitive sectors of the economy. Both of these conclusions are suspect.[8]

In general, the return to innovation to the incumbent firms exceeds that to an entrant. Were the entrant successful, the market would then be characterized by two firms. In the duopoly, profits would be lower than under monopoly, so it would pay the incumbent to engage in just sufficient R&D to deter others. Once a firm becomes established, it would pay to maintain a monopoly position. Schumpeter, it appeared, was wrong in his characterization that markets would normally be followed by a succession of monopolists. Of course random events (the discovery of new products like transistors or lasers) mean that monopoly positions are not sustained forever.

The conclusion of the previously described view that entry would occur until average profits were driven to zero is also incorrect. Competition drives profits to the marginal entrant to zero, but the profits of the inframarginal firm—the incumbent—is, at that point, strictly positive.

A Fourth View: Limits of Schumpeterian Competition

According to the view I have just described, while Schumpeter was wrong in his view about the temporary nature of monopolies, he was, however, correct in his contention that potential competition served as an important goad for engaging in research. For the incumbent firm to maintain its monopoly position, it must engage in sufficient research that it is not worthwhile for any other firm to enter.

But an essential assumption in that conclusion[9] is that R&D competition is not "sequential"; that is, it does not entail a series of decisions taken over time. Rather, a once-and-for-all decision is made about the speed of research. Once we make the more realistic assumption that the speed of research can be revised, then even the conclusion that potential competition forces firms to engage in "fast" research is thrown into doubt. The incumbent can take a lead in an R&D program and then pursue a policy of pacing this R&D at the (slower) monopoly rate. Potential entrants know that, should they enter the race, research will be accelerated (it is not only that a threat to do so is made, but that the threat can be shown to be credible), and given the monopolist's lead, it will win. Since potential entrants know this, they do not enter. Potential competition may have only limited effects in goading on research.[10]

The same conclusion follows in the case where technological change is the result of learning by doing.[11] Learning by doing implies, as we have suggested, a kind of decreasing costs, much as in the usual story of natural monopoly. This gives an advantage to the firm that produces the largest output. Of course, if there are 100 percent spillovers, the firm that produces the largest output will not have an advantage, since all other firms will share equally in the learning. But so long as there are not 100 percent spillovers, market equilibrium will be characterized by imperfect competition, with the dominant firm earning profits. Since the dominant firm will have lower costs, it can undercut any rival (actual or potential), and even under less fierce forms of (ex post) competition,[12] such as with Cournot competition, a firm with a small competitive advantage (which initially will produce only slightly more than its rivals) may wind up dominating the market, as its greater production gives it a further cost advantage.[13]

A Fifth View: Further Complications

My argument of the preceding section suggests that there will be underinvestment in R&D in a market economy. Three further considerations complicate the analysis, though on balance they probably serve to reinforce the conclusions concerning underinvestment.

Spillovers

First, I have ignored the often large spillovers associated with R&D. Even with a fairly strong patent system firms appropriate only a fraction of the social returns to their invention. An innovation may suggest ideas to others, and the value of those ideas can be thought of as a part of the marginal return to the innovation. Yet the return on those ideas cannot normally be appropriated. Because of these spillovers—positive externalities—there is likely to be underinvestment in R&D.

Rent Seeking

On the other hand, some R&D activity is nothing more than an attempt to capture rents away from some other firm. This is seen quite commonly in drugs. A pharmaceutical company will spend a considerable amount of money to invent "around" a patent, that is, to invent a product that is like an already existing product but not covered by the patent protecting that product. This is an example of socially wasteful R&D.

Nature of Competition in the Product Market
As is well known, when competition is limited, it can take a variety of forms.

A third determinant of the relationship between social and private returns to expenditures on R&D is the nature of competition in the product market after the innovation has occurred. Suppose that there is competition among a group of firms looking for cost-saving innovations, and suppose that there is Bertrand competition in the product market. Then the return to the firm that succeeds in finding the lowest-cost technology is simply the difference between its cost of production and the cost of production of the next highest cost producer (times the scale of production). This is exactly the social return to this invention.

The level of innovation may differ from what it would be under competition with government-financed research, because the scale of production may differ. If the government can levy lump-sum taxes, then price would be set equal to the marginal cost of production, which is lower than under Bertrand competition, where price would be set equal to the marginal cost of production of the producer with the second lowest costs of production. Accordingly there will be less innovation in the market than would have occurred in the first best (with lump-sum taxation).[14]

Government Remedies

The moral of these stories is simple: Market processes, in the presence of innovation, do not automatically ensure fierce competition or rapid R&D. As dubious as we might be about government regulation to limit the exercise of monopoly power in utility natural monopolies, we must be even more skeptical about the ability of direct regulatory powers to solve the problems posed by natural monopolies arising out of technological change. Still that does not mean that *some* policies—antitrust policies aimed at limiting the abuse of monopoly power—might not only be welfare enhancing in the static sense but might even play a role in promoting innovation. These are areas of ongoing research: a research agenda that only recently has been pursued, given the long dominance of the standard paradigm which simply ignored technological change.

Other Reasons That the Arrow-Debreu Model Cannot Embrace Innovation[15]

In the discussion of this chapter, I have focused on the fact that technological change necessarily entails nonconvexities, from learning by doing or from the fixed sunk costs associated with R&D expenditures which result in the lack of competition, and that competition must be imperfect for firms to obtain a return on their investment. But there are other ways in which the Arrow-Debreu model is fundamentally inconsistent with the natural ways in which information, in general, and technological change, in particular, should be modeled.

Differences between the Production of Knowledge and the Production of Other Goods

The production of knowledge is different from the production of ordinary goods in several important ways. It is important to bear this in mind because all too often there is a tendency to minimize these differences, to suggest that we can write down a production function for knowledge, with inputs producing outputs, and having done that, we can then treat the production of knowledge just like that of any other good—just as Arrow and Debreu extended the static framework of competitive analysis to time, location, and risk by adding subscripts and superscripts, so too advocates of the production function approach sometimes seem to suggest that the framework can be extended still further to embrace technological change, whether it occurs by learning by doing or by the allocation of resources to R&D. The attempt to extend the standard neoclassical framework to problems of innovation has proved to be even more misguided than the attempt to extend it to problems of uncertainty, where "all" that was required was the existence of a complete set of risk markets.

Beyond the basic problems posed by nonconvexities,[16] there are several other major difficulties, which I discuss in the following sections: (1) the essentially inevitable absence of a complete set of markets, (2) the absence of markets for information, (3) the problems posed by the necessarily non-homogeneous nature of the output of R&D, and (4) the public good nature of knowledge.

Absence of a Complete Set of Markets

The first of these problems I have touched upon in preceding chapters: There cannot exist a complete set of markets, and in particular there cannot exist competitive markets for commodities that have not yet been conceived of, let alone invented. Once we recognize the importance of innovation, we realize that the conception of the price system embodied in the Arrow-Debreu model simply cannot provide an adequate description of competitive markets. To return to the theme of the preceding chapter, competition involving R&D is much more akin to *real competition*, contests, than to the rarified conception of perfect competition reflected in the price-taking assumptions of the Arrow-Debreu model. But there are other reasons why markets for information are not likely to exist, or when they exist, are not likely to be perfectly competitive, or to look anything like the markets envisaged in the Arrow-Debreu model.

Lack of Homogeneity
At a fundamental level knowledge production differs from the production of conventional goods which can be marketed in competitive markets: The standard model requires *homogeneous* commodities. (The lack of homogeneity gives rise, for instance, to the adverse selection problems discussed in earlier chapters.) But every piece of information produced must be different from any other piece of information produced (otherwise it is not new knowledge).

Asymmetric Information and the Existence of Markets
Indeed markets for knowledge are an extreme case of a market in which the buyer and sellers have asymmetric information, and such markets behave in qualitatively different ways than markets with symmetric information. The seller knows what is being sold (though sometimes the buyer may be better informed of the uses to which the information may be put). The buyer obviously does not know the piece of information that the seller is selling —otherwise, it would not be bought. Since before being told the piece of information, the buyer cannot know what the seller is selling—and since after being told precisely what it is that the seller has to sell, the buyer has no reason to pay the seller for it, for the buyer has by then already received it and could claim that (1) it was already known or (2) if it had been known what it was that the seller was selling, nothing would have been offered for it—markets for information/technology cannot work in the way that standard competitive markets for homogeneous products work.

This is obviously an extreme way of putting the matter: Markets for information, though imperfect, do exist. In practice, the seller gives some indications to the buyer of what is being sold but does not provide all the details. Markets with reputation/repeat sales obviate some of the difficulties, but, as I noted above, markets that work on the basis of reputation mechanisms are markedly different from standard competitive markets and, in particular, are different from the kinds of markets that either the Arrow-Debreu model, or the model of market socialism, well describe.[17]

Knowledge as a Public Good

Knowledge differs in other ways from conventional goods. This makes it both less likely that markets for knowledge exist and more likely that such markets, when they exist, differ markedly from markets for conventional goods. Perhaps the most important of the ways in which knowledge (information) differs from a conventional commodity are the difficulties of appropriating (all of) the benefits and the lack of desirability of doing so. In a sense, information, in general, and technological change, in particular, are public goods.

Appropriability (Exclusion) Problems
Information and technological change have, to some extent, both of the attributes of pure public goods: First, it is usually *impossible* to exclude others from enjoying all of the benefits, and therefore impossible to appropriate a fraction of the benefits (the property of nonexcludability). With government intervention, through the patent system, *some* degree of appropriability is possible. The difficulty of excluding others, and thereby appropriating the returns, has also been recognized for a long time. The framers of the American Constitution included a provision for patents, specifically to provide incentives for innovation which in the absence of these intellectual property rights would be greatly attenuated.

The property rights granted by patents, as I have already noted, do not correspond well to the *incremental* value of the researcher's contribution, which may be more related to the extent, as a result of his or her efforts, innovations are earlier than they otherwise would have been. But beyond that, they almost never capture—nor could they feasibly ever capture—all of the social benefits associated with knowledge production. The fact that a firm succeeds in producing something conveys what in many cases turns out to be an extremely valuable piece of information: that the thing which the firm is producing can be produced. For instance, the knowledge that synthetic fibers can be produced in an economically viable manner has a significant effect on the expected returns to searching for a synthetic fiber. More generally, there are almost always spillovers from an innovation, both within a sector and to other sectors.

It is not only that returns are imperfectly appropriated; it is also the case that the costs of appropriation can be very high, as the story of Eli Whitney's invention of the cotton gin, perhaps one of the most important innovations of his day, illustrated. Eli Whitney, with a great deal of effort, was able to enforce his patent rights, but the legal cost—much lower in those days than now—virtually consumed all of the returns he obtained.

Nonrivalrous Consumption
Inventions have the second property of public goods—sometimes referred to as "nonrivalrous consumption." It is undesirable to exclude others, since the marginal costs of others enjoying the benefits is zero. The fact that knowledge had this second property of a pure public good was recognized even before the concept of pure public goods had been formalized. Thomas Jefferson, writing almost two hundred years ago, likened knowledge to a candle, which even as it lights another candle, does not reduce the strength of its own flame.

Market Socialism and Innovation

In the preceding sections I explained not only that the Arrow-Debreu model did not incorporate endogenous technological progress but also why that framework could not be modified (at least without changing the basic spirit of the model) to incorporate it. I described the incentives provided within the market economy for innovation, why those incentives were in general imperfect, and why, as a result, there was some presumption that there would be too little expenditure on R&D. I also explained why, in those sectors of the economy in which R&D was important, there was likely to be imperfect competition in the product market.

At first blush, all of these might seem to strengthen the argument for market socialism. Innovation, like other forms of investment, would be directly under the control of the government. The government would thus be able to correct these obvious market failures. Yet, as I suggested earlier, the failure of the socialist economies to innovate except in selected areas suggests a fundamental problem with the socialist "solution" to this market failure.

It is not so much that the government could not organize and direct R&D. The success of the Soviet and Chinese governments in certain areas of military research is certainly suggestive that it can. Indeed, among the most successful research programs within the West have been those organized by the government: from the agricultural research programs, which did so much to increase productivity in that sector, not only in the United States, but throughout the world, to the space programs; from the Manhattan project developing the nuclear bomb, to the more recent military programs developing the smart bomb, many of the most important advances have occurred in government laboratories and government-financed laboratories.

The failure appears to be the lack of market signals to direct the attention of researchers to innovations that reduce costs and improve the quality of life. When there is a well-defined social objective—building a nuclear bomb in a short period of time—resources can be marshaled and directed in an effective way. But the far more difficult task of thinking up ideas and, equally important, *evaluating* them seems beyond the scope of government.

Part of the reason undoubtedly has to do with bureaucratic incentives: When a government department attempts to evaluate an Airbus, or a proposal for a supersonic transport, it is not the bureaucrats' own money that is at stake. These projects are so long-lived and there are so many uncertainties associated with their success that there is no way that those approving projects can be punished for bad mistakes (or rewarded for good decisions). To be sure, similar problems arise in large corporations in which managers do not have a large ownership stake. Still, the fact that it is the corporation's future that is at stake alters how projects are evaluated: When everyone pays for a project through tax dollars, it often is as if no one is bearing the cost. Prospects of "externalities" and "spillovers" loom large, even in the face of prospects of large losses. This may be because of the role of special interest groups, who have an incentive to plead the cause of these externalities and spillovers. In the case of a project being undertaken by a firm, these special interest groups never get a chance to sit around the table: It is only the direct profits that are of concern.

Beyond that, there is a fundamental fallacy in the dichotomy between investment (including investment in R&D) decisions, and production decisions envisaged by market socialism. Market socialism is premised on the economy of information/communication afforded by the price system. *All* relevant information, between consumers and producers and among producers, is communicated through the price system. But with technological change, this simply isn't so! Firms need to have contact with their customers, whether they be other producers or final consumers, in order to know what kinds of products their customers might like. It is here that perhaps Hayek's criticism of central planning becomes most relevant. It is essentially impossible for all the relevant information to be communicated to a central planner. There is really no alternative other than some form of decentralization and a far more fundamental form of decentralization than envisaged by the market socialism model.

This brings us to the broader issue of decentralization, and the question of, to what extent do the neoclassical models of competition accurately reflect the strengths, and limitations, of decentralization. This is the subject of the next chapter.

Centralization, Decentralization, Markets, and Market Socialism

Market economies are decentralized: Production decisions occur in millions of firms, and consumption decisions occur in millions of households. No one has to know the preferences of all consumers. No one has to know the production capabilities of all firms. This is one of the great advantages of market economies.

The concept of decentralization, like the concept of competition, has many meanings, only some of which are adequately reflected in the standard neoclassical model. Market economies are decentralized, but the nature of decentralization—and the advantages which are derived from it—are only imperfectly captured in the Arrow-Debreu model. Again, to resound my theme, if the standard model had correctly reflected the nature and advantages of decentralization, then market socialism would have provided an alternative way of decentralizing that would have captured all of the advantages of decentralization found within the market.

In this chapter I explain the limitations on the traditional conceptions and present a broader perspective on the nature and advantages of decentralization.

Decentralization in the Arrow-Debreu Model and under Market Socialism: A Possibly Efficient Computer Algorithm

Market socialism attempted to capture some of the same advantages as market economies. The central planner did not have to have all the information concerning preferences and technology. Communication between the central "planners," firms, and households was mediated by the price mechanism. The "messages" sent were fairly simple: Prices are sent, and quantity demands and supplies are given in response.

As I noted earlier, in chapter 1, decentralization in this context has a very limited meaning: It is essentially a (possibly) efficient algorithm for calculating the equilibrium of the economy. If this were the central advantage of decentralization, then market socialism would indeed have reflected that advantage, at least in the determination of current output levels.

The fundamental theorems of welfare economics provided the underlying theoretical foundations for this belief in decentralization: They established that the decentralized market economy using the price mechanism was not only efficient but every Pareto-efficient allocation could be obtained using the price mechanism (with the appropriate lump-sum redistributions). In chapter 4, I questioned the validity and generality of these conclusions in the presence of imperfect information. I showed, for instance, that whenever information is imperfect and markets incomplete, actions by one individual (firm) give rise to externalities, limiting the extent to which the economy could be efficiently decentralized. Indeed the externalities were not only pervasive, they could not be corrected by simple interventions by the government. Moreover I pointed out that the key mathematical assumption of convexity required for decentralization was not, in general, satisfied in economies where information was imperfect and could be changed.

What the Arrow-Debreu model does capture is the sense that (1) it is desirable for there to be some devolution of decision making and (2) individuals involved in decision making have only limited information. But while the Arrow-Debreu model assumes unlimited capacities to process and transmit information, it establishes that only limited information must actually be transmitted (the information conveyed by the price system).

I argue in this chapter that there is much more to the issue of decentralization: The advantages to decentralization are greater, though so too are its limitations. Indeed, in chapter 4, I suggested that the Greenwald-Stiglitz theorem[1] might be thought of as the fundamental nondecentralizability theorem. Despite this I believe that decentralization is essential. But my analysis begins from precisely the opposite perspective of the standard model, which argued that decentralization was possible because only limited information was required. In the view developed here, decentralization is motivated by the limited capacities of individuals and firms to process and transmit information.

The Meanings of Decentralization

More popular discussions of centralization and decentralization involve a broader range of concerns. Decentralization represents the devolution of decision-making power from the center of an organization to subunits (and from subunits into the subsubunits of which they are composed).

Two important points need to be raised: First, whether an organization is decentralized or centralized is not a black-or-white matter. There is always some degree of decentralization. In no organization can all decisions be taken centrally, and the degree of centralization may differ in different matters. Thus an organization may centralize financial decisions but may decentralize marketing decisions.

Viewing the market economy as an organization, we see that it is a mixture: It consists of many seemingly independent subunits (firms), each of which has considerable control over its own decisions. In that sense it is decentralized. But many, perhaps most, firms, employ a high degree of centralization.

Second, it may not even be clear the extent to which any particular decision has been decentralized. Subunits may be given powers to make certain decisions, but the central authority may insist on being consulted, or may reserve the right to intervene. While it may be clear who "signs off" on the decision, who participates—or what it means to participate—in the decision making is often ambiguous. We can refer to these situations, quite common in all organizational structures, as *shared governance*. Rather than focusing on this, perhaps the most common situation, discussions tend to center on the polar cases where decision-making authority is unambiguously assigned, where either the central authorities retain the right to make the decision, or where they delegate that right to subunits. In the ensuing discussion we follow the common pattern, but with emphasis on the limitations of that approach.

Once again, we observe that the failures of market socialism closely paralleled those of the reigning economic paradigm. In both, as I have said, decentralization had a particularly narrow meaning—the ability to delegate "production" decisions to individual firms, guided by prices, and "consumption" decisions to individual households, again guided by prices. In fact the decisions that each made (as I argued above) were relatively simple, and so the issue of decentralization was not very central.

The failure of the standard model (and the market socialism model which was based on it) to address the central questions of decentralization should have been obvious from the onset: For few firms make extensive use of the price system for the allocation of resources within the firm. As I have noted, many, perhaps most, decisions within a firm are made centrally. Just as Coase emphasized that the standard theory did not address the question of the boundary of firms, so too I would argue that the standard theory did not address the relative merits of centralization versus decentralization. Coase's theory emphasized the importance of transactions costs for determining the boundary of firms. But the issue of the boundary of firms is not coterminous with issues of centralization/decentralization; for firms can (and some firms do) organize themselves internally in a more or less decentralized way. Transactions costs undoubtedly play a role in determining whether decisions are made in a centralized or a decentralized way, but there is more at stake in the centralization decision than that, as we will shortly see.

The analysis of this chapter attempts to identify the basic advantages and disadvantages of centralization and decentralization. The central thesis of the chapter is simple: The existence and pervasiveness of externalities would—in the presence of unlimited ability of a centralized authority to gather, process, and disseminate information—provide a strong argument for centralization. But the ability of any centralized authority to gather, process, and disseminate information is limited. These limitations form the basis of the argument for decentralization.

The chapter is divided into six major sections. In the first, I attempt to formalize the sense in which and the conditions under which decentralized decision making, in the presence of imperfect information, results in better decisions. In the second, I consider several other economic advantages of decentralization. In the third, I consider briefly the other side, the advantages of centralization. In the fourth, I address a seeming paradox, which would suggest that in general, centralized decision making is superior to decentralization, and I uncover the basic fallacy in the "centralization paradox." In the fifth I ask, Why is it that when economies face a crisis, they seem to abandon confidence in decentralization, and often resort to more direct control structures? In the final section, I consider noneconomic rationales for decentralization and several of the broader social implications.

Human Fallibility and the Architecture of Economic Organizations

Over the past five years, Raaj Sah and I (see Sah and Stiglitz 1985a, 1985b, 1986, 1987, 1988a, 1988b, 1991; Sah 1991; Stiglitz 1989d, 1989e, 1991a) have been investigating the consequences of different forms of organizational design for the quality of organizational decision making. Our analysis is predicated on three observations:

1. Individuals' capacity to gather, absorb, and process information is limited.

2. The transmission of information is noisy and incomplete. I cannot, to use modern computer language, give you a complete dump of what is in my brain, and even if I tried, what you receive would coincide only imperfectly with what was in my brain. Indeed, in this lecture, I can only give you but broad hints of what is on my mind. (You may find this reassuring, for you may be asking yourself—surely there must be more here than he has succeeded in conveying. The answer is, there is; whether I succeed in conveying it is another matter.)

3. As a result there are reasonable chances that others will make errors. As the old saying has it, "To err is human." As I have grown older, I have increasingly become conscious of the importance—at least in others—of human fallibility.

Different ways of organizing decision making represent different ways of aggregating the different, and fallible, information of each of the members of the organization. In our work, we contrasted, in particular, hierarchies and polyarchies. Hierarchies are organizations in which approval (in our model, the adoption of a project) entailed passing through a sequence of approvals, which in polyarchies, decisions to undertake a project could be taken by each individual (or suborganization). Figure 9.1 portrays schematically these two organizational forms. We contrast these organizational forms with respect to the costs of decision making, the likelihood that bad projects (those whose expected value is negative) are adopted, and the likelihood that good projects (those whose expected value is positive) get rejected. The different organizational forms differ in all three respects.

That there are such differences is simple enough to see. If it takes two approvals to go ahead with a project, the probability of a bad project getting through the approval process is lower, and the probability of a good project being wrongfully rejected is, at the same time, higher. While the probability of one type of error is reduced, the probability of the other type of error is increased, and the cost of two approvals is obviously greater.

These differences are reflected in one of the popular arguments in favor of decentralization: that it involves giving individuals and projects a second chance. If there were only one journal in mathematical economics, then if a paper failed to pass muster with the editor of that journal, that would be the end of the matter. There would not be an *independent* second chance. When there are several journals, a paper that is rejected by one journal has a chance for an independent review.

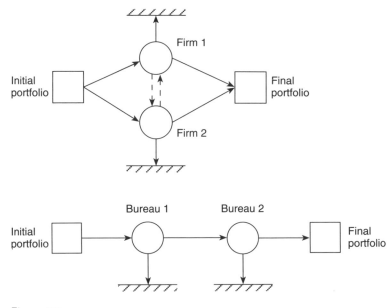

Figure 9.1
Schematic representation of alternative organizational structures—polyarchy (*top*) and hierarchy (*bottom*). Each organization takes a given set of projects (referred to as the "initial portfolio"). In polyarchy, firm 1 first screens a set of projects. If it approves a project, the project is undertaken (it becomes part of the "final portfolio"). If it rejects a project, the project returns to the original portfolio, and firm 2 screens it. If firm 2 approves, the project is undertaken. In other words, a project is undertaken if *either* firm 1 or 2 approves is. Under hierarchy, the lower level (here "bureau 1") first screens projects in the initial portfolio. If it approves a project, the project is passed on to bureau 2. If that bureau also approves it, the project is undertaken (i.e., it becomes part of the final portfolio). In other words, a project is undertaken if and only if *both* bureaus approve.

These results are perhaps obvious for the case where the probability of errors (of a good project being viewed badly, or conversely) are fixed, independent of the organizational form, but they also hold for the case where the criteria for acceptance or rejection are endogenous and respond to the environment in which the decision maker is found. Knowing that there will be another check on a judgment is likely to lead to a lower standard of acceptance than if the decision maker knows that he or she is the only decision maker.

Hierarchical decision making (with multiple decision makers involved in any decision, with decisions being passed on from one level in the hierarchy to the next) involves higher costs (in terms of more decision makers) and delay. The latter problem can be obviated—at the expense of still higher costs—by employing committees. A committee of two, requiring unanimity of approval, is analogous to a hierarchy, where both levels must approve a project, but the latter entails the second level only reviewing projects that have passed the first level.

More generally, a hierarchy of N individuals, all of whom have to approve a project, is similar to a committee of N individuals, all of whom have to approve a project with two differences: Since projects must pass from one level of the hierarchy to the next, the time to make a decision may be much greater, but in a committee all N individuals must obtain information required to form an opinion about the desirability of undertaking the project while in a hierarchy, as soon as any level turns the project down, no further resources are expended at vetting the project. Similarly a polyarchy of N individuals is similar to a committee of N individuals, in which only one vote is required for the project to be undertaken; again there is a trade-off between resources devoted to screening projects and delay. Once we see polyarchies and hierarchies as two limiting cases of committees, it is apparent that there may be in between cases, such as a committee of N in which a project is undertaken if k or more approve the project, just as there can be mixtures of hierarchies and polyarchies, such as a polyarchy in which each unit is itself a hierarchy.

While, as I have said, the fact that these organizational forms perform differently is obvious, identifying circumstances under which one or the other performs better is a far more subtle task. When Sah and I embarked on our research program, we had a predilection for establishing that, under a wide variety of "reasonable" conditions, polyarchical structures dominated hierarchical. The mathematics, however, did not confirm our prejudices, and as we thought about it more, we were glad that this was the case: What we actually observe in market economies is not pure decentralization, but a mixture of centralization and decentralization in which hierarchical firms interact "polyarchically" (to invent an adverb) with each other. What the mathematics did confirm was that this mixture was efficient (which is not to say that the *precise* mixture we observe is "optimal").

One of the central results of our analysis was to establish that for large organizations, mixed structures, for instance, involving polyarchies in which each unit is itself a hierarchy, dominate either polar form of organization.[2]

The problem with the market socialist model here is not that it was wrong but simply that it failed to address the central questions of how production and decision making should be organized. Thus the market socialist economy never addressed the question of where should be the boundary of firms, within which production would be organized hierarchically, making limited use of the price mechanism.

Self-perpetuating Organizations

The arguments about centralization and decentralization of *decision making* with respect to projects extends, with even greater force, to decision making with respect to project selectors. There is an amplification effect: if decision makers make bad decisions concerning their successors, then not only will that have an adverse effect on the performance of the organization during the reign of those successors, but those successors themselves are more likely to appoint incompetent successors. Thus incompetence can perpetuate itself.

Other Arguments in Favor of Decentralization

There are several other economic arguments in favor of decentralization, to which I now turn.

Risk Diversification

More decentralized decision making reduces the variability of the quality of the overall system-organization. For instance, the above analysis suggested that if the top manager is given more power, that is, a greater ability to appoint successors (both high- and low-level successors), then if that manager is good, the expected average ability of the successor organization is likely to be higher. But, by the same token, if the person in that critical decision-making position is bad, the expected average ability of the successor organization is likely to be lower. Greater decentralization represents a form of *risk spreading*.[3]

In practice, we see the great harm, as well as the occasional good, that has resulted from strong leadership: Mao's great *economic* failures —the backyard furnaces and the conversion of land to wheat—involved untold costs; Stalin and Hitler must be included in the roster of strong leaders whose negative net product must be tallied against the occasional good leadership, such as that of Lee Kuan Yew in Singapore. (The fact that the losses seem to exceed the gains may not be an accident: There is a general principle that leaders seem to like to stay on beyond the point where their net product is positive.[4] This accounts for the fact that the value of firms with dominant leaders seems to increase upon their retirement.)

Competition

Still another aspect of decentralization is competition: In earlier chapters I discussed the marked advantages that arise from competition. But if there is to be competition, there must be at least two units engaged in similar activities. My earlier discussions emphasized the importance of competition in providing appropriate incentives, particularly in situations where information about the difficulty of the task may not be readily available or obtainable. Competition also provides the basis of *selection*, of deciding who has a comparative advantage in performing a particular task.

These functions of competition (and of decentralization) are not those recognized, let alone emphasized, within the traditional Arrow-Debreu paradigm, or within the market socialism models derived from it.

Localized Information

Earlier chapters stressed that the information problems addressed by the economy were far richer than those envisaged by the standard model, which focused only on scarcity. I emphasized, for instance, the rich dimensionality of the product space: Firms must know not only how much to produce but when and where to deliver the product. Moreover there are myriad characteristics describing any commodity, and the producer must adapt the product to the preferences of the user/consumer. This information is not conveyed by prices (though, in principle, it could be if there were a complete set of prices for all commodities; but there are not, and for good reason, as we saw in chapter 5). There is no way that a centralized authority could ever gather, process, and disseminate this kind of information.

Experimentation

A fourth argument for decentralization is that it is more conducive to experimentation. Each of the decentralized units may engage in "random trials"; the outcome of all these random trials provides valuable information. Good outcomes may be imitated, and even bad outcomes may yield important lessons.

The Advantages of Centralization

There are two important respects in which "centralization" is alleged to have a great advantage: coordination and the internalization of externalities.

Coordination

One of the alleged great advantages of the price system is its ability to coordinate the production decisions of firms and the consumption decisions of households. But, as I argued earlier, the set of information problems confronting the economy is much richer than that with which the standard Arrow-Debreu model has been concerned. The Arrow-Debreu model was not designed to answer questions concerning the efficiency with which the economy gathered and distributed new information, for instance, about changes in the economic environment, and at least in some highly idealized models—the most simple models we have been able to construct—the pure price model does not live up to the high standards of "constrained Pareto efficiency."

In practice, when firms put teams of people together to design new products, they do not use price mechanisms, though "cost" information is obviously relevant. The kind of coordination that is required *cannot* be mediated through the price mechanism.

Externalities

Externalities represented one of the important classical cases of market failures. A standard solution for externality problems was the "internalization" of externalities, that is, forming large organizations that can take into account *all* of the effects of the various actions.

Internalization is of course not the only solution: One can *sometimes* deal with externalities within a decentralized framework, for instance, by the use of Pigouvian corrective taxes or Coasian bargaining. But each of these has its problems: Pigouvian taxes cannot attain efficient outcomes in the presence of nonconvexities, which are pervasive in the presence of externalities (Starrett 1972) and, more generally, moral hazard problems.[5] While Coase *asserted* that parties imposing externalities on each other could arrive at an efficient solution, provided property rights were properly defined, we now know that is not true if there is imperfect information, such as about the extent to which any particular party is affected by the externality, which is likely to be especially relevant in large-group situations (see, e.g., Farrell 1988).

Nevertheless, while decentralized solutions may not work, evidence suggests that neither may internalization (centralization): Pollution problems within Eastern Europe are among the worst in the world, and in the United States public bodies are among the worst polluters. A little thought, using our information-theoretic paradigm, reveals why this should not be that much of a surprise: The *organization* might, in principle, have reason to "internalize the externality"—taking into account all the ramifications of the action—but decisions within organizations are taken by individuals, and the problem is making the individuals within the organization act in such a way as to internalize the externality. This entails designing incentive structures that take into account the full consequences of the action, which is an extremely difficult task. Though modern incentive theory has devised ways by which, in principle, payments can be made to any individual depending on the entire organizations' output (thereby making the individual fully internalize all the externalities), such incentive structures are virtually never implemented, partly because of the extreme risks that they would impose on any individual.[6]

In practice, most individuals' pay is only weakly tied to the performance of the entire organization. Individuals within a large organization identify (to use Simon's term) with some subgroup, and when they are not pursuing their own selfish interests, it is the subgroup's interests (or, as they would put it, the organization's interests, but seen through the perspective of the subgroup) that they are pursuing. The marketing department will argue that it needs more resources; the research department will argue for its needs. Each will of course justify its claims on resources by the benefits that it confers to the other, but there is little evidence that they are fully integrating all the consequences. This was brought home forcefully to me some years ago when I was a consultant to AT&T's Bell Labs. The economics research group within the Labs, besides doing first-rate basic research, had played an important consultative role to AT&T's headquarters. But, from the perspective of the management of Bell Labs, this was an externality, one that they saw little need to take into account in their decision to eliminate the research group.

The military provides some of the most interesting examples of subgroups pursuing their own self-interests, to the detriment of the overall organization. Each of the branches of the military—the army, the air force, and the navy—looks at defense problems from its own perspective. Each takes limited account of how its actions might benefit others. There are dramatic accounts of the consequences of this, even in wartime.

If, of course, it were easy to design incentive schemes to make each of the participants internalize the externality, decentralization would be feasible. We have here a seeming paradox: Centralization only resolves the problems with which decentralization cannot deal when decentralization would itself work. I now come to the other side of this paradox, and a partial resolution.

The Fundamental Centralization Paradox

Recent discussions of the appropriate role of government, and the appropriate degree of decentralization, often seem to go in a circle. While one group of economists has been trying to argue that anything the government can do, the private sector can do as well if proper recognition of the (same) set of constraints (information and transactions costs) is given, there is another set of results arguing that whatever a decentralized system can do, a centralized regime can do as well. The first result, which is enjoying a certain amount of popularity in certain circles, is simply wrong, as we saw in chapter 3. Markets are not, in general, constrained Pareto efficient; there exist government interventions that are welfare enhancing (even if we greatly restrict what the government can do, and even if we recognize the limitations on the government's information), and government does have powers (of compulsion and proscription) that private organizations do not have.

The Importance of Commitment

But now let me turn to the countervailing result, that whatever can be achieved within a decentralized mechanism can be achieved within a centralized framework. The argument underlying this is simple: A centralized system could, in principle, organize itself in a decentralized way so that, if there were advantages to decentralization, they could be attained. But the centralized authority can do more (and our earlier discussions suggested that it might well be desirable to do more, to intervene to counter externalities or to coordinate).

If this argument were correct, it would suggest a distinct advantage to economies that did not *restrict* themselves to market mechanisms. But there is one fundamental flaw in this reasoning: It omits the value of commitment. Centralized (nonmarket) systems have a difficult time committing themselves. For example, if the central authority has the power to intervene, it finds it difficult to commit itself not to intervene; if it has the authority to provide a subsidy, it finds it difficult to commit itself not to provide a subsidy, under certain conditions. Market systems can be thought of as constituting commitments: If, for instance, the firm cannot make its payments, it goes bankrupt. There is a hard budget constraint.

This argument of course exaggerates the difference; the U.S. government did intervene with the Chrysler and Lockheed bailouts, and with the S&L bailout. But different "rules" of the game imply different transactions costs associated with different interventions. These transactions costs are what constitute the commitments. And knowledge of these "commitments" affects behavior, both ex ante and ex post: Anticipations of the possibility of interventions can have real effects.

In a sense the foregoing explanation underlies the "residual" control approach to ownership (Grossman and Hart 1988). Earlier I observed that large organizations have the same problem, in motivating their "agents" to do what they would like, that one firm would have in motivating a firm with which it is dealing to do what it would like. With a complete set of contracts, the two problems might be equivalent. That is, by making payments to one's own agent depend on performance in exactly the same way that one's contractors' payments depend on performance, the distinction between "employees" and "contractors" becomes completely obfuscated. (The fact that the distinction is a weak one is apparent to tax authorities who attempt to tax the two differently.) Contracts are not complete. In capital markets equity owners bear the "residual return," that is, returns that are not committed elsewhere go to equity owners. The contract does not need to say what they get: What they get is defined by the difference between profits and what others get as a right. The owners of an asset get all the residual returns. The heart of ownership, Grossman and Hart contend, however, is not in residual returns, but residual control: All those rights to do particular things with the asset in different states of nature that are *not* stated in the contract belong to the owner; that is, if the contract does not *obligate* the owner to do a particular thing, then anything can be done with the asset.

Of course, in practice, different individuals may have different degrees of discretion over an asset in different circumstances, and I suppose that Grossman and Hart would then say that ownership is shared. This is not the common usage of the term "ownership," but this need not detain us here.

Thus, when one firm takes over another firm, it obtains the residual returns. Having obtained the residual return, it has a stronger (or at least different) vested interest in the firm. It will find it difficult to commit (and to make any commitments it makes credible) itself not to intervene. Knowing this certainly affects behavior ex ante and may indeed make the intervention more likely than if it could have made others believe that it would not in fact intervene.

Here is where the transactions costs make such a difference. Assume the shareholders of firm *A* and firm *B* are the same. Then the claims on residual returns of, say, *B* are the same whether *A* buys *B* or not. Since the same shareholders own *A* and *B*, if we were so naive as to say that "shareholders own the company," ownership (and, in that sense, residual control) would be the same whether A buys B or not. But it *does* make a difference whether A buys B: The manager of A can intervene in the affairs of B more easily. If A did not own B, the manager of A, thinking B should be doing something different in the interests of shareholders, could appeal directly to the shareholders and persuade them to intervene with B's managers. But the probability of intervention is likely to be affected (and indeed should be) if this circuitous route does not have to be followed. Changing the costs of intervention changes behavior. Organizational form does matter.

Centralization and Crises

There is an anomalous aspect of behavior in many modern societies: While professing a faith in democracy, in times of crises they call for a strong leader. Faced with a drug crisis, there is a demand for a drug czar. In times of war they want to make sure someone is in charge. The remarkable thing about decentralized economies is that *no one is in charge, and yet they work marvelously well.* To put it another way[7] there is a commonly held view that democracies—and polyarchical organizations—are fine if you can afford them, but when things must get done quickly, as in a time of war or in a country engaged in rapid development, more centralized control is called for.

It is certainly the case that most countries in times of war do resort to more centralization of control, but it is not clear whether this is because centralization is more efficient in making quick decisions or because there is a mistaken belief in the efficacy of centralized control. There may perhaps be a false sense of security in such times from knowing that someone is in control. In this perspective an explanation for the proclivity for centralized control in times of emergency is more likely to be found in Freudian psychology than in economic analyses.

The proclivity to resort to centralized control seems particularly odd, given the widespread perception, at other times, that government bureaucracies are subject to delays and inefficiencies. Why should an organizational form that is so maligned in normal times suddenly become virtuous?[8]

It also seems odd when the great merit claimed for the price system is its informational efficiency. When the world is not changing very much, capabilities of a system in information processing are not that important; even an inefficient information processor might converge to an efficient resource allocation. It is in times of change that we make demands on the information-processing capabilities of the system, and it is at times such as these there so many societies seem to abandon the price system.

There is in fact some merit in the traditional skepticism of the use of markets in times of crisis.[9] Underlying this argument is the observation that time, that scarcest of commodities, is frequently not well allocated in organizations. The kinds of prices that are used to allocate scarce resources simply do not exist for the allocation of time within an organization. This is not to say that there are not implicit prices on time: I have observed that typically department meetings of the philosophy department are longer than those of the economics department. While the depth of the problems that have to be resolved may account for some of the differences, I suspect that the value of time of the participants of the meetings provides a more cogent explanation. (I once proposed to my department chairman that each chair of a committee or department within the university be given a time budget, as well as a dollar budget. A meeting could be called, but the chair would be charged for the time of the faculty members. I proposed too that a clock be placed on the wall, with the units being dollars, rather than minutes, so that each faculty member should weigh whether, for instance, a five-minute speech was worth the $1000 of aggregate faculty time that it used. Needless to say, my suggestions were not taken up.)

Earlier I noted the important disparity between individual and organizational objectives: In virtually no organization are incentive schemes adequate to make the two coincide, or even nearly so. One aspect of this concerns the use of time within an organization. Since others' time is an unpriced resource, there is a natural tendency for an excessive amount of consultation, or for managers using meetings, not for efficient decision making, but for "broadcasting" their competencies. Several studies (e.g., Hannaway 1989) show that the amount of time spent by managers in meetings is enormous—on average, almost two-thirds of the time of the typical manager. *Some* degree of consultation is of course desirable; "two heads are better than one." This indeed is a corollary of our earlier proposition that the individual's ability to collect and process information is limited. The question is, How much better are two—or four—heads than one? Is the improvement in the quality of decision making worth the cost? Because markets do not provide an adequate way of evaluating or coordinating decisions concerning time, there may be advantages in central coordination. For instance, in many decision-making situations, input from several individuals is required. It is more costly to obtain information early, and information that is not used deteriorates in value quickly. Deciding on the "optimal" speed of decision making is a difficult task. One balances the additional cost of making a fast decision with the value of having a decision earlier. There is no presumption that the market makes the "right" decision concerning the speed of decision making. Indeed there is some reason to believe that the uncoordinated market equilibrium may entail too-slow decision making. In cases where each needs the others' input, and where there are insufficient rewards for "early" information, each worries more about the waste due to the obsolescence of information gathered too early than the benefits that result from "freeing" a bottleneck. The manager bears the cost of the "duplicate" information gathering required in the latter case but shares far more imperfectly in the benefit which the organization enjoys in those circumstances where the particular "piece" of information was the bottleneck. In wartime the difficulties of coordinating decisions in a decentralized environment are increased (because so many more new problems have to be solved), and the value of quick decision making is enhanced. Thus both the magnitude of the market's bias and the social cost from this inefficiency are increased.

Nonetheless, there are costs from the abandonment of market mechanisms, costs that tend to increase over time. Almost all centralized systems of allocation run into increasing trouble over time. This is popularly attributed to the difficulty of sustaining "enthusiasm" in a crisis situation: Initially people are willing to make sacrifices, but eventually self-interestedness wins out. There is even more to it than that: The price system provides important information. I noted in earlier chapters how competition (contests) provides us with information about the relative difficulty of tasks in changing circumstances. More generally, market mechanisms provide us with information about appropriate "norms": How many stamps should a post office clerk sell an hour? Norms of work set in this manner continue to operate even when the market mechanism is "suspended" during the crisis. When the market mechanism is suspended for an extended period of time, the information that the market brings to bear, and that the nonmarket mechanisms make use of, becomes increasingly obsolete. Nonmarket mechanisms may work for an extended period of time, making use of the information that was provided during the period in which markets worked. But it is essential to update this information, and eventually markets have to be reinstituted. Thus under some circumstances it may make sense to abandon markets during a crisis. Doing so, however, does not represent a rejection of market processes, rather a recognition of the imperfection of markets and a recognition that *for a short time*, some of the advantages of market mechanisms—or at least the information that they provide—can be combined with the advantages of centralization.

Beyond Economics

The discussion of centralization/decentralization so far has touched on a variety of issues, focusing narrowly on economic concerns and economic motivations. But issues of centralization and decentralization go beyond these standard economic concerns. I wish to touch briefly on two of these.

Participation

Few questions touch us as much in our everyday lives as those concerning organizational design, or what Sah and I have called organizational architecture. The sense of control over our own lives, our ability to fulfill ourselves as individuals, our sense of individuality, may all in large measure depend on the extent of centralization or decentralization in our society. There is something dehumanizing about being a cog in a bureaucratic machine, and there is something correspondingly energizing about being an entrepreneur, bringing to the market a new product based on a new concept or new insight. The proportion of individuals within any society who have one experience or the other depends critically on the organization of society—a perspective that is totally outside the purview of either the Arrow-Debreu model or market socialism.

Economic Consequences

While decentralization may in many circumstances have a profound effect on the "quality of life," there is a direct feedback effect on economic outcomes. I noted earlier that the Arrow-Debreu model left out all those subtler aspects of motivation that are so much the concern of managers. In many contexts workers who have a say in the nature of their job may work harder and more effectively; there is an increase in efficiency. In education, parents who choose their school are more likely to take an active role in ensuring that administrators and teachers do a more effective job of educating. The choices that decentralized decision making affords result in commitments and involvements that make organizations more effective.[10] (It is not just that the schools are better matched with the preferences of the consumers, as suggested by the standard model.) Principals and teachers that have more autonomy over their schools may, by the same token, be more effective educators. For instance, since they have chosen the textbook or the curriculum, they are more likely to have more incentive to make it "work."

Centralization, Decentralization, and Liberty

It is these political concerns, as well as our belief in the importance of competition (the broader conceptualization of competition depicted in chapter
7 rather than the narrow construct underlying the standard model) that
is associated with decentralization that ultimately underlies our belief in
decentralization.

There is undoubtedly a relatedness among economic decentralization,
political democracy, and freedom. It is precisely the perception of this
relationship that, above all, has provided the motive for those within Eastern Europe to abandon not only centrally controlled socialism but market
socialism as well. As decentralized as it may seem, enterprises within market socialism are state controlled and owned, and this control gives the
state enormous powers, powers that can be, and frequently are, abused.

10

<h1 style="text-align:center">Privatization[1]</h1>

A central problem facing all the Eastern European countries in the process of making the transition to market economies is the privatization of the currently "publicly" owned and operated firms. I put the word "publicly" in quotation marks deliberately. In different countries there are different patterns and forms of ownership and control—as we would normally use those terms. While *nominally* all the property may belong to all of the people, the "people" do not directly exercise control, and even in democratic governments, the link between those who actually make decisions and those on whose "behalf" they exercise control may be very weak. In some countries control may be exercised directly from the planning "center" or the relevant industry ministry; in others a plant may be under the control of a large "firm," or the plant may be more directly under the control of its managers. In all of these cases there are myriad influences that affect the decisions, including the interests of the workers at the plant. When plants are establishment controlled, it is more common for the managers to be exercising their control nominally on behalf of the workers, with some limited attention being paid to the *remote* interest in the state as the provider or "owner" of the capital. The theme of "public" companies not working in the interests of the public is a theme to which I will return later in this book.

Public Production versus Public Finance

Curiously enough, the fundamental theorems of welfare economics and the associated theoretical analyses in the economics of the public sector have not been directed at the question with which most of the recent discussions on the role of government have been focused: public versus private *production*. The market failures approach derived from the fundamental welfare theorems focuses on arguments for government intervention (usually financial interventions such as government subsidies, taxes, or purchases), but they never address the question of when the government should *produce* a particular good or service. Indeed until my textbook, *Economics of the Public Sector* (1988b), standard textbooks made little mention, let alone devoted a chapter, to this central topic. There, and in subsequent work, I have attempted to identify what differentiates public from private production, and what the consequences of those differences are.

Private Production and Social Objectives

Standard criticisms of *private* production begin with the premise that private firms will not pursue social objectives. Adam Smith's invisible hand conjecture explains why that conclusion is not, in general, valid, and it is the objective of the first fundamental theorem of welfare economics to show more precisely the conditions under which that objection is or is not correct. But even when prices do not provide the correct signals, it is not an argument for public production: Under the assumptions of standard (perfect information) economics, Pigouvian taxes and subsidies will induce the socially desirable outcomes; public production is not required.

Similarities between Public and Private Production

Although the labels "public" and "private" may elicit images of very distinct modes of operation, many similarities exist between the everyday operations of public and private enterprise. Both models involve substantial delegation of responsibility. Neither members of Congress nor shareholders (in large companies with wide diversification of ownership) directly control the daily activities of an enterprise that is, in principle, under their control. Instead, oversight of the firm's operation is delegated to a commission or board of directors. A chief executive officer or president is also endowed with considerable discretion to influence the firm's operations. There generally follow many additional layers of authority under both forms of ownership. The hierarchy of authority terminates in both cases with managers who use their precise knowledge of local conditions to make daily decisions that directly affect the firm's performance.

In earlier chapters I discussed at length the problems arising from managerial discretion: Managers have considerable autonomy to pursue their own interests regardless of who is the "owner" of the enterprise. I suggested there might be little difference, in this respect, between a

largely publicly owned corporation (Petrofina), a privately owned corporation (Texaco), and a corporation that was half-owned by the government
(BP).

The fact that there is "little" difference cuts both ways: It suggests that
the benefits of nationalization are weaker than its advocates claim, but it
also suggests that the benefits of privatization may be weaker than *its*
advocates claim. For instance, publicly held enterprises in Eastern Europe
failed to internalize the externalities of pollution to an even greater extent
than those in the West did. The most "unsafe" nuclear reactors in the
United States are in the public sector. Racial and sexual discrimination in
the military was (and in some cases remains) as, or even more, rife than in
the private sector. Recognizing that nationalized firms often pursued the
interests of their managers and workers more than the national interest,
Andreas Papandreou, while prime minister of Greece, used to speak of the
necessity of socializing the nationalized enterprises, though he never succeeded in finding a way of providing an incentive mechanism that could do
this. Exhortation, if it worked at all, did not have lasting effects.

These general theoretical arguments, as well as the empirical evidence,
do not make the case for privatization as compelling as some of the
stronger advocates for market mechanisms would suggest. At least one of
the Eastern European countries has suggested explicitly that the economic
case for privatization is unconvincing (the minister for privatization for
Czechoslovakia, at a meeting of IPR/IRIS in Prague, March 1991). The case
for privatization is a political one.

Coase's Theorem and the Role of Private Property

This conclusion that privatization does not guarantee good economics runs
counter to one of the results often cited as at the center of modern economics, what I referred to in chapter 1 as Coase's conjecture. This holds that *all*
the government has to do is to assign property rights clearly. Once this is
done, economic efficiency will naturally follow. In this Coasian view, then,
the essential problem with socialism is the failure to assign property rights
clearly. When everyone owns property, through the state, no one does. No
one has the incentive to ensure that capital goods are used efficiently. No
one has the incentive to design efficient incentive structures. To use the
colloquial phrase, no one has the incentive to "mind the shop." Thus the
one *essential* virtue of socialism (in particular, market socialism), its abolition
of private ownership of the basic means of production, is its one essential
flaw. There is no hope of reforming socialism. In this view too the first

thing the former socialist economies should do—and almost the only thing that they need to do—is to privatize.

The Critical Error: Ignoring Information and Transactions Costs

Coase went wrong in assuming that there were no transactions costs and no information costs.[2] But the central contention of this book is that information costs (what can be viewed as a special form of transactions costs) are pervasive. Assuming away information costs in an analysis of economic behavior and organization is like leaving Hamlet out of the play. With perfect and costless information there would be myriad ways of achieving perfect economic efficiency. Assigning property rights would be one way, but centralized control under socialism would be another. Incentive problems could easily be resolved.

Coase's analysis provides us with no perspective on whether the assignment of property rights is the key to resolving incentive problems in the presence of imperfect information.

Why Property Rights/Ownership May Be Less Important Than Coase Suggests

Recent analyses suggest that ownership/property rights may be more or less important than Coase suggested. Ownership (the assignment of well-defined property rights) may be less important in large organizations, where almost all members are not themselves owners. All must be confronted with incentive structures; principal-agent problems arise, but the nature of those principal-agent problems may differ little depending on whether ownership is public or private.

Some have argued that it makes a difference who bears *ultimate* responsibility. Private owners, it is contended, have an incentive to design good incentive structures, and accordingly privately owned firms are likely to be more effective. There is little theoretical or empirical evidence in support of this contention. To be sure, public organizations often operate in a different economic environment than that typically confronting private enterprises. For instance, they are often immune from competition or subject to soft budget constraints, and these conditions will alter behavior. Still the fraction of any improvements in productivity that would be appropriated by the managers in either a public or private firm is small. This might suggest that neither has an incentive to design good incentive structures. But the "effort" required to design incentive structures is not so great as to impose a major impediment, in either case. It seems implausible to think, in either case, of managers mulling over whether to exert the little effort to design a good incentive structure that will make the organization function better, carefully balancing the returns they will obtain with the extra effort they will have to exert.

Privatization and People's Capitalism

Several of the countries in transition have proposed and begun to implement voucher schemes that would result in firms owned by large numbers of shareholders, creating a form of people's capitalism. Earlier I suggested that when "everyone" owns a firm through the state, effectively no one owns it. Perhaps it would have been more accurate to say that in such a situation managers are the effective owners, for they are the ones who exercise effective control. Would it make much difference if everyone in society received a little piece of paper, saying that they owned one share of the firm? Probably not. Nor would it make a difference whether those pieces of paper were tradable for other pieces of paper (money), except if, as a result of that trade, ownership shares got sufficiently concentrated that some shareholder(s) could exercise effective control. "Clarifying" property rights, by mailing out these pieces of paper, even making them tradable, is unlikely to have any significant effect on the efficiency of the enterprise.

Many of the countries in transition have recognized this problem and have proposed putting these firms under the control of holding companies. Later in the chapter I discuss these proposals, as well as alternative proposals that leave a significant fraction of the shares under the control of public entities. Those who believe that the essential problem is having well-defined private property rights would not be sanguine about the second approach. In contrast, I express reservations concerning the first.

The Experience of the People's Republic of China

The recent experience within the People's Republic of China provides the most dramatic evidence of economic success in the absence of well-defined property rights. Guodang Province has been experiencing growth rates in excess of 12 percent per year for more than a decade (from 1979 to 1992). One can *feel* the sense of rapid growth, the rising standards of living, a pace perhaps unparalleled in economic history. At the center of the growth are publicly owned enterprises (often operating in joint ventures with Hong Kong and Taiwanese firms, though these typically are minority shareholders). Most of the publicly owned enterprises are not "state" enterprises, owned and operated by the central government and its ministries. Rather they are "owned" by provinces, townships, municipalities, and other local bodies. Nonetheless, they are public enterprises. (There are some private firms and some collective enterprises, the nature of which is often ambiguous.) Even the smallest of these public units may have tens of thousands of members.

Ownership/property rights are even more ill-defined than this would suggest. In many cases there is what we have referred to elsewhere as *shared governance*. Oversight, in one form or another, can be exercised both vertically (by higher level authorities within the same sector) or horizontally (by other authorities, e.g., the party or the finance bureau within the same community). There are often several "shareholders"—each a communal organization (a province, township enterprise, etc.)—with no shareholder having a majority share.

Traditional economic theory (including Coasian analyses) would suggest that this system is a recipe for economic failure. Yet the success is palpable. (This does not mean that the system is well designed for sustained economic growth, and there are moves afoot to make property rights more well defined. Nonetheless, what has been achieved under ill-defined property rights cannot be ignored.) This analysis, and the results cited earlier, suggest that for these large organizations property rights play a far less important role than is conventionally ascribed to them.

Why How Property Rights Are Assigned May Be More Important Than Coase Suggests

There are circumstances where property rights are more important than Coase seems to have suggested. Coase argued that once property rights were well defined, outcomes (in interdependent situations) would not only always be efficient, but they would be *independent* of the assignment of those property rights. One of the basic messages of chapter 3 was that *both* of these conclusions are not general; they may not, and indeed are likely not, to hold in the presence of imperfect information. Information costs are but one form of transactions costs, and transactions costs more generally imply that the assignment of control rights can make a difference.

In the previous chapter I noted the Grossman-Hart view that the assignment of residual rights of control has serious consequences for a firm's behavior. Assigning residual rights to income and control can be thought of as *defining* property rights. Thus, we see again, from a different perspective (though again, information problems underlie the analysis), that how property rights are assigned can make a difference.

With costly contracting, principal-agent problems arise whenever those who own physical assets must rely on others to make use of them. Economic efficiency—in two senses—may accordingly be affected by the assignment of property rights. The first sense corresponds more to the ordinary (noneconomists') usage. The "solution" to principal-agent problems generally entails incentive structures that give the agent less than perfect incentives. For instance, under sharecropping, tenant farmers obtain only a fraction of their marginal returns. Borrowers do not bear the full costs of their decisions, so long as there is some chance of bankruptcy: They do not care about the return to the project in those states in which they go bankrupt.

The second sense is that of the economist, (constrained) Pareto efficiency. We saw in chapter 3 not only that, in general, would markets not be constrained Pareto efficient but also that whether they were or not might depend on the wealth distribution. How property rights are assigned makes a difference for whether principal-agent problems arise, and thus whether the economic system is, in either of the senses just described, efficient. With distributions of wealth that give rise to principal-agent problems (e.g., in an agricultural society, in which there is a marked discrepancy between the distribution of human and physical resources), the economy is likely not to be constrained Pareto efficient.

These results make it clear that Coase's view that it makes no difference how property rights are assigned is wrong. In Coase's world, if property rights are initially "wrongly" assigned, trade will occur until they are held in an efficient way. But this simply assumes away the cost of markets—of transferring property—and ignores the consequences of disparities between ownership of physical and human capital.

The Political Argument for Privatization: Weakening the Power of the State

One of the bases of the Communist party's strength was its monopoly in both political and economic spheres. The ability of the party to provide economic rewards for those who complied with its wishes, and to provide economic punishments for those who crossed it, was a major source of its coercive powers: It could exercise these powers even without having to engage in the brutality associated with Stalinism. Decentralization of economic power is an important check on political power, and it is this hard-learned lesson of their political experience, as much as anything else, that may motivate the drive for rapid privatization.

But there are some important economic aspects of privatization, and an understanding of those may affect the *design* of the privatization program, including the speed with which it is pursued. The remainder of this chapter is divided into two parts. In the first, I discuss a variety of theoretical issues—general principles concerning privatization. In the second, I discuss a variety of more specific issues in the design of privatization programs within Eastern Europe.

The Fundamental Privatization Theorem

David Sappington and I set out several years ago to ask whether the government could attain whatever objectives it wanted through the privatization of state enterprises. The striking result was that the conditions under which privatization could fully implement public objectives of equity and efficiency were extremely restrictive—and indeed the conditions bear a striking resemblance to the conditions under which competitive markets attain Pareto-efficient outcomes.

The problem of course is not unlike that of a principal trying to elicit desirable behavior out of an agent (an employee). In some cases the principal can "sell" the agent the job and be done with it, but more generally, if the agent is risk averse (and the principal is not) and/or the agent faces capital constraints, then the principal (the employer) has to give up something if the job is "sold." In this context there is a cost to privatization: The state receives less than the expected present discounted value of the profits of the enterprise.

Moreover, the state may not be able—even with a complicated set of Pigouvian taxes—to induce the privatized industry to act in the way that it would like. Simple social objectives (like increased employment) can easily be attained. But more complicated social objectives, like the "right" amount of risk taking or innovation, may not be obtained so easily, and it may be difficult to proscribe socially undesirable activities, such as discriminatory pricing (the firm of course claiming that price differentials are due to differences in the costs of serving different customer groups).

These concerns have intuitively been recognized in some of the social choices that we observe for public production. There is a concern in the United States, for instance, that some of the social objectives of public education cannot be obtained through a private school system, even with the best-designed Pigouvian taxes/subsidies. How can we "measure" the extent to which a school district promotes "social integration" or "good citizenship"? Indeed recent concerns about how *public* schools can provide incentives for their teachers (whether merit pay, based on students' performance on standardized tests, will promote good education or simply divert teachers' attention to improving test scores, a poor measure of a "good" education) reflect similar difficulties of using prices (taxes, subsidies) to encourage socially desirable behavior.

The fundamental privatization theorem, like the fundamental theorems of welfare economics, helps delineate the circumstances under which one or the other sector (public or private) has a *potential* advantage. Neither theorem provides an adequate characterization of the government. Thus the fundamental theorem of welfare economics sets out conditions under which no government, no matter how benevolent and efficient, could do better than the market (though, admittedly, as I have argued in earlier chapters, the model of the market is not a particularly accurate description of the actual economy). Given that *no* government could do better, there was little necessity to model the government. But, as we have seen, the Greenwald-Stiglitz theorem reversed that presumption: It established that government could *potentially* almost always improve upon the market's resource allocation. Whether it would or not then depends on a more careful modeling of the strengths and weaknesses of the government.

Similarly the Sappington-Stiglitz fundamental privatization theorem establishes that an *ideal* government could do better running an enterprise itself than it could through privatization. Again it forces us to focus more closely on actual government behavior and on actual markets—not the idealized government and idealized markets of these welfare theorems and the Lange-Lerner-Taylor theorem.

The Economic Advantages of Privatization

There is, I believe, an economic argument for privatization: The government does indeed have a marked disadvantage relative to private firms, but it is not based on differences in managerial incentives, as usually defined.

Enhanced Commitments

The economic advantages of privatization are derived from the inability of the government to make certain commitments, in particular, the commitment to competition and the commitment not to subsidize. To be sure, even with privatization the government cannot make such commitments.

Private enterprises are constantly seeking government assistance, in attempts both to reduce competition and to receive direct subsidies. From time to time the U.S. government has provided bailouts of isolated firms, such as Chrysler and Lockheed—and of whole industries, such as railroads and the S&Ls. The government has helped protect the automobile industry and the computer chip industry from foreign competition. Hence privatization is no panacea, no protection against protection and subsidies.

What privatization does is to increase the "transactions cost," to use the fashionable phrase, of obtaining government subsidies and government protection from competition.

Enhanced Incentives

Clearly privatization makes it more credible that soft budget constraints will be replaced with hard budget constraints. But this is not the only advantage of privatization. Despite our discussion emphasizing the *common* problem of incentives under both private and public ownership, those problems are, I suspect, worse under public than private ownership. The main reason for this is that the restrictions on the incentive devices and salary schedules as well as civil service restrictions ensuring job security[3] place public sector enterprises at a marked disadvantage relative to private sector firms and contribute to the inefficiencies frequently found in those enterprises. Both organization and individual incentives are attenuated.

The essential problem facing the government is associated with one of the ways which the Arrow-Debreu model fails to capture the essence of market economies (and accordingly fails to capture the essence of the difference between markets and government). I stressed earlier the role of rents in providing incentives under imperfect information (the importance of rents in ensuring the effectiveness of the reputation mechanism). The problem is the difficulty of distinguishing between those rents that are *necessary* to promote economic efficiency and those rents that are the reward to unproductive rent-seeking activities within the political process. To limit the latter, governments put restrictions on the salaries that can be paid, and these restrictions, while they prevent one "evil," do affect both the quality of workers that the government can attract and the incentives that those that it does attract have to work hard.

Selection Effects

The commitment to hard budget constraints that privatization facilitates not only has incentive effects. Tough budget constraints are also important as part of the selection mechanism, through which it is decided not only which enterprises survive but which enterprises garner additional resources to expand. Those who cannot meet the market test are weeded out.

The Design of Privatization

The design of privatization programs must attempt to (1) ensure economic efficiency while (2) retaining as much "rent" for the government as possible and (3) ensuring that other social objectives are effectively pursued. The following paragraphs describe several aspects of this.

Speed of Privatization

One key issue is the speed of privatization. To some extent, the issue of fast versus slow privatization is a matter of perspective: There is a joke about the debate on the speed of privatization in Hungary, with those who advocate rapid privatization arguing that privatization must be achieved in five years while those who advocate slow privatization urging that matters be taken calmly—privatization should take place over five years. Those who advocate rapid privatization have found the practicalities of organizing massive sales to be overwhelming. It is these practicalities that are determinative, not the balanced considerations of the appropriate sequencing that entail answering questions such as, Should price liberalization, "cleaning balance sheets" (described below), creating capital markets (see chapter 12), and enacting a legal framework to ensure enforceability of contracts and the viability of competition precede, go along contemporaneously with, or follow privatization? It is the overwhelming practical problems of organizing sales that may not only determine the speed of privatization but its form: Those who (for a variety of reasons) believe in rapid privatization see the direct distribution of shares or a voucher system for the purchase of shares as the only practical solution.

On the other side, those who advocate slow privatization have found overwhelming practical problems in pursuing that strategy as well: In many cases the government has quickly lost control over the enterprises that it nominally owns. It simply does not have the information to prevent managers from diverting the firm's resources to their private use. There are a variety of ways in which managers can use the autonomy they have gained as the control of the central ministries has declined to their own advantage: With limited future horizons they have no incentive not to waste the firm's assets and every incentive to convert the firm's assets into their own. They can, for instance, use transfer pricing.

As the government announces its intention to privatize, managers' incentives to behave well are attenuated: They see their employment as terminating shortly, so incentives to shirk, if not to "steal" (usually conducted in a more subtle way than outright embezzlement, but theft—in the form of diverting the firm's resources—nonetheless), are greatly enhanced.

In cases where the managers do not divert resources to their own benefit, workers may effectively seize control of the firm and exercise it for their own benefit. Capital is depleted, with the firm's profits going to pay wages rather than being reinvested in the firm. Indeed they have no incentive to do otherwise. It is "spontaneous privatization" (spontaneous because they are not controlled by the government and privatizations, because they represent the effective devolution of control of the firm) that may dictate the necessity for rapid privatization. (It is worth noting that American firms, once they have announced that they are being sold, customarily attempt to complete the transaction as quickly as possible. The limbo period is one that is trying on the firm, since many of the "long-run incentives" essential in the functioning of the firm get greatly attenuated. Key employees leave, and effort is reduced, or at least diverted, as employees focus their attention on seeking jobs elsewhere or entrenching themselves within the firm.)

Recapitalization of Industry

The enterprises inherit financial debts and assets from the previous regime. Financial relationships under the previous regime bear little resemblance to those under capitalism.[4] Keeping track of financial positions is important for both incentive and selection reasons. Any society has to know how well each of its units is doing so that the less efficient may be weeded out and the more efficient can be allocated more resources to manage. The carrot and the stick—of being rewarded with more resources or of being "weeded out"—provide strong incentives. These organizational incentives are perhaps as powerful as the profit motive itself.[5]

Unfortunately, inherited financial assets and liabilities provide no information concerning firms' abilities, since they were accumulated under a quite different set of rules. What's worse, these inherited assets and liability will obfuscate the signals provided by the market mechanisms concerning current enterprise performance. Thus the future success or failure of enterprises may be determined as much by the randomness of the valuation of those claims as by the efficiency of management in running its enterprises. The extensive interfirm lending means that the fortunes of all the enterprises are (unless there is an extensive recapitalization) closely intertwined. Whether firms get repaid their loans may have as much to do with the vagaries of government policy—for instance, whether the government allows government-owned enterprises to renege on their loans—and, if it does not, on the speed of privatization, which will affect the likelihood that reneging will occur (since private enterprises are more likely to default).[6]

The fact that there is such "noise" makes it less likely that the government commitment not to subsidize in the event of a default is credible. After all, if a default occurs through no fault of the enterprise, but through a default of borrowers from the firm, there is a more persuasive argument for government intervention than if the default is a result of managerial incompetence. When there are large loans, the government may not be able to distinguish well the source of the default—default on loans will be blamed on them even when the real reason lies elsewhere.

Moving back one step, the fact that the government commitment not to subsidize will be less credible has in turn real incentive effects. For those enterprises that inherit large amounts of debt—augmented possibly by the debt that was acquired in the process of privatization—a further incentives problem arises: The by-now familiar moral hazard problem confronting firms with high debt, the incentives to undertake undue risk, to maximize returns in the nonbankruptcy states at the expense of returns in the bankruptcy state.[7] These problems became all too evident in the case of S&Ls in the United States. Among the dangers is that such enterprises extend credit to others—a form of contagion of soft budget constraints which I will discuss in greater detail in the next section.

(At least one of the former socialist countries has recognized the problems discussed in this and the next section: Rumania has provided a partial recapitalization; the government has exchanged the liabilities of firms for government liabilities—thus removing this source of uncertainty concerning each firm's net worth. Firms will pay money to the government and receive money from the government. Since firms are both borrowers and lenders from each other, what is important is the *net* positions. The firms whose outstanding debts are less than what is owed to them by other firms are granted in effect an endowment of government bonds as part of their capital; those with net liabilities are having their slates wiped clean.)

Recapitalization of the Financial System

The problems just discussed are all the more important within the financial sector: The *main* assets that they inherit are financial assets and liabilities.

Kornai (1990) has emphasized the debilitating effect of soft budget constraints, and the inability of the government not to commit itself to subsidize enterprises. But we now have recognized that soft budget constraints can arise not only from government but also from the financial system. In the United States, firms were able to borrow huge amounts of money, and borrow to make up for losses, on the enhanced chance that they would subsequently be able to repay those loans,[8] partly because banks saw their only hope of getting out of their positions of negative net worth was undertaking large risks. (As Ed Kane has put it, the Zombie institutions—the institutions which, in any real sense, were dead, though they remained among the living—were gambling on resurrection.) So long as there are some institutions within the society that have the capability of making loans—and that have an incentive to make large gambles or believe that any losses they will incur will be made good by the government—then there is an effectively soft budget constraint. The soft budget constraint of one enterprise gets translated into the soft budget constraint of other enterprises. Institutions with soft budget constraints will be "softer" in granting loans to others. Given the importance of interfirm lending, the disease of soft budget constraints—and the resulting softening of incentives—can spread quickly through the economy.

Hard Budget Constraints and the Selection Mechanism in the Process of Transition

Earlier, I emphasized both the selection and incentive effects of the government's commitments, particularly its commitment to tough budget constraints. Selection problems are likely to be acute in the process of transition for two reasons. First, under socialism there was no process of weeding-out comparable to what occurs in capitalist economies. Second, the characteristics that formed the basis of selection under socialism—such as the ability to survive within the bureaucratic structure—may be imperfectly correlated (or even negatively correlated) with characteristics that are important for good performance in a market economy. On both accounts, there would appear to be a need to engage in a process of weeding-out that is of greater than normal intensity.

Unfortunately, there are several factors that will make the process of weeding-out also far more problematic. There are two kinds of mistakes that occur in the selection process: Good firms may be weeded out, or bad firms survive. The market test is always an imperfect indicator: Competent firms may fail the market test as a result of bad luck, and bad firms may pass, as a result of good luck. Still, in market economies, the process of weeding-out that results from tough budget constraints is important because it improves the average quality. Those weeded out are, on average, of lower quality than those who survive. But the process of weeding-out is costly.

There are several reasons, some of which we have already touched upon, which are likely to make profits a relatively poor indicator of competence. First, solvency is likely to depend on the valuation of assets at the time of privatization, and this in turn is as likely to depend on political decisions concerning how liabilities are to be treated as on the underlying economics. (There is not, in any case, much of a market for used capital goods, so there would be valuation problems even in a more developed market economy.) Second, profitability may not be a good indicator of the "true" value of the underlying assets if prices do not reflect "true" scarcity values. In the transition period market prices are likely to deviate markedly from their longer-run equilibrium values. Profitability, at current market prices, may accordingly be a poor predictor either of the competence of management or the true contribution of the establishment to social economic product; and thus it may be a poor basis for selection.

Voucher Schemes as Negative Lump-Sum Transfers

We have noted that a number of former socialist economies are in the process of privatizing through the use of voucher schemes. These can be viewed as negative lump-sum capital transfers—transfers of wealth from the public sector to private individuals. Public finance economists have an ingrained revulsion at such transfers. In traditional public finance theory the optimal tax is a lump-sum tax or a capital levy. Such a tax raises revenue without causing distortions. The reason that lump-sum taxes are not employed is that they are generally viewed to be inequitable, since in practice they have to be uniform. The reason that capital levies are not employed is the inability of the government to commit itself to employing such taxes once. Thus, if it imposes a capital levy once, investor/savers may well reason, it is likely that the government will do so again, and this adversely affects savings and investment behavior. While such taxes, when unanticipated, are (by definition) nondistortionary with respect to past behavior, the anticipation of such taxes is itself distortionary.

The give-away of the nation's capital, through vouchers, will necessitate the imposition of higher, distortionary taxes in the future.

Government Retention of a Large Equity Share

Even when the government sells its ownership claims through, say, an auction process, it is unlikely that it will be able to appropriate the full expected present discounted value of the revenue stream. A major disadvantage of privatization is thus the loss of potential rents from the government, which the government must recoup with distortionary taxation. A major advantage of privatization (if done properly) is the enhanced commitment of government not to subsidize (the hardening of the budget constraint) and whatever advantages private management can provide. In balancing these advantages and disadvantages, the optimum is not necessarily a "corner solution"—all private or all public. Rather, there seems little reason for the government not to retain a large minority interest.

Lowered Capital Requirements

There is another strong reason for government retaining a strong minority interest: Less finance is required to buy the company, implying that the purchaser is likely to have to undertake less debt. We have already discussed the marked disadvantages of excessive debt. The same argument suggests that the government interest should be an equity interest.

Limiting Government Abuses

A large minority interest can still exercise considerable control and power. We suggested that one of the motives for privatization was the limiting of government economic power. The question is how government can maintain a strong equity claim while limiting its ability to exercise its control.

As Domar and Musgrave (1944) pointed out some fifty years ago, the corporation profits tax represents an equity claim on corporations. It is an equity claim with, however, a few peculiar characteristics. The government-as-partner does not share in the losses, a fact (as Alan Auerbach has emphasized) that causes significant distortions; the government has no commitment as to the share that it will take, another fact that may give rise to considerable distortion; and the government does not exercise any voting rights over its "share." The government could "replicate" its equity interests by, ex post, imposing a corporate profits tax, but it seems better for the government to commit itself, ex ante, to a share.

As a large minority shareholder the government might be able to exercise its influence to prevent managerial abuse. The question is, how to do this without at the same time opening up the possibility of government abuse? One suggestion is to divide the government interests among different government units—using the checks and balances provided by appropriately designed governmental structures.

For instance, some of the shares could be given to the workers' pension fund, some to a county enterprise board, some to a national enterprise board, some to fund the state pension scheme, some to the state hospital system. All of these will have an interest in making sure that the enterprise maximizes profits. Though it is possible that all of these come under the control of a single "party," it is unlikely, and the division of power will work to make it less likely that the power of government ownership will be abused.[9]

The Importance of a Commitment not to Renationalize, and the Implications for the Design of Privatization
A basic problem facing all governments is the difficulty of making credible commitments. No government can bind its successors. This provides a major disadvantage to the government. One implication of this is that the government cannot really bind itself not to renationalize the firms that are being privatized.

We began with the theme that privatization affects the transactions costs, the costs of government intervention. By the same token, the design of the nationalization program can affect the likelihood of renationalization. For instance, widespread ownership of shares, obtained at below-market prices, as in the British privatization, makes it less likely that there will be renationalization; the government has created a strong lobby for remaining private, as voters see vividly their potential losses, without the same conviction of a possible gain. The proposed programs of vouchers, with widespread ownership, in several of the Eastern European countries, provide the same credibility.

Selling enterprises to foreigners on the cheap, on the other hand, lays open a real possibility of renationalization in the future, unless other commitments not to do so can be made, such as through joining the Common Market. One of the major ways that Western Europe can help the Eastern European countries is through the commitments that joining the Common Market would provide—commitments with respect to trade and competition policies, taxation, and renationalization.

Financing Privatization

There has been much confusion over the issue of financing privatization. In some cases concern has been raised about who has the funds to purchase the enterprises. In a perfect capital market that issue would be irrelevant:

The enterprise would be purchased by the individual or group of individuals who would most effectively make use of those assets. No country—let alone the Eastern European countries—has a perfect capital market, so there is some cause of concern that enterprises will go not to those who are most competent at running them but to those who have the most capital, or the best access to capital. These are legitimate concerns, but they can be partially alleviated by the government providing finance itself. Where, it may be asked, does the government receive the funds to make the loans, given the budget stringency under which it already is? Such questions show a confusion between the macroeconomic roles of government finance and the role of financial accounting. The government will lend the firms money to buy the firm and then receive the money back again.[10] It is a pure wash, with no direct macroeconomic consequence (though not *relative* to selling the firm for cash, which can decrease the outstanding money supply). It has real microeconomic consequences—those that arise from control and ownership.

There are some serious problems with government-provided loans, in the absence of adequate equity on the part of the buyer: The kinds of moral hazard problems discussed briefly earlier, which are likely to be particularly severe given the government's limited ability to screen applicants, to distinguish which of the potential loan applicants see the purchase of the firm with government-provided credit basically as an "option." If things turn out worse than they think, they can simply walk away, perhaps having first stripped the firm of its assets.

In some countries with a large monetary overhang, selling enterprises, it has been argued, has a further advantage: It absorbs some of the extra money. Alternative ways, such as monetary reforms and taxation, are likely to be more distortionary or undesirable for other reasons.

For both of these reasons government loan programs will not provide a perfect substitute for private funds. Those with private funds or access to private funds will be at a marked advantage. This in turn suggests that opening up the auction process to foreigners and encouraging cooperative ventures between nationals and foreigners will be desirable. It will enhance the competition, thus ensuring that the government receives a larger share of the total potential value of the assets. At the same time it may provide greater access to foreign managerial skills.[11]

Corporate Governance

Throughout this book I have emphasized the potential abuse of managerial prerogatives. This is particularly important in situations where no single shareholder owns a significant fraction of the shares. Financial institutions, such as pension funds, have, at least until recently, been reluctant to intervene in the governance process. This presents a real problem for "people's capitalism," a problem that several of the Eastern European countries have recognized and tried to grapple with in the design of their privatization programs. It has been proposed that control of each company be vested in a holding company, whose responsibility will be to manage enterprises. Individuals will own shares in holding companies, and holding companies will compete against each other to maximize share market value.

Why Holding Companies May Not Be the Solution
At a theoretical level the solution seems suspect. RJR-Nabisco could be viewed as a holding company. It was responsible for the management of firms in the tobacco, food, and other industries. There were a large number of separate enterprises. Yet managerial abuse was rife throughout the enterprise. Who monitors the monitor?

Shared Governance
One solution is "mutual" or "peer" monitoring[12]—an economic version of the old political solution of "checks and balances." In peer monitoring each member of the group monitors other members of the group. It is possible to design reward structures that provide incentives for this kind of mutual monitoring. Peer monitoring is an example of a wider class of governance structures that involves multiple participants and often nonhierarchical relations.

This is the case for modern corporations, where shareholders, lenders, suppliers, customers, and workers all are stakeholders, and all exercise some influence in the decisions undertaken by the firm. Traditional discussions focused on shareholders because formally control is vested in them. Free-rider problems, however, mean that shareholders have limited incentives to obtain information required to intervene intelligently, or to bear the costs of those interventions. Management of the enterprise is a public good.

Banks as Monitors
Banks may exercise more effective control than do shareholders, or bondholders for that matter, a point made long ago by Berle (1926).[13] For banks the costs of intervention will be smaller and the free-rider problems will be less severe than for shareholders.[14] Because most bank lending is short-term, banks can quickly withdraw their funds if they believe the firm is "misbehaving."[15] There is an extensive literature arguing that Japanese banks actively perform this monitoring role, and do so more effectively than do American banks.

Capital structures in the United States, Japan, and Western Europe differ markedly from each other. There is more than one form of capitalism, and one of the problems that the Eastern European countries face is the choice of the appropriate form. For those countries that see themselves as evolving toward a form of people's capitalism, I see marked advantages in the Japanese main bank system, combined with large ownership shares by the government and an important role for holding companies. Large levels of indebtedness to the bank will give the bank both an incentive to monitor and a means of control—the threat of withdrawing credit is an effective discipline device. It will provide an important check on the abuse of managerial prerogatives, should the holding company not do its job properly. Oversight by the government units that have significant ownership shares will provide further checks. The question is the delicate balance of maintaining checks on incompetence, without hindering the effective exercise of managerial discretion for taking advantage of profitable opportunities, and without providing the "checkers" with an opportunity of abusing their power to their own advantage. The United States has not yet found that delicate balance in the case of enterprises with widely held share ownership. We should not expect the Eastern European countries to find, at the first try, the right balance. An awareness of the issue, and a willingness to adapt, is what is most important at this juncture.

The Auction Process

Organizing the sale of enterprises so as to maximize value received has been the subject of extensive discussion—and litigation—within recent years. In virtually every major sale of an American firm, there has been litigation by shareholders that the firm did not receive what it should (could, might) have, had the auction process been run differently. There is widespread consensus that Great Britain, in its privatization program, received far less from its sales than it could have received.

There have been extensive developments in auction theory in recent years, and some of these insights can be brought to bear, and the experiences of firm sales provides us further insight. One issue, raised both by the theoretical literature and auction experience, is the importance of asymmetric information. Inside management has more knowledge concerning the true value of the assets, which provides them an inside track. It is not only that this enhances the likelihood that they will win. If other bidders believe that there are important information asymmetries, bidding will be less intensive. The winner's curse raises its head with a vengeance: Outside bidders only beat the insider when they have bid too much.[16]

Two of the most important determinants of the success of the bidding process (in terms of sellers maximizing value) are maintaining a level playing field and enhancing the number of bidders. In the United States an attempt to level the playing field is provided by a process of due diligence in which potential buyers are provided access to the company's books, a process that is typically managed by a disinterested outside third party (an investment bank). The investment bank also has the responsibility of drumming up bidders.

The consequences of the asymmetries of information may be reduced by structuring the "object" over which bidding occurs. Thus, in oil leases, it can be shown that royalty and net profit bidding succeeds in garnering for the seller a substantially larger fraction of the potential rents than does bonus bidding, with no royalty. While organizing the bidding process as a net profit auction (bidding over the fraction of the net profits which accrues to the government) may not be desirable,[17] setting a large preassigned share of profits to the government (the equity share discussed earlier) will result in a larger fraction of the total potential rents going to the government in the auction process.

The Advantage of Liberalizing Prices and Resolving Institutional Uncertainty First

There are several other factors that are relevant to the sequencing and speed of the privatization process. Bidders are likely to be risk averse. The greater the risks that they perceive, the less they will be willing to bid. The risks that they perceive are likely to be greater if the course of government policy is not clear. Issues of competition, trade, finance, and tax policy all impinge in an important way on a firm's profitability and, to the extent that they have not been resolved, confront bidders with a high degree of uncertainty. If the government has not engaged in a recapitalization, there is further uncertainty associated with all of the enterprise's financial assets (what it is owed by other firms).

One particularly important aspect of government policy is price liberalization. If prices are not at their "equilibrium" level, buyers may buy the firm more to take a speculative position on the price of assets than to enhance the efficiency with which the firm is managed. The winner of the auction may not be the best manager, but the individual who is most optimistic about the future price of those assets. Though this problem arises in the case of the auction of any enterprise, it is particularly acute when prices are very far from equilibrium.

Privatization in Eastern Europe: Some General Perspectives

The changes in economic structure which Eastern Europe is undertaking are among the most interesting economic experiments to have occurred. We have limited experience with privatizations, and the experiences we have are all within the context of economies that are otherwise dominated by private markets. Unfortunately, these are experiments whose success or failure will touch the lives of millions of people, and so they cannot be approached with a dispassionate perspective. It is all the more important that all we know from economic science—both theory and practice—be brought to bear, that ideological commitments—such as beliefs that markets always work and work quickly and efficiently—be put to the side. It is also imperative that political judgments be cleanly separated from economic judgments: Much of the debate on timing is based on a balance of political judgments concerning the political consequences of an excessively rapid privatization, and its consequent unemployment, with the consequences of an excessively slow privatization, and the possibility that in the interim the commitment to privatization and markets may be weakened.

In this part of the chapter I have attempted to set forth some of what I see as the central theoretical considerations. To put what I have said in context, let me make four concluding remarks.

First, I have focused my attention on the privatization of large-scale enterprises. Some of the issues that I have discussed also arise in the privatization of small-scale enterprises, but by and large, the privatization of small-scale enterprises is a far easier task, one that is already well underway.

Second, privatization itself is only one means of achieving a market economy: Establishing new enterprises is the other. Establishing institutions to facilitate that deserves at least as much attention as does the privatization process. In some cases, such as financial institutions, an argument can be made that the countries may be better off starting anew, rather than attempting to reform institutions that were designed with quite different functions in mind than those served by financial institutions in capitalist economies. China's remarkable success is based more on the creation and growth of new enterprises, than on the privatization of extant state enterprises. As I noted earlier, incentives for work and entrepreneurship can and have been provided, without resolving many property rights issues. As new firms have been created, and communal and collective firms have expanded, the relative importance of the "state"-run enterprises (those controlled by the central government) has declined markedly. Moreover the state-run enterprises have been forced by competition from these other firms to become more efficient. Beyond that there is now a base of well-run enterprises that can be (and are being) used to take over less well-run enterprises.

There are good reasons to postpone the decision concerning privatization. Privatization issues are inextricably linked with issues of distribution: How should claims on existing assets be distributed? It is well known (both as a matter of theory[18] and empirical observation) that pure redistributions are always a contentious affair. Thus, giving workers the right to farm the land, without vesting them with full ownership, provides them with strong incentives, and avoids, or at least mitigates, some of these sources of contention. To be sure, not all incentive problems are fully resolved: Workers will not have full incentives to maintain the quality of the land. In the long run it will be important to resolve these issues, but when the size of the pie is bigger and growing—as it has been in China—it is undoubtedly easier to reach consensus.

Third, reforms and policies once undertaken may be difficult to undo. It is important to get things right the first time—or, at least, as right as possible. Property rights quickly get established, and any reform is likely to destroy some of this implicit property. Indeed, such property rights, created under the old regime, even now serve as an impediment to the reform process. In some Eastern European countries, such as Rumania, the position in the queue for buying consumer durables (e.g., a car) at below "free-market" prices is an asset that will be destroyed under price liberalization, and is evidently a considerable source of political pressure resisting price liberalization.

At the same time concern about getting things right can lead to a paralysis: There is no single best way, no single right way. V. Klaus, in a talk at the World Bank's Annual Bank Conference on Development Economics (ABCDE), provided a metaphor—reform was like playing a chess game. No one, not even the best players, can, at the beginning of the game, see all the way to the end. Better players can, however, see more steps into the future than can worse players. It is my hope that my remarks will help those who are engaged in the real life game of economic reform play that game a little better.

This brings me to my final concluding remark: The "next move" in the game may be dictated as much by political imperatives—for instance, the

concern about weakening the power of the state—as by economic judgments. In one sense, the two are intertwined: the loss of strong control by
the central authorities, combined with the likely prospect of privatization,
provides managers with incentives to grab what rents their current positions afford them while they can; and as a result delay in privatization may
be extremely costly. As I have suggested, in many cases, it is these costs of
delay, perhaps more than anything else, which may—and should—be
central in determining the speed of privatization.

Concluding Remarks

I began this chapter with a presentation of the fundamental theorem of
privatization. That theorem showed that the twin objectives of economic
efficiency and full rent acquisition could be attained only under highly
restrictive conditions. Full rent acquisition is important, of course, because
it is costly for the government to raise revenues: Any giveaway entails a
real social cost, for it necessitates the government raising more money
through distortionary means. Whenever potential bidders for the firm are
risk averse or whenever there is limited competition (conditions which are
likely always to be satisfied), the government, through the *best*-designed
auction process, cannot obtain full rents.[19]

The government may not even be able to ensure that the winning bidder
is the most efficient producer. With limited liability and imperfect enforceability of commitments, the producer bidding the most, and promising
to conform most closely with government objectives, may neither carry
out those commitments nor be the one for whom the asset is truly the most
valuable: A willingness to bid higher may simply reflect a higher probability of defaulting on promises.

The moral of this theorem (and the discussions of this chapter) can be
briefly summarized: We cannot, in general, be assured that private production is necessarily "better" than public production. Privatization involves
costs and benefits, which, as always, must be weighed against each other.

I have argued that the differences between public and private production have been exaggerated. Yet there are important differences, arising
from *commitments* and *incentives*. As Sappington and I concluded our paper,

... neither public nor private provision can fully resolve the difficult incentive
problems that arise when considerations of imperfect information result in delegation of authority. The choice between models of organization simply defines the
transactions costs of future interventions into these delegated relationships, and
thereby influences the likelihood of such interventions. (p. 581)

This chapter completes our discussion of the Lange-Lerner-Taylor theorem, asserting the essential equivalency of market economies and market socialism. The observation that a socialist economy could use the power of prices was an important insight, but there is more to a market economy than just the use of prices. My basic contention has been that by focusing on prices, the Lange-Lerner-Taylor theorem, as well as the Walrasian model on which it was based, badly mischaracterized the market economy. Neither the model of the market economy nor the model of the market socialist economy provided a good description of the economies they were supposedly characterizing.

Pieces of my criticism have, of course, been remarked upon before. Critics of market socialism have commented on the lack of managerial incentives, just as critics of markets have commented on the imperfections of competition. I have tried to provide a balanced account, showing that many of the underlying problems with *both* models can be traced to the inadequacy with which they treat information problems. In this and the previous five chapters I have taken up six of the major failings of both sets of models and have suggested how recently developed theories—constituting a major departure from the Walrasian tradition—have addressed these problems.

All societies face major incentive problems, which are not fully addressed by standard systems of prices and property rights. There are managerial incentive problems in market economies just as there are in socialist economies. In both markets and market socialism, limited use is made of the price system for allocating investment. In markets this is because the necessary futures and risk markets do not, in general, exist. In both, then, more than price information (and the knowledge of one's own technology) is employed by firms in making decisions. In all societies some degree of decentralization is employed, and no society—even among the most market-oriented economies—is completely decentralized: There exist firms within which transactions are not mediated by prices. In no society are property rights perfectly clearly assigned, and even when they seem to be clearly assigned, de facto rights may differ from de jure rights. The heads of large American corporations can be thought of as exercising (imprecisely defined) property rights no less than did the managers of socialist enterprises.

The market does have some instruments—such as takeover mechanisms —which socialist economies do not have, but the takeover mechanism is far from perfect. Some institutions, such as banks, which they both have, operated (as I will comment in chapter 12) markedly differently under socialism. It is my contention, however, that the fundamental difference between markets and market socialist economies lies not just in these institutions but in the broader array of mechanisms by which market economies handle information problems. While, as we saw in chapters 3 and 4, the market did not solve these information problems perfectly—the market economy was in general not constrained Pareto efficient—markets do a better job than did the market socialist economies. For instance, markets provide incentives for firms to produce high-quality products, through the reputation mechanism. But nowhere are the differences between the two systems so apparent as they are in the special kind of information/knowledge acquisition associated with innovation. Again, I noted the failure of the standard theories describing market and market socialist economies even to address these issues, and indeed I argued the conceptual framework of the Arrow-Debreu model could not be readily adapted to accommodate it. The basic economic issue is that markets in which innovation is important will inherently be imperfectly competitive. It is the force of innovation itself that limits the degree of competition.

Thus those who advocated market socialism on the grounds that market economies were imperfectly competitive did not inquire deeply enough into why this was so. To be sure, at the time that many of these earlier discussions occurred, one of the reasons for imperfect competition in many industries was the presence of significant returns to scale (relative to the market size at that time). But it was innovations that formed the basis of the industrial revolution, and it was innovations—in organizational practices as well as technology—that led to the evolution of large enterprises. Given the Marxian tradition from whose roots market socialism was derived, the failure of socialist theorists to pay adequate attention to technology—and changes in technology—is particularly hard to understand.

In the next chapter I use the theoretical framework I have developed thus far to provide us further insights into what went wrong with the socialist experiment.

11   The Socialist Experiment: What Went Wrong?

Most of this book is about economic theories: about the failures of the neoclassical model, and about how the failures of that model were closely related to the failures of the market socialism model. The neoclassical model had many of the right ingredients: incentives, competition, decentralization, prices. Yet the particular meaning that it gave to these concepts were at best incomplete, at worst misleading. Market economies are characterized by competition, but not the price-taking behavior associated with the perfectly competitive model. Market economies are *partially* decentralized, but there was more to the decentralization of decision making than the passive response to price signals. Indeed the appropriate mix of centralization and decentralization of decision making is one of the key questions facing market economies. Prices are central to the functioning of market economies, but prices do more than just equilibrating supply and demand, conveying information about scarcity values. They have effects on the quality of goods being traded. Beyond that, much of economic activity is regulated by mechanisms other than the price mechanism. Incentives are important, but, again, the Arrow-Debreu model in which everyone is paid either on the basis of observed output or input provides an inaccurate characterization of the role of incentives in modern economies. Finally, we have seen that the Coasian presumption, that all that is required to ensure economic efficiency is making property rights well defined, is simply not correct.

Market socialism took seriously the neoclassical model, and that was its fatal flaw. But the socialist economies never really took seriously the market socialist ideal. We need to ask, What does our interpretation of what makes market economies work have to say about the failure of the socialist experiment?

Many of the results of my earlier analysis would have suggested that socialism, or at least a economic system in which government took a more active role, would have had a running chance of faring better than the market economy. I showed, for instance, in chapter 3 that the economy was essentially never constrained Pareto efficient. Imperfect information and incomplete markets give rise to externalitylike effects that cannot be easily internalized by firms. Some form of government intervention is required. At the heart of the *economic* failure were a variety of information problems, which, interpreted broadly, include incentive issues. In the following I briefly analyze the most important of these issues.

Excessive Centralization

Perhaps the most important reason for failure was the very reason that Hayek argued that central planning would fail: The central authorities simply did not have the information required to run the entire economy. Yet, probably for political reasons, the government insisted on keeping decision making centralized.

We need to go further and inquire into what kind of information was lacking. Central planning focused on ensuring that the material balance equations were satisfied, that the outputs of intermediate goods were appropriately coordinated with the production of goods using those intermediate goods. This kind of planning required information about the input requirements per unit output—the Leontief matrix. It was not, I suspect, the failure of this planning exercise that was at the heart of the failure of the socialist experiment. To be sure, the information required to carry out these planning exercises was often not accurate, and accordingly there were shortages of some inputs. In the more open economy of the 1980s, however, these mistakes should have been of little moment: Shortages of inputs could easily have been made up by imports, and surpluses (were international trading markets truly competitive) could have been sold abroad. The failures were more *microeconomic* in nature.

Product Quality

Problems of product quality provide an important class of examples. It was hard for the central authorities to specify, in their central planning exercises, the precise nature of every commodity, including the quality of the product. We saw earlier (chapter 6) that the limitless number of possible commodities and the impossibility of precisely specifying most commodities provided part of the explanation for why there was an incomplete set of markets—one of the reasons that the neoclassical model fails. Exactly the same factors are at work in explaining why socialism fails.

Market economies can be thought of as having a far more finely tuned control mechanism. Each buyer monitors each seller's quality. If the seller's quality falters, the buyer switches sellers, or gets a price concession. The seller knows this, and thus has a strong incentive to provide goods of the appropriate quality. It is *not* that (or just that) socialist economies produce low-quality goods. In some cases it might be appropriate to produce low-quality goods, where the (marginal) costs of increasing quality exceed the (marginal) benefits. The problem is that firms had no incentive to make the appropriate marginal benefit—marginal cost calculations. Rather, since they had a given target to produce, they had an incentive to get by with the lowest acceptable quality. The economic structure was such that there were strong incentives for quality deterioration.

Incentives

Also high on the list of standard explanations for the failure of the socialist economies was their failure to provide incentives. It would perhaps be more accurate to say that they provided incentives—for in almost any society some types of behavior get rewarded and others punished, and thus there is an incentive structure—but the incentives were not those that were directed at increasing economic efficiency.

I view incentive problems as a problem of information. If the centralized authorities had the information with which to ascertain what each individual was doing at each moment of time, and with which to judge what each individual *should* be doing, say, in order to maximize output, then there would be no incentive problem. The individual would be instructed to do that, and he would either be sent off to Siberia if he failed (the stick), or he would be paid his wage if he did (the carrot). Interesting incentive problems arise because (1) input (effort) is not observable, (2) outputs are either not observable or not a perfect predictor of the level of effort (input), and/or (3) there is imperfect information about what the individual should be doing, so that it is difficult to assess directly whether he has done the "right" thing.

The socialist economists, like their counterparts in Western academia, did not fully recognize the importance of these incentive problems. If there were no information problems, one could directly control behavior. The socialist economies—like market economies—tried to structure production in such a way as to mitigate the control problems. One of the advantages of assembly lines is that they provide an easy way of monitoring workers' performance: It is easy to detect when a worker falls behind. Collective farms might have been justified in terms of the communist ideology, but the advantages derived from the greater ability to control levels of effort that "industrial farming" provided surely did not elude the Soviet planners. In industries in which close monitoring can be instituted, and where there is little scope for quality variability, the socialist economies attained some success. Nonetheless, in many industries of modern economies, in service sectors like computer programming, these techniques are of little avail.

Equality

An essential aspect of any incentive structure is that pay must vary depending on performance (however measured). With varying pay there is ample scope for inequality. The socialist economy's ideological commitment to equality precluded instituting effective incentive structures.

Political Control Mechanisms

While what may be viewed as conventional economic incentives were thus limited, there were other control mechanisms in place. The party system provided a reward structure and, at the same time, a control mechanism.

In earlier chapters I noted that in many large corporations, direct economic incentives play a limited role. Firms try to get their workers to "identify" with them. So too in the early days of the Revolution workers identified with it, and economic incentives were less important. At the same time, work norms from the prerevolutionary period survived. But as time went on, social fervor waned, and the norms established during the prerevolutionary days became increasing irrelevant. The consequences of the lack of direct economic incentives became more pronounced.

Misdirected Incentives

I said before that the problem was not that there were no incentives within the socialist system—there were—but that many of the incentives were misdirected. This was true both at the individual and the institutional level.

We have already encountered some examples of this. The system provided incentives to produce as low a quality a product as one could get away with. Because firms could never be sure of adequate or timely deliveries of inputs, and because they faced no interest changes, they had incentives to inventory all excess inputs.

Though bribery was a crime, there were all kinds of incentives for individuals to do favors for each other. A manager of a firm with a shortage of some input, but which had control over its scarce output, had an incentive to provide preferential access to his output to a manager of a firm that could provide him additional inputs.

The political system, while it acted as a partial substitute for economic incentives, at the same time contributed to the problem of misdirected incentives: Promotions were less related to performance in economic measures than to political criteria, and this had the natural consequences for incentives and behavior.

Selection Problems

The socialist economists—like many economists in the West during the period—took what I call an engineering approach to economics. As Paul Samuelson tried to suggest in his *Foundations of Economic Analysis*, economics was nothing more than a constrained maximization problem. We have seen how this was reflected in views concerning decision making: All the manager had to do was to look up in the book of blue prints the page corresponding to the observed factor prices.

Given that decision making was so limited, the quality of decision making was of little relevance. Hence the issue of who should be the decision maker, and more important, how to make the decision about who should be the decision maker, received no prominence. Indeed, in Samuelson's classic textbook, the question about who decides or how decisions are to be made was not even included in the standard list of the basic questions of economics. While decision makers in the socialist economies paid more attention to these questions, they had neither the information nor the incentives to make good decisions.

Information about technology—the nature of the input/output matrix —can, as I have suggested, easily be obtained by centralized authorities. But information about individuals cannot. There is not a single number that describes how well an individual will perform a particular job, which those in the producing units could convey to the central authorities, and on the basis of which they could make an informed decision. There is a complex vector of characteristics that determine whether an individual will be successful in a particular job; the characteristics may in fact depend on the complex vector of characteristics of the other individuals with whom that individual will be interacting. That is why even in organizations with a reasonably high degree of centralization, personnel decisions are often made in a fairly decentralized way.

Underlying both the failures to provide appropriate incentives and effective selection were two further failures—the failure to have an adequate accounting (price) system and the lack of competition.

Accounting and the Price System

In earlier chapters I repeatedly noted that the market economy has an incomplete set of prices and that prices do not work in the magical way sometimes suggested by neoclassical theory. But while the price system may be imperfect, it performs a number of vital roles. Among these roles is the basis of an accounting system. If we think of the economy as a game, prices and profits provide a basis of telling who is winning at the game. Prices thus provide the basis of an incentive structure and a selection mechanism.

In the socialist economies prices were set in a sufficiently arbitrary manner that the resulting profit numbers were essentially meaningless. Ideology prohibited using interest rates (though partial substitutes, using different terminology, were employed). If this were the only problem, then one would have had a bad accounting system, but one which still could be used to ascertain who was doing well according to the peculiar scoring system.

Of course the more fundamental problem was that the government attempted to control directly firm behavior: It specified inputs and outputs. The system of accountability was a simple one: Did one meet the target? Firms had an incentive not to exceed their target (another example of misdirected incentive schemes),[1] since the target would be increased if firms exceeded their targets.

We have seen other ways in which the accounting system misdirected incentives, such as the incentives to hold excess inventories, since there was no capital charge for holding inventories. Inventories facilitated meeting targets in subsequent periods when firms could not be assured of the supply of required inputs.

It is now widely recognized that accounting systems (including the price system) are an essential part of the market economy's control mechanism. It has increasingly been recognized that inventories themselves are part of the economy's control mechanism as well as indicators of the failure of the economy's control mechanism. This is seen most clearly in the just-in-time inventory system that was pioneered by Toyota and other Japanese firms. Manufacturers keep only two hours of inventories. Failures of suppliers to respond quickly to orders would impede the firm's ability to maintain its production line. With just-in-time production, any weaknesses in the production system of suppliers or the communication system between the firm and its suppliers are quickly detected and corrected.

The huge inventories within the Soviet system were necessary because of the lack of communication and the prevalence of problems in the production system; they prevented problems in a supplier cascading downstream. But at the same time, they enabled problems to remain hidden, or at least not to be remedied quickly. In the traditional market economy moderate levels of inventories provided a buffer—cushioning the impact of production failures while weakening the signals concerning production problems. At the same time inventories have played an important signaling role. It is changes in inventory levels as much as, or perhaps more than, changes in prices that provide the signals for firms either to increase or to decrease production.

Lack of Competition

The absence of competition—the monopoly of the state not only in political matters but also in economic affairs—had debilitating effects both on the ability of the economy to perform the essential functions of providing appropriate incentives and selection. As I stressed in chapter 7, what is important is not the perfect competition of the neoclassical model, but the *real* competition that I attempted to describe there. Thus I argued there that the information provided by looking at the relative performance of two or more firms engaged in similar economic activities is critical both for the design of incentives and selection. In the early days of the Revolution, information about reasonable work or performance norms was perhaps carried over from prerevolutionary days or from comparisons with performance in other countries. But as time moved on, and the path that the Soviet Union increasingly departed from that of the rest of the world, these experiences became increasingly irrelevant, and the Soviet Union was left without relevant reference points. They knew, for instance, that their agricultural sector lagged far behind that of the more advanced countries. But should that be attributed to the sloth of their workers, the differences in climates, or the lack of investment?

Innovation and Adaptability

Perhaps the most important characteristic of an economy is its ability to adapt to changing circumstances. An economy may do well under one set of circumstances but, when circumstances change, may lack the ability to adapt, and thus fail under the new set of circumstances. Some of the changes in circumstances are endogenous, a result of what happens within the system itself, and some exogenous, a result of the changing world environment.

In analyzing the failure of the socialist economies, we should not forget the remarkable achievements of the Soviet Union. In the face of a hostile world, a worldwide recession, and a devastating World War, and beginning from a weak industrial base, an economy ravaged by World War I, and a political upheaval of enormous proportions, the Soviet Union's growth between 1917 and 1960 has to be given reasonably high marks (particularly if one does not take off for the huge costs imposed on their citizens). Savings were mobilized, and the process of industrialization moved rapidly along. Unlike previous experiences of development, this rapid growth was achieved with a reduction, rather than a large increase in inequality.

Heavy industry was perhaps particularly well suited for the control mechanisms employed by the socialist system. The scope for individual discretion was limited, and accordingly so too was the scope for decision making. Technology (at least from current perspectives) was relatively simple, and the requisite technological knowledge could easily be acquired abroad or developed at home (making using of publicly available information.) With heavy industry there were relatively few establishments (plants).

But the last fifty years has seen a marked change in industrial structure, the growth of the service and high-technology sectors and the decline in heavy industry. Heavy industry itself has become markedly more technology oriented. Specialty steels, for instance, have grown in importance. These sectors are particularly ill-suited to the control mechanisms of socialism.

Thus it is not only that the system failed in its ability to innovate—a failure that can partially be understood in terms of the theories presented in chapter 8, including the lack of incentives, the lack of competition, and the lack of communication between those who might make the innovation and those who might use it. But equally important, the system failed to adapt to the innovations that were occurring elsewhere in the world. It is not clear of course that it could have adapted. In the evolution of the world's economy, there may have been a short window of time, the period of heavy industry associated with steel, autos, coal, and so on, in which some variant of a socialism may have been able to work.

This may then be the ultimate irony: Marx may have been right in his theory of economic determinism, in his view that technology determined the nature of society, the economic and social systems that would prevail. Where he erred was in his ability to forecast how technology would evolve. But how could he! No one, even a hundred years ago, could have forecasted the twists and turns that modern technology has taken, from computer-driven manufacturing to genetic engineering. It is these changes, in the end, that doomed socialism.

12   Reform of Capital Markets[1]

If capital is at the heart of capitalism, then well-functioning capital markets are at the heart of a well-functioning capitalist economy. Unfortunately, of all the markets in the economy, the capital markets are perhaps the most complicated and least understood. They correspond even more poorly to the conception of competitive markets captured by the Arrow-Debreu model than do product and labor markets. The discussion in this chapter of the central issues facing the Eastern European countries, as they attempt to design new financial institutions, will reveal how far off the mark—and accordingly how unhelpful—the traditional competitive model is in thinking about what is the central set of institutions of capitalism.

Few governments leave capital markets to themselves—they are affected by a host of regulations and government policies. Moreover the structure of capital markets appears, in some important respects, vastly different among major capitalist economies. Are the differences inessential, perhaps a consequence of different historical experiences, but having no more substance beyond that? Are they important, with each country's markets reflecting an adaptation to the particular cultural or economic circumstances of their own? Or are some more conducive to economic success, with the solid economic performance of some countries being a consequence of their well-designed capital markets and the poor performance of others being in part a consequence of ill-designed capital markets?

To a large extent the form of capital markets observed in the more developed countries is the consequence of a historical process. Technologies have changed everywhere, but nowhere so much as those that affect capital markets. These markets are transactions-intensive; banks are involved in recording millions of debits and credits a day. The computer revolution has, first and foremost, lowered the costs of such transactions. To those in the more developed countries, it is not apparent that the capital markets that they have inherited are the appropriate ones for the technologies of the twenty-first century. But change is not costless, and the evolution of financial systems, even when confronted with quite serious problems, appears to be a slow process.

The newly emerging democracies of Eastern Europe face difficult choices in designing capital markets. The choices they make will have a bearing not only on the efficiency with which capital is allocated, but also on the macroeconomic stability and performance of their economies. In a way, though, they have an advantage over other developed economies: They may have wider scope for choice, less encumbered by current institutional forms. This too places a heavier burden on them: They should know that the choices they make now may not be easily undone. Institutions once established are not easily or costlessly altered. My objective in this chapter is not to lay out a blueprint for the ideal set of capital markets but rather to help frame the discourse and, in so doing, to illustrate the central role of the kinds of considerations upon which I have been focusing in this book— considerations that are, for the most part, totally absent from the standard competitive paradigm.

On an occasion at the beginning of the discussions of transition, when I was asked to talk about agricultural policies for these economies in transition in Budapest,[2] I found myself in the uncomfortable position of an American saying, "Do as we say, not as we do." Our agricultural policies are hardly a model of economic rationality. Americans asked to comment on the design of financial institutions find themselves in much the same position. Parts of the capital market in the United States are, to put it mildly, in disastrous shape. One major part of our financial system, our Savings and Loan Associations, has gone belly-up. The S&L debacle has cost the taxpayers hundreds of billions of dollars. That is a financial loss. But beyond that financial loss is a real loss: Resources were misallocated. The government's losses are only a part of the total losses to society. Even if we take a middle ground in the range of estimates of the loss, it is as if a substantial part of one year's investment of the United States was completely squandered. It is hard to fathom mistakes of this magnitude.[3] While the S&L debacle is the most obvious problem with our financial markets, other parts of the U.S. banking system are also not healthy, though their weaknesses may not be fundamental and they may be restored to at least a modicum of health within a few years. This experience may put me in an advantageous position, for I can relate from the American experience the consequences of ill-functioning capital markets and some of the causes.

The Functions of the Capital Market

To help frame the discussion, I need to spend a few minutes reviewing the central functions of capital markets. These have been variously described:[4]

1. *Transferring resources* (capital) from those who have it (savers) to those who can make use of it (borrowers or investors). In any capitalist economy there is never a perfect coincidence between those who have funds and those who can make use of those funds.

2. *Agglomerating capital.* Many projects require more capital than is available to any one (or any small set of) saver(s).

3. *Selecting projects.* There are always more individuals who claim that they have good uses for resources than there are funds available.

4. *Monitoring.* This ensures that funds are used in the way promised.

5. *Enforcing contracts.* Those who have borrowed must be made to repay the funds.

6. *Transferring, sharing, and pooling risks.* Capital markets not only raise funds, but the rules that determine repayment determine who bears what risks.

7. *Risk diversification.* By pooling a large number of investment projects together, the total risk is reduced.[5]

8. *Recording transactions.* Banks, in particular, can be thought of running as the medium of exchange, including activities such as check clearing.

Notice that almost all of these are economic functions that are of no importance within the standard competitive paradigm. Transactions costs simply do not exist, so no attention is paid to the institutions involved in transferring resources or in recording transactions.[6] Institutions are not required to transfer, share, and pool risks, since, in the absence of transactions costs, individuals can do that on their own. The existence of a full set of risk markets (*assumed* by the theory) ensures that the market does this efficiently. There are no returns to scale, and so no necessity to agglomerate capital. Most important, there are no information problems, so the central information problems of selecting projects and monitoring simply do not arise; and it is simply assumed that there are no problems in the enforcement of contracts.

Capital markets are engaged not only in intertemporal trade but also in risk. The two are inexorably linked together, partly because intertemporal trades involve dollars today for promises of dollars in the future, and there is almost always the chance that those promises will not be fulfilled. Thus, even if we would like to separate the two, we cannot. As a practical matter, in all capital markets, the two are combined.

The various functions I have described are linked together, but in ways that are not inevitable. For instance, banks link the transactions functions and the functions of selecting and monitoring. With modern technologies, the transactions function can easily be separated. In cash management accounts (CMAs), which are run by the various brokerage houses in the United States, money is transferred into and out of "banks" instantaneously. The brokerage house's bank performs the transactions function, but no balances are kept, and accordingly no loan function (e.g., selecting and monitoring projects) is performed.

Some investment banks perform selection functions. They certify, in effect, bond or equity issues, but they play a very limited role in subsequently monitoring the borrower. Today mutual funds provide risk diversification services, though few of the other services of capital markets.

The array of financial institutions recognizes the advantages that come from specialization, as well as the possibilities of economies of scope.[7] Thus one of the traditional arguments for the interlinking of the medium of exchange function of banks and their loan functions was that in the process of mediating transactions, banks acquired considerable information that might be of value in loan assessment and monitoring. This argument still has considerable validity, though the presence of a large number of alternatives for processing transactions vitiates some of the information content. Observations of a small fraction of the transactions of a potential borrower may have little if any information value.

Some of the interlinkages among functions arise from particular characteristics of information. Judgments about whether a particular loan candidate is worthy have a lot more credibility when the persons or organizations making the judgments are willing to put up money, than when they are only willing to make a recommendation. Monitoring is enhanced when the borrower is likely to be returning to the lender for additional funds.

At the same time it is important to bear in mind the distinctions among the various financial institutions and the roles they play. Thus, while the capital market as a whole raises and allocates funds, much of the activity in bond and stock markets consists in trading existing assets. The stock market in particular is a relatively unimportant source of funds in the United States and the United Kingdom—two of the countries with the most developed equity markets.[8] New firms typically raise their capital through venture capital firms or from friends and relatives of the entrepreneur, and established firms finance themselves through retained earnings, resorting to bank loans and debt if they should need outside funding. Though the liquidity provided by the stock market to shareowners may affect the attractiveness of firm's reinvesting its retained earning, the equity market itself does not exercise a primary role in raising and allocating investment funds.

The Distinctive Aspects of Capital Markets and the Role of Government

What are the distinctive aspects of capital markets that result in government regulation in almost all countries? Capital markets are different from ordinary markets, which involve the contemporaneous trade of commodities. As I have noted, what is exchanged is money today for a (often vague) promise of money in the future. This distinction has played an important role in explaining why capital markets cannot be, and are not run as, conventional auction markets, and why as a result there may be credit (and equity) rationing.[9] It also explains some of the important roles described in the previous section that financial institutions perform, such as monitoring and selecting: In conventional markets, there is no need to select; the item goes to the highest bidder.

We can begin our analysis of the role of the government with an examination of the primary roles that government has already assumed. There are five distinct roles.

Consumer Protection

The government is concerned that investors not be deceived. Thus, if a bank promises to repay a certain amount upon demand, the government wants it to be likely that it will repay that amount. There is a public good —information—that merits government intervention: Information about the financial position of the firm is a public good.[10] Of course there are private incentives for disclosure (at least by the better firms),[11] and in many areas, private rating agencies, such as Best for insurance, Moody's and Standard and Poor's for bonds, and Dun and Bradstreet for other investments, do play a role. The question is whether they are adequate; most governments have decided that they are not.

Government attempts to protect consumers have taken four forms:[12] (1) By ensuring the solvency of financial institutions,[13] governments make it more likely that financial institutions keep the promises they have made (e.g., banks will return the capital of depositors upon demand, insurers will pay the promised benefits when the insured against accident occurs). (2) Deposit insurance and government-run guaranty funds protect consumers in the event of the institution's insolvency. (3) Disclosure laws make it more likely that investors know what they are getting when they make an investment.[14] (4) The market is regulated in such a way as to ensure that certain individuals (insiders) do not take advantage of others. In the United States there are a variety of such regulations, from those prohibiting inside trading to those that regulate the operation of the specialists (market makers), to those that attempt to prohibit unsavory practices, such as cornering a market.

The government's interest in consumer protection in this area goes beyond looking after the interests of investors. The government is concerned that without such protection, capital markets might not work effectively. If investors believe that the stock market is not fair, then they will be not be willing to invest their money. The market will be thin, and firms may have greater trouble raising capital. Episodes when investors have been cheated —from the South Sea Bubble of the eighteenth century on—have been followed by a drying up of equity markets. Honest firms trying to raise capital are hurt by the potential presence of scoundrels: There is an externality. Government policies, in protecting investors, are thus aimed at making capital markets function better.

Government Enhancing the Solvency of Banks

The United States has periodically been plagued with bank runs, perhaps more frequently than have other countries. The government has employed three sets of instruments to enhance the solvency of banks.[15]

1. *Insurance.* Government insurance for depositors was one way of trying to maintain confidence in banks, and thus prevent bank runs. The government has undertaken this insurance role for two different reasons. One is to enhance the viability of the banking institutions, by increasing consumer confidence, making runs less likely. In this role the insurance reduces the likelihood of illiquidity causing the default of a basically solvent bank. Here the question is whether the other mechanisms (to be described below)

suffice; whether there is much value added by government insurance. The second role is consumer protection. Today it is hard, in principle, to see a justification for the latter role because individuals can put their money in money market funds, investing in Treasury bills for which there is no default risk (apart from that which might arise as a result of fraud.)

Given that the government does provide insurance, the government, like any other insurer, has a vested interest in making sure that the insured against event does not occur—that is, the government in its capacity as insurer has a vital interest in ensuring the solvency of those that it has insured. This provides one (but only one) rationale for government intervention.

2. *The lender of last resort.* Another mechanism for preventing bank runs was provided with the establishment of the Federal Reserve System which serves as a lender of last resort, ensuring that banks could obtain funds if they had a short-run liquidity problem. With this assurance, it was hoped, bank runs would be less likely. Obviously this does not resolve problems if the bank is truly insolvent; its only intent is to prevent short-run liquidity problems from bringing down a bank.

3. *Regulations.* Various regulations have been designed to prevent banks from becoming insolvent. Such regulations are (or should be) based on the following principles. Monitoring banks is costly and necessarily imperfect. Accordingly the regulations must be designed to make it more likely that those in control of banks make the kinds of decisions that enhance the solvency of the institution, and make it possible to detect problems before the bank is actually insolvent. Regulations must also be based on the recognition that there are important asymmetries of information between the bank and the bank regulators, that the "books" of the bank are largely in the control of the bank, and that accordingly, the information presented to the bank regulators may quite possibly be "distorted." Thus banks are in a position to sell undervalued assets but to keep overvalued assets on their books at book value. When banks systematically engage in this practice, "book" value will systematically overestimate true value.[16]

The first objective, making it more likely that those in control of banks take solvency-enhancing decisions, is aided by requirements that the bank have substantial net worth—so that it has much to lose if losses do occur—and by restricting the kinds of loans and investments which the bank may make, for example, by restricting insider lending and restricting purchases of junk bonds.

Government Attempting to Enhance Macroeconomic Stability

One of the reasons that the government has been concerned about bank runs is that the collapse of the banking system has severe macroeconomic consequences. Banks and other financial institutions are a repository of specialized information about their borrowers. When banks fail, there is a concomitant decline in the economy's information-organizational capital. This translates into a decrease in loan availability. Note that bank failure would not be a problem if capital markets were just auction markets. But they are not. A decrease in information not only impairs the efficiency with which funds get allocated but also may lead to more extensive credit rationing, so the effective cost of capital is greatly increased.

One of the functions that banks (and other financial institutions) are engaged in is certifying who is likely to repay loans, that is, whose promises to pay should be believed. If too many people are so certified—if there are too many who can get funds, and they decide to exercise that option—then the demand for goods can easily exceed the supply. Since the price system (interest rate) is not functioning to clear the capital market, there is, within the market system, no automatic market-clearing mechanism. This provides an important role for a central bank.

Competition Policy

In the United States, perhaps more than in other countries, there is (or least has been) a concern that without government intervention, the banks would be able to exercise undue concentration of economic power. Many of the restrictions imposed on banks, such as those relating to interstate banking (American banks are allowed to have branches only *within* one state) and those relating to the activities banks can engage in, are intended to limit their ability to exercise economic power.

Rationale for Government Intervention

This, perhaps by now familiar, litany of the roles that government regulation plays in financial markets is one way we could approach the problem of government regulation. Another way is to ask if there is any reason to believe that free and unfettered capital markets result in the efficient allocation of resources. Until fifteen years ago there was a quick and easy answer: Adam Smith's invisible hand theorem said that competitive markets would ensure efficient resource allocations. But research over the past decade has analyzed in depth the functioning of the capital market. What makes capital markets interesting and important is that information is imperfect. With imperfect information, markets are, in general, not constrained Pareto efficient, as I explained in chapter 3. There is no presumption in favor of unfettered markets. Now is not the occasion to review all the reasons why this might be so. Let me just briefly mention one that I perhaps did not sufficiently emphasize in the earlier discussion of the inefficiency of market economies: that much of the return in capital markets consists of rent seeking. Your knowing a minute before anyone else does that Exxon has made a major oil discovery may make you a fortune buying Exxon stock, but it does not increase the efficiency with which society's resources get allocated.[17] Much of the innovation in the financial sector entails the recording of transactions more quickly, but is society really that much better off as a result? Someone might get the interest that might otherwise have accrued to someone else, but have more goods been produced? Or have they been allocated more efficiently?[18] In short, there is no a priori basis for arguing that the government should not intervene in the market, and there seem to be strong arguments for government intervention. It is this *potential* value that must be balanced against the possibility of "government failure." Since some government intervention is likely, the questions to be answered are what kinds of financial institutions to establish and what role should government play.[19]

Perspectives for the Newly Emerging Democracies: Issues of Transition

Most of the problems discussed in the previous section are generic: They arise in virtually any economy, though with more force in some than in others. The problems take on a particular color within the newly emerging democracies of Eastern Europe, and it is upon these distinctive features that I want to concentrate my attention.

We can distinguish two sets of issues—those that relate to the form of the financial institutions that will eventually emerge in these countries and those that relate to the particular problems associated with the *transition* from their current situation to a market economy. The two problems are in a sense inseparable: Views about the ultimate destination impinge on how some of the short-run problems ought to be addressed, and answers provided to the short-run transition problems will almost undoubtedly have a major impact on the ultimate destination. Indeed earlier in this chapter I urged an awareness of this interaction: Decisions made in the short run may not easily be reversed.

I begin with a discussion of the transition problems, noting in particular the instances where how these are resolved are critically dependent on the conception of the eventual structure of the financial system. The discussion of this section will recall, here from the perspective of the capital market, several of the themes raised in the previous chapter on privatization.

There are five related central problems facing these economies in the process of transition: (1) The most apparent problem is that of establishing *hard budget constraints*. The importance of the other four has only gradually been recognized. (2) Historically the banks and other so-called financial institutions did not perform any of the central functions (other than that of mediating transactions) that we associate with financial institutions. In effect completely new institutions have to be created. Yet in most of the countries there have been attempts to adapt old institutions rather than creating new institutions. The extent to which their *historical institutional legacy* will impair them remains to be seen: Will the old modes of thinking impede their ability to recognize their new economic functions? At the very least, a process of re-education is required. (3) Under the old regime not only did banks not perform the same role (e.g., screening loan applicants), but those taking out loans did not view them in the same way. After all, given that the government owned the bank and owned the enterprise, it was like the left pocket owing the right pocket money. Both sides looked upon the transaction as simply an accounting exercise. This raises important questions of what are we to make of the *inherited loan portfolios* of the financial institutions? How we treat these inherited debts has obvious consequences for, and is obviously affected by, the process of privatization. (4) Under former socialism the state had an economic monopoly and did not use *competition* as an instrument of policy. Developing effective competition may prove to be a difficult task. (5) The relationship between finance and *corporate control* has increasingly drawn the attention of economists.[20] The special problems that are likely to arise in socialist economies that decide to privatize by means of schemes that result in a wide distribution of equity ownership have implications for the role and design of financial institutions. I elaborate on the first three issues in the discussion below, leaving the last two to the next part in which I focus on the ultimate shape of the financial system.

Underlying much of the discussion of the design of financial systems for the newly emerging democracies is the extent to which reliance should be placed on the reform and reorganization of existing institutions, the extent to which reliance should be placed on the creation of new institutions, and the extent to which a clean slate should be declared, with old debts and credits, created under a very different economic regime, being wiped out. Many of the issues that form the basis of this debate turn on politics and expectations and bring us beyond the scope of economics. Still there are basic economic issues that are relevant to this discussion, and it is upon these economic issues that I focus. A perhaps disproportionate share of the discussion will center around the reform of existing institutions rather than the distinctive problems of creating new institutions.

Soft Budget Constraints, Bank Solvency, Selection Processes, and Inherited Assets and Liabilities

Many of the financial institutions have been run with soft budget constraints: Deficits have been made up by the government. Soft budget constraints within the financial sector can have disastrous effects for the entire economy. Soft budget constraints are like a disease: They can be highly contagious. If the banks face soft budget constraints, they will not impose discipline upon their borrowers. If a borrower has a zero or negative net worth, they may not care if they make a loss: Even if the government will not make up the difference, they may be able to borrow to keep themselves operating. There is a more direct mechanism by which the disease of soft budget constraints is spread: Firms are constantly extending trade credit to suppliers and customers. If some firms are not on a tight leash, they may not put their suppliers and customers on a tight leash. If there is a widespread belief that the state stands behind state firms, and will honor their debts, then any state firm is in the position of being able to create credit.

The difficult question is how best to harden the budget constraint. There is no easy answer. Here I want to suggest some problems with some of the often proposed solutions. The seeming simplest solution is privatization. Once a firm is in the private sector, it has no more "entitlement" to the public purse. It must sink or swim.

Problems of Valuation
The problems of privatization have been widely discussed (see chapter 10). I want to focus here on some of those problems that arise acutely in the privatization of the financial sector. Suppose, for the moment, that the government were to decide to sell the financial sector in open competition. One central problem is that of valuing the assets of financial institutions. The risks associated with valuing those assets imply that with risk-averse bidders the government is likely to get considerably less than the actuarially fair value. This of course is true for all privatizations. But the risks are,

in a fundamental sense, different from the risks associated with privatizing industrial firms. One of the central aspects of the risks associated with valuing a banks' assets is how, in the process of privatization of the "firms" that owe the bank money, the liabilities of those firms are to be treated. Will the government honor the loans taken out by state enterprises? Will it insist on those purchasing state enterprises "honoring" these debts? These are issues that, at this juncture, have not been resolved. Thus the principal valuation risk is a political risk, and it makes little sense for the government to transfer—at a cost—that risk to the private sector.

Moreover the consequences of valuation errors are likely to be particularly severe. If, on the one hand, the bidders overestimate the value of their net assets, the financial institutions will be undercapitalized. Undercapitalized financial institutions have strong incentives to undertake undue risks. This is the familiar moral hazard problem, whose consequences were all too clear in the case of the S&L debacle in the United States as near-bankrupt banks gambled on their resurrection. If such undercapitalization is widespread, then the likelihood of a government bailout becomes very high. The financial institutions will know this and act accordingly: Privatization will not harden budget constraints. If, on the other hand, the bidders underestimate the value of the assets, there will be charges of a government giveaway. It may be hard for governments to resist the temptation to recapture these profits, for example, by a special tax on the industry.

Insolvency of Financial Institutions
With either a significant under- or overvaluation of assets, the success or failure of the financial institution will not convey much information—other than about the luck (or lack of it) of the bidders or their skill (or lack of it) in predicting political winds. If a bank appears to be solvent, it may not be because it is making good lending decisions. It may only be because its assets were undervalued. By the same token the government faces severe problems in deciding what to do with a bank facing a liquidity crisis. First, it must ascertain whether it is insolvent. Determining insolvency gets us back to the basic problems of asset valuation discussed earlier. The value of the bank's loan portfolio depends to a large measure on government policies. If it is ascertained that a bank is insolvent, should one presume that it is incompetent, and therefore be shut down? It could be simply that it made a political misjudgment on how government would treat bank loans. Similarly the failure of an unprivatized bank does not *necessarily* imply incompetence. After all, there have been drastic changes in economic circumstances that could not reasonably have been anticipated. Moreover, the grounds

for granting loans by state-run banks had little to do with standard commercial principles. As was noted, banks under socialism did not perform the central functions of screening and monitoring that they do under capitalism.

Assume one concludes that the insolvency is not a mark of incompetence: What then? There is (perhaps) valuable organizational capital[21] that would be lost if the bank were dissolved. One needs a once-and-for-all capital infusion. But without some method of ensuring that such a capital infusion would not be repeated, incentives would again be distorted.

Public Distribution of Shares: A Negative Capital Levy?

The problems I have just described would arise—even more strongly[22]— if the banks were privatized but the shares distributed publicly. This is, in effect, a negative lump-sum grant, or a negative capital levy. Traditional tax theory has argued for the desirability of capital levies, were it not for the distortionary consequences arising from the expectation that they might be repeated. Proponents of these negative capital levies argue that the gains in managerial incentives from privatization more than outweigh the subsequent costs arising from the distortionary taxation which will be necessary to raise the requisite revenue. But a partial privatization, with the government retaining a substantial fraction of the shares, would presumably do as well. (Any managerial incentive scheme could be as effectively employed; indeed in most large private corporations in the United States, managerial pay is only weakly related to managers' contributions to firm performance, as we saw in chapter 3.[23])

To mitigate the effect of a negative capital levy, the government might, alternatively, treat the current liabilities of a nonfinancial firm being privatized as debt of the firm to the government.[24] But then the government itself would be involved in the difficult question of valuation, with all the untoward consequences of misvaluation which I have previously noted.

The Timing of Privatization of Financial Institutions

In short, the potential viability of any newly privatized bank may depend as much on its competence in valuing the old assets, or on luck, as prices and market values change unpredictably—as on the competence of the institution in performing its *on going* roles (described earlier in this chapter). Particularly during the early stages of the transition, where government laws, regulations, and policies affecting the private sector are not clear, market values may change in hard to predict ways. For instance, the government might decide that the high debt of some firms represents an impediment to their ongoing operation, and either repudiate that debt or assume that debt as its own obligation. These alternatives have obviously drastically different implications for the holders of the debt paper.[25]

In the days of socialism, financial structure made no difference. Here at last was a domain in which the Modigliani-Miller theorem was correct, though for quite different reasons: All obligations were simply obligations of one part of the government to another.[26] Firms produced what they were told to produce; finance simply accommodated the "orders."[27] In market economies financial structure makes a great deal of difference.[28] Again there is no incentive or sorting reason to impose the inherited financial structure of firms upon the ongoing operations of the firm. Some kind of recapitalization is required, as I argued in chapter 10. While privatization represents one form such recapitalization can take, government assumption of debt (as in the restructuring of the S&L's in the United States) and debt for equity swaps (as in the restructuring of some third world debt) may represent interim measures to be taken as the government reexamines some of the more fundamental issues associated with privatization. But these recapitalizations, as desirable as they may be, can have profound effects on the value of outstanding liabilities of these firms to the financial institutions. There seems to be a case for resolving these uncertainties before proceeding with the privatization of financial institutions. If privatization is postponed, some alternative interim method of "hardening" budget constraints may be required. McKinnon (1992) provides one thoughtful possibility.

Leaving for the moment the question of the timing of privatization of the financial institutions, there are some important caveats to be borne in mind in the design of what might be viewed as the "privatization package."

Other Issues in the Hardening of Budget Constraints

There are obvious macro as well as micro advantages to enforcing tough budget constraints. The excessive expansion of credit can clearly lead to inflationary pressures. I want to put a word of caution against hardening the budget constraint too rapidly or, perhaps I should say, in the wrong way. For the reason explained in chapter 10, in the process of transition current profitability may be an unreliable signal on which to base a decision to weed out.

Credit Constraints and Aggregate Supply
The standard macro model focuses on the effect of monetary (credit) constraints on aggregate demand. But such constraints also have effects on
aggregate supply. If firms cannot get sufficient working capital, then production will be cut back.[29] If interest rates are raised sharply, and there has
not been a recapitalization, high-debt firms may be thrown into bankruptcy. But these problems have nothing to do with their current operating
efficiency, only with an inherited financial structure.[30] If the reduction in
aggregate supply exceeds that of aggregate demand, the monetary (credit)
constraints can actually be inflationary. More broadly, it is important that
credit be cut off to those for whom the return is lowest. In the transition
process that is difficult to ascertain.

Macroeconomic Control Mechanisms
There are problems with controlling both the allocation of credit and
its total volume. When there is a single bank, the volume of credit is,
in principle, easy to control. But a central part of establishing a market
economy is having at least a few competing banks and other financial
institutions. In the United States and many other capitalist economies, the
government relies on indirect control mechanisms for controlling the
quantity of credit: open-market operations, discount rates, and reserve
requirements. Even in the United States, the relationship between these
instruments and the volume of credit becomes tenuous, when the economy
faces considerable uncertainty, as in the event of a downturn. In newly
established financial systems there is likely to be even greater uncertainty
about these relationships, and thus indirect control mechanisms may be
viewed as an excessively risky way of controlling the volume of credit. On
the other hand, the central bank may not be in a position to allocate credit
targets efficiently among the various banks. One suggestion is "marketable
quantity constraints." The central bank would control the quantity of credit,
either auctioning off the right to issue loans or granting the rights to
various banks, with the proviso that banks could trade the rights among
themselves. Such marketable quantity constraints combine the certainty of
quantity targets with the allocational efficiency of market mechanisms.[31]

Perspectives for the Newly Emerging Democracies: The Ultimate Shape of the Financial System

There are some basic issues concerning the design of the financial system
that must be faced as part of the transition but that are as much issues of

the ultimate shape of the financial system. My discussion is divided into three sections. The first deals with the role of competition, the second with the set of regulations that are concerned with the solvency/liquidity of the banking system, while the third focuses on issues of corporate control.

Banks and Competition

Chapter 7 emphasized the importance of competition—a broader conception of competition than that conveyed by the price-taking behavior of the standard competitive paradigm. There are two separate, but related, issues involving the relationship between banks and competition: competition among banks, and banking practices that affect competition among firms. The United States has clearly been worried about the possible deleterious effects of banking practices that limit competition among firms. A variety of laws and regulations have encouraged competition within the banking system—far more competition than in other countries—and there are proposals to dismantle some of the regulations that were intended to limit the economic power of banks.

The problem of establishing viable competition in the newly emerging democracies of Eastern Europe is a bone of some contention. There are some who believe that allowing foreign competition is all that is required: There are enough firms in the international marketplace to ensure that competition within a country will be strong, if only these international firms are allowed to compete. Others see a variety of barriers to entry, of a kind that have been well documented within capitalist economies, resulting in at best imperfect competition. Chapter 7 explained why I am inclined to the latter view.

Banks can serve, and have served, the function of limiting competition in product markets. They are in an ideal position for coordinating decision making. Moreover it is even in the bank's narrow interest as a lender to limit competition: The fiercer the competition, the more likely the less efficient firms within the market will go bankrupt, and thus the more likely that some loans will not be repaid. While the vitality of capitalism does not depend on the existence of perfect competition in the textbook sense, a high level of competition is essential, to ensure both economic efficiency and that the fruits of that efficiency are passed on to consumers. Farmers will find little relief if instead of receiving low prices for their goods from the government, they receive low prices from monopsonist food processors. In either case low prices will depress production and inhibit development of the agricultural sector.

There is a general presumption that competition among banks is no less desirable than competition in other sectors of the economy. But while *some* competition among the banks is desirable, excess competition may have its problems. Banks, perhaps more than other institutions, depend on their reputation. Reputation is an asset worth preserving—provided that there is an economic return. For there to be an economic return, competition has to be limited. The limitation may come from natural economic forces— establishing a reputation may act as a barrier to entry.[32] (Though this argument holds, to some extent, in many other markets, it holds with particular force in financial institutions, where what is being exchanged is dollars today for *promises* of dollars in the future. A buyer of a TV can see quickly what he or she is getting; if the TV wears out in two years, the producer will quickly lose its reputation. With financial markets, the promises are frequently much longer term.) It is worth noting that in the United States one of the effects of deposit insurance was to reduce or eliminate this barrier to entry, facilitating entry and competition. But the resulting competition, and the ensuing reduction of reputation rents, encouraged banks to pursue shortsighted policies, and this contributed to the S&L debacle and the related banking crisis.

There seems a real possibility of either excessive entry—driving rents to zero, and thus eliminating the incentives for maintaining a reputation— or of insufficient entry—leading to insufficient competition within the financial sector. Nor do we have any confidence in the government's ability to set the "right" level of entry. Are observed levels of profit just those rents necessary to ensure economic efficiency? Or is there an element of monopoly profit beyond that? Out of this no clear prescription emerges, simply a word of caution: The financial sector needs to be carefully watched, for evidence of significant "errors" in either direction.

Regulations for a Banking System

There is now widespread recognition (for the reasons given earlier) that even in the best run of capitalist economies, banks need to be regulated. Earlier I discussed the general form and objectives of this regulation. To translate these into concrete proposals for the financial institutions of the newly emerging democracies would take me beyond the scope of this chapter. But I would like to dwell on a couple of key issues, relating to the twin problems of "market failure" and "government failure," both well illustrated by the problems that have confronted the S&Ls and banks within the United States. The standard diagnoses attribute the problems facing American financial institutions to eight factors:

1. Deposit insurance, which removed the incentive of depositors to monitor banks.

2. Inadequate capital requirements, which resulted in insufficiently capitalized institutions having an incentive to take excessive risk. (Some financial institutions found themselves with negative net worth, were they to be evaluated at market values; the low net worths were partly the result of bad investment decisions, partly the result of changes in interest rates that decreased the value of their assets, which consisted largely of long-term debt at fixed interest rates.) Firms with negative or low net worth gambled on their resurrection.

3. Inadequate restraints on how financial institutions could invest the funds that were entrusted to them, allowing those who wished to gamble on their resurrection to do so. Indeed, in an attempt to *help* the failing S&Ls the Reagan administration had, in the early 1980s, actually loosened the regulations.

4. Inadequate incentives for banks not to engage in risk taking. Their premiums on deposit insurance were not adjusted according to the risks being undertaken. Indeed a process of Gresham's law was at work: Firms that offered high interest rates could attract more funds (since depositors only cared about the interest rate—with deposit insurance all were equally safe)—and to pay the high interest rates, financial institutions in effect had to undertake high levels of risk.

5. Inadequate monitoring by regulators.

6. Inadequate accounting procedures. Assets were not valued at current market value, so firms whose net worth was low or negative—and who therefore had an incentive to engage in excessive risk taking—were not shut down.

7. Regulatory forbearance. Regulators, having noticed a problem, had every incentive to try to "patch things up" rather than face an immediate crisis.

8. Corrupt bankers.

The last problem is more a consequence rather than a cause: Bankers used to rank among the more boring and more steadfast members of the community. It was the incentives and opportunities provided by the banking climate in the 1980s that attracted, if not corrupt individuals (by most accounts they accounted for a relatively small fraction of the total losses), then at least more "entrepreneurial" activities (to put a positive light on their risk-taking actions). They should not be blamed for pursuing their self-interest, for taking advantage of incentive opportunities provided by the system, even if it meant the government had to bear much of the risk and they reaped much of the potential reward.

The problems facing the regulators are inherent: They have less information than the banks, and they will therefore always be at a disadvantage. (The problems are exacerbated by the low pay which regulators receive, both absolutely, and relative to those received by those they are regulating. But these restrictions in pay are part of the almost inherent limitations on government, to which I referred earlier.)

The effect of deposit insurance on monitoring is a red herring: Individuals have neither the capacity nor the incentive, even in the absence of deposit insurance, to monitor effectively. The fact is that monitoring is a public good, individuals do not have access to the relevant information, and they are not in as competent position to judge as regulators should be. Rating services go only a little way to fill the gap. They certainly did not perform stellarly in the crises of the late 1980s.

Any insurance firm, when it provides insurance, knows that insurance may give rise to a moral hazard problem: Insurance attenuates incentives to avoid the insured against accident. Insurers attempt to impose "regulations" to mitigate these effects; fire insurance companies attempt to mitigate the losses of fire by insisting that commercial insureds have sprinkler systems. The regulatory system should be designed to reduce the likelihood that government will have to pay off on its deposit insurance and to take account of the fact that the government and depositors have limited abilities to monitor banks. They should be designed to alter incentives, to exercise control at points where observability is easy, and to reduce the magnitude of residual risk bearing by the government. Government regulations of insured accounts can be viewed in the same way as any insurer's attempts to reduce its exposure: Capital requirements, restrictions on interest paid to attract funds, and restrictions on risky investment reduce the likelihood of defaults that will necessitate the government paying up on the insurance it has provided. Ownership restrictions, limiting potential conflicts of interest, and the abuse of banks' fiduciary responsibilities reduce "temptation" and therefore, once again, the burden on monitoring.

With capital requirements set at a sufficiently high level, many of the other problems become alleviated: Since the government will be bearing less risk, the consequences of adjusting premiums to the risk being borne becomes less important,[33] and the consequences of failing to value the bank correctly also become less important[34]—problems will still be detected before it is too late, that is, before the government's risk exposure has increased. Incentives for excessive risk taking by banks will be reduced, and the banking system will seem less attractive to the kind of risk loving entrepreneurs which found their haven in the S&Ls in the 1980s.

I noted above that one of the indirect restrictions that may be effective is that on ownership of banks. But on this last point, I have less confidence, for reasons to which I will now turn.

Banks and Corporate Control: Two Views

The view that I have just expressed—the desirability of maintaining strong walls between the financial and production sectors of the economy runs counter to what many observers see as the very successful models of financial structure of Japan and Germany. These provide very viable alternative models for designing financial systems, models that are particularly attractive in the context of "people's capitalism" to which some of the emerging democracies may be evolving. In my view, there is not just one viable financial structure. On the other hand, there are many nonviable financial structures. The United States has one that has certain marked problems.

The Japanese financial system is usually characterized as involving production groups, in each of which there is a bank at the center. These banks are closely involved with production firms. When Mazda had trouble, its bank stepped in, changed management, and successfully turned the company around. There is competition across these groups, cooperation within the groups.

The Japanese model has received considerable attention as resolving a problem plaguing American managerial capitalism, to which we have repeatedly referred. With widely diversified shares, managers have considerable autonomy. Good management is a public good: All shareholders benefit if the firm is run better. No shareholder can be excluded from these benefits. Each shareholder thus has an inadequate incentive to monitor the firm. Indeed there are great barriers to small shareholders doing an effective job. The alleged control mechanisms work most imperfectly—management is seldom replaced through the voting mechanism, and there are fundamental problems with the takeover mechanism.[35]

While banks nominally do not have control, they may actually exercise more effective control. They have a credible threat of withdrawing credit;

information problems mean that credit markets are inherently imperfect, and when one firm withdraws credit, others will not normally rush in.[36] Moreover credit is normally more concentrated than equity (there is normally a lead bank, the number of banks in a lending syndicate is limited, and they have a variety of reciprocal relationships which help reduce the importance of free-rider problems). Thus banks have both the incentives and the means to exercise control.[37]

In this perspective the appropriate way to view the firm is as a multiple principal-agent problem—the various principals being all those who provide capital to the firm as well as the workers (essentially, anyone who would be adversely affected by, say, the bankruptcy of the firm.) In this view, the manager is the "agent" of all these principals. While the bank may not induce the firm to take actions that maximize the welfare of these other groups—ensuring that there is a relatively low risk of bankruptcy may not maximize expected returns to shareholders—the control that they exercise does confer external benefits on other groups, at least in ensuring the solvency of the firm. One could argue that, when the bank also is a shareholder, the bank is more likely to pursue actions that enhance the overall return to capital. This is one of the essential advantages of the "Japanese model." A single bank has the incentive to exercise the critical monitoring function, and because it also has an ownership stake, it does this in a way that reflects both the interests of lenders and owners of equity.

One might imagine that if the shares of the large enterprises within the newly emerging democracies were widely distributed, there would be real problems of managerial control. The worst kinds of abuses—the kinds that have been documented in the case of RJR-Nabisco—could become prevalent. The Japanese system *may* limit these—at the expense of an agglomeration of enormous amounts of corporate power. Some of these abuses will be limited by ensuring that there are several such groups, and that there will be competition among them. (Thus one's view of the desirable financial structure may be affected by how effectively one believes antitrust laws will be enforced.) International competition may provide further discipline. Yet one cannot be blind to the possibility that the concentration of large amounts of capital under the control of relatively few individuals (even if they do not "own" the capital) can be used to obtain political influence, possibly to restrict competition (though always of course in the name of some other more sacred principle).

Perhaps a hybrid system—one in which there are holding companies, performing managerial roles over those who are part of their group, as well as *separate* financial institutions—would provide the needed checks and balances.[38] The financial institutions would provide an important role in monitoring the monitors; at the same time the separation would serve to limit somewhat the concentration of economic power.[39]

In recent years within the United States, venture capital firms have played a vital role in providing finance, particularly to new high-technology industries (especially in computers and biomedical and related areas). There the monitoring and selection functions are intimately inter-connected with the provision of capital. Whether there is a greater poten-tial scope for these firms, and whether variants of these firms could be adapted to the process of privatization, is not yet clear.

Equity Markets

I have focused my attention primarily on banks, not on equity markets. The choice is deliberate. To a large extent equity markets are an interesting and fun sideshow, but they are not at the heart of the action. Relatively little capital is raised in equity markets, even in the United States and the United Kingdom.[40] One cannot expect equity markets to play an important role in raising funds in the newly emerging democracies. Equity markets are also a sideshow in the allocation of capital. As my colleague Robert Hall once put it: The *Wall Street Journal* finally got it right, when they split the financial section from the business section. The two are only very loosely connected. As I noted earlier, managers do not look to the stock market to determine whether another blast furnace should be built, or whether further exploration for oil should be undertaken. The stock price is relevant—they do look to the effect of their decisions on the stock market price. But it does not, and should not, drive their behavior. It simply provides information that is too coarse to direct investment decisions. In the transition process of the Eastern European countries, it is even less likely that equity markets will play an important role in providing information that is of relevance for investment decisions.

While the stock market enhances liquidity, and the enhanced liquidity makes investment in equities much more desirable, the stockmarket is not an unmitigated blessing. If the stock market becomes important, instability in the stock market[41] can contribute to macroeconomic instability, in ways that are by now familiar. The policy implications of this (e.g., for transac-tions taxes on the stock market) remain a subject of considerable debate. (See, e.g., Stiglitz 1989c and Summers and Summers 1989.)

There has also been concern that to the extent that managers do pay attention to stock market prices, it leads them to behave in an excessively shortsighted manner (presumably because stock prices are excessively sensitive to short-run returns). Advocates of this view—a view that can be traced at least back to Keynes—look for ways to encourage long-term investment in securities, perhaps using the tax system to discourage short-term trading (e.g., a turnover tax). Though this is not the occasion to enter into that debate (aspects of which turn around practical problems in implementing such a tax), it should be noted that there is little evidence that such taxes, which have been implemented in several countries, have had any adverse effects on market volatility or indeed on the ability of the market to perform any of the other functions that it performs.

Conclusions

Financial markets play a central role in any capitalist economy. The design of capital markets affects the ability of the economy to raise capital and to allocate it efficiently. Beyond that the design of capital markets affects the efficiency of enterprises in all other sectors of the economy. Even if one has little confidence in the efficiency or effectiveness of the "market for corporate control," the monitoring function of financial institutions provides essential discipline on managers, a discipline that is particularly important in economies in which shares are widely held.

While there are an array of financial structures found in different capitalist economies from which the newly emerging democracies can choose, it is not evident that any represent the "optimal" financial structure, or indeed that any of them has fully adapted to the new technologies that have revolutionized the processing of information. In the case of some capitalist countries, the defects in the financial systems are all too apparent. The newly emerging democracies have ahead of them a delicate balancing act: Once they settle upon a financial structure, they will find that change is difficult and costly. Vested interests arise and attain political and economic influence quickly. The dangers of settling too impetuously upon a financial structure seem clear. But the process of privatization and establishing a well-functioning market economy requires effective capital markets. Delay is costly, perhaps impossible. At the very least it is hoped that the remarks in this chapter may prove of some help in thinking through some of the key aspects in the design of financial markets and institutions.

13 Asking the Right Questions: Theory and Evidence[1]

Traditionally the debate about socialism, market socialism, and capitalism has been couched as the choice of alternative economic systems. This, I would like to suggest, is not the correct way of posing the question. The real question is, What should be the economic role of the state? Posed this way, one immediately recognizes the possibility of a continuum of roles that it might assume, from the all-encompassing role assumed in some centrally planned socialist economies, to the very limited role that it undertakes in Hong Kong. The government can take an interventionist role, imposing corrective Pigouvian taxes, for instance, and engaging in massive redistributions, yet it may take a very limited role in production. Government ownership of the means of production is neither necessary nor sufficient for ensuring equality, or even for ensuring limitations on the political power of certain elites.

Thus the question is not just "how large a role" the government should undertake but what specific roles? What should be left to the market? What forms should government intervention take? Even in the most ardent market-oriented state, the government has an active role in production: While the government buys defense equipment from private contractors, it does not contract out the actual provision of "fighting" services. In this chapter we enquire briefly into why this is so.

I suggested earlier that belief in the market system is based partly on analytic results, on theory, and partly on empirical evidence. Support for market-based systems is largely based on the fact that they have worked so well, in so many dimensions. Yet for many this observation is not sufficient: They would like to be assured that this is not a happenstance, a matter of luck, but rather a fundamental consequence of the economic structure. It is the objective of the "theorems" to provide that assurance. In previous chapters I have tried to argue that the standard theorems, those that in recent years been relied upon for that assurance, do not, upon closer examination, provide the intellectual basis, for either the sweeping conclusions of the invisible hand or the associated conclusions concerning decentralization and the ability to separate issues of efficiency and equity.

The Historical Record

I now want to take a closer look at the empirical evidence. Unfortunately, history does not provide us with controlled experiments. We have an enormous number of historical episodes, on the basis of which we might form some generalizations. The problem is separating the general from the particular. While it may be true that those who do not study the lessons of history are condemned to repeat its mistakes, the lessons of history are not always writ plainly. Like data, they do not speak for themselves. The lenses through which we see the world, the conclusions that we want to draw, often affect how we interpret the historical record. It sometimes seems as if even our collective memory is selective.

Thus, as I noted earlier, textbooks of only a decade ago read the historical record as saying that socialist economies and countries with "strong governments" (often a euphemism for something worse) could grow faster than market economies, at least at the early stages of development. Today's textbooks read the historical record quite differently. Were Bayesian priors held with such low confidence that but ten years of experience, possibly to the contrary, lead to such changes in how we read the historical record? If so, the historical record provides at best a shaky basis for proceeding to the future.

What history teaches us is that there is a huge range of experiences: Economic success and economic failure have occurred in a variety of situations and circumstances. There is no simple key without which failure is guaranteed, and with which success is assured.

The Ubiquitous Role of Government

I want to venture four generalizations germane to the issues at hand. First, governments have played an important role in almost all of the major success stories. The American government played a major role, through its land grants, in financing the railroads. The central role of the Japanese government, and in particular the role of MITI, and of the Korean government in those success stories is by now well documented.

The view, popular in recent years among development economists, that governments necessarily *impede* progress, particularly as a result of the socially unproductive rent seeking to which government activities give rise, has at best limited support. There are, to be sure, some cases in which government activities have not had the success that they have had in Korea and Japan. (Even in these countries the fact that there have been some notable *bad* decisions has led some critics to claim that growth would have been even better were it not for the government intervention. The most notable example was the Japanese government's attempt to prevent Honda from entering the auto industry. But this perspective ignores the nature of "human fallibility" which I stressed in chapter 5. Errors are present in every system. The issue is not whether errors are made, but the prevalence and consequences. While the question of whether Japan without MITI would have done even better belongs to the land of counterfactual history, the consensus is that it would not—a consensus with which I agree.) In short, while there are many cases in which government activities have been counterproductive, there are few cases where the private sector has, without major help from the government, succeeded on its own.

Government Inefficiency?

This brings me to the second empirical generalization: While there are many instances of inefficient government enterprises, there are some instances of apparently efficient enterprises. The state enterprises in France provide the standard examples, but there are others, such as in Singapore. By the same token, there are plenty of instances of inefficient private enterprises.

Theoretical Quandaries

We have already noted that the differences between public and private large-scale enterprises may frequently be exaggerated: Both entail extensive delegation, with limited incentives. Herbert Simon, who received his Nobel Prize for his important contributions to understanding how organizations behave, recently put the matter this way:

Most producers are employees, not owners of firms.... Viewed from the vantage point of classical [economic] theory, they have no reason to maximize the profits of the firms, except to the extent that they can be controlled by owners.... Moreover, there is no difference, in this respect, among profit-making firms, non-profit organizations, and bureaucratic organizations. All have exactly the same problem of inducing their employees to work toward the organizational goals. There is no reason, a priori, why it should be easier (or harder) to produce this motivation in organizations aimed at maximizing profits than in organizations with different goals. *The conclusion that organizations motivated by profits will be more efficient than other organizations does not follow in an organizational economy from the neoclassical assumptions. If it is empirically true, other axioms will have to be introduced to account for it.* (emphasis added)[2]

Making the Relevant Comparisons: Inefficiency in Administrative Activity
One of the reasons that it is difficult to find convincing empirical evidence[3] concerning the relative inefficiency of government is that, by and large, the public sector produces different goods and is engaged in different economic activities than the private. While detailed studies of those few instances where direct comparisons might be relevant—such as garbage collection—are of some interest, they do not provide direct evidence to the relative efficiency of government in the kinds of services in which it is primarily engaged. In most of these services output measures are notoriously difficult to come by. This is not only true of the administrative activities that occupy many government bureaucrats but also of education, and even defense.

Private sector performance in administrative areas too is often criticized for inefficiency: Try getting a refund from an airline or collecting money for lost luggage. I suspect that the Internal Revenue Service processes claims faster than many airlines.

There are theoretical reasons why we might not be surprised at the seeming widespread inefficiency in both the public and private sectors in administrative work. Standard economic theory has emphasized the importance of incentives. Implementing incentives in administrative activities is no easy matter.

We need to distinguish between incentives at the organizational level and at the individual level, though some of the problems in designing incentive structures are common to both. We need to ask how, for the kinds of activities the public sector engages in, the organization is rewarded for "success" or punished for lack of it, and how individuals are similarly rewarded and punished.

Multiple Objectives
The first problem is determining what is meant by success. What are the objectives of the organization? What tasks is the individual supposed to perform? Problems arise because, in general, there are *multiple objectives*. A school is supposed not only to impart knowledge but to build citizenship. An employee is supposed not only to produce goods but to train new

employees. Traditionally firms have an unambiguous objective: to maximize profits. Were there a complete set of prices (for all dates, all states of nature), there would be no ambiguity about what this would entail. But there is not. Firms (or more accurately, firm managers) must make decisions about short-run profits versus long-run profits, about risk versus safety. There will not, in general, be unanimity concerning the weights to be attached to the various objectives that the organization should pursue.[4]

Measuring Outputs

Second, there are difficulties in *measuring outputs*, in ascertaining how successful the organization or individual has been in attaining any of its objectives. In the case of firms there are some well-defined criteria—the effect on the firms' market value or profits. (These are not synonymous, and the conflict between the two illustrates the problem of multiple objectives. Managers might, by releasing misleading information, increase the current market value, but this might have adverse effects on market value and profits in the long run. Practical illustrations of this conflict were noted in earlier chapters where I discussed the tax paradoxes, cases where firms took actions that increased current reported profits, increasing current market value but at the same time the present discounted value of tax liabilities.)

While in the case of firms organizational goals like maximizing value or profits can easily be quantified, in the case of many public organizations measuring performance of goals is not so easy. How are we to measure the success of an educational institution? Certainly scores on standardized tests do not even measure well such narrowly defined objectives as contributions to an individual's earning capacity (human capital).

In the case of subunits, such as the administrative department of a firm or some unit in the government bureaucracy, again there may be no good measure of output. The number of pieces of paper processed is not a good surrogate for the achievement of the true purposes of the organization.

Measuring the Contributions of Individuals and Suborganizations to Organizational Output

But the problems do not stop here: Even were it possible to measure the organization's performance, ascertaining the individual's or the suborganization's contribution to that performance is frequently an almost impossible task. Every firm needs an administrative staff, but how can we assess the marginal contribution of that staff? Some studies suggest that when the head of an organization dies, on average the value of the firm increases. Does this mean that his or her marginal contribution was negative? Among the more important administrative functions in both the private and public sectors are those which I will simply refer to as *management*—selecting the members of the organization, organizing them in productive ways, assigning them to tasks based on comparative advantage, motivating them to do well (whether by incentive structures or other means), and so on. As I noted earlier, the fraction of firm's incremental value captured by management—that is, the strength of managerial incentives—is quite weak. While there is a wide range in these estimates, the consensus is that at most managers get but a few percent of the returns from their efforts. This is perhaps understandable, given that measured output (the short-run increase in market value) is a noisy measure of the firm's objective (which may be more concerned with long-run performance) and given that there is such a weak link between what management does and the firm's value.

Measuring Inputs

Finally, there are administrative activities to consider; just as output is difficult to measure, so too is input. We can measure time, but we cannot measure effort. Output is often not closely linked with effort so that output cannot be used as a good surrogate for input. Even when actions are observable, ascertaining how much credit should be given for each is hard. Some of the tasks to be undertaken may be difficult and time-consuming; others may be simple. Even in manufacturing, where output is often well defined, piece rate systems run into difficulty because over time, with technological change, the effort required to produce a given output changes. This necessitates changing the piece rate, a process that, to say the least, can be contentious.

Rent-Seeking Activities: Private and Public

There is a large literature that focuses on the role of rent seeking within the public sector, and it attributes the inefficiency of public sector activities to this rent seeking. Rent seeking is obviously important[5] within the public sector: Special interest groups and bureaucrats have incentives to use the powers of the state to divert resources to themselves. Many of the constraints on employment practices can be interpreted as attempts to limit the rents available, and thus the extent of rent-seeking activity. But we now realize that rent seeking also goes on within the private sector. In the older theory where owners of firms perfectly monitor and control those who work for them, this cannot occur. Workers or managers who tried to divert resources of the firm to their own benefits—to get more than the value of their marginal product—would be fired instantly. In the new theory of the firm, emphasizing owners' imperfect control over managers, managers can, and do, divert firm resources to their own benefit; they are engaged in rent seeking, gains to themselves at the expense of shareholders.[6]

Informational constraints not only limit the ability of shareholders to control rent-seeking behavior on the part of top managers, they also limit the ability of top managers to control rent-seeking behavior on the part of their subordinates. How much of the time spent by a middle-level manager to prepare a report was absolutely necessary? To what extent was it devoted to acquiring information, of marginal value to the firm, but which would make that manager look relatively good compared to other managers? To what extent are the efforts and resources spent by a manager to cultivate a client really being directed to enhance that manager's job opportunities? Private and organizational objectives are intricately intertwined, and in many cases they are not conflicting. But at the margin they frequently are, and there seems little reason to doubt that private objectives frequently, perhaps usually, win out.[7]

The Distinguishing Features of Public Sector Activity: Lack of Competition and Difficulties in Making Commitments

The force of the argument so far has been that (1) what scanty evidence we have concerning the relative efficiency of the different modes of production is ambiguous—particularly when account is taken of the *nature* of the activities involved—and (2) there are theoretical reasons for suggesting considerable similarity. Both face delegation problems, in both limited use of incentive schemes is employed, and in both rent seeking is prevalent. Yet I do think that the popular prejudice is, by and large, correct: *Private sector activities, while not necessarily more efficient, are on average so.* The question is why? I would argue that the distinguishing features of the private sector, which accounts for the fact that government activities are, frequently, if not in general, less efficient are

1. competition in the public sector is weaker,

2. the threat of termination of the organization—the threat of bankruptcy in the case of private firms—is weaker,

3. government enterprises often face additional constraints not imposed on private sector firms,

4. government often faces problems making commitments.

The Role of Competition

Chapter 7 argued for the importance of competition. Monopolies, whether in the public or private sector, are frequently inefficient.[8] Perhaps the most telling example, to which I referred earlier, is the study comparing the performance of the Canadian National Railways and the Canadian Pacific Railways, one public, one private, which compete against each other. There is no evidence that the state enterprise was less efficient than the private. The discussion of earlier chapters, on the importance of incentives and the role of competition in providing incentives, makes such results not unexpected.

Commitments to Hard Budget Constraints

We have also repeatedly referred to the problems that the government has in making credible commitments. Perhaps the most important commitment is to terminate inefficient enterprises. In a private market economy firms face hard budget constraints: If they are unable to compete effectively, to sell their goods at prices that exceed the average costs of production, they cease functioning. Incompetent firms thus get eliminated. There is no automatic selection mechanism working within the public sector. Indeed in many public enterprises financial and social objectives get mixed up, making it difficult to tell whether a firm is being efficient. If a steel company is instructed to keep a plant open, to avoid the loss of jobs, and then records a loss, it will try to attribute its loss not to a lack of efficiency, but to these external constraints imposed upon it. We then replace hard budget constraints with soft budget constraints: The firm appeals to the government to cover any losses.

Implications for Incentives

Earlier I referred to the importance of organizational incentives, the carrots that organizations receive for performing well, and the sticks, for poor performance. In the market economy there is a big stick: bankruptcy. With soft budget constraints there is no comparable incentive device in government enterprises.

Further Consequences of Limitations on Ability to Make Commitments

The difficulty government has in making commitments has further consequences. The importance of contracts—binding commitments between two parties—is important for the functioning of capitalist economies; otherwise, intertemporal trade is virtually impossible. Government ensures that others live up to their contractual commitments. But who is to ensure that the government lives up to any commitments it makes? Moreover a basic principle of democratic government is that each government is sovereign, each has the right to make its own decisions.[9]

Are These Limitations Inherent?
Some of these widely observed limitations of government, I would suggest, are not *inherent*. Government can allow, perhaps even encourage, competition, either with private sector firms or among governmental units. Government can create government enterprises that are given hard budget constraints; it can set up a set of procedures that can at least increase the transactions costs associated with softening the budget constraint. It can impose procedures and rules that *effectively* increase the ability of government enterprises to make commitments. Government-owned corporations can be made to have the same legal status of privately owned corporations, differing only in who owns the shares. While these changes will not obliterate the differences between private and public enterprises, they will reduce the differences, to the point where behavior will be indistinguishable.

The Distinguishing Features of Government: Fiduciary and Equity Constraints

So far I have emphasized the absence of constraints on the public sector that the private sector faces: the constraints imposed by competition and the threat of bankruptcy (hard budget constraints). To make matters worse, the public sector faces constraints that the private sector does not. These constraints arise, as I noted briefly earlier, from the greater powers of government: The fact that the government has the power of compulsion, to force individuals to pay taxes, means that constraints have to be imposed in order that those powers not be abused. Among the resulting constraints are those attempting to ensure equity and the proper exercise of government's fiduciary role.

Information and Equity Constraints
To a large extent the problems that these constraints engender arise from imperfect information. In the world of neoclassical economics it would be easy to determine whether or not government was abusing its powers. In the world of imperfect information—the world we live in, and upon which I have focused in this discussion—it is not so easy.

Mistakes

Consider first the problem of mistakes. The public outcry when a mistake is detected is understandable: It is their money that is being wasted. (They may even suspect that the mistake was not an accident: There was a diversion of funds. An incompetent contractor got the job because of a payoff.) Voters do not see the costs that would have to be incurred—and are incurred—to make such mistakes less likely. Businesses can take a more cold-hearted look at the matter. They balance out the costs and benefits of mistakes. In some cases they can be quite explicit about the trade-offs: One can obtain a more reliable product though at a higher cost. The market responds to consumer evaluations of the trade-off. But in the public sphere, the link is harder to see, partly because costs and benefits are often borne by different individuals.

In an interview with one major manufacturer of jet engines for airplanes, the firm reported significantly higher costs for making precisely the same engine for the government than for the private sector. Government engines cost 30 to 50 percent more. These were engines that were of exactly the same design. The government, however, wanted to make sure that there were no mistakes, and that none of the money that was to be spent on the engine was spent on anything else. The government monitored the private firm closely and imposed many rules designed to prevent waste and mistakes. The lesson seems to be that it is expensive to save money: One can spend more than a dollar to ensure that a dollar is not wasted. Because it is difficult to distinguish among mistakes indicating incompetence, mistakes reflecting optimal decisions with respect to monitoring, and mistakes representing a true violation of fiduciary responsibility, and because the costs of the mistakes, when they are detected, are borne by politicians, while the costs of preventing the mistakes are borne by the populace, there is, I suspect, an excessive concern about mistakes within the public sector.

Inequities

Among the "mistakes" that most arouse public ire are those associated with inequities. Any of us with more than one child knows the importance of issues of equity. No charge is heard more often than "It's not fair." (Indeed I cannot recall an occasion on which I have heard the complaint, "It's not efficient.") Most of us—having passed on to the role of the parent—quickly grasp that fairness, like beauty, is in the eye of the beholder. All sides can, simultaneously and quite righteously, claim to have been unfairly treated.

The greater powers of government—its power to tax—lead to a strong obligation, in democratic societies, that the funds so raised be spent equitably. No one wants—or would stand for—their child being treated different from another child of equal ability. To ensure that funds are spent equitably, we impose significant constraints on government, constraints that in many cases interfere significantly with economic efficiency.

Competition and Equity
The absence of competition exacerbates concerns about equity. There is a choice of airlines. If a person thinks that an airline has unfairly treated him—being assigned an undesirable seat, for example—the option is open to use another airline. The fact that such inequities may also arise in the private sector teach one an important lesson: Perceived (and perhaps actual) inequities are inevitable. But when the government has a state monopoly on some activity, there is nowhere to turn in the event of an inequity.

Constraints on Wages
Constraints imposed on salaries are an example of such equity-driven constraints facing the government that arise from imperfect information. It is difficult for the general populace to ascertain whether a particular person's productivity is so high that it is actually efficient for the government to pay her $500,000 a year. Such a salary would instantaneously arouse suspicions of rents—rents even beyond the minimum required by efficiency wage theory to ensure that she puts out a high level of effort. Such a salary might even arouse suspicions of kickbacks, bribery, or other such scandalous activity.

When one government official decides to pay her that salary, it does not come out of that individual's pocket but out of the pocket of the public, and that is the fundamental difference between attitudes toward high salaries within the public and private sectors. When a private firm pays her that salary, there is a presumption that the firm would not pay that much unless she were worth it, since the money comes directly out of the firm's pocket. If the firm is incorrect in its judgment, it bears the cost. This is quite different than when taxpayers are *compelled* to pay the cost.[10]

There may be a high cost to these constraints. For instance, we now recognize that firms often pay wages in excess of opportunity costs (the efficiency wage theory).[11] Higher wages lead to greater effort; they motivate workers to work harder. At the very least, the threat of being fired becomes more effective because the cost of being fired is greater. Higher wages lead to reduced labor turnover. Higher wages lead to larger applicant pools, from which employers can select higher-ability employees who are better matched to the needs of the firm.

The efficiency wage is the wage that minimizes total labor costs, taking account of the benefits of paying higher wages. The problem is that there is no easy way of ascertaining whether a government agency is paying a higher wage because (1) the worker's opportunity wage is high, (2) the "efficiency wage" is high, or (3) the worker is simply receiving pure rents. Accordingly civil service rules restrict the ability of government agencies setting wages. That implies that the government cannot pay efficiency wages, even when it would pay to do so, and it cannot hire high-wage individuals, even when their higher productivity would more than warrant the higher wage.

Concern about abuses of power similarly have led to civil service regulations that restrict the ability to fire workers. Thus government is unable to provide effective incentives—either the carrot of high pay for high performance or the stick of termination for low performance.[12]

While the existence of constraints on government induced by the concern for equity and the abuse of its fiduciary responsibilities is inevitable, the strength of those constraints is not. The issue is one of trade-offs: If we were somewhat more relaxed about possible inequities, that one person might get a little more than another, might we gain significantly in economic efficiency? We have no hard evidence on this matter, but I am inclined to believe that we have indeed gone too far. Just as greater tolerance of mistakes—or more accurately, the recognition that mistakes are inevitable and costly to avoid—would enhance the efficiency and effectiveness of public organizations, so too would greater tolerance of inequities—or more accurately, the recognition that (perceived) inequities are inevitable and costly to avoid.

Government and the Capital Market

The third empirical generalization is that almost all governments have played a central role in capital markets. Earlier I referred to the fact that capital markets are almost always imperfect. They are concerned with the allocation of capital. The problem of allocating capital is an important and interesting one, precisely because there is imperfect information. If we knew exactly the outcome from each investment project, if we knew precisely the managerial abilities of each firm, then decisions about the allocation of capital would be trivial. Capital markets are concerned with information, and markets for information do not work perfectly, at least not in the way that the standard neoclassical model suggests.

Government and Direct Production

Finally, as I noted earlier, governments in almost all countries have assumed some direct role in production. Perhaps the most dramatic re-thinking of the role of the state during the past decade has been with respect to these roles.

The Failure of Regulation and Deregulation

On the one hand, the deregulation movement questioned the ability of the government to exercise efficient indirect control over private firms. For a while some economists thought that such indirect control was unnecessary: Efficient outcomes could be obtained with potential competition, and in the absence of government barriers, potential competition was essentially always present. These conclusions must now be viewed as suspect: The theoretical arguments presented in chapter 7 (the presence of even small sunk costs vitiate these conclusions) and the experience within the United States following the deregulation of the airlines have shown that unre-gulated markets may face serious problems and that profits may not be driven to zero. Still doubts about the capacity of the government to regulate effectively, and in the general interest, are sufficiently strong that the failures of deregulation have not led to a strong feeling (among economists) that there should be reregulation. We live in an imperfect world in which often we face nothing but the choice of the lesser of two evils!

On the Scope of Public Production

While confidence in the efficiency of private markets left to themselves may have waned during the past half-century, so too has confidence in government's ability to regulate private producers, and confidence in gov-ernment's capabilities as a producer has waned even more. The last decade has seen a strong movement toward privatization. Ultimately the problems to which I have referred repeatedly—inadequate incentives, caused by soft budget constraints and restrictions on acceptable compensation and firing policies, and lack of decentralization and competition—lie behind the fail-ure of government enterprises; but of these at least the two last limitations do not appear to be inherent in government action.

While there is by now general rejection of the view that there are any marked advantages of government ownership of the essential means of production, there is still a consensus that the government should not contract out for military services. In between there remains a debate about the scope of government: its role in activities like education and health. Within the United States there was a strong movement (supported by President George Bush) for a voucher system in education, where the government would provide a voucher that could be used at either a public or a private school to pay for educational services. Were it adopted, the system would likely result in a major shift from public to private production of elementary and secondary education.

General Principles

The major argument for the private provision of such services is that government is less efficient; the major argument against it is that private production cannot be used to reflect adequately social objectives. I have dwelled at length on the uneasy case for government inefficiency. Let me turn briefly to the second issue, the problem of adequately reflecting social objectives.

Again I want to stress the link between the view of the government's appropriate role, and the models we have, until recently, employed to describe the economy. *If* there were a complete set of markets, *if* compliance with a contract were costlessly enforceable . . . then there would be no problem of the government using markets to implement social objectives. There might indeed be discrepancies between *free* market solutions and socially desirable outcomes—the unfettered market might produce too much pollution. But it would be an easy matter to correct that distortion, by the imposition of Pigouvian taxes. No change in economic organization is required.

How can we use the price system to guide a private contractor to fulfill national objectives with respect to defense, particularly in time of war? We have explained why there is not a complete set of securities for all risks. Surely it would be impossible for the government to figure out the complete set of state-contingent securities, which would convey through the price system the government's attitudes toward all the risks that the society might face. By the same token, it would be impossible for the government to write a complete contract, specifying what the contractor should do in every contingency. Or consider the problem posed by the limitations on liability. What would happen if the costs of providing the services for which the producer had contracted were far in excess of what was estimated. The producer might simply renege on the contract. The social losses that might arise from failure to provide adequate defense could be astronomical—far in excess of any bond that a private producer could conceivably post to ensure performance. With feasible penalties for failure that are dwarfed by the social losses that would result from failure, private producers cannot be induced through monetary means to invest the appropriate level of effort to prevent failure.

When a failure occurs, it is difficult to tell whether it is because of a lack of effort on the part of a contractor or because of an event outside its control. So long as incentives for avoiding failures are attenuated, there will be a suspicion that it is lack of effort. But so long as effort cannot be monitored very accurately, it is not possible to design contracts to reward contractors on the basis of their efforts rather than their performance. (More accurately, given risk aversion, the cost to the public for relying heavily on noisy input or even output signals is sufficiently great that only limited reliance on input or output measures is employed.)

The list of comparative strengths and weaknesses of government and private production noted so far is not meant to be exhaustive. Another issue frequently raised concerns monitoring: Often with private production the system of monitoring is more effective. When households contract directly for the purchase of garbage removal services, they have an incentive to make sure that the job gets done right. When the service is provided publicly, then it is likely that it is provided uniformly. In that case there is a free-rider problem. If the service improves for me, it improves for everyone. Everyone hopes that someone else will put out the effort required to improve the quality of service. For the most part, however, differences in monitoring relate more to the nature of the good being produced than to how it is provided. When it is a publicly provided private good, such as garbage collection, then private monitoring is feasible, and even when it is publicly provided, there is often a strong feedback from the recipient to the provider. When it is a publicly provided public good, like defense, private monitoring is, to say the least, more difficult.

This brings us back to the theme struck earlier in this chapter: Much of the difference between public and private sector efficiency is related to the nature of the service that is being provided. Efficiency problems are more likely to arise in administrative activities, where monitoring is more difficult, and in the provision of public goods, where free-rider problems in monitoring arise.

Yet there are differences, for instance, in the constraints facing each sectors, and not surprisingly, these constraints result in differences in behavior. Our central concern should be first to understand those areas in which government is likely to have an advantage, and second, recognizing the disadvantages facing government, to see how government programs can be designed that suffer least from those disadvantages, while at the same time reaping whatever advantages might arise from government involvement.

For public services like defense there are fundamental problems with "contracting out" (i.e., using private production) that limit its scope. Some public production is inevitable. This does not mean, however, that the present "assignments" are correct: There may be scope for more private production (current estimates are that around a quarter of defense expenditures are contracted out), or it might conceivably be more efficient for more of production to occur within public firms.

Education: A Case Study

Many of the issues I have raised in this section are well illustrated by education. Whether in the public or private sector, financial incentives play a relatively small role for the workers (teachers) and the managers (principals and superintendents.) Whether in the public or private sector, almost no one's pay is based on performance.

Because the output of educational institutions is difficult to observe, "mistakes" and inefficiencies—in the conventional sense of those terms—are hard to detect. Inequities in resource allocations are easy to observe. Hence attention is directed to avoiding those.

I mentioned earlier that in the United States there has been a small, but determined, effort to introduce a voucher scheme—the vouchers could be used at either public or private schools—that would allow individuals to make choices. Proponents argue that one should let the market work. Markets for education, critics claim, are not like markets for standard goods. In this, they are undoubtedly right. The assumptions of well-informed consumers buying homogeneous commodities in perfectly competitive markets, necessary to obtain the standard efficiency results associated with competitive markets, simply do not seem relevant to education markets.

I believe that competition would be beneficial for education. But in arguing for competition, I do not rely on the weak analogy between education and other commodities, for which competition can be shown to ensure efficient outcomes. Rather, I see competition as a way of resolving what would, in conventional terms, be viewed as market failures, such as the inability to design financial incentive schemes that effectively reward either inputs or outputs, and the lack of information about the technology making it difficult to know whether or not an organization is efficient.

We now understand clearly the distinction between public funding and public production. While there are good arguments for public funding of education, the argument that public funds should be used almost exclusively (in the United States) for publicly produced education seems far less compelling. Even if, for some reason or other, we restrict funds to publicly produced education, there is no reason why we cannot reorganize the educational system to allow for more interschool competition and choice.

Concluding Remarks

In this chapter I have attempted to put into perspective the issue of the role of the government in production. The socialist-versus-market debate posed the question the wrong way. The correct question is not which mode of production is superior, but what are the comparative advantages of each sector, what should be the appropriate scope of each? In defining the appropriate scope for each, one needs to take into account the scope for, and limitations of, government regulation of private production, as well as the limitations on its control of public production (as anomalous as that might seem).

Government is different from private organizations. It has powers they do not. The existence of those powers leads to constraints, constraints that the private sector does not face. These powers and constraints give rise to natural comparative advantages: Certain economic activities may be assigned more effectively to one sector or to another. An important objective of the economics of the public sector is to discover those comparative advantages.

At the same time I have noted that *some* of the differences between the public and private sector may have been exaggerated—they are differences among the activities being pursued, not differences of the sector within which they are pursued. Private sector organizations face incentive (principal-agent) problems no less than do public organizations.

Some of the differences are not innate but are more a consequence of common practice. The most important of these is the absence of competition and the high degree of centralization. Government organizations no less than private organizations dislike competition. The difference is the government has the power to forbid competition, which private organizations do not—and indeed government sees one of its roles as curbing unfair practices aimed at reducing competition.

I have described how the constraints imposed on government, in response to its greater powers, naturally lead to a focus on equity and avoiding mistakes, concerns that in turn lead to bureaucratic red tape and inefficiency. Because the system does not appropriately take into account the costs of ensuring equity and avoiding mistakes, I have argued that concerns about equity and avoiding mistakes are *excessive*. I suspect that verbal injunctions to public organizations to be more balanced, to take costs as well as benefits into account, are unlikely to have much effect. The economic environment in which public organizations operate must be changed for individual and organizational behavior to change. The environmental change that would have the most dramatic, and I think effective, results would be inducing more competition. Even short of that, there are alterations that would improve the efficiency and effectiveness of the public sector. A more widespread recognition of some of the trade-offs that I have identified in this chapter would be a good place to start.

14   Five Myths about Markets and Market Socialism

Among academic circles, at least in America, there has been little debate for decades over the need or role for socialism. Convinced by the success of capitalist economies, a belief reinforced by the most stunning intellectual triumph of economic theory—the fundamental theorems of welfare economics—why spend one's time trying to answer the concerns of thinkers of an earlier generation? Yet outside these circles there remain lingering doubts about markets, doubts that, in some sense, the earlier theorems have done little to resolve. As I have emphasized, if we wish to be helpful to those seeking a new basis for their economy, we cannot simply resort to ideology.

It may be helpful, at this juncture, if I address directly some widespread myths that have confused discussions aimed at attempting to define an appropriate role for the government. In discussing these myths, I hope that I can convey a better sense of what the new information economics paradigm says about how the economy functions. This discussion will repeat several of the notes and themes already struck, but I hope that this restatement, focusing on these widely believed myths, will help sharpen our perspective.

The Pricing Myth

The first myth, to which I have already alluded briefly, is that economic relations in capitalist economies are governed primarily by prices. There are several senses in which this is a myth. First, it ignores the large fraction of economic activity that occurs within firms, economic activity that is governed only to a limited extent by prices. We need to recall that the size of the largest capitalist firms exceeds that of many economies. Second, it ignores the many nonprice sources of information used by firms. Firms look at quantitative data—like what is happening to their inventories, and the inventories of other firms. Third, it ignores the many nonprice aspects of economic transactions between unrelated parties: the role, for instance, of reputations and contracts which I emphasized in earlier chapters.

But there are further reasons why economic relations cannot simply be governed by prices. Earlier I discussed a variety of nondecentralizability results. These results say, in effect, that economic relations cannot be (optimally) governed through *linear* price relationships. For instance, optimal incentive schemes entail, in general, payments that are nonlinear functions of output. Such nonlinear schemes are often hard to implement, and may not be robust to changes in the underlying environmental parameters. Nonprice (quantity) relations may be preferable to linear price relations.[1]

The Myth of Socialized Industries

Earlier I discussed the objection to private ownership, that private firms pursued their objectives at the expense of public objectives. While the fundamental theorems of welfare economics are directed at correcting this misconception, there is a corresponding myth, that state enterprises pursue "social" objectives. There is an enormous disparity here between ideology and reality. As I noted earlier, state enterprises are frequently more interested in improving the welfare of their workers (and managers) than in pursuing national objectives (however those might be defined). Thus it comes as no surprise that the least safe atomic energy plants in the United States are those run by the government, that state enterprises (including the Department of Defense) have at times been among those most ardently opposed to more stringent pollution laws, that pollution by state enterprises in the socialist bloc has been far worse than in the West, and that state enterprises have been accused of sex discrimination, just as have private enterprises.

The principal-agent literature, to which I referred earlier, provides a framework within which we can understand these problems: Those involved in making decisions maximize their own payoffs, and those payoffs are seldom coincident with more broadly conceived social objectives. (Of course some of the problems arise from the fact that it is not easy or even feasible to design managerial payoffs that adequately reflect social objectives; were it easy to translate social objectives into quantifiable criteria that could be used as a basis of compensation, then presumably the government could obtain those objectives *without* resort to public ownership, by the use of Pigouvian taxes. But some of the problems, e.g., those concerned with pollution, cannot be explained away on this basis.)

The Planning Myth

Another standard criticism of market economies (within the socialist tradition) is that markets cannot plan, and without planning, one cannot obtain efficient resource allocations. In earlier days economists might have responded that prices provide the coordinating mechanism. But the new paradigm has laid to rest this response: Markets can, at best, perform these tasks imperfectly without a complete set of futures and risk markets.

Nonetheless, the criticism of the market is to a large extent misplaced. In market economies there is planning and coordination—the planning occurs within firms, and there is extensive coordination among firms. The issue is not whether there is planning, but rather the locus of planning. When US Steel decided to build its plant on the southern shores of Lake Michigan, it did extensive planning. It made forecasts of future demand. It coordinated the construction of railroads, the opening of iron ore mines, the construction of housing, the expansion of limestone quarries, and the development of shipping facilities.

In an open economy the material balance equations, which were the focus of old planning models, become largely irrelevant, and in any case, the level of aggregation required for countrywide planning models may be of limited use for the development of particular projects. Firms need to know not just that there will be steel available; they need to know the particular kind of steel. (This is parallel to the point made in chapter 6, that the information contained in price signals in the stock market had only limited relevance for investment decisions.)

Within the industrial sector, producers, their suppliers, and their customers, all coordinate decisions through informal networks (and sometimes through formal contracts). When planning is concentrated at the very "local" level, those who have the detailed knowledge of production capabilities and potential needs interact, in a way that simply cannot occur within a countrywide planning framework.

The Centralization Myth

The question of the choice of an economic system often focuses on the extent to which decisions are made in a decentralized or centralized manner. We contrast the "centralization" within the (former) socialist system with the decentralization within the market economy.

As with the planning myth, the distinction may be overdrawn: All societies involve *some* decentralization. It would be impossible for *all* the information required for all decision making to be concentrated in the hands of any single individual. Some decisions, even in the most centralized societies, occur in a decentralized manner.

By the same token, in even the most decentralized of market economies, there are firms that employ, within themselves, a fair degree of centralized control. Thus the issue is not *whether* there should be decentralization, but how much and in what form. This is not to say, of course, that there are not many differences among alternative forms of decision structures, a point I hope I argued forcefully in chapter 9.

The work to which I referred earlier addresses many of the traditional arguments for centralization. Those advocating centralization and hierarchical decision structures worry about the duplication that can result in "polyarchical" (decentralized) structures. They worry about the problems of coordination, and the failure to internalize externalities, and they worry about the absence of "checks" on the adoption of bad projects. (The more recent literature on the economics of information has identified a broader range of externalitylike effects that arise whenever information is imperfect or markets incomplete.[2])

Yet the thrust of that work was that there are offsetting advantages of decentralization: the diversification of risk, the absence of bureaucratic waste, the multitude of opportunities provided by polyarchic organizations (the opportunities for a second chance), and the ability that it provides for competition, which can be used as a basis of both selection and incentives.

The mixture of polyarchical and hierarchical organizations that we observe in market economies reflects the advantages and disadvantages of these alternative modes of organizing decision making. (I do not, however, want to suggest that the particular mix we observe is optimal.) Firms and the government seem always to be struggling to find the balance that is appropriate for the particular conditions facing them.

The Property Myth

Perhaps no myth in economics has held such sway as that which I will refer to as the *property myth*. This myth holds that *all* that one has to do is correctly assign property rights, and economic efficiency is assured. How property rights are assigned makes no difference, except for the distribution of welfare, and if one is dissatisfied with that, one can easily remedy the matter, by lump-sum transfers. This myth is a dangerous one because it has misled many of the countries engaged in transition to focus on property rights issues, on privatization, rather than a broader set of issues (of the sort discussed in the next chapter). In the preceding chapters I have explained why resolving property rights is certainly not sufficient, and may not even be necessary.

The Myth of the Two Ways

The final myth that I want to dispose of has played a prominent role in recent discussions. As I suggested earlier, the seeming failure of market socialism has led many to conclude that there is no third way between the two extremes of markets and state enterprises. As the popular joke puts it, you can't be a little bit pregnant! I want to suggest that this way of framing the question is misleading. The fact of the matter is that government plays a prominent role in all societies. The question is not *whether* there will be government involvement in economic activity but what that role should be.

Moreover the way the question is usually posed does not give appropriate attention to institutional arrangements that do not fall squarely within the two "extremes." Let me illustrate by noting several "intermediate" institutional arrangements.

In recent years there has developed a large literature on local public goods and clubs, the voluntary agglomeration of individuals to pursue common interests. In the United States nonprofit organizations play a prominent role. In many other economies cooperatives are important. Even in the United States they have played an increasingly important role in joint ventures in research.

The problems encountered by "worker cooperatives" in Yugoslavia— and the forced so-called cooperatives in many so-called socialist economies —has perhaps dampened enthusiasm for these intermediate institutional arrangements. But that should not detract from the role that these institutions can potentially play in an economy. There are local public goods, which can most efficiently be provided by local communities.[3] The organization of these intermediate institutions is often a public good itself, and it may be an appropriate role for the central government to facilitate (though not coerce) their organization.

Still another example of a intermediate way is provided by the countries of East Asia, whose remarkable economic performance over the past two decades has attracted so much attention. There is a widespread consensus that government played an active role, a far more active role than that of governments in most of the developed countries. In most of the East Asian countries, they created marketlike institutions, such as banks. In some, such as Korea, they controlled the allocation of much of the capital. Even today the government there appoints the heads of all the private banks. They encouraged private firms to undertake certain activities (and used economic instruments, both carrots and sticks, to obtain private sector cooperation). When the private sector did not undertake the desired activities, they undertook them: Both Korea and Taiwan constructed highly efficient steel mills. They picked entrepreneurs to undertake some projects and lent them the requisite capital.[4] Government interventions were, if not heavy-handed, at least ubiquitous.

We are increasingly recognizing the diversity of capitalist institutions. I noted earlier the marked differences in financial institutions among the United States, Germany, and Japan. There are differences in educational systems and in legal systems. There are differences in the welfare systems, the extent of redistribution undertaken by the government, the safety net it provides, the size of the public sector, and the range of activities that it undertakes. These different institutional structures may have a profound effect on how the economy functions. It is not apparent at this stage that one of these systems is unambiguously better than the others. There are real choices to be made.

15   Some Tentative
Recommendations

The problems facing the former socialist economies, as they try decide which roads to take, are so fascinating and of such importance that it is hard to resist the temptation, to offer advice if asked—or to speculate about what one would advice, were one asked. I have not resisted that temptation. (But the advice may be worth roughly what the countries may be paying for it—nothing, or next to nothing—perhaps the first hard lesson of market economics.)

In chapters 10 and 12, I have discussed a range of issues associated with privatization and the reform of the financial system. Here I want to take a broader perspective. My principle objective in these lectures has been to explain, from the information-theoretic perspective, the inadequacies of the conventional paradigm and to suggest that the perspectives on comparative economic systems provided by the conventional paradigm are fundamentally misguided. Here I want to strike a somewhat more positive note: to ascertain what lessons, if any, can be drawn out of the new economics of information. There are seven lessons which I tentatively, cautiously, and speculatively put forward. They are "informed" by economic science, but they are not general propositions and universal generalizations derived within economic science. To a large extent they repeat themes already struck within these lectures.

On the Central Importance of Competition

The first is to emphasize the importance of competition—not pure price competition but simply old-fashioned competition, the rivalry among firms to supply the needs of consumers and producers at the lowest price with the highest qualities. As I argued in earlier chapters, the difference between competition and monopoly is the distinction of first-order importance, rather than the distinction between private and state ownership. (The two issues may of course not be completely unrelated: It may be hard for the government to commit itself to competition, when it "owns" the state enterprise and has the power to exclude competition, but these are political economy matters, to which I will come shortly.)

The distinction between monopoly and competition may also be more important than the distinction between allowing free trade or not. Free trade is important in a small economy because it provides the discipline of competition, a discipline that the country's own market may not be able to supply, simply because there are too few firms. But there may be cases where there is sufficient internal competition and where, apart from political economy concerns, I think a convincing "infant industry" case for protection might be made.[1,2]

Thus the first objective of state economic policy is to ensure competition. This needs to be taken into account in the process of privatization or reorganizing state enterprises, as well as in the laws allowing the formation of firms, cooperatives, and partnerships. The government must take actions to minimize the barriers to entry.

In the United States and other Western economies, governments have imposed a variety of taxes and regulations that serve as an important impediment to small firms. While these impediments have a significant cost to these more advanced countries, the costs to the former socialist economies—beginning with virtually no competitive structures—may be far greater.

At the same time it is important, as the former socialist economies draw up the "rules of the game" by which firms will play in the future, that they include within those rules effective antitrust policies. They must not succumb to the argument that to compete effectively on international markets, large enterprises are required, and therefore antitrust policies should be shunted aside. Taiwan has shown that one can have rapid growth without relying on large enterprises. Korea has shown that *if* there are advantages to large enterprises, one can attain those advantages and still have competition among the large enterprises. In any case for years to come there will be few enterprises within most of the former socialist economies which, based on domestic production alone, might attain a scale comparable to the larger firms in the OECD. But, as I emphasized earlier, there is another danger: that of excessive concern about monopoly, attributing all profits to monopolistic behavior and, under the ruse of protecting consumers from rapacious monopolists, reinstituting state-controlled regimes.

On the Importance of Establishing and Enforcing the Rules of the Game

I argued earlier that the appropriate way the question should be framed is not markets versus government, but the appropriate balance between the two. There is one vital role that the government must perform in any economy, and that is establishing the rules of the game—rules that will govern both the interactions among private parties and between these private parties and the government.

The importance of this should be evident both from the theory to which I referred earlier, as well as from historical experience (though I did not include this in my short list of major historical generalizations): An inadequate legal system has been, and remains, a major impediment to development in many countries.

In my theoretical discussion I emphasized the importance of contracts within the market system. (Most transactions do not involve contemporaneous trades; one party gives up something today in return for a promise in the future. It is essential that those promises be fulfilled, and that disputes about whether contracts are fulfilled be equitably and efficiently resolved.) I have also emphasized the importance of competition. Again the "rules of the game"—the antitrust laws—need to be specified.

Another related set of regulations pertains to financial markets. Different economies have chosen to regulate their financial institutions in different ways, with important differential effects. In the United States concern about antitrust problems has resulted in strong constraints being imposed on the activities of banks and similar holding companies, constraints that have not been imposed in Japan. Yet despite the heavy dose of regulation (though some would say because of it) the financial institutions in the United States spent much of the 1980s in a precarious state, and there is considerable evidence that they have not done a good job in allocating resources. By the same token, the experience of Chile—as well as the general theories of financial markets, based on imperfect information—has made it clear that an unregulated banking system can be an absolute disaster.

Some of those in favor of a quick transition argue that more important than determining *which* set of rules is fixing on some set of rules: Uncertainties about the rules of the game will impede the economy. There is considerable truth, I think, in that conclusion. But at the same time, there are sunk costs associated with establishing rules, and once rules have been established, they are difficult to change. Changes involve not only large transactions costs but may have large distributional consequences. Hence it is important to think through at least some of the major elements of the "rules of the game," before announcing them.

On the other hand, it is impossible to anticipate every contingency: We live in a world of incomplete contracting. The former socialist economies are engaged in a process of change, not in the determination of a new equilibrium, and this too needs to be borne in mind.

The Importance of Commitment

In the discussions of tax reform in the United States in 1985, Treasury Secretary Donald Regan announced that the proposals were written on a word processor, signaling the lack of commitment of the Reagan administration to those proposals. Laws can be changed, and the possibility of such changes can affect behavior. Sovereign governments cannot commit their successors. I have already called attention to the consequences of these commitment problems. In their absence, as we saw, a centralized economy might dominate a market economy.

Nonetheless, while governments cannot commit their successors, they can engage in actions that reduce the likelihood of certain changes, for instance, by changing the transactions costs or by changing the political constituencies in favor of particular changes. In chapter 10 we saw how the design of the privatization program might affect the likelihood of a renationalization. If done appropriately, there would be an effective commitment against renationalization (short of a major, unanticipated change in the political climate).

An essential commitment, which virtually all observers have emphasized, is not to subsidize enterprises that are making losses. While the standard remedy for this is "privatization," it should be recognized that this is neither necessary nor sufficient for imposing hard budget constraints. Governments in many countries have subsidized private producers (e.g., of steel), and governments in some countries have imposed hard budget constraints on government enterprises.

Price and Institutional Reform

A precondition for imposing hard budget constraints is that profit measures be meaningful. Unfortunately, this is often not the case. Prices are often not meaningful: A price reform is one of the first orders of reform. Firms inherit assets and liabilities; assessing whether a firm is doing well requires assessing those assets and liabilities in a meaningful way. If a firm is given a large capital stock, for which it is not "charged," then it can have strongly positive cash flows, and yet in an economically meaningful sense, it can be doing very poorly. On the other hand, if a firm is given few assets, but inherits debts upon which it has to make high interest payments, it could have a negative cash flow, yet its true performance could be quite strong. If profit data are to be meaningful, firms' balance sheets must be put in order, a point I emphasized in earlier chapters.

Privatization is, at best, only a partial solution. Privatizations in which vouchers are given, and there is not a recapitalization, do not address this problem at all. Privatizations in which the firm is sold are likely, in the presence of limited competition for the firm, to provide an underestimate of the true value of the firm's assets. Accordingly good performance, based on this undervaluation of the firm's assets, does not provide a true measure of the firm's efficiency.

Soft budget constraints can come not only through government grants but also through financial institutions, as I emphasized in chapter 12. Thus an essential feature in the transition must be a reform of the financial institutions. This is particularly important because the economic roles played by financial institutions under socialism were markedly different from the roles that they must perform under capitalism.

Macrostability and Microtransformation

A stable unit of account is also important: Inflation has to be kept in check. The two major culprits in causing inflation are excessive expansion of credit—a consequence in part of an unreformed financial system—and insufficient government tax revenue.

McKinnon (1991) has emphasized how, in the early stages of transition, government revenues are eroded. Under socialism government imposed implicit taxes: the difference between producer prices (the costs of production) and consumer prices. The government appropriates the profits of the government enterprises. With price liberalization, these "profits" quickly vanish, and the government is left without an adequate source of revenue. Thus tax reform too must be high on the order of transition.

The problems posed by inflation have seemed so formidable that many countries, during the early days of the transition, have focused their attention on macroeconomic stability. Advisors recommending a cold turkey approach seem almost to have taken pride in the pain that the countries have gone through, as tight government policies have resulted in high unemployment; it has sometimes been presented almost as part of the rites of initiation into capitalism.

The general view is that as part of the process of transition, resources have to be transferred from one use to another. Two arguments are frequently put forward for why, in the process, there must be high unemployment and extraordinarily low wages. One is that before resources can be deployed where they are more productive, they have to be released from where they are less productive; the transition takes time—and this is the intervening period of unemployment. The second is that those in unproductive sectors must be induced to move out. Firms must be induced to fire workers, and workers must be induced to search for more productive employment. The only way that workers can be so induced is to lower their wage, and the only way that firms can be induced to get rid of their employees is to face them with hard budget constraints.

There may be some truth in these arguments, but they need to be qualified in two important ways. First, the fundamental problem in many former socialist countries may be the structure of capital. The patterns of employment may be wrong because the patterns of investment may have been wrong. But *given* the current stock of capital goods, the allocation of labor may not be as inefficient as it might seem. The stock of capital goods will not change overnight. Hence the gains from reallocating labor in the short run may be much less than the gains that accrue in the long run.

Second, we have come to understand in recent years that workers' productivities may be sensitive to the wages they receive. Lowering wages may lead to lowered productivity, perhaps not in the very short run, when there is a special mentality, akin to that of wartime, where workers are willing to put out special efforts as part of the process of defending the country; here there is the excitement of building a new society. But in the longer run, when that excitement passes and day-to-day life resumes, the efficiency wage effects, which have come very much to the center of our understanding of macroeconomic adjustments, may play a more prominent role.

In much of the discussion of the speed of adjustment, there has been a confusion between macroeconomic and microeconomic issues: It may indeed be necessary to stop inflation and to get the government budget in control, but solving these problems is not the same as restructuring the economy. The macroeconomics of these economies in transition—with capital markets that hardly function and labor markets where mobility is impeded by the lack of free markets for housing—may be markedly different from standard Keynesian macroeconomics. Again, as I emphasized in chapter 12, supply responses may be more important, or at least different.

Tightening credit may result in a reduction in supply at the same time that it reduces demand, with limited effects on inflationary pressures. (This is not true, of course, if credit does not expand production of goods for which there is a demand, but rather, for instance, it simply enables the enterprise to pay higher wages than it otherwise would have paid. There is little double that the rapid credit expansion in Russia in 1993 was a major factor contributing to this high rate of inflation.)

Promoting New Enterprises

Much of the discussion of the transition process has focused on reforming and changing old institutions. Equally or perhaps even more important is the creation of new institutions and enterprises. China presents an interesting case study in this respect. It did not focus its attention on privatizing existing state enterprises. The existing state enterprises have declined in importance as a result of the growth of new enterprises, such as joint ventures and village, township, province, and private enterprises. Institutional reforms were required to facilitate this growth. The communes transformed themselves radically, to the point where there is little resemblance between the agriculture communes of the cultural revolution and the modern industrial communes.

On Privatization[3]

There are some free marketeers who say that the first step to success is to privatize the state enterprises. Whether they are right or wrong I do not know; what I do know is that they have no scientific basis for that conclusion.

As I argued earlier, I view competition as far more important than privatization. I see little difference in behavior between BP and Texaco (the former appears to be far better run than the latter, but I do not want to attribute this to the large ownership share of the British government), and (perhaps more controversially) some of the major gains in efficiency at British Telecom and British Airways occurred before privatization.

Theory tells us that in both cases we will face incentive problems (principal-agent problems). The first order of importance is changing the incentive structure of managers—and this can be done while the firms remain within the public sector.

I would have liked to have said that the first order of business is putting into place new managers, but it is not obvious from where the new managers are to come, and how are they to be chosen. (In any case, it must be recognized that there may be a shortage of competent managers in the short run.) Would a board of directors somehow elected by shareholders be any more competent at choosing new managers than would some alternative mechanism within the state enterprise system, such as the establishment of holding companies with boards of directors chosen by some other selection process (perhaps with participation by domestic and foreign banks, domestic and foreign business leaders, and possibly even academics in related areas)? In the interim, while privatization is proceeding, it may be important to have a change in the institutional structure, such as ensuring that the state enterprises are not controlled by the ministries who formerly operated them.

As I noted in chapter 10, a number of countries have embarked on a program of privatization using vouchers, establishing a form of people's capitalism. Here my advice is a word of caution, one that most of them have already taken to heart: Beware of the corporate governance problem. But while they have recognized the problems, too many seem to believe that the establishment of holding companies and stock markets will provide the information and incentives to ensure efficient management. In chapter 10, I expressed some skepticism concerning whether these will suffice.

Issues of political economy may, in the end, be more important in driving the pace of privatization than the factors discussed so far. Privatization will reduce the political power of the ministries (and their bureacrats), and it will create a new class of individuals for whom the continuation of the reform process is in their interest.

Sequencing

The discussion so far has highlighted the importance of the sequencing of reforms. It is hard to have market-based incentives without price liberalization. If because of hyperinflation, the price system fails to function, again market-oriented reforms cannot succeed. Beyond this, there appears to be considerable room for discretion.

China has shown that a successful market reform can proceed without privatization, without even clearly defining property rights. They have placed heavy emphasis on competition. There have been reforms in the financial system. How important they have been in the short run is not clear: Much of the investment is financed (as it is elsewhere in the world) through retained earnings. Though there has been much fanfare surrounding establishing a stock market, this has not played an important role in the remarkable growth that was experienced from 1979 through 1992. China has paid considerable attention to the issues of sequencing (and, as I will comment below, to those of timing as well). Before introducing a full-fledged price reform, China introduced a two-tier price system. The "flexible" part of the price system gave firms information, without simultaneously and instantaneously disrupting the entire economic system. The information (signals) could then be used to allow for a more thorough reform of prices.[4]

Broad-based incentive structures/market reforms were put into place *before* privatization. At the same time China came to recognize that in the long run, property rights issues would have to be addressed, if investment was to be sustained. There began a process of corporatization of enterprises, where, first, shares were issued to workers and members of the commune. Once the current ownership structure becomes well-defined, it will be an easier matter to go into "full capitalism."

There are good reasons for postponing the privatization issue: Issues of property rights assignment are highly contentious. There is no easy solution to how you divide a pie up fairly. This is particularly true when there are lingering questions about historical property rights. When the pie is growing rapidly, distribution issues became less contentious. People are (relatively) content, since they are getting a bigger piece than they ever anticipated having. However, with the imminent threat of spontaneous privatization, the issue may be not so much when to privatize but how, and who should control the process.

Transition Speed

No question is more controversial than the speed and manner in which the transition is to be done. There are the advocates of the cold turkey approach—as they put it, you never cross a chasm in two jumps. There are the advocates of a more gradual transition—it takes nine months even to have a baby. What is a fast or a slow transition is also a matter of dispute.

Many of the central issues in this debate are beyond the scope of economics; they involve political judgments. Are the political forces in the country such that the only way to attain an irreversible commitment to markets is to plunge ahead? Or are the political forces in the country such that the opposition that will be engendered through the cold turkey approach may threaten the very commitment to the market? The answers to these questions will, undoubtedly, differ among countries. Some of the former socialist countries seem—perhaps as a reaction to their foreign occupation for many decades—so committed to the market alternative that nothing will stop them, no matter what the costs.

Standard economic theory has indeed remarkably little to say about these matters. The Arrow-Debreu model—as inapplicable as I have argued it is to analyzing equilibrium—does not even attempt to characterize itself as a model of an economy in transition. While stability analysis has, from time to time, enjoyed moments of popularity within mathematical economics, the underlying models (with their explicit dynamics) seem completely inappropriate for modeling the problems of transition.

Still, economic theory has a little to say about the matter. Unless one is brought up in a tradition that values suffering for its own sake—and there is no reason to believe that most of the former socialist economies lie within that tradition—suffering is to be endured only as the inevitable price to be paid for some gains that cannot be attained in some other way. In my earlier discussion I suggested that in some cases, there was a confusion between macroeconomic and microeconomic adjustments: Little change in economic structure was being achieved (in the short run) at relatively high costs.

There are two other sets of arguments that suggest the desirability of a more gradual approach. The first emphasizes problems of government committing itself not to reverse reforms. In the absence of such a commitment, if investors believe that they will not be permanent, then they will not make the requisite investments, and if they do not make the requisite investments, it becomes more likely that the reforms will not be permanent. Gradual reforms have the advantage that the government can select areas in which it is more likely to be successful. With rational expectations investors will take this into account and, expecting success, will be willing to make the investments. These investments will help confirm their expectations. (This particular argument has been developed at greater length in a Stanford Ph.D. dissertation by Xinghai Fang.)

The second set of arguments focuses on learning. In going from a socialist to a market economy there is both individual and organizational learning. Individuals have to learn how to respond to market signals. Society has to learn which institutions work most effectively, and organizations must learn how to adapt to the new environment. A gradual transition may facilitate this learning process, for several reasons. First, it avoids the problem of "information overload." When excessive demands are placed on a system, its effectiveness may actually be impeded. The general principle is one that should be familiar to all teachers: Material is presented in small steps. What is learned one day is built upon in the next. Indeed it may not be possible to solve (or at least solve easily) the problems at later stages without first going through earlier stages. This is illustrated by the problems of pricing. In the early days of the transition in China, there was a great deal of discussion about how they were to know the correct prices. They recognized that they faced a huge general equilibrium problem. They knew that the prices of many of their goods (including primary products, like coal) were far from equilibrium. They had—in my judgment, for good reason—little confidence that computable general equilibrium models would be of much help. They introduced a two-tier price system. Production over the basic quotas was sold in markets. In the first tier (the quota) prices remained set by government. In the second tier prices were flexible. They began to provide good signals concerning scarcity. They operated at the margin, but there was not the huge dislocation that might have occurred had all prices been instantly freed. (There is a large literature in general equilibrium theory questioning the stability of the movement of prices toward equilibrium. These theoretical reasons perhaps reinforced the practical views questioning such a dramatic reform.) But the marginal prices provided the information that enable further price reforms to proceed, to the point that in a few years the two-tier system was effectively replaced by a single, flexible price system.

Second, a gradual transition avoids the loss of information that occurs when organizations are destroyed, as inevitably happens when there is a dramatic and rapid transformation. Evolution, from this perspective, is superior to revolution. Thus organizations embody information about the relative capacities of different individuals to perform various tasks. While in the process of transition the tasks assigned may alter, the information at one stage still may have relevance to subsequent stages. It is better to have *some* information than to proceed *ab initio*. The arguments are not meant to be conclusive,[5] only to suggest that economic arguments can be brought to bear on the question of the speed of transition, though they do not seem to have been extensively employed.

Stretch for Equality

The former socialist economies are in the perhaps unique position of being able to obtain a degree of equality of ownership of wealth unattained, and perhaps unattainable, in other market economies. The often-noted goal of a "people's capitalism" may indeed be within their reach, in a way that most other countries cannot even remotely approach, given their concentrations of wealth. They should not lose this opportunity: The damage of the "wealth" reform has already been done; now is not the occasion to lose the advantages that such a reform can afford. (In my earlier discussion I argued against the contention that it was possible to separate out equity and efficiency concerns; and for the advantages which are attendant upon a more equal distribution of wealth.)

From a strictly political perspective, the long-run legitimacy of democratic governments would, I suspect, be enhanced if they could succeed in maintaining a more egalitarian wealth distribution.

Yet the spontaneous privatizations that have occurred and the private wealth that has been created by entrepreneurs that have taken advantage of the huge opportunities for arbitrage profits that characterize many of the economies in transition have already created a group of wealthy that make the task of attaining equalitarian capitalism far more difficult.

There are some difficult issues in how to privatize land, industrial capital, and housing in an equitable manner. But the fact that the task is difficult does not mean that it should not be attempted. Going back to earlier land rights at a particular date—rights that often had existed for but a brief moment in history—as several countries seem to be doing, is hard to justify on grounds of either equity or efficiency. One cannot obliterate the scars of communism by rolling back history: The task is to take advantage of whatever has been done, however misguided it may have been. There has been a massive wealth redistribution. That may have been a mistake. The challenge is to grasp the opportunity that it now provides to construct a more egalitarian society.

Democracy and Economic Progress

Earlier textbook discussions often saw rapid progress and democracy as conflicting. Governments in wartime almost universally resorted to more direct controls, and to limited markets. They seemed to believe either that markets were luxuries that could not be afforded in times of emergency or that markets were not good as mechanisms for adapting to new situations—both appropriately damning criticisms of markets. Earlier I tried to argue that this belief in centralized authority may be misplaced.

Totalitarian governments may be good at suppressing consumption, but they do not seem to have any virtue in promoting economic efficiency. To a large extent, the high rates of savings simply served to offset the massive economic inefficiencies. For a while the socialist economies grew faster (if their statistics were to be relied upon), but only barely so. The disadvantages of limited freedom become particularly important as an economy develops into stages where greater individual decision making must occur. The kind of free intercourse required for the efficient exchange of products and market-related ideas can only be impeded by regimes that restrict other forms of social intercourse.[6]

Pose the Problem Correctly

The final word of advice is, "pose the problem correctly." Do not see the question of "markets" versus "government," but the appropriate balance between markets and government, with the possibility of many intermediate forms of economic organization (including those based on local government, cooperatives, etc.).

Imperfect and costly information, imperfect capital markets, imperfect competition: These are the realities of market economies—aspects that must be taken into account by those countries embarking on the choice of an economic system. The fact that competition is imperfect or capital markets are imperfect does not mean that the market system should not be adopted. What it does mean is that in their choices, they should not be confused by theorems and ideologies based on an irrelevant model of the market economy. Most important, it means that in deciding on what form of market economy they might adopt, including what role the government ought to play, they need to have in mind how actual market economies function, not the quite irrelevant paradigm of perfect competition.

16 Philosophical Speculations

The dream of a better world here on earth has been a central theme in the development of Western civilization since the Reformation. The nineteenth century saw some of these utopian visions translated into experiments of rather limited success. But the nineteenth century also saw the development of ideologies, which replaced the religious doctrines that had so long held sway over humankind but were held with the same emotional fervor; indeed the fervor was reinforced by the false sense that the ideologies rested on scientific premises. The sway that the Marxist ideology had over the minds—and eventually the lives—of so many for more than a century should give us pause: It is surely a sign of the importance of human fallibility, which I have stressed in this book. It should make us cautious in the confidence with which we hold our views, and cautious in our appeal to "science" to justify our beliefs about the organization of society. But, beyond that, we need to seek the deep-seated reasons for the depth and persistence of the appeal of these doctrines.

The neoclassical model and the ideologies with which it was associated did not speak to many of these fundamental concerns: It spoke of the efficiency (albeit "Paretian") of the market. Such views have little appeal to a society experiencing 25 percent unemployment in the Great Depression, say, or to one that has been mired in stagnation for centuries. Nor do they have much appeal to those who face a life of squalid poverty in the midst of the plenty of America or Western Europe, nor to the youth of these countries, whose ideals of social justice have not yet been shunted aside in the pursuit of self-interest which seems to come along with the so-called maturation process.

Is this the best of all possible worlds? Perhaps, but these individuals do not, and do not want to, believe it. As a society we do not want to believe it. We cannot accept this view, if for no other reason than that the creative struggle to solve these problems has a value itself, even if we make little progress.

Shaping Individuals

The popular success of the Marxist ideology was partly the hope of a more efficient economy, one that would bring more goods to more people. But the success among intellectuals went beyond that: It was partly based on the belief of the effect of the economic system on the nature of the individual. The concern was well-founded: One of the most damning criticisms of the socialist experiment has been what it did to the human spirit—the cynicism that developed among the young, the bureaucratic mentality, the lack of innovation.

Similarly one cannot simply dismiss Marxist concerns about the effects of market economies on the alienation of workers. In the discussion below, I will comment briefly on these broader effects of competition and cooperation; trust, self-interested behavior, and altruism; alienation; and decentralization.

Competition

Competition is important, not only because of its ability to promote economic efficiency but also because of the zest that it gives to life. Here we encounter one of the many ambivalences that characterizes our views about market economies: Competition is good, but we have our doubts about excessive competition. We encourage cooperation within teams but competition among them. We frown upon people who are excessively competitive. Yet the competitive market environment may encourage and bring out these aspects of individuals' personalities. If ruthlessly competitive people are successful, such behavior may be imitated. At the same time those who are (excessively) cooperative may be taken advantage of, derogated as pansies. Accordingly such behavior will be discouraged.

Self-interested Behavior

One of the reasons that we frown upon people who are excessively competitive is our ambivalence toward self-interested behavior. Adam Smith may have been right that we can rely on self-interestedness to lead to the public interest being served more surely than we can rely on benevolence.

There are some special conditions in which the reliance on self-interested behavior results in economic efficiency.

Yet trust is essential in the world in which we live; to be earned, trust often requires acting in a less than perfectly self-interested manner. Trust was essential for the early development of capital markets. In "imperfect" markets certain types of self-interested behavior impair economic efficiency. Indeed we know that we must provide incentives that are often quite costly to make self-interested individuals act in a trustworthy way (the wages of trust).[1]

There is, in this, a certain irony: Capitalism, as it promotes self-interested behavior, may create an environment less conducive to efficiency. Capitalism prospers best in an environment with a peculiar combination of self-interested behavior—enough to induce individuals to look for profitable activities—and non-self-interested behavior, where one's word is one's honor, where social rather than economic sanctions suffice to enforce contracts.

The critique of capitalism, that it promotes self-interested behavior, goes beyond, of course, the self-interest of capitalism in itself. A long-standing tenet of civilizations, both East and West, is that individuals must care about others. Capitalism may encourage self-interestedness, but is that really desirable?

We view charity as a virtue,[2] but does it remain a virtue when we compel charity upon others? There is something different, certainly for the giver, perhaps for the receiver, about giving money to a poor person voluntarily rather than being compelled to do so. By changing the locus of caring and responsibility from the individual to the government—not only for the needy, but for oneself, one's parents, one's children—we change society and we change ourselves. Here again we see a certain irony: Attempts to *improve* society by having the government undertake a greater role in redistribution, may ultimately—through their effects on individuals and the nature of the social contract—have more ambiguous consequences.

Alienation

Marx and his followers focused on workers' alienation from their work and from the product of their work. Today we talk about job satisfaction and worker involvement. These too are real concerns. We now know that changing the ownership of the means of production does not solve these problems: It may make matters worse. At least within capitalist systems, to the extent that job satisfaction and worker involvement affects worker productivity, there are strong incentives for firms to develop production arrangements that enhance job satisfaction. But should they only do so to the extent that it pays? Arguments to that effect are based on the assumption that preferences and personalities are unaffected by what goes on within the firm.

Decentralization

I have emphasized that competition has effects well beyond the narrow benefits upon which the standard model has focused. The same can be said of decentralization. I have emphasized the narrow efficiency effects of decentralization. But decentralization may also be important for the effect it has on individuals' perceptions of their effectiveness, their sense of "control." While these perceptions themselves may have effects on productivity, they may also have consequences that go well beyond that.

One of the aspects of modern society that individuals often complain about is the sense of powerlessness. How the economy is organized may contribute to, or mitigate, that sense. Decentralization almost surely gives more individuals a sense that they can have some effects. I suspect it is better to have a sense of control, even if limited to a small domain, than to have a sense of being but one cog within a larger system.

At the same time the analysis of human fallibility (discussed in chapter 9) points to the virtual inevitability of some sense of powerlessness in a well-organized society. We do not, and we should not, rely on one individual for making important *collective* decisions. These decisions are almost always made by committees, or within hierarchies, with any single individual having but a marginal effect on the outcome. It is only on unimportant matters—where mistakes are of little consequence—that we can turn over the decision making to a single individual. This is perhaps an argument for limiting, so far as possible, the domain of collective decision making.

Endogeneity of Human Nature

I have spoken of how the design of the economic system may foster certain characteristics—self-interestedness and competitiveness. In modern vocabulary, we say that certain aspects of human nature are endogenous to the system. The concern about what the economic system does to the human spirit, while it has disappeared from modern economics, was present in Adam Smith's writing:[3]

The understandings of the greater part of men are necessarily formed by their ordinary employments. The man whose whole life is spent in performing a few simple operations...generally becomes as stupid and ignorant as it is possible for a human creature to become. The torpor of his mind renders him, not only incapable of relishing or bearing a part in any rational conversation, but of conceiving any generous, noble, or tender sentiment, and consequently of forming any just judgment concerning many even of the ordinary duties of private life.... His dexterity at his own particular trade seems, in this manner, to be acquired at the expense of his intellectual, social, and martial virtues. But in every improved and civilized society this is the state into which the laboring poor, that is, the great body of the people, must necessarily fall, unless government takes some pains to prevent it.

Yet, while traditional economic theory is clearly wrong in treating individuals as immutable—"tastes" no less than technology were the primitives of the model—we have no scientific basis on which to judge one set of moral values, one set of personality types, as superior to others. Thus, while Hayek may have been right in stressing the moral dimension of markets—the kind of consequences in shaping human nature that I have just described—he fails to provide us with a systematic approach for addressing these issues (e.g., see his 1989 book).

The Narrowness of Neoclassical Man

The criticism of neoclassical economics is not only that it fails to take into account the broader consequences of economic organization on the nature of society and the individual, but that it focuses too narrowly on a subset of human characteristics—self-interested, rational behavior. To be sure, this model of behavior can go a long way in helping us to understand economic behavior. Indeed it can go a long way in helping us to understand the failures of the socialist experiment. But, as my discussion of the role of incentives should have made clear, there are many aspects of *economic* behavior that are left unexplained. I have shown how economic incentives, narrowly construed, seem to provide an insufficient explanation for why many individuals work as hard and as effectively as they do. I have stressed the importance of cooperation, honesty, and trust, virtues that make *economic* relations run more smoothly but that themselves frequently (and thankfully) lead to behavior that goes well beyond that called for by self-interestedness.[4]

The Evolutionary Approach[5]

Neoclassical economists have attempted to defend capitalism on the narrow ground of economic efficiency. I have shown how the claims for Pareto efficiency cannot be justified, as soon as we introduce more realistic assumptions concerning incomplete markets and imperfect information.

There are other strands of thought in economics that argue for market processes, but decry the neoclassical defense as too narrow, and indeed even misguided. I have already noted Hayek's argument for the "moral" dimension. One long-standing tradition, which includes Hayek and his followers, and Alchian, has emphasized an evolutionary argument for markets.

There is a natural analogy between competition among species and competition among individuals in the marketplace. Spencer and others extended Darwin's ideas on natural selection and survival of the fittest to a social context. Terms like "fittest" have an essentially normative overtone: The term "survival of the fittest" is obviously meant to convey more than just the observation that those who survive are the ones who survive. In some essential respect the "fittest" who survive are better than the less fit who do not. There is a teleological aspect of evolutionary processes: Nineteenth-century views of progress were reflected in the motion of constant, albeit slow, "improvement" in species and societies resulting from evolutionary forces. Callous policies that entailed governments ignoring the suffering of the poor were justified in the name of social Darwinism.

Within economic theory, more narrowly defined, evolutionary ideas have also long played an important role.[6] To the objection that many firms did not seem consciously to maximize profits, evolutionary economics responded that those firms that, consciously or unconsciously, acted as if they did maximize profits would, in the long run, be the only firms to survive. Profit maximization and competition were of course both essential parts of the argument for why market economies were efficient.

Evolutionary forces work not only to select firms within an economy, they work to select institutions. As society has evolved, it has moved from primitive social exchange to sophisticated markets. Market economies, having evolved later, and having replaced these other institutional arrangements, are presumably "better" in some sense.

As important as these ideas are, they are not based on a well-formulated dynamic theory, nor is there a well-articulated normative basis for the widespread belief in the "desirability" of evolutionary forces—or the often-drawn policy conclusion that government intervention in the evolutionary process would either be futile or, worse, be a retrograde step. It seems nonsensical to suggest that we should simply accept the natural outcome of the evolutionary process. What does "natural" mean? How do we know whether or not any particular perturbation that we might propose, such as more or less government, is or is not part of the "natural" evolutionary process? Can we only tell in hindsight—if it does not survive? The evolutionary process has involved enormous changes over the past centuries, so we cannot simply reject all change. Change is the very essence of the evolutionary process.

Indeed it is only with hindsight that we may be able to tell whether a particular policy had survival value. Certainly the hypothesis that governments constitute a positive evolutionary step is supported by the observation that societies with governments have survived, and those without have not. By the same token, certain types of government intervention in the market may, from an evolutionary perspective, enable a society to survive better. While we might conclude from the demise of socialism that it did not have survival value, we cannot conclude that therefore market institutions are superior. Supporters of socialism could equally well argue that it simply showed that the particular forms of socialism that we tried did not have survival value. By the same token, one can argue from the success of the East Asian countries, that "managed markets" and strong government intervention have survival value, in comparison with market institutions with much more limited government intervention.

More broadly, we now recognize that there is more than one form of capitalism, that the conduct, structure (organization), and performance of the Japanese economy—both the private sector, and the relationships between government and the private sector—differ, for instance, in important ways from those of the United States. Evolutionary theory does not give us much basis for choosing among these institutions.

By the same token, those who appeal to the evolutionary process also claim too much: There is no reason to believe that evolutionary processes have any optimality properties. Indeed there are strong arguments suggesting that evolutionary processes are far from optimal. Biologists stress the randomness of the process, the seeming redundancies so frequently observed, the vestigial elements that often lead to problems (such as the human appendix).

Economists note that in the absence of a capital market, a species with strong long-run prospects simply cannot "borrow" to carry it through a temporary change in the environment. A species—or a firm—with greater long-run adaptability can be wiped out in the competitive struggle by one better-suited for the particular environment. Thus more competitive environments—environments in which competition is more ruthless so that any but the most efficient firms, in that environment, are weeded out—may in the long run actually be less productive.

One can view natural selection as a screening process. It attempts to screen "good" (productive) individuals (species, firms) from "bad" (unproductive) ones. But like any screening process, the screening is imperfect. Some good firms are eliminated: Under ruthless competition an efficient firm with a run of bad luck will be sent into bankruptcy. Some bad firms manage to survive, at least for a long time: The story of GM surviving for years after it became inefficient, squandering in the process by some estimates more than $100 billion, has already become legendary.

As in any screening process there are trade-offs; one can normally reduce one type of error (e.g., reducing the probability of bad firms surviving) only at the expense of increasing the other type of error. By allowing firms that are making losses to survive for long, one accumulates more information; one becomes more confident that the reason that they are making losses is that they are incompetent. Thus one is less likely to make the mistake of terminating an efficient firm. In the meanwhile the inefficient firm allowed to survive longer may be badly misallocating resources.

The fundamental point is that there is no reason to believe that market economies "naturally" make the right trade-offs or that, in particular, market economies with more ruthless competition are more efficient than economies in which competition is more gentle. Moreover, since whether a particular trait (species) survives depends on the environment, which itself is endogenous, there is no reason to believe that the system as a whole has any optimality properties. The system simply ensures that those who have characteristics that are rewarded, in the particular environment which the system has created, survive. Thus one can imagine a world in which there are two types of individuals, bureaucrats and innovators. Bureaucrats make life difficult for innovators, and innovators make life difficult for bureaucrats. There are multiple equilibria to such a society. Bureaucrats may dominate; in that environment innovators do not prosper. The bureaucrats create an environment that is favorable to their own type. But, conversely, innovators might dominate. They create an environment that is favorable to their type. Though the economy, from different initial conditions, could evolve toward either equilibrium, one of these might be (under some welfare criterion, such as long-run economic growth) clearly superior to the other. (It is only when the two societies come in direct conflict or comparison with each other that the disadvantages of bureaucracy become revealed.)

Good mutations (new social institutions) may not survive on their own, for they require accompanying changes in other social institutions. There is a coordination failure. Many changes have to occur at the same time, and market processes may not be able to provide the necessary coordination. There is thus no presumption that evolutionary forces, left to themselves, have any desirable welfare properties. Moreover, if we take seriously the observations made in the first part of this chapter, concerning the endogeneity of preferences, we have fundamental problems even ascertaining what are appropriate criteria for judging evolutionary processes.

Of course, if evolutionary forces "naturally" led to desirable outcomes (whatever that might mean), then the economist's task would be a simple one: to observe and comment on the process. But as economists, we are called upon to analyze a variety of proposed changes in policies and institutions. As our tools of analysis have improved, we are in a better position to ask of any proposed change, what are its effects? In evolutionary terms we can ask, is it likely to survive? We are even in a position of engaging in social engineering, of asking. can we design institutions or policy reforms that are likely to be welfare improving, or, again in evolutionary terms, that are likely to have survival value?

Judging whether a particular social innovation—including a changed role for government—is "evolutionarily sound" is a difficult task, and one for which history will only provide limited guidance. For many innovations I hope that the insights provided by this book will be of some help.

The great socialist experiment is coming to an end: We have learned a lot from these experiments, but because they were hardly controlled experiments, what we learned remains a subject of some dispute. While government ownership is clearly no panacea, there remains scope for further experimentation. For instance, we need to study forms of economic organization involving more worker participation and ownership. Not too much should be read into the failures of the worker-managed firms in the former Yugoslavia, for these involved peculiar (and obviously unsatisfactory) arrangements with respect to the transfer of property rights, as well as other institutional details which, both ex ante and in hindsight, were not conducive to success. To return to the theme with which I began these speculations, the question is whether the insights of modern economic theory and the utopian ideals of the nineteenth century can be brought closer together?

17 Conclusions

Whither socialism? Mark Twain was once reported to have said that "Reports of my death have been greatly exaggerated." But if I were to claim that socialism as an ideology can now be officially declared dead, I do not think it would be an exaggeration. The Mitterand victory in France and the resulting nationalizations might be considered its last gasps: The subsequent rejection of socialism in France and the privatization movements throughout the developed world signaled its death knell.

The answer that socialism provided to the age-old question of the proper balance between the public and the private can now, from our current historical perspective, be seen to have been wrong. But if it was based on wrong, or at least incomplete, economic theories, theories that are quickly passing into history, it was also based on ideals and values many of which are eternal. It represented a quest for a more humane and a more egalitarian society.

There is a poem by the great American poet, Robert Frost, that begins, "Two roads diverged in a wood, and I—/ I took the one less traveled by, / And that has made all the difference." As the former socialist countries embark on their journey, they see many paths diverging. There are not just two roads. Among these there are many that are less traveled by—where they end up no one yet knows. One of the large costs of the socialist experiment of the past seventy years is that it seemed to foreclose exploring many of the other roads. As the former socialist economies set off on this journey, let us hope that they keep in mind not only the narrower set of economic questions that I have raised in this book but the broader set of social ideals that motivated many of the founders of the socialist tradition. Perhaps some of them will take the road less traveled by, and perhaps that will make all the difference, not only for them, but for the rest of us as well.

Notes

Chapter 1

1. There is even some controversy about the extent to which market socialism was a failure, as in Hungary, for example, where it was assiduously tried. In Hungary growth rates immediately after the initial reforms of 1968 were quite high. The reduction in growth rates in later years may be partly attributed to the retrenchment from the commitments to reform, and partly to worldwide economic conditions that resulted in a slowing down of growth in most countries. Indeed the slowdown in Hungary was less than in many other countries, though critics claim that this was because Hungary failed to adjust to the changed oil prices, borrowing extensively abroad. This international indebtedness constitutes one of the major problems facing Hungary today.

2. Or, for that matter, the kind of poverty that characterizes the black ghettos in the United States. It is perhaps worth noting that, at least by conventional measures of inequality, some of the most successful of the developing countries, such as Korea and Taiwan, exhibit a high degree of equality.

3. See, for instance, Wade (1990) and Amsden (1989).

4. I will discuss later what is meant by market socialism.

5. In emphasizing the information paradigm, I do not intend to dismiss or slight other important critiques of the neoclassical paradigm that have developed over the past quarter century. Some of these, such as those emphasizing the importance of imperfections in competition, are not only consistent with the information paradigm; in many ways, to be noted below, they are complementary.

Limitations of time and space force me to focus on the information paradigm, which, in my judgment, provides the most well-articulated and far-reaching alternative to the standard paradigm developed to date.

6. For surveys, see Stiglitz (1975a, 1985c, 1990a), or Hirshleifer and Riley (1979). More extensive accounts of many of the models can be found in Laffont (1989) and Milgrom and Roberts (1992).

7. See, for instance, Stiglitz (1985a, 1988a) and the collections of papers representing the newly emerging theory of rural organizations edited by Bardhan (1989) and Hoff, Braverman, and Stiglitz (1993).

8. See, for instance, Greenwald and Stiglitz (1987).

9. For a survey, see Stiglitz (1987a).

10. In this new theory, divergences between the interests of shareholders and managers, and between managers and workers, are explicitly recognized. The limitations on the ability of markets to provide discipline for managers is explained, and new questions concerning how firms are and should be organized, to take into account both incentive problems and the problems arising from the fact that information is limited and costly both to obtain and transmit are addressed. I will touch on many of these issues later in this book.

11. My criticism of the earlier Austrian work goes beyond the contention that they provided an incomplete theory; as I will show, some of the basic ideas, such as those concerning evolutionary processes and the informational efficiency of the economy, were somewhat misconceived.

12. When I wrote these lectures, the process of transition was just beginning. As these lectures go to press, more than two years later, most of what I said then seems still relevant. The debate about the transition process remains a lively one.

13. The standard reference for this is Francis Bator's (1958) paper. This approach now forms the basis of standard textbook expositions in the economics of the public sector. See, for example, Stiglitz (1988b).

14. The U.S. government has recently done this, and the Chicago Board of Trade has actually created markets for these permits, facilitating not only trade but also speculation on the future value of these rights.

15. The early literature on market socialism developed before more recent advances in public finance, in which optimal taxation might entail differences between producer and consumer prices. But the Lange-Lerner-Taylor theorem could easily be extended to embrace these differences. See, in particular, Dasgupta and Stiglitz (1972).

16. As we will see later, there were good reasons for the difference in the treatment: The futures and risk markets necessary for the efficient allocation of capital did not exist in capitalist economies, and it would presumably be hard to make the analogues work within market socialism. Indeed, capitalist economies rely heavily on direct allocative mechanisms, albeit decentralized ones.

17. In the Soviet model, not much emphasis was placed on consumer preferences, but presumably, in a more consumer oriented economy, information about preferences would also have to be communicated to the central planner.

18. A word of caution is in order: Political considerations, particularly in the mid and late 1970s, put constraints on the extent to which the market socialism model could be implemented, even in Hungary.

19. That is, that there is a precise optimization problem for which all competitive market allocations are in fact the solution.

20. Lange, one of the pioneers of market socialism, had high hopes for these new technologies, as evidenced in his book (Lange 1967). (Lange, it should be noted, served for a long time as a high official within the Polish Communist government, and by all accounts had considerable influence in the evolution of economic policies there.)

21. It is also perhaps worth noting that even strong critics of neoclassical economics, such as Joan Robinson, fell into that same mentality, as she described the problem of the firm's manager as looking up in the book of blueprints the correct page corresponding to current (and future) factor prices.

22. In the absence of rent control, the owner has an incentive to maintain the building because it affects the rent that can be extracted.

23. And, as I argue later, public good problems are more general than the conventional discussions often suggest: For instance, they arise in knowledge acquisition and in the monitoring of enterprises.

24. Strikes are examples where mutual advantageous deals fail to be consummated, as each party tries to get a larger fraction of the surplus from the relationship for itself. The outcome of bargains depends in part on each parties perceptions of how the other party would be affected by the failure to consummate a deal (the threat point). If one party can convince the other that it has good outside opportunities, then it can obtain a better deal for itself. Each party to the bargain tries to signal such information, but to be effective, such signals must be costly (talk is cheap, and thus statements are often not taken at face value). One common way of signaling such information is to show that one is willing to delay arriving at an agreement, even (or particularly) when such delay is costly.

25. Later I will discuss a theorem showing that shareholders in firms will generally not agree about what actions the firm should take.

Chapter 2

1. I will return to this general theme later in this book. Here I simply want to set the stage: Too many economists today dismiss market socialism out of hand, saying that it was "obviously" flawed.

2. There also must exist markets for all risks. In chapter 3 I will take up the issue of why futures and risk markets do not exist, and will discuss more extensively the consequences of the failure of such markets to exist.

3. In indicative planning, various firms in the economy tell the government how much they plan to invest and produce in the future, and what their corresponding needs are for factor inputs. In principle, then, the government could use this information—for instance, to inform firms that there will be an imbalance in some future market, or, that given current plans, the supply of steel will exceed the demands. For indicative planning to have worked, firms would have had to reveal their factor demand and output supply curves—that is, what they "planned" to do—contingent on what prices might emerge on the market. Most firms of course do not have such well-articulated plans. But probably the more fundamental reason for the failure of indicative planning was that firms simply had no incentive to reveal the requisite information, even if they had it.

4. This literature, growing out of the papers by Ross (1973) and Stiglitz (1974), has become enormous. For a brief overview, see Stiglitz (1989a).

5. Indeed, as I noted in my Tokyo lecture (1972b), in the absence of a complete set of markets, there will not, in general, be unanimity among shareholders concerning the objective that the firm should pursue.

6. Until recently, majority interest in BP (British Petroleum) was held by the British government. Texaco, a private American oil company, had earned a reputation among those in the industry for a combination of managerial arrogance and incompetence; when Texaco lost a multibillion dollar suit that Pennzoil had filed against it, for inducing Getty oil to breach a contract to sell itself to Pennzoil, there was little sympathy for Texaco.

7. Evidence that it is not is provided in Caves and Christensen (1980). (Canadian National Railways is government owned; Canadian Pacific, privately owned.)

8. RJR-Nabisco was a major American conglomerate, originally known for its two principal product lines—the cigarettes sold by R.J. Reynolds, and the bakery products produced by Nabisco (but it included other products, such as Dole Pineapple)—but increasingly known for the life style of its managers, which included a large fleet of corporate jets and vacation homes at ski resorts. For a popularized version of this takeover story, see *Barbarians at the Gate* by Bryan Burrough and John Helyar. There is a growing theoretical and empirical literature discussing the conflict of interest between managers and shareholders. See, for instance, Morck, Shleifer, and Vishny (1989, 1990), Shleifer and Vishny (1986, 1989), and Jensen (1986).

9. See Persky (1989).

10. The theoretical literature in the late 1920s and early 1930s reflects this concern with increasing returns and the importance of overhead costs. See, for instance, Lewis (1928) and Clark (1923). Among the concerns were the nature of equilibrium. See, for instance, Young (1928). Out of these concerns arose the theory of imperfect competition. In this respect, while Chamberlin's (1933) contribution may have been the more original, Robinson's (1933) was more directly concerned with the central issues.

11. I should perhaps mention one development which argued that imperfections of competition had far fewer consequences than had previously been thought—the contestability doctrine which held that potential competition was all that was required to ensure economic efficiency; even with one firm, the benefits of competition would be passed on to consumers, since profits would be driven to zero. But a closer examination of how markets function showed that competition was even less robust than economists had thought earlier: There were numerous strategies that incumbent firms could use (beyond outright collusion) to deter entry and to restrict competition among themselves. Competition might be limited even with very small sunk, fixed costs. See, for instance, Stiglitz (1987g).

12. For an overview, see Greenwald and Stiglitz (1993) or Stiglitz (1992b).

13. In the absence of a perfect capital market, for instance, firms finding it difficult surviving —but who know that in future circumstances they would prosper if they could only hold out until then—cannot borrow against their future prosperity. See Stiglitz (1975a, 1992c). For a discussion of problems in "learning," see Bray and Kreps (1987).

Chapter 3

1. A. Smith, *Wealth of Nations*, bk. 1, ch. 2.

2. Greenwald and Stiglitz (1986, 1988) develop a general methodology for analyzing the welfare consequences of imperfect information, limited markets, and other market imperfections. They apply their methodology to economies facing problems of adverse selection, signaling, imperfect risk markets, moral hazard, costly transactions, efficiency wages, and search. Unpublished work shows how the analysis can be extended in a simple way to models with incentive compatibility (self-selection) constraints. (See Arnott, Greenwald, and Stiglitz 1992.)

3. It is perhaps remarkable that not only does Debreu (1959), in his classic statements of the competitive model, pay no attention to the implicit information assumptions, but he does not even seem to recognize this as an important limitation of the theory. For instance, in

concluding the basic statement of the theory, he lists what he considers to be (presumably) the two most important limitations of the theory: the failure to integrate money into the theory of value and the exclusion of indivisible commodities.

The *economic* significance of the assumption of a complete set of futures and risk markets is passed over with the statement, "The assumption that markets exist for all the uncertain commodities . . . is a natural extension of the usual assumption that markets exist for all the certain commodities. . . ." (p. 102)

4. Using the term "competitive" in the natural way, referring to a market in which there are a large number of participants on both sides. Of course some equilibrium theorists take it as a *definition* of competitive markets that there be perfect information. This assertion can be thought of as either a semantic quibble or an admission that, unless it could have been shown that markets with imperfect information behave very much like markets with perfect information, competitive equilibrium theory is of limited relevance as a description of actual economies.

5. In these cases prices (interest rates, wages) affect the quality of what is being traded (the risk of the borrower not repaying the loan, the productivity of the labor). It does not pay firms to raise interest rates charged, even when there is an excess demand for credit (so that it could do so, and still make all the loans it wished to); doing so would result in a higher probability of default, and thus a lower expected return. It does not pay firms to lower wages, even when there is an excess supply of workers; doing so would result in a labor force of lower productivity. In chapter 4 I will discuss these issues at greater length.

6. Firms make prices depend on quantity in order to discriminate among different kinds of customers. Insurance firms thus use the quantity of insurance purchased as a basis in making inferences concerning the likelihood of having an accident. On average, those more prone to having accidents will want to have more extensive coverage (see Rothschild and Stiglitz 1976; C. A. Wilson 1977). In other cases firms may simply do this to increase their profits: With perfect information they would engage in perfect price discrimination. With imperfect information they can glean information about individuals from the quantity that they purchase For instance, if those who buy large quantities have a lower consumer surplus per unit purchased than do those who buy small quantities, a nonlinear price system, with charges per unit purchased declining with quantity purchased, may yield a monopolist higher profits than would a conventional "linear" price system. This issue too will be discussed at greater length in chapter 4. See also Stiglitz (1977b) and the vast subsequent literature. The same argument also applies in cases where there is some, but imperfect, competition. See, for example, Salop (1977) or Salop and Stiglitz (1982).

7. In standard reputation models (to be discussed in the next chapter) profits are necessary to induce firms to produce high-quality goods (otherwise there is no penalty for producing shoddy merchandise.) In the context of adverse selection, the argument is more subtle. The equilibrium contracts, say, in the insurance market with two types of risks, can be described as follows: The high-risk individual gets complete insurance, at his or her actuarially fair odds. The contract for the low risk is that policy that maximizes the low-risk individual's expected utility, subject to the high-risk individuals preferring their own policies to this policy (the self-selection constraint) and the policy's profits being nonnegative. If the low-risk individual is more risk averse than the high-risk individual, the latter constraint may not be binding. The equilibrium policy offered to the low-risk individual makes a profit, but were a firm to lower the premium or raise the benefit, all the high-risk individuals would demand the policy, and with that mix of applicants (remember, it is assumed that the insurance firm cannot distinguish between high-risk and low-risk individuals) the expected profits of the policy drop precipitously: The slight reduction in premium or increase in benefits results in the policy now making an absolute loss.

Precisely the same reasoning applies in the context of moral hazard. Suppose that individuals have the choice of two different activities, a "safe" activity or a risky activity. Which activity the insured undertakes depends on the insurance policy. With more complete insurance, the insured undertakes the risky activity. The equilibrium insurance contract may be described as that contract that maximizes the expected utility of the insured, subject to the insured undertaking the safe activity and subject to profits being nonnegative. Again the solution to this maximization problem may entail the latter constraint not being binding. The equilibrium contract makes a profit, but a slight increase in benefits, say, results in the insured's switching from the safe activity to the risky activity, with profits dropping precipitously from positive to negative. For a fuller discussion, including the formal argument, and a more complete statement of the assumptions, see Arnott and Stiglitz (1988a).

8. The lump-sum transfers are identical for *all* individuals, regardless of differences in observable characteristics.

9. The general analysis is due to Greenwald and Stiglitz (1986, 1988). The first paper shows the constrained Pareto inefficiency of market economies in which markets clear, and the second (1988) shows the result in efficiency wage, search, and other models in which markets do not clear. (For a more extensive discussion of market equilibrium when markets do not clear, see Stiglitz 1987b.) A third paper (Arnott, Greenwald, and Stiglitz 1992) extends the analysis to models with self-selection and incentive compatibility constraints.

The more general Greenwald-Stiglitz results were anticipated by a number of papers considering special cases. These papers provide insight into the nature of the market failure in each of these instances. For the analysis of inefficiency in the presence of moral hazard, see Arnott and Stiglitz (1985, 1986, 1989, 1991); for the analysis of inefficiency in stock market models, see Stiglitz (1972b, 1982a); for the analysis of inefficiency in more rudimentary economies, in which there is not even a stock market, see Newbery and Stiglitz (1982, 1984); for the analysis of inefficiency in models with implicit contracts, see Newbery and Stiglitz (1987); for the analysis of inefficiency in search models, see Mortenson (1989); for a discussion of the inefficiency within efficiency wage models, see Shapiro and Stiglitz (1984a). A more thorough discussion of the general problems of welfare economics in the presence of asymmetric and imperfect information is contained in my Lindahl lectures on "Welfare Economics with Asymmetric Information" (forthcoming, Oxford University Press).

10. See below for further elaboration on the sense in which popular interpretations of the insights provided by the Arrow-Debreu model are and are not correct.

11. Thus the Greenwald-Stiglitz analysis explains why representative agent models are simply of no use in evaluating the efficiency of market economies. (Of course a result establishing conditions under which markets with representative agents should turn out to be inefficient would tell us something, but results showing that a particular representative agent model is efficient are of little, if any, value.)

12. Still a third example is the stock market economy with no bankruptcy and a single good studied by Diamond (1967). Stiglitz (1982a) showed that with just two goods, the stock market economy was essentially never constrained Pareto efficient. Greenwald and Stiglitz showed how the Stiglitz (1982a) result could be seen as a special case of their more general theorem. Other, rather different problems with the efficiency of economies with an incomplete set of risk markets (e.g., the possibility of multiplicity of equilibria, one of which might be Pareto dominated by another) were studied by Stiglitz (1972b), Drèze (1974), and Hart (1975).

13. This example helps clarify the special nature of Diamond's result, showing the constrained Pareto efficiency of stock market economies with a single good. In his model the actions of each investor has no effect on the probability distribution of returns, since the relative prices of different goods are, *by assumption*, fixed.

14. This is the case in the standard adverse selection model. See Akerlof (1970).

15. It is a somewhat more subtle matter to show that the government can effect these changes in such a way as to make everyone better off—given that the government faces the same limitations on information that employers do. But if there are enough different commodities (over which the groups with different abilities differ in their preferences), then one can show that the government can indeed attain a Pareto improvement.

16. This discussion makes clear why earlier results, such as that of Shavell (1979) asserting the constrained Pareto efficiency of market economies with moral hazard with a *single* good are not general: With a single good there is no scope for government policy to induce greater care through differential tax rates on different commodities.

17. For a derivation of the optimal rates of taxes/subsidies, see Arnott and Stiglitz (1986).

18. A folk theorem is a widely known theorem, the origins of which cannot easily be traced. It is part of the oral tradition in a particular field. The most famous folk theorem of recent vintage is that in repeated games, which states that for an infinitely repeated prisoner's dilemma, the strategy "cooperate–cooperate" is a subgame perfect equilibrium of the supergame.

19. Several years ago, when I was assigned the task of setting the comprehensive Ph.D. exams in microeconomics, I was so foolish as to ask what were the central economic assumptions of the fundamental theorems of welfare economics that might be questioned. At least a third of the students, well trained in the mathematics of the theorem, responded with an extended discussion of the role of the nonsatiation assumption, totally omitting any discussion of the issues with which I have been concerned in these lectures.

20. If there were no nonconvexities, as assumed by the standard theory, then presumably there could be many firms producing at each date, location, and state of nature. In a sense the theory is consistent in making a series of unreasonable, but "coherent," assumptions. With small fixed costs associated with the production of each of these state-location-time dated commodities (or with each set of such commodities), not only will there not be many firms producing each, many such commodities will not even be produced.

21. This point was first made by Radner (1968).

22. This is not quite accurate. So long as there is some chance of default, creditors bear some residual risk.

23. See Stiglitz (1992b).

24. See Asquith and Mullins (1986).

25. This is sometimes referred to as the problem of "hidden knowledge," as opposed to the moral hazard problem, which is referred to as one of "hidden action," but I think the description is somewhat misleading. The moral hazard problem arises because of a particular type of hidden knowledge problem—hidden knowledge concerning the actions taken by the individual.

Why we use the terms "selection problem" or "screening problem" can be seen most clearly in the context of the insurance or labor market. The insurance firm wishes to select (or screen) for the lowest risks; the employer wants to select (or screen) for the highest productivity workers. In the product market the buyer of used cars wishes to select for the most underpriced car, that is, the car that represents the greatest value. All of these problems share in common that there is a characteristic of the commodity relevant to one side (e.g., the buyer) that is not costlessly or directly observable to that individual.

The term *adverse selection* is used to denote the fact that as certain terms of the contract change, there is an adverse effect on the quality mix of those offering themselves on the market; for instance, raising the premium adversely affects the mix of those who wish to buy insurance, raising the interest rate charged on a loan adversely affects those who apply for a loan, with an increase in the proportion of those who are bad risks—who have a high probability of default.

26. This is sometimes referred to as the hidden action problem because one side of the contract cannot observe the actions taken by the other side, and accordingly cannot make contracts contingent on those actions. Contracts can only be made contingent on the observable outcomes, or on observable actions (which may be related to the hidden actions).

27. Curiously some insurance firms do attempt to distinguish between smokers and non-smokers, trusting that those that it sells insurance to will report honestly whether they do or do not smoke.

28. A more rigorous development of this point is contained in Arnott and Stiglitz (1988a, 1990), where it is shown that not only is insurance, in general, incomplete, but in some instances no insurance may be provided. (At a more technical level, in some cases no competitive equilibrium exists. The reason for the failure of equilibrium to exist is quite different from that noted in Rothschild and Stiglitz 1976.)

29. Moral hazard arguments also are used to explain the thinness of the equity market: The fixed obligations associated with debt provides an incentive for managers to work hard.

30. This discussion has a curious history. Grossman (1975) and Grossman and Stiglitz (1976), after setting out some simple models in which prices fully revealed all the relevant information, viewed these as "limiting cases" helping us to fix our ideas on how to construct more relevant models of how prices convey information; we quickly moved on to construct such models. A subsequent literature (see, e.g., Radner 1979) seemed to get fixated on what we viewed as the wrong question: the conditions under which prices could convey all the relevant information.

It should have been obvious from our analysis that not only were the assumptions concerning the dimensionality of the commodity-marketed security space critical but so too were the assumptions concerning the utility function. For instance, we explored one model in which different farmers had information about their own crops. This affected their demand for futures, and *with a constant absolute risk aversion utility function*, the futures price conveyed all the relevant information, that is, provided a perfect predictor of the future supply. The reason was simple: Demand for futures was *linear* in each farmer's crop size, and hence the equilibrium futures price could be shown to be a function only of total crop size. With virtually any other utility function, demand for futures will not be linear in crop size, so that a low price might represent either a higher aggregate supply, or a more or less disparate distribution in crop sizes. (See Jordan 1983 or Gale and Stiglitz 1985.)

31. That is, markets in which participants have information other than that which arrives at zero cost.

32. See Grossman and Stiglitz (1980a).

33. Of course, in principle, the Arrow-Debreu model involves states of nature that are exogenous, and it is not apparent whether we should take the discovery of atomic energy as "exogenous" or "endogenous." To the extent that it depends on the allocation of resources to research, it is endogenous. But the outcome depends not only on the allocation of resources but on an underlying unknown "state"—the world that the research is supposed to uncover. Thus there are formalisms that could embrace these risks—if they could have been articulated—within the state-of-nature formulation. Nonetheless, research will alter subjective probabilities concerning the various states of nature, and these endogenous changes in the probabilities are themselves precluded from the theory. Thus these formalisms fail to rescue the central results of the conventional paradigm.

34. With the dominance of Keynesian economics within macroeconomics and the perfect competition paradigm within microeconomics, the monopolistic competition model remained relatively unexplored until its formal revival by Spence (1976) and Dixit and Stiglitz (1977). The similarities (and differences) between these models and the imperfect competition generated by imperfect information is evident in the studies by Salop (1976), Salop and Stiglitz (1977, 1982, 1987), Stiglitz (1986a, 1989b), Wolinsky (1986), and Diamond (1971). These results were anticipated by Arrow (1988) and Scitovsky (1950). For other references, see Stiglitz (1989b).

35. See Dixit and Stiglitz (1977).

36. See Salop and Stiglitz (1977, 1982).

37. Except to the extent that market socialism emphasized the market's failure to allocate investment efficiently, partly as a result of the absence of the requisite futures and risk markets.

Chapter 4

1. These points are developed with greater rigor in Brito, Hamilton, Slutsky, and Stiglitz (1990).

2. See Stiglitz (1987a).

3. First developed in Stiglitz (1982b), and exposited more fully in Stiglitz (1987a). This literature on Pareto-efficient taxation was a natural outgrowth of the earlier literature on optimum taxation, initiated by Mirrlees (1971).

4. See Stiglitz (1974, 1987h).

5. These are not perfect incentives, so long as workers do not have the capital to pay for the entire rent at the beginning of the period, and punishments for defaulting are limited. With payment at the end of the period, the rental contract can be thought of as a combination of a loan and a rental contract, and loan contracts with limited liability give rise to important incentive problems, as Stiglitz and Weiss (1981) have emphasized.

6. Cheung (1963) gives an alternative interpretation of sharecropping contracts, in terms of transactions-cost efficiency. He argued that labor is efficiently supplied. The difference between our two models was that he assumed that the amount of labor that the worker supplied was (costlessly) observable, and therefore the contract could specify the amount of labor: There was no incentive problem.

7. This is one of the main points of the principal-agent literature. For a brief survey, see Stiglitz (1989a).

8. Shapiro and Stiglitz (1984), for instance, show that in their model of an economy in which it is costly to monitor workers, whether the economy is constrained Pareto efficient depends on whether wealth is equally distributed.

9. Sah and Stiglitz (1991) provide a method of partially ranking organizations/economic systems by the degree of decentralization in decision making.

10. It is well known that cross-subsidization may be necessary in this case.

11. There is no simple intuition behind the Radner-Stiglitz theorem. In the absence of information the individual optimizes by taking the same action in response to any signal. A small amount of information leads the individual to revise slightly this action in response to observing different signals. But since the individual has optimized his or her action, given the information, by the standard envelope theorem, the change in expected utility (conditional on observing the particular signal) is zero. Moreover, the individual's expected utility, conditional on observing different signals, is the same, so there is no change in expected utility resulting from the revision of the probabilities associated with different outcomes/ signals (resulting from the improved information).

12. For earlier discussions, see Stiglitz (1982c). In the context of moral hazard, see Arnott and Stiglitz (1988a, 1988b).

13. See Stiglitz (1982c) and Arnott and Stiglitz (1988b).

14. See Arnott and Stiglitz (1990).

15. See Stiglitz and Weiss (1983).

16. See, for instance, Stiglitz (1987g), where I show that even though there may be very many consumers and very many producers, the number of "free" consumers is sufficiently small that markets do not behave competitively.

17. For instance, if individuals have constant absolute risk-aversion utility functions, then linear contracts will be optimal (Milgrom and Roberts 1988), but constant absolute risk-aversion utility functions imply that individuals' marginal propensity to hold safe assets as their wealth increases is one. As people become wealthier, they are unwilling to hold additional risky assets.

18. See Stiglitz (1992a) for a more extensive discussion of the implications of asymmetric information and the legal structure for changes in the standard contractual forms.

Chapter 5

1. See Stiglitz (1982d, 1985b).

2. See Stiglitz (1972a, 1975a).

3. In particular, the above analysis assumed fierce "Bertrand" competition, with identical information and risk neutral bidders. Under more general conditions, with a limited number of bidders, the bidders will bid less than the full value. The fact that we see such high values being bid may be a reflection more of the irrationality of bidders, as they get carried away in the auction process (including the hubris of the takeover specialists), than of the ability of the bidding mechanism to extract full rent.

The general issue concerning divergences between private and social returns to the gathering of information has been discussed, for instance, by Hirshleifer (1971) and Stiglitz (1975c, 1985c).

4. For other problems with the takeover mechanism, see Stiglitz (1972a). There is by now a large literature analyzing when and under what conditions takeovers may provide some partial discipline on managers. The literature is too extensive to review here. Suffice it to say that while the takeover mechanism provides some discipline, it is limited.

The most dramatic example of firms that were "undervalued" but were not being taken over is provided by closed-end mutual funds. At times, particularly in the 1970s, these firms sold at a marked discount from the value of the underlying shares. There was accordingly a simple policy that would have enhanced market value—buy the firm and distribute the shares. Yet this did not occur.

5. Such schemes have the property that each individual receives the full marginal value of his or her contribution.

6. As in all rental contracts, the "renter" bears all the residual risk.

7. Borrowing does not resolve the agency problems. At most, it shifts them to the lender. See, for instance, Stiglitz and Weiss (1981).

8. See, for instance, Stiglitz (1975b).

9. The other tax paradoxes, discussed below, provide further evidence on this.

10. See Stiglitz (1987e).

11. My discussion in chapter 3 has already suggested one aspect of this, beyond the nonlinearity of compensation schedules. There I noted that effort may be enhanced by subsidizing complements to effort and taxing subsidies. Firms may be able to use similar devices. Landlords may enhance the effort of their sharecropping tenants (which increases the landlords' expected return) by providing fertilizer (which may increase the marginal return to effort) or by providing credit at below market interest rates (which may lead the tenant to buy more inputs, which in turn may lead to enhanced effort.) Thus concerns about incentives may lead to "interlinkages" across markets. Although this point was first made in the context of less developed countries (Braverman and Stiglitz 1982, 1986), it provides part of the rationale for certain vertical restraints in industrial economies.

12. This is a central theme of my forthcoming book with Richard Arnott.

13. The general point that (even optimally chosen) piece rates direct attention in particular ways, not necessarily commensurate with the interest of the firm, was made in the early discussions of piece rates, both at the theoretical level (e.g. Stiglitz, 1975b) and at the practical level of implementation. Workers would not have an incentive to train new workers. Unless quality could be accurately measured, and piece rates accurately reflected these quality differences, there might be a bias toward low-quality production. For more recent discussions, see Holmstrom and Milgrom (1991), and for an interesting application to the design of educational systems, see Hannaway (1992).

14. Indeed, when there is an incomplete set of risk markets, there will not be unanimity among shareholders concerning what objectives the firm should pursue (see, e.g., Grossman and Stiglitz 1980b). When there is a complete set of futures and risk markets, not only will there be unanimity concerning what objective the firm should pursue—maximizing market value—there is also no ambiguity about what that entails (see Stiglitz 1970, 1972a, 1972b). When these conditions are not satisfied, managerial judgment about what actions will maximize "long-run market value" is required, and this provides enormous scope for managerial discretion, making it difficult to ascertain whether the actions are being undertaken because of private or organizational objectives.

15. This was a point made in the earliest principal-agent literature, for instance, Stiglitz (1974) where it was pointed out that a manager is like a tenant farmer: The manager obtains but a fraction of the output that is due to his or her effort.

16. See Nalebuff and Stiglitz (1983b).

17. See Edlin and Stiglitz (1992).

18. Similar arguments apply for managers' incentives to discourage takeovers.

19. This particular part of the paradox is less—but only slightly less—paradoxical than it seems: In a perfect capital market risk-averse executives could divest themselves of the stock market risk, say, by selling short the S&P 500 index fund. In actual markets executives can imperfectly divest themselves of some of the risk. The question remains, however, why alternatives that reduce both transactions costs and (as we will see below) tax burdens are not employed.

20. If a firm pays a manager a $100 in pay, it is deductible from the corporation income tax. Before 1986 the federal government paid approximately 50 percent of the managers' pay. The combined corporate and individual taxes on $100 paid to the employee would be (for an individual in the 50 percent tax bracket) zero (the $50 reduced corporate income tax offset by the $50 increase in individual income taxes). By contrast, with a stock option the net tax paid would be approximately $25, with capital gains taxed at 50 percent of the ordinary rate. With capital gains and ordinary income taxed at a rate of 28 percent, a state income tax rate of, say, 6 percent, and a corporate income tax rate of 36 percent, the net tax paid with performance-based pay is $2, while with stock options that are not deductible from the corporate income tax the net tax paid is approximately $34; though, by deferring realization, the effective tax may be reduced, except under unusual circumstances it remains tax disadvantaged.

21. There are two criticisms of this argument. The first is that these uninformed individuals are a sufficiently small fraction of all investors that they have no effect on the market price. In most stock markets the number and importance of what would appear to be relatively uninformed traders seems quite large. The second is that prices are determined by the informed speculators, not the uninformed. The argument that all that it takes is a few informed individuals to ensure that the market behaves as if all individuals were informed is simply not correct (see Salop and Stiglitz 1977). Indeed, if information is costly, prices cannot fully reflect the information of the informed if there is to be any incentive to obtain information (Grossman and Stiglitz 1976, 1980a).

Chapter 6

1. The discussion of this section parallels certain aspects of the analyses of earlier chapters, where we argued that the assumption that there be a complete set of markets was implausible. One of the reasons we put forth was that there were simply too many *possible* commodities for there to be a competitive market for each.

2. As I noted earlier, the fact that competition is limited must be attributed not only to the high dimensionality of the product space but also to fixed costs of production (without such fixed costs, any firm could produce *all* commodities), and to costs of search/negotiation. (It takes time to find the firms producing the particular characteristics that one is interested in. So, even if there were many such firms, finding them might be difficult.)

There have been several extensions of the standard Arrow-Debreu model to include a continuum of commodities. These mathematical extensions might suggest that the model could handle quite complex product spaces, but they demonstrate the important distinction between economic and mathematical "limits" of the standard model. The problem with the Arrow-Debreu model is *not* that it assumed a finite number of commodities. I have stressed here the *economic* problems of defining commodities, and of how the presence of even small fixed costs will, in a world of product differentiation, lead to imperfect competition.

3. There are other explanations, one of which is discussed more fully later. As I showed in earlier chapters, in the presence of imperfect information, efficient economic relations cannot be "supported" by (linear) price relations.

4. As I noted earlier, we often distinguish between the observability of a variable by the parties to the contract (required for reputation mechanisms to work) and the verifiability of a variable, required for disputes to be resolved by third parties (courts). See, for instance, Newbery and Stiglitz (1987) or Hart and Holmstrom (1987).

5. This basic insight was noted and modeled independently, in different contexts, by Becker and Stigler (1974), Klein and Leffler (1981), Shapiro (1983), and Eaton and Gersovitz (1981). For a model analyzing the implications for the labor market, see Shapiro and Stiglitz (1984), and for a discussion of the implications for macroeconomics, see Stiglitz (1992a). For a discussion of more formal game theoretic analyses, see Kreps (1990).

The earlier analyses of reputation in product markets were not complete in that they omitted an adequate discussion of the entry conditions (the conditions for long-run equilibrium). While profits might be positive in the short run, long-run profits might be zero. For an analysis of the relation between short-run and long-run profits, see Stiglitz (1989b).

6. Those who believe in markets often find it difficult to be dissuaded from this belief by the evidence. In the case of these so-called coordination failures, they might point out that ex post excess capacity is not itself evidence of a misallocation of resources. After all, decisions must be made in the presence of uncertainty. In the presence of uncertainty, there will be some states of nature in which the level of investment is such that there is excess capacity.

7. The points in this section are discussed at slightly greater length in Stiglitz (1989c).

8. If one thought that providing information of this kind was of critical importance, then presumably the various units of large firms would have separate listings, but there is very little evidence of this.

9. This point was first forcefully made by Hirshleifer (1971). The relationship between social and private returns to information acquisition is discussed in Stiglitz (1975c).

10. For a more formal discussion, see Stiglitz and Weiss (1990).

11. The points in this paragraph are developed at greater length in Stiglitz (1982e). Formal proofs of related results are contained in Milgrom and Stokey (1982), and Tirole (1982).

12. There is a wider set of tax paradoxes, entailing the interaction of the corporate and individual income tax structures: For instance, firms pay dividends rather than buying back shares (the dividend paradox) (Stiglitz 1973b). These paradoxes are sometimes interpreted as reflecting managers' maximizing share market value, with irrational investors. In either case the view that stock markets lead to efficient behavior (in any meaningful sense), is questioned.

13. See Edlin and Stiglitz (1992) for a discussion of how managers can make decisions to manipulate the information available in the market to increase managerial rents.

14. One could of course argue that the problem was not one of incentives but incompetence. This is an equally damning criticism: Somehow the market did not do a good job in selecting evaluators.

15. By the same token, some econometric tests of the capital asset-pricing model seem to indicate that own-variance has an effect on price, contrary to the predictions of that model. There remains, however, considerable controversy over these findings.

16. In principle, by making incentive pay increase more than proportionately with income, the firm could induce the manager to act in a risk neutral manner. But firms do not seem to do this.

17. See Greenwald, Stiglitz, and Weiss (1984), Myers and Majluf (1984), Jensen and Meckling (1976), among others.

18. The argument is essentially an application of Akerlof's (1970) analysis of the market for lemons (used cars) to the capital market.

19. There is a clear analogy with a farmer renting his land (and getting all the marginal proceeds of his efforts) and entering a sharecropping contract with the landlord. See Stiglitz (1974).

20. See Jensen (1986). This list of explanations for why firms make limited use of equity is not meant to be exhaustive. Another theory that has enjoyed some popularity, largely I suspect because of its analytic simplicity, is called the costly state verification theory. The theory picks up on an old idea, that the information required to implement an equity contract is much larger than that required to implement a debt contract. With an equity contract, firm profits have to be observable, while with a debt contract, they do not. Only when the firm goes bankrupt does the debtor have to be able to ascertain what the borrowing firm's profits are. If it is costly to verify the state (the profits of the firm), then debt contracts clearly have an advantage.

This theory ignores the fact that there are a variety of other reasons that firms' profits have to be verified, for instance the firm must pay taxes, and it already has outstanding shares. Thus the marginal verification cost associated with issuing additional shares may be small, or zero. The theory is consistent with the emphasis put on the development of auditing standards and fraud laws (Greenwald and Stiglitz 1992), and the absence of equity markets for farms and other very small enterprises.

21. Alternatively, reputation mechanisms can work, but the profit margin (prices) have to be increased to make them effective.

22. It should be emphasized that this is an assumption not made just to simplify the analysis; it is essential to the conclusions concerning the efficiency of market resource allocations, as I pointed out in chapter 2.

23. There was even an attempt to provide a theoretical justification of this conclusion, by Diamond (1967), who constructed a model of an economy producing a single commodity which, under extremely restrictive conditions (outputs in every state of nature increased proportionately when firms increased investment, firms could not change the patterns of output, and there was no bankruptcy). But it was soon shown that when any of his assumptions were dropped—for example, if there were just two commodities, and firms maximized their stock market value—the economy would, in general, not be constrained Pareto efficient. See Stiglitz (1972b, 1982a).

24. I need to express a word of caution: Greenwald and Stiglitz do not show that there is a discontinuity in welfare with the "degree" of informational imperfection. Such a discontinuity does arise in the problem of existence (Rothschild and Stiglitz 1975, 1976; C. A. Wilson 1977) and in some of the characterizations of equilibrium (Diamond 1971; Salop and Stiglitz 1982).

Chapter 7

1. This chapter draws heavily upon Stiglitz (1992d).

2. As we saw in chapters 1 and 3, the Arrow-Debreu paradigm is important because it provides the rigorous intellectual basis of most of our faith in the market system: With perfectly competitive markets (provided a number of other conditions are satisfied) markets are Pareto efficient.

3. See Lazear and Rosen (1983), Green and Stokey (1983), Nalebuff and Stiglitz (1983a, 1983b), and Holmstrom (1982). These authors study incentive-based systems in which rewards depend on *relative* performance. In some cases rewards are based on *rank ordering*, that is, the person who produces the most gets a larger financial reward than the person who produces the second most. Nalebuff and Stiglitz (1983a) show that under certain conditions the optimal incentive structure entails a penalty for the worker with the lowest output, rather than a reward for the worker with the highest output.

4. The marginal return to effort in a contest is the increased probability of winning the prize times the size of the prize. The size of the risk is associated with the size of the prize.

In contests, by adjusting the size of the prize appropriately one can increase incentives to the level that they would have been with "perfect" incentives, that is, if the worker obtained all the marginal returns from his or her effort. The requisite prize will entail a lower level of risk bearing by the worker than if the worker's pay depended on his or her own output and all the marginal returns were obtained from the worker's effort.

5. This property is referred to by Nalebuff and Stiglitz (1983a) as *incentive flexibility*.

6. See Salop and Scheffman (1983).

7. The price-taking assumptions ensure exchange efficiency (goods are consumed by those who value them the most, in such a way that all individuals' marginal rates of substitution between goods are identical), production efficiency (goods are produced by those who can produce them most cheaply, in such a way that the economy operates along its production possibilities schedule), and product mix efficiency (the marginal rate of transformation— how much of one good must be reduced to produce one more unit of another—is equal to the marginal rate of substitution—how much of one good individuals are willing to give up to get one more unit of another.)

8. Consumers lose more than producers gain, but the difference is small.

9. See Baumol (1982) and Baumol, Panzar, and Willig (1982). See also Grossman (1981b).

10. Their argument went beyond this to the case of a multiproduct firm, where they argued that the structure of prices would coincide with that of a government trying to raise money to pay the overhead costs by taxing efficiently, that is, in such a way as to minimize deadweight loss. They argued that firms would charge prices in excess of marginal costs, according to precisely the same formula that Ramsey (1927) had suggested optimal taxes should have prices in excess of marginal costs. Though there is a certain superficial similarity

between the Ramsey problem and the monopolists' optimal pricing problem, there are some important differences, for instance, arising from the monopolists' inability to forestall entry of competitors and the necessity of setting prices to take that into account. See Sappington and Stiglitz (1987a).

11. There is a slight inconsistency here: At the margin, in competitive markets, price equals marginal cost, so at the margin the producer and distributor do not bear any loss from a loss in sales. Of course more realistically price exceeds marginal costs, and both do bear losses.

12. We will discuss the limitations on competition policy at greater length below.

13. The ideas I refer to as the "new view" are sometimes discussed under the rubric "post-Chicago" views.

14. *Wealth of Nations*, bk. 1, ch. 10, pt. II.

15. I differentiate between monopolistic competition and oligopoly: In the former there are a sufficiently large number of firms that each does not take into account any strategic interactions with other firms. Chamberlin provided the original analysis of monopolistic competition. As we noted above, the theory was revived by Spence (1976) and Dixit and Stiglitz (1977).

Several of the classic studies, such as Salop (1979b), used the spatial representation, with firms differentiated by location, located at points along a circle. This representation has been criticized because any firm has only two neighbors and thus should be aware of strategic responses. This objection, however, is not valid for spatial representations in higher dimensional spaces. See Stiglitz (1986a).

16. See Salop and Stiglitz (1977, 1982), Stiglitz (1979, 1987c), for further references. For a survey, see Stiglitz (1989b).

17. Salop and Stiglitz (1982) showed that, under the assumptions employed by Diamond, if firms could use nonlinear prices (e.g., charge a fixed fee plus a "price" equal to marginal cost), it would pay them to do so. If they did that, and there was a fixed cost to entering the market, then there would exist no equilibrium. In their efforts to extract all the consumer surplus out of their customers, the greedy stores actually destroyed the market.

What prevents this from happening is "noise" in the market—the existence of product diversity and price dispersions. See below and Stiglitz (1989b).

18. Early examples of this approach include Dixit (1980), Spence (1979), Salop (1979a), and Stiglitz (1981a).

19. Stiglitz (1987g) and Dasgupta and Stiglitz (1988a).

20. See Salop (1979). Dasgupta and Stiglitz (1980a), and Gilbert and Newbery (1982), among others.

21. In some cases the threat of potential competition—with its induced response by the incumbent firm to deter entry—may be welfare decreasing. The incumbent firm may, for instance, construct new capacity early enough that it deters new entrants from entering. In the extreme case, profits may be driven to zero, but this is not a sign of economic efficiency: Rents are simply being dissipated by excess capacity. See Stiglitz (1981a, 1987g).

22. Dasgupta and Stiglitz (1988a) and Stiglitz (1987g).

23. In the United States the notion of the small farmer (and by extension, the small entrepreneur) has played a central role in conceptions of the "American ideal" society often associated with Thomas Jefferson.

24. See the discussion in the first part of this chapter.

25. Stiglitz (1987g) illustrates this with a case where firms build excess capacity to deter entry to such an extent that virtually all of profits are dissipated.

26. Salop and Scheffman (1983) develop the theory of raising rival costs, as well as providing examples of where it has occurred.

27. The following paragraphs are from Stiglitz (1993a).

28. In particular, he did not explain well why it is that some regulators are captured by consumer interest groups, while others are captured by industry interest groups.

29. States typically do not allow firms from outside the state to sell within their borders, thus limiting entry. Many states even have laws requiring firms to post prices, thus facilitating collusion.

30. It is curious that much of the early discussions of the formulation of competition in this model worried not about whether this accurately captured the nature of competition in market economies, but whether the price-taking assumption was consistent with assumptions of there being a finite number of firms or households. Even if there were a billion firms, surely each must have a detectable effect (in a world of perfect information) on the price level. Only if there were a continuum of agents would the model be coherent.

31. Firms were simply ordered to maximize profits, given the prices announced by the central planning agency. More recent discussions have noted that firms would recognize that the government agency revises the prices it calls off in response to firms' announcements of planned inputs and outputs at the announced prices; if there were not a continuum of firms, firms might behave strategically, attempting to affect the prices the government announced. Of course, since managers in the market socialist economy had no objective other than maximizing social welfare—and followed instructions carefully, playing according to the rules set forth by the central planners—if the central planner told the managers not to act strategically, presumably they would not. By the time we have arrived at this juncture in the world of market socialism, the departure of the model from reality is so great that it is hard to know which of the assumptions to fault most.

Chapter 8

1. While there is some debate about what fraction of growth in per capita incomes is due to technological change (versus capital accumulation)—with Solow (1957) arguing that more than 80 percent of it can be traced to changes in technology—few would deny its central importance.

2. See Arrow (1962a).

3. R&D competition is much better described as a "patent" race (see Barzel 1968; Stiglitz 1971; and Dasgupta and Stiglitz 1980a) or, more broadly, by the general theory of contests (see Nalebuff and Stiglitz 1983a; Lazear and Rosen 1981). For an application of the theory of contests to R&D, see Stiglitz (1986b).

4. See Stiglitz (1987d) and Dasgupta and Stiglitz (1980b).

5. For a study exploring this idea, see Dasgupta, Gilbert, and Stiglitz (1983).

6. For a fuller discussion of these issues, see Stiglitz (1969).

7. See Stiglitz (1971), Samuelson (1965), or Barzel (1968).

8. This issue is known as the "persistence of monopoly" (Dasgupta and Stiglitz 1980a; Salop 1979; Gilbert and Newbery 1982).

9. As Dasgupta and Stiglitz (1980) noted in a footnote.

10. See Stiglitz (1987g) and Harris and Vickers (1987).

11. See Dasgupta and Stiglitz (1988b).

12. The somewhat surprising implication of this analysis, paralleling that of Stiglitz (1987g) is that the stronger the ex post competition, the weaker will be the ex ante (potential) competition. Firms will not enter, even when current profits are observed to be high, because they believe that given the fierceness of ex post competition, those profits will quickly be bid away.

13. Of course, if the firms have perfect foresight, the relevant marginal cost for determining the current production decisions is their long-run marginal costs, so even slight differences in *current* marginal costs of production can result in large differences in current levels of production.

14. See Sah and Stiglitz (1987).

15. For a fuller discussion of the issues presented in this section, see Stiglitz (1987b).

16. Radner and Stiglitz (1984) showed that there was a fundamental nonconvexity associated with the *amount* of information; it never paid to acquire just a little bit of information, or to put it another way, "ignorance, if not bliss, is a local optimum."

17. In some overly simple models, one can devise well-defined solutions to the problem of devising incentive-compatible contracts: If there is common knowledge about the profits that the buyer would have made in the absence of the innovation, the seller can offer a contract that provides returns in excess of that amount, so the buyer would have nothing to lose.

Chapter 9

1. As I pointed out in chapter 6, investment funds are not allocated simply by giving them to the firm that *promises* to pay the highest interest rate.

2. The intuition behind the result is simple: When the hierarchy is long, too few projects pass all the requisite approvals. There are in a sense too many errors of one type (rejecting good projects) relative to the errors of the other type (accepting bad projects). By dividing the hierarchy into two, and constructing a polyarchy of two hierarchies, one moves to restore the balance.

3. See Sah and Stiglitz (1991).

4. Recent advances in the theory of options suggest that with high sunk costs of transition, this may not be as irrational as it seems. See Dixit (1992).

5. For instance, Arnott and Stiglitz (1990) show the limits on the extent to which a tax on insurance can correct the problem of "overinsurance" in the presence of moral hazard (without observability of the insurance purchases of any individual).

6. Such schemes typically require the worker to pay a fixed amount but to receive, in return, an amount equal to the total value of the output of the organization. Thus the individual acts to maximize the value of the organization's output.

7. The following paragraphs draw heavily from my NOG lecture, delivered to the annual meeting of the Austrian Economic Society, Vienna, September 29, 1988, subsequently published as Stiglitz (1989d).

8. Of course a century ago bureaucracies were not such a focus of opprobrium (cf. the discussion in Weber). They were thought to represent a devolution of control upon the meritocracy, an improvement over the aristocracy and, for those who have less faith in market mechanisms, of the commercial classes.

9. In my NOG lecture (1989d), I provide a more extensive discussion of this point.

10. This point—and the more general perspective concerning the importance of decentralization for reasons other than those considered in standard economic and information models—has been emphasized by Hannaway (1989).

Chapter 10

1. This chapter draws heavily from two papers, Sappington and Stiglitz (1987b) and Stiglitz (1991b). Much of the chapter, while raising issues of general principle, is devoted to particular issues associated with the management of transition and may be omitted without loss of continuity.

2. Perhaps I should more accurately say that popular interpretations of Coase go wrong in these respects: Coase was careful to point out that his conclusion depended on the absence of transaction costs and information costs.

3. In Stiglitz (1989f) I provide some rationale for these restrictions.

4. See McKinnon (1992) and Stiglitz (1991b, 1992e).

5. In either case, organizational objectives have to be translated into individual objectives, requiring the design of individual incentive structures.

6. A host of other government policies are likely to affect profitability in an important way, such as the extent of protectionism, competition policy, and the speed of price reforms.

7. See Stiglitz (1972a) and Myers (1977).

8. There has been a limited theoretical literature concerning this problem of "hooking" onto a lender: Once the lender has made an initial loan, it is "forced" to provide additional loans, to recover the initial loan. See Hellwig (1977) and Stiglitz and Weiss (1981).

9. This system of "shared governance" has seemingly proved extremely effective within the People's Republic of China.

10. A problem arises when the enterprise is "owned" by a subunit of the government in which case the money is not received back by the central government.

11. Alexander Dyck, in a Ph.D. dissertation recently completed at Stanford, has argued forcefully that the essential problem facing East Germany was acquiring good managers. He argued that because of problems of adverse selection (see Akerlof 1971 or Greenwald 1986),

state enterprises within East Germany were at a marked disadvantage in acquiring good managers, compared to West German firms.

12. See Stiglitz (1985b, 1990c) and Arnott and Stiglitz (1991).

13. And revived more recently in Stiglitz (1985b).

14. For a more extensive discussion of the limited control of shareholders and the limitations of takeover mechanisms, see, for instance, Stiglitz (1972a, 1981b) and Grossman and Hart (1980).

15. This is not quite accurate: Though they have the right to demand their funds back, whether they can actually get their funds back is often more questionable, as Hellwig (1977) and Stiglitz and Weiss (1981) point out. They can, of course, force the firm into bankruptcy. Compared to long-term lending, short-term lending has a decided advantage as a control mechanism. See Rey and Stiglitz (1992).

16. These are just manifestations of the adverse selection–lemons problem. In the case where the original owners are more informed and are selling equity, and buyers are risk neutral, the only equilibrium price for shares is zero. More generally, equity markets will be thin. See Greenwald, Stiglitz, and Weiss (1984) and Myers and Majluf (1984).

17. There are severe problems with monitoring net profits. Excessively high royalty rates give rise to large distortions when net profits are not monitored perfectly.

18. There never exists a majority voting equilibrium in the context of pure redistributions.

19. This list of limitations is not meant to be exhaustive. Sappington and Stiglitz (1987b) discuss a third important category of problems, that which arises when the government has more information concerning the value of the asset being sold than do bidders.

Chapter 11

1. This phenomenon is known as the ratchet effect. It is discussed in Stiglitz (1975b) and in Weitzman (1974).

Chapter 12

1. This chapter is devoted to a discussion of particular problems of the transition to a market economy. The chapter may be omitted without loss of continuity. This chapter was originally presented at a conference sponsored by the Institute of Policy Reform and IRIS (University of Maryland) on "The Transition to a Market Economy—Institutional Aspects" Prague, Czechoslovakia, March 24–27, 1991, and published as "The Design of Financial Systems for the Newly Emerging Democracies of Eastern Europe," in *The Emergence of Market Economies in Eastern Europe*, C. Clague and G. C. Rausser (eds.), Basil Blackwell, Cambridge, 1992, pp. 161–184.

2. See Stiglitz (1993a).

3. This may overestimate the true social loss. Much of the loss is in real estate, and some of these expenditures were for the purchase of land. The banks' borrowers (and thus, with default, the bank) made speculative mistakes. They overpaid for the land. But these are pure transfer payments. Of course these transfer payments may adversely affect the level of real savings of the economy, and thus have a deleterious effect on the economy's growth path.

4. For a more extensive discussion of these various functions see, for instance, Stiglitz (1985b), Greenwald and Stiglitz (1992), Stiglitz and Weiss (1990); Fama (1980), and the references cited in these papers.

5. This can be viewed (like some of the other functions) as "economizing on transactions costs, including information costs." Individuals can diversify without using financial intermediaries, but at greater costs.

6. In a sense this is but a minor objection to the standard theory: It is easy to extend the standard theory to include at least some forms of transactions costs. See, for instance, Foley (1970) and Hahn (1971). The other objections are far more serious.

7. Again, this is an aspect of technology that is *assumed away* in the standard competitive paradigm where nonconvexities are ruled out.

8. See Mayer (1989, 1990).

9. See Stiglitz (1988b,c), Stiglitz and Weiss (1981), Greenwald, Stiglitz, and Weiss (1984), and Myers and Majluf (1984).

10. In addition there may be an economy of scope between the enforcement of fraud laws and this kind of regulation. It is easier to enforce fraud if there are clear (and compulsory) standards of disclosure.

11. See, for instance, Stiglitz (1975c) or Grossman (1981).

12. Beyond fraud laws, which prohibit outright deception.

13. We will discuss later how the government attempts to do this.

14. In the United States there are laws intended to make sure that borrowers know the true rate of interest they pay on loans and that purchasers of equity know the true risks that they are undertaking in making an investment.

15. The government takes a less active role in ensuring the solvency of most other financial institutions, with the possible exception of insurance. Insurance firms are highly regulated, and the government in most states has established a guaranty fund to protect those who purchase insurance against the consequences of insolvency of insurance firms.

16. Tax considerations may limit the extent to which they do this. But when a bank is in difficulties, regulatory considerations are likely to dominate tax considerations.

17. See Hirschleifer (1971). For a more general discussion of the principles of "information and rent seeking," see Stiglitz (1975c).

18. See Stiglitz and Weiss (1990) for a formal model of this.

19. See Stiglitz (1994) for a more extended discussion of market failures in financial markets.

20. See, for instance, Stiglitz (1985b).

21. My earlier remarks suggested that there may be "negative" organizational capital: The outmoded ways of thinking associated with banking under socialism may tinge the banks in the new economic situation, and thus impair their ability to perform their new, different, and more important economic role.

22. Because, unlike what happens when a bank is sold, there has been no outside assessment of the value of assets and liability (as unreliable as those assessments might be) and no infusion of additional equity from the outside (which might normally be expected to occur in the event of a privatization of a bank).

23. Again the difficulties of valuing the financial institution's existing assets make it difficult to ascertain whether the financial institution is doing a "good" job.

24. It is worth noting that the nationalization of the Rumanian debt, to which I referred in the previous chapter, represents an interesting compromise: No attempt was made to value physical assets; financial obligations of the firm to other firms (previously government owned) were converted into financial obligations of the firm to the government.

25. An important issue in the transition process is how to deal more broadly with these inherited obligations. Inflation is obviously one way of reducing their importance, but this obviously has its own disadvantages. A fuller discussion of this issue would take us beyond the scope of this chapter.

26. This undoubtedly oversimplifies the situation, particularly in countries such as Hungary and the former Yugoslavia where firms had some autonomy, where there were bankruptcy laws, and where the government did not as a consequence serve as the ultimate guarantor of all loans.

27. For a more extensive discussion of this, see McKinnon (1992).

28. See, for instance, Stiglitz (1988c).

29. See Greenwald and Stiglitz (1993) for a model in which the effect of capital market conditions on aggregate demand and supply are analyzed simultaneously. Calvo and Frankel (1991) have emphasized the role of these supply effects in the transition process.

30. Although there is some debate about the significance of the costs of bankruptcy, in the process of transition, when all of society's resources are being reorganized, the disruption in the use of resources following a bankruptcy may be particularly costly. The external costs of bankruptcy are especially large when there is only one supplier of a good, as was often the case under central planning.

31. Such marketable quantity constraints have been introduced in the United States for the control of certain kinds of pollution. Weitzman (1974) provides an analysis of the advantages of the use of quantities versus prices as control mechanisms in the presence of uncertain benefit and cost functions. Such an analysis can be extended to the problem under consideration here.

The kinds of criticisms raised against the use of the price system for the allocation of credit (Stiglitz 1988d) can be raised here, for the use of the price system in allocating the rights to allocate credit among financial institutions.

32. See Eaton (1986), Shapiro (1983), Schmalensee (1982), or Stiglitz (1989b).

33. The government would, in any case, have a difficult time adjusting premiums to reflect risk: Is it likely that the government could charge higher premiums for deposit insurance in one state than in another, declaring that, in its estimate, the risks are greater?

A number of recent proposals have suggested ways by which the government can employ market mechanisms to provide "objective" determinations of the appropriate premium levels. For instance, the government can "sell" a portion of the insurance in the re-insurance market, using the prices determined there as the basis for levying premiums.

34. Banks complain that marking to market assets is "unfair" since, in practice, not all assets are marked to market; some assets, such as the physical assets the bank owns, typically are not revalued. But there is less justification in this complaint than at first seems the case. Under current practice banks have, in effect, the option of revaluing assets at their own discretion. An asset that has increased in value can be marketed, and thus the capital gain

recorded; an asset that has decreased in value can be kept on the books at the original value. Accordingly "book" value can present a strongly biased view of the firm.

35. For discussions of these problems, see Stiglitz (1972a, 1982d, 1985b) and Grossman and Hart (1980).

36. For a theoretical analysis of why this is so, and of the incentive effects of credit termination, see Stiglitz and Weiss (1983).

37. See Berle and Means (1932) and Stiglitz (1985b). Part of the reason for the concentration of debt is that, given the limited extent of risk, risk diversification is less important than in the case of equity.

38. Some people envisage the holding companies as having only a role in the transition process. While eventually shares are widely held, they see a process of concentration, with eventually some ownership shares being sufficiently large to play an effective role in control. There is little evidence on the speed with which such concentration would occur, or indeed whether it would eventually occur, in which case the holding companies would become a permanent part of the scene.

39. To some extent, designing financial institutions that "work well" with those of Western Europe may be as important as any of the factors we have listed, if the Eastern European countries want to be integrated quickly into Europe.

It is perhaps worth noting that the United States quite explicitly tried to restrict the extent to which one firm could own or control other firms (at least in related industries)— because of its concern over the resulting potential for collusive behavior. On the other hand, having firms own other firms (as seems prevalent in Japan) may provide a more effective system of "peer monitoring." See Arnott and Stiglitz (1991) for a discussion of the role of peer monitoring in mitigating moral hazard problems.

40. For a review of the data for recent years, see Mayer (1989).

41. Of the kind that can result from speculative bubbles.

Chapter 13

1. This chapter draws in part on a paper delivered to a joint meeting of the Chinese Academy of Social Sciences and the National Academy of Sciences, held at Wingspreads, Wisconsin, in December 1980.

2. Simon (1991), p. 28.

3. For citations to some of the relevant evidence, see Stiglitz (1988b, 1991c). Many of the better studies make a valiant effort to adjust for the differing circumstances of the communities in which public and private services are provided, but the corrections are usually (in my judgment) not fully convincing. The communities in which private provision has been chosen often differ in numerous ways from other communities, and not all of the ways may be picked up in the statistical adjustments used in the econometric studies. (There may accordingly be a significant sample-selection bias.) Moreover a Hawthorne effect may arise in those cases where private provision of public services is being tried on an experimental basis. Thus the often-cited results on the greater efficiency of fire protection in Scottsdale, Arizona, appear to suffer from both sources of bias.

4. In the case of the firm, in general, in the absence of a complete set of markets, shareholders will not agree about the objectives, as I noted in chapter 2.

5. See, for instance, Bhagwati (1987), Kreuger (1987), and Buchanan (1986).

6. See the discussion in chapters 5 and 6.

7. These points have been emphasized in Hannaway (1989).

8. Of course standard theory says that a private monopoly is perfectly efficient. It wishes to maximize profits, and it does so by minimizing costs. The criticism of monopoly is not that it is inefficient, but that it produces too little. Casual observation of monopolies suggests that this conclusion is simply wrong. Leibenstein (1966) provided an explanation, in terms of what he called X-inefficiency. Modern information economics has provided a rigorous basis for understanding this kind of inefficiency, in terms of theories of managerial discretion.

9. Earlier I discussed the implications of this for the process of privatization. See chapter 10. There I noted that governments can affect the transactions costs facing subsequent governments, and hence affect their behavior.

10. In recent years, in the United States, there has been a substantial weakening in the presumption that higher pay for top executives reflects higher productivity. In the previous paragraph, I anthropomorphized the firm. I spoke, for instance, of the money coming out of the pocket of the firm. As I have repeatedly stressed, the shareholders exert only limited control over the actions of the firm's managers, and when the board of directors (over which management often exerts effective control) decides to pay their executives higher pay, it comes out of the pocket of shareholders. Shareholders are compelled to pay. Yet there is a fundamental difference: No one is compelled to be a shareholder in any particular firm, but everyone is compelled to pay taxes.

11. Discussed briefly in chapter 6.

12. Some of the observed lower productivity of government employees may not represent a social loss but simply a form of redistribution. These workers might have been unproductive in any job to which they were assigned. It is only that in the private sector their wages would have reflected the lower productivity.

Chapter 14

1. This point was made most forcefully in an early paper by Weitzman (1974), providing conditions under which quotas dominate prices. Dasgupta and Stiglitz (1977) similarly show, in the quite different context of international trade, that quotas may dominate prices (tariffs).

2. This was the thrust of the fundamental theorem on the nondecentralizability of the economy discussed in chapters 3 and 4. There we noted that the externalities implied the desirability of government intervention. (In some cases the externalities can be internalized. This provides the rationale for the interlinkage of credit, land, and product markets observed in less developed countries, as Braverman and Stiglitz 1982, 1986, observe.) Beyond this, information problems provide two further reasons why decentralization may not work. First, the second welfare theorem requires convexity, while information problems in general, and moral hazard in particular, gives rise to nonconvexity (see Arnott and Stiglitz 1988). Second, in the presence of information problems (in particular, moral hazard problems), cross-subsidizations are desirable; that is, welfare is increased by taxing output in one sector to provide subsidies to another (see Arnott and Stiglitz 1989).

3. At one time it was hoped that one could find a set of conditions under which, say, a set of theorems, corresponding to the fundamental theorems of welfare economics, could be established for local public goods provided competitively by different communities. Competition among communities would always result in Pareto efficiency, and any Pareto-efficient allocation of local public goods could be provided by means of competitive communities. In a series of papers (Stiglitz 1977a, 1983a, 1983b) I establish that the conditions under which such theorems could be established were far more stringent than those of the standard welfare theorems. If those conditions were satisfied, one could make certain predictions about community voting patterns and compositions, predictions that were easy to refute. Nonetheless, Tiebout's basic insights on the usefulness of local communities and the role of competition among communities remain, I believe, of value.

4. Formosa Plastics, which has grown into one of the major world producers, is an example.

Chapter 15

1. The standard reasoning against the infant industry argument (other than that based on political economy—the inability of the government to distinguish in practice among the truly deserving and those not deserving of protection) typically overlooks the fact that the informational problems that underlie infant industry arguments are such that market equilibria will not, in general, be (constrained) Pareto efficient; the imperfections of capital markets, which I have discussed above, imply that firms may not be able to borrow the funds required if they are to obtain the requisite skills to compete effectively. See Dasgupta and Stiglitz (1988b).

2. Governments can provide protection and at the same time encourage competition among domestic producers. Many suggest that the Japanese automobile market was effectively protected, but competition among the automobile firms was very keen.

3. See chapter 10 for a more extensive discussion of the issue of privatization.

4. In the very early days of the reform, I participated in discussions with economists from China who were concerned about how one could figure out what the equilibrium prices were. They knew that the prices they had were wrong, but solving the requisite computable general equilibrium model was not viewed to be feasible, and the information that it might yield, given all the strong assumptions that go into such a model, would probably be of limited value.

5. An analogy may make clear the ambiguities. In reconstructing a house, two approaches are often compared. Sometimes it is suggested that it makes more sense simply to tear down the old house and start from scratch. At other times it is suggested that it is preferable to renovate one part of a house, then another, gradually moving through the entire structure, until at the end, little of the original building is left. This is generally the preferred method when one needs to use the structure—one cannot do without it for the extended period required in the first scenario.

6. Drèze and Sen (1989) have emphasized the role of democracy in imposing political constraints impeding the occurrence of famines of the magnitude of those in China under Mao.

Chapter 16

1. This notion was emphasized in the reputation models (including the efficiency wage theories) I discussed earlier.

2. We should note the extensive literature arguing that certain forms of altruism have survival value in an evolutionary context. (The critical issue in that context is, What is the relevant unit of analysis?)

3. Quoted by Heilbroner, in "Reflections: Economic Predictions," *New Yorker*, July 8, 1991.

4. George Akerlof, in a conversation, put forth a possible explanation: Because these are virtues that have economic value, employers and others screen individuals to find out whether they have them. Parents, who "believe" in self-interested behavior, might like to be able to train their children to *seem* to have those characteristics but at the same time to be *really* simply self-interested. But this turns out to be difficult. Dissembling is not an easy matter. The only way effectively to make children *seem* to be cooperative and honest is *actually* to possess those characteristics. Of course, once so trained, they are sincere in training their children to possess those characteristics.

There are other examples where the standard model of the economic individual fails. For instance, there is evidence showing that individuals may be more effectively motivated by intrinsic than extrinsic rewards. Advocates of the central place for "self-interested" behavior in economics dismiss these results as special cases, or wrinkles on the basic theory: They argue that, by and large, most economic behavior can be explained by the simple hypothesis that individuals are self-interested.

5. This section borrows heavily from Stiglitz (1992c).

6. Earlier contributions to this literature include Farrell (1970), Alchian (1950), Winter (1971, 1975), and Nelson and Winter (1974, 1982). There have been at least three large, more recent strands of literature: one growing out of the Nelson and Winters work and focusing on technology (and including works such as Dosi et al. 1988 and Hanusch 1988), the second growing out of recent work in sociobiology (including the work of Maynard-Smith 1976, 1982 and Hirshleifer 1977), which has been further refined within game theory under the concept of evolutionarily stable equilibrium, and the third growing out of the organizational literature (as exemplified by the work of Hannan and Freeman 1977, McKelvey 1982 and Pelikan, 1982, 1989).

References

Akerlof, G. 1970. The market for "Lemons": Qualitative uncertainty and the market mechanism. *Quarterly Journal of Economics* 86:488–500.

Akerlof, G. 1991. Procrastination and obedience. *American Economic Review* 81:1–19.

Alchian, A. 1950. Uncertainty, evolution and economic theory. *Journal of Political Economy* 58:211–221.

Amsden, A. H. 1989. *Asia's Next Giant: South Korea and Late Industrialization*. Oxford University Press, Oxford.

Arnott, R., B. C. Greenwald, and J. E. Stiglitz. 1992. Information and economic efficiency. Paper presented at AEA annual meeting in New Orleans.

Arnott, R., and J. E. Stiglitz. 1985. Labor turnover, wage structure and moral hazard: The inefficiency of competitive markets. *Journal of Labor Economics* 3:434–462.

Arnott, R., and J. E. Stiglitz. 1986. Moral hazard and optimal commodity taxation. *Journal of Public Economics* 23:1–24.

Arnott, R., and J. E. Stiglitz. 1988a. The basic analytics of moral hazard. *Scandinavian Journal of Economics* 90:383–413.

Arnott, R., and J. E. Stiglitz. 1988b. Randomization with asymmetric information. *Rand Journal of Economics* 19:344–362.

Arnott, R., and J. E. Stiglitz. 1989. The welfare economics of moral hazard. In *Risk, Information and Insurance: Essays in the Memory of Karl H. Borch*, Henri Louberge (ed.). Kluwer Academic Publishers, Norwell, MA, pp. 91–122.

Arnott, R., and J. E. Stiglitz. 1990a. Price equilibrium, efficiency, and decentralizability in insurance markets. Working Paper, Stanford University.

Arnott, R., and J. E. Stiglitz. 1990b. Equilibrium in competitive insurance markets with moral hazard. Working Paper, Stanford University.

Arnott, R., and J. E. Stiglitz. 1991. Moral hazard and non-market Institutions: Dysfunctional crowding out or peer monitoring. *American Economic Review* 81:179–190.

Arrow, K. J. 1951a. *Social Choice and Individual Values*. Wiley, New York.

Arrow, K. J. 1951b. An extension of the basic theorem of classical welfare economics. In *Proceedings of the Second Berkeley Symposium on Mathematical Studies and Probability*, J. Neyman (ed.). University of California Press, Berkeley, pp. 507–532.

Arrow, K. J. 1962a. The economic implications of learning by doing. *Review of Economic Studies* 29:155–173.

Arrow, K. J. 1962b. Economic welfare and the allocation of resources for invention. In *The Rate and Direction of Inventive Activity*. Princeton University Press, Princeton, pp. 609–625.

Arrow, K. J. 1974. *The Limits of Organization*. Norton, New York.

Arrow, K. J. 1988. Toward a theory of price adjustment. In *The Allocation of Economic Resources*, P. A. Baran, T. Scitovsky, and E. S. Shaw (eds.). Stanford: Stanford University Press.

Arrow, K. J., and G. Debreu. 1954. Existence of an equilibrium for a competitive economy. *Econometrica* 22:265–290.

Asquith, P., and D. W. Mullins. 1986a. Equity issues and stock price dilution. *Journal of Financial Economics* 13:296–320.

Asquith, P., and D. W. Mullins. 1986b. Equity issues and offering dilution. *Journal of Financial Economics* 15:61–89.

Bain, J. S. 1956. *Barriers to New Competition*. Harvard University Press, Cambridge.

Bardhan, P. (ed.). 1989. *The Economic Theory of Agrarian Institutions*. Clarendon Press, Oxford.

Barzel, Y. 1968. Optimal timing of innovations. *Review of Economic Studies* 35:348–355.

Bator, F. 1958. The anatomy of market failures. *Quarterly Journal of Economics* 72:351–379.

Baumol, W. J. 1959. *Business Behavior, Value and Growth*. Harcourt Brace, New York.

Baumol, W. J. 1982. Contestable markets: An uprising in the theory of industry structure. *American Economic Review* 72:1–15.

Baumol, W. J., J. C. Panzar, and R. D. Willig. 1982. *Contestable Markets and the Theory of Industry Structure*. Harcourt Brace Jovanovich, San Diego.

Becker, G., and G. Stigler. 1974. Law enforcement, malfeasance, and compensation of enforcers. *Journal of Legal Studies* 3:1–18.

Berle, A. 1926a. Management power and stockholders' property. *Harvard Business Review* 5:424–432.

Berle, A., Jr. 1926b. Non-voting stock and "bankers" control. *Harvard Law Review*.

Berle, A., and G. Means. 1932. *The Modern Corporation and Private Property*. Commerce Clearing House, New York.

Bhagwati, J. 1987. The generalized theory of distortions and welfare. In *International Trade*, J. Bhagwati (ed.). Cambridge University Press, Cambridge, pp. 265–286.

Blinder, A. S. 1987. *Hard Heads, Soft Hearts: Tough-Minded Economics for a Just Society*. Addison-Wesley, Reading, MA.

Braverman, A., and J. E. Stiglitz. 1982. Sharecropping and the interlinking of agrarian markets. *American Economic Review* 72:695–715.

Braverman, A., and J. E. Stiglitz. 1986. Cost sharing arrangement under sharecropping: Moral hazard, incentive flexibility and risk. *Journal of Agricultural Economics* 68:642–652.

Bray, M., and D. M. Kreps. 1987. Rational learning and rational expectations. In *Arrow and the Ascent of Modern Economic Theory*. New York University Press, New York, pp. 597–625.

Brito, D., J. Hamilton, S. Slutsky, and J. Stiglitz. 1990. Pareto-efficient tax structures. *Oxford Economic Papers* 42:61–77.

Buchanan, J. 1986. *Liberty, Market and State, Political Economics in the 1980s*. New York University Press, New York.

Burroughs, B., and J. Helyar. 1990. *Barbarians at the Gate*. Harper and Row, New York.

Calvo, G, and J. Frankel. 1991. Credit markets, credibility, and economic transformation. *Journal of Economic Perspectives* 5:139–148.

Caves, D. W., and L. R. Christensen. 1980. The relative efficiency of public and private firms in a competitive environment: The case of Canadian railroads. *Journal of Political Economy* 88:958–976.

Chamberlin, E. 1933. *The Theory of Monopolistic Competition*. Harvard University Press, Cambridge.

Cheung, S. 1963. *The Theory of Share Tenancy*. Chicago University Press, Chicago.

Clark, J. B. 1923. *Studies in the Economies of Overhead Costs*. Chicago University Press, Chicago.

Coase, R. 1937. The nature of the firm. *Economica*: 386–405.

Coase, R. 1960. On the problem of social cost. *Journal of Law and Economics* 3:1–44.

Dasgupta, P. 1993. *An Inquiry into Well-being and Destination*. Oxford: Oxford University Press.

Dasgupta, P., and J. E. Stiglitz. 1972. On optimal taxation and public production. *Review of Economic Studies* 39:87–103.

Dasgupta, P., and J. E. Stiglitz. 1977. Tariffs vs. quotas as revenue raising devices under uncertainty. *American Economic Review* 67:975–981.

Dasgupta, P., and J. E. Stiglitz. 1980a. Uncertainty, market structure and the speed of R&D. *Bell Journal of Economics* 11:1–28.

Dasgupta, P., and J. E. Stiglitz. 1980b. Industrial structure and the nature of innovative activity. *Economic Journal* 90:266–293.

Dasgupta, P., and J. E. Stiglitz. 1988a. Potential competition, actual competition and economic welfare. *European Economic Review* 32:569–577.

Dasgupta, P., and J. E. Stiglitz. 1988b. Learning by doing, market structure and industrial and trade policies. *Oxford Economic Papers* 40:246–268.

Dasgupta, P., R. Gilbert, and J. E. Stiglitz. 1983. Strategic considerations in invention and innovation: The case of natural resources. *Econometrica* 512:1439–1448.

Debreu, G. 1951. The coefficient of resource utilization. *Econometrica* 19:273–292.

Debreu, G. 1959. *The Theory of Value*. Wiley, New York.

Demsetz, M. 1968. Why regulate utilities? *Journal of Law and Economics* 11:55–66.

Diamond, P. 1967. The role of the stock market in a general equilibrium model with technological uncertainty. *American Economic Review* 57:759–776.

Diamond, P. 1971. A model of price adjustment. *Journal of Economic Theory* 3:156–168.

Dixit, A. 1980. The role of investment in entry-deterrence. *Economic Journal* 90:95–106.

Dixit, A. 1992. Investment and hysteresis. *Journal of Economic Perspectives* 6:107–132.

Dixit, A., and J. E. Stiglitz. 1977. Monopolistic competition and optimal product diversity. *American Economic Review* 67:297–308.

Domar, E., and R. Musgrave. 1944. Proportional income taxation and risk taking. *Quarterly Journal of Economics* 58:388–422.

Dosi, G., C. Freeman, R. Nelson, G. Silverberg, and L. Soete. 1988. *Technological Change and Economic Theory*. Pinter, London.

Drèze, J. 1974. Investment under private ownership: Optimality, equilibrium and stability. In *Allocation under Uncertainty: Equilibrium and Optimality*, J. Drèze (ed.). Macmillan, New York, pp. 261–297.

Drèze, J. 1987. *Essays on Economic Decisions under Uncertainty*. Cambridge University Press, Cambridge.

Drèze, J., and A. K. Sen. 1989. *Hunger and Public Action*. Oxford University Press, Oxford.

Eaton, J. 1986. Lending with costly enforcement of repayment and potential fraud. *Journal of Banking and Finance* 10:281–293.

Eaton, J., and M. Gersowitz. 1981. Debt with potential repudiation: Theoretical and empirical analysis. *Review of Economic Studies* 48:289–309.

Edlin, A., and J. E. Stiglitz. 1992. Discouraging rivals: Managerial rent seeking and economic inefficiencies. Presented at CEPR Conference on Corporate Governance, Stanford University, May 1992.

Fama, E. 1980. Banking in the theory of finance. *Journal of Monetary Economics* 6:39–57.

Fang, X. 1993. Essays on the processes of economic transitions. Ph.D. dissertation. Stanford University.

Farrell, M. J. 1970. Some elementary selection processes in economics. *Review of Economic Studies* 37:305–319.

Farrell, M. J. 1987. Information and the Coase theorem. *Journal of Economic Perspectives* 1:113–129.

Farrell, M. J. 1988. Puzzles: Sylvia, ice cream and more. *Journal of Economic Perspectives* 2:175–182.

Foley, D. K. 1970. Economic equilibrium, with costly marketing. *Journal of Economic Theory* 2:280–284.

Gale, I., and J. E. Stiglitz. 1985. Futures markets are almost always informationally inefficient. Princeton University Financial Research Center Memorandum No. 57. February.

Gilbert, R. J., and D. M. G. Newbery. 1982. Preemptive patenting and the persistence of monopoly. *American Economic Review* 72:514–526.

Green, J., and N. Stokey. 1983. A comparison of tournaments and contracts. *Journal of Political Economy* 91:349–364.

Greenwald, B. C. 1986. Adverse selection in the labor market. *Review of Economic Studies* 53:325–347.

Greenwald, B., and J. E. Stiglitz. 1984. Informational imperfections in capital markets and macro-economic fluctuations. *American Economic Review* 74:194–199.

Greenwald, B., and J. E. Stiglitz. 1986. Externalities in economies with imperfect information and incomplete markets. *Quarterly Journal of Economics* 101:229–264.

Greenwald, B., and J. E. Stiglitz. 1987. Keynesian, new Keynesian and neoclassical economics. *Oxford Economic Papers* 39:119–133.

Greenwald, B., and J. E. Stiglitz. 1988. Pareto inefficiency of market economies: Search and efficiency wage models. *American Economic Association Papers and Proceedings* 78:351–355.

Greenwald, B., and J. E. Stiglitz. 1990a. Macroeconomic models with equity and credit rationing. In *Information, Capital Markets and Investments*, R. Glenn Hubbard (ed.). Chicago University Press, Chicago.

Greenwald, B., and J. E. Stiglitz. 1990b. Asymmetric information and the new theory of the firm. Financial constraints and risk behavior. *American Economic Review* 80:160–165.

Greenwald, B., and J. E. Stiglitz. 1992. Information, finance and markets: The architecture of allocative mechanisms. *Journal of Industrial and Corporate Change* 1:37–63.

Greenwald, B., and J. E. Stiglitz. 1993. Financial market imperfections and business cycles. *Quarterly Journal of Economics* 108:77–114.

Greenwald, B., J. E. Stiglitz, and A. Weiss. 1984. Informational imperfections in the capital markets and macro-economic fluctuations. *American Economic Review* 74:194–199.

Grossman, S. J. 1975. The existence of future markets, noisy rational expectations and informational externalities. Ph.D. dissertation. University of Chicago.

Grossman, S. J. 1976. On the efficiency of competitive stock markets where traders have diverse information. *Journal of Finance* 31:573–585.

Grossman, S. J. 1981a. The informational role of warranties and private disclosure about product quality. *Journal of Law and Economics* 24:461–484.

Grossman, S. J. 1981b. Nash equilibrium and the industrial organization of markets with large fixed costs. *Economica* 49:1149–1172.

Grossman, S. J., and O. Hart. 1980. Takeover bids, the free rider problem and the theory of the corporation. *Bell Journal of Economics* 11:42–64.

Grossman, S. J., and O. Hart. 1986. The costs and benefits of ownership: A theory of vertical and lateral integration. *Journal of Political Economy* 94:691–718.

Grossman, S. J., and O. D. Hart. 1988. One share–one vote and the market for corporate control. *Journal of Financial Economics* 20:175–202.

Grossman, S. J., and J. E. Stiglitz. 1976. Information and competitive price systems. *American Economic Review* 66:246–253.

Grossman, S. J., and J. E. Stiglitz. 1977. On value maximization and alternative objectives of the firm. *Journal of Finance* 32:389–402.

Grossman, S. J., and J. E. Stiglitz. 1980a. On the impossibility of informationally efficient markets. *American Economic Review* 70:393–408.

Grossman, S. J., and J. E. Stiglitz. 1980b. Stockholder unanimity in the making of production and financial decisions. *Quarterly Journal of Economics* 94:543–566.

Grossman, S. J., and J. E. Stiglitz. 1986. Information and competitive price systems. *American Economic Review* 66:246–253.

Hahn, F. 1966. Equilibrium dynamics with heterogeneous capital goods. *Quarterly Journal of Economics* 80:133–146.

Hahn, F. 1971. Equilibrium with transaction costs. *Econometrica* 39:417–400.

Hahn, R. W. 1989. Economic prescriptions for environmental problems: How the patient followed the doctor's orders. *Journal of Economic Perspectives* 3:98–114.

Hall, R. E. 1988. The relation between price and marginal cost in U.S. industry. *Journal of Political Economy* 96:921–947.

Hannan, M. T., and J. Freeman. 1977. The population ecology of organizations. *American Journal of Sociology* 82:929–964.

Hannaway, J. 1989. *Managing Managers: The Working of an Administrative System.* Oxford University Press, Oxford.

Hannaway, J. 1992. Higher order skills, job design, and incentives: An analysis and proposal. *American Educational Research Journal* 29:3–21.

Hannaway, J. 1993a. Decentralization in two school distributions: Challenging the standard paradigm. In *Decentralization and Education: Can We Fulfill the Promise?* J. Hannaway and M. Carnoy (eds.). Josey-Bass, San Francisco.

Hannaway, J. 1993b. Political pressure and decentralization in institutional organization: The case of school districts. *Sociology of Education* 66:147–163.

Hannaway, J., and Carnoy, M. 1993. *Decentralization and Education: Can We Fulfill the Promise?* Josey-Bass, San Francisco.

Hanusch, H. 1988. *Evolutionary Economics.* Cambridge University Press, Cambridge.

Harberger, A. C. 1954. Monopoly and resource allocation. *AEA Papers and Proceedings* 44:77–87.

Harris, C., and J. Vickers. 1987. Racing with uncertainty. *Review of Economic Studies* 54:1–21.

Hart, O. 1975. On the optimality of equilibrium when the market structure is incomplete. *Journal of Economic Theory* 11:418–443.

Hart, O., and B. Holmstrom. 1987. The theory of contracts. In *Advances in Economic Theory*, T. Bewley (ed.). Cambridge University Press, Cambridge, pp. 71–155.

Hayek, F. A. 1989. *The Fatal Conceit*. University of Chicago Press, Chicago.

Heilbroner, D. 1991. Reflections: Economic predictions. *New Yorker*, July 8.

Hellwig, M. 1977. A model of borrowing and lending with bankruptcy. *Econometrica* 45: 1876−1906.

Hirschman, A. O. 1970. *Exit, Voice, and Loyalty*. Harvard University Press, Cambridge.

Hirshleifer, J. 1971. The private and social value of information and the reward to incentive activity. *American Economic Review* 61:561−574.

Hirshleifer, J. 1977. Economics from a biological viewpoint. *Journal of Law and Economics* 20:1−52.

Hirshleifer, J., and J. Riley. 1979. The analytics of uncertainty and information: An expository survey. *Journal of Economic Literature* 17:1375−1421.

Hoff, K., A. Braverman, and J. E. Stiglitz. 1993. *The Theory of Rural Economic Organizations*. Oxford University Press, Oxford.

Holmstrom, B. 1982. Moral hazard in teams. *Bell Journal of Economics* 13:324−340.

Holmstrom, B., and P. Milgrom. 1987. Aggregation and linearity in the provision of intertemporal incentives. *Econometrica* 55:303−328.

Holmstrom, B., and P. Milgrom. 1991. Multitask principal-agent analyses: Incentive contracts, asset ownership, and job design. *Journal of Law, Economics and Organization* 7 (special issue): 24−52.

Jarrell, G. A., J. A. Brickley, and J. M. Netter. 1988. The market for corporate control: The empirical evidence since 1980. *Journal of Economic Perspectives* 2:49−68.

Jensen, M. 1986. Agency costs of free cash flow, corporate finance and takeovers. *American Economic Review* 76:323−329.

Jensen, M., and W. Meckling. 1976. Theory of the firm: Managerial behavior, agency costs and ownership structure. *Journal of Financial Economics* 3:305−360.

Jensen, M., and K. Murphy. 1990. Performance pay and top management incentives. *Journal of Political Economy* 98:225−264.

Jordan, J. 1977. Expectations equilibrium and informational efficiency for stochastic environments. *Journal of Economic Theory* 16:354−372.

Jordan, J. S. 1983. On the efficient markets hypothesis. *Econometrica* 51:1325−1343.

Keynes, J. M. 1936. *The General Theory of Employment, Interest and Money*. Macmillan, London.

Klein, B., and K. B. Leffler. 1981. The role of market forces in assuring contractual performance. *Journal of Political Economy* 89:615−641.

Knight, F. 1921. *Risk, Uncertainty and Profit*. Houghton Mifflin, Boston, 1921.

Kornai, J. 1980. *Economics of Shortage*. North Holland, Amsterdam.

Kornai, J. 1986. The soft budget constraint. *Kyklos* 39(1):3−30.

Kornai, J. 1990. The affinity between ownership forms and coordination mechanisms: The common experience of reforms in socialist countries. *Journal of Economic Perspectives* 4:131–147.

Krattenmaker, T., and S. Salop. 1986. Anti-competitive exclusion: Raising rivals' costs to gain power over price. *Yale Law Journal*, December.

Kreps, D. 1990. *A Course in Microeconomic Theory.* Princeton University Press, Princeton.

Kreuger, A. 1987. The political economy of the rent-seeking society. In *International Trade*, J. Bhagwati (ed.). Cambridge University Press, Cambridge.

Laffont, J. -J. 1989. *The Economics of Information and Uncertainty.* MIT Press, Cambridge.

Lange, O. 1967. *Essays on Economic Planning.* 2d ed. Asian Publishing House, Bombay.

Lazear, E. P., and S. Rosen. 1981. Rank-order tournaments as optimum labor contracts. *Journal of Political Economy* 89:841–864.

Leibenstein, H. 1966. Allocative efficiency and X-efficiency. *American Economic Review* 56: 392–415.

Lerner, A. P. 1944. *The Economics of Control.* Macmillan, New York.

Lewis, A. 1928. *Overhead Costs.* Holt & Rinehart, New York.

Lucas, R. E., Jr. 1972. Expectations and the neutrality of money. *Journal of Economic Theory* 4:103–124.

March, J. G., and H. Simon. 1958. *Organizations.* Wiley, New York.

Marris, R. K. 1964. *The Economic Theory of Managerial Capitalism.* Free Press, New York.

Marschak, J., and R. Radner. 1972. *Economic Theory of Teams.* Yale University Press, New Haven.

Mayer, C. 1989. Financial systems, corporate finance and economic development. CEPR. Mimeo.

Mayer, C. 1990. Financial systems, corporate finance, and economic development. In *Asymmetrical Information, Corporate Finance, and Investment*, R. G. Hubbard (ed.). University of Chicago Press, Chicago.

Maynard-Smith, J. 1976. Evolution and the theory of games. *American Scientist* 64:41–45.

Maynard-Smith, J. 1982. *Evolution and the Theory of Games.* Cambridge University Press, Cambridge.

McKelvey, W. 1982. *Organizational Systematics: Taxonomy, Evolution, and Classification.* University of California, Los Angeles.

McKinnon, R. 1991a. Financial control in the transition to a market economy from classical socialism. In *The Emergence of Market Economies in Eastern Europe*, C. Clague (ed.). Basil Blackwell, Oxford.

McKinnon, R. 1991b. *The Order of Economic Liberalization: Financial Control in the Transition to Market Economy.* Johns Hopkins University Press, Baltimore

McKinnon, R. 1992. Taxation, money, oil credit in a liberalizing socialist economy. *Journal of Economic Perspectives* 5:107–122.

Milgrom, P., and J. Roberts. 1988. An economic approach to influence activities and organizational responses. *American Journal of Sociology* 94 (July suppl.): S154–S179.

Milgrom, P., and J. Roberts. 1992. *Economics, Organization, and Management.* Prentice Hall, Englewood Cliffs, NJ.

Milgrom, P., and N. Stokey. 1982. Information, trade and common knowledge. *Journal of Economic Theory* 26:17–27.

Mirrlees, J. 1971. An exploration in the theory of optimum income taxation. *Review of Economic Studies* 38:175–208.

Mirrlees, J. 1975. The theory of moral hazard and unobservable behavior. Mimeo. Nuffield College, Oxford, 1975.

Morck, R., A. Shleifer, and R. W. Vishny. 1989. Alternative mechanisms for corporate control. *American Economic Review* 79:842–852.

Morck, R., A. Shleifer, and R. W. Vishny. 1990. Do managerial objectives drive bank acquisitions? *Journal of Finance* 45:31–48.

Mortensen, D. 1989. The persistence and indeterminacy of unemployment in search equilibrium. *Scandinavian Journal of Economics* 91:367–372.

Musgrave, R. 1959. *The Theory of Public Finance.* McGraw-Hill, New York.

Myers, S. 1977. Determinants of corporate borrowing. *Journal of Financial Economics* 4:147–175.

Myers, S., and N. Majluf. 1984. Corporate financing and investment decisions when firms have information that investors do not have. *Journal of Financial Economics* 13:187–221.

Nalebuff, B., and J. E. Stiglitz. 1983a. Prizes and incentives: Towards a general theory of compensation and competition. *Bell Journal of Economics* 14:21–43.

Nalebuff, B., and J. E. Stiglitz. 1983b. Information, competition and markets. *American Economic Review* 72:278–284.

Nelson, R. R., and S. G. Winter. 1974. Neoclassical vs. evolutionary theories of economic growth: Critique and prospectus. *Economic Journal* 84:886–905.

Nelson, R. R., and S. G. Winter. 1982. *An Evolutionary Theory of Economic Change.* Harvard University Press, Cambridge.

Newbery, D., and J. E. Stiglitz. 1981. *The Theory of Commodity Price Stabilization.* Oxford University Press, Oxford.

Newbery, D., and J. E. Stiglitz. 1982. The choice of techniques and the optimality of market equilibrium with rational expectations. *Journal of Political Economy* 90:223–246.

Newbery, D., and J. E. Stiglitz. 1983. Information, competition and markets. *Economic Review* 72:278–284.

Newbery, D., and J. E. Stiglitz. 1984. Pareto-inferior trade. *Review of Economic Studies* 51:1–13.

Newbery, D., and J. E. Stiglitz. 1987. Wage rigidity, implicit contracts, unemployment and economic efficiency. *Economic Journal* 97:416–430.

Pelikan, P. 1982. *An Evolutionary Theory of Economic Change.* Harvard University Press, Cambridge.

Pelikan, P. 1989. Evolution, economic competence, and the market for corporate control. *Journal of Economic Behavior and Organization* 12:279–303.

Persky, J. 1989. Adam Smith's invisible hands. *Journal of Economic Perspectives* 3:195–201.

Persky, J. 1991. Lange and von Mises, large-scale enterprises, and the economic case for socialism: Retrospectives. *Journal of Economic Perspectives* 5:229–236.

Prescott, E. C., and R. M. Townsend. 1984. Pareto optima and competitive equilibria with adverse selection and moral hazard. *Econometrica* 52:21–45.

Radner, R. 1968. Competitive equilibrium under uncertainty. *Econometrica* 36:31–58.

Radner, R. 1972. Existence of equilibrium of plans, prices, and price expectations in a sequence of markets. *Econometrica* 40:289–303.

Radner, R. 1974. A note on unanimity of stockholders' preferences among alternative production plans: A reformulation of the Ekern-Wilson model. *Bell Journal of Economics* 5:181–184.

Radner, R. 1979. Rational expectations equilibrium: Generic existence and the information revealed by prices. *Econometrica* 47:655–678.

Radner, R., and J. E. Stiglitz. 1984. Nonconcavity in the value of information. In *Bayesian Models in Economic Theory*, vol. 5, M. Boyer and R. Kilstrom (eds.). Elsevier, Amsterdam, pp. 33–52.

Ramsey, F. 1927. A contribution to the theory of taxation. *Economic Journal* 37:47–61.

Rey, P., and J. E. Stiglitz. 1992. Short-term contracts as monitoring devices. Stanford University mimeo.

Robinson, J. 1933. *The Economics of Imperfect Competition.* Macmillan, London.

Romer, C. P. 1986. Is the stabilization of the postwar economy a figment of the data? *American Economic Review* 76:314–334.

Ross, S. 1973. The economic theory of agency: The principal's problem. *American Economic Review* 63:134–139.

Rothschild, M., and J. E. Stiglitz. 1975. Existence and equilibrium in markets with imperfect information. Paper presented to World Congress of the Econometric Society, Toronto.

Rothschild, M., and J. E. Stiglitz. 1976. Equilibrium in competitive insurance markets. *Quarterly Journal of Economics* 90:629–649.

Rotter, C. 1988. World War I and the postwar depression: A reinterpretation based on alternative estimates of GNP. *Journal of Monetary Economics* 22:91–115.

Sah, R. 1991. Fallibility in human organizations and political systems. *Journal of Economic Perspectives* 5:67–88.

Sah, R., and J. E. Stiglitz. 1985a. Human fallibility and economic organization. *American Economic Review* 75:292–297.

Sah, R., and J. E. Stiglitz. 1985b. Perpetuation and self-reproduction of organizations: The selection and performance of managers. Presented at World Congress of Econometric Society, Cambridge, August.

Sah, R., and J. E. Stiglitz. 1986. The architecture of economic systems: Hierarchies and polyarchies. *American Economic Review* 76:716–727.

Sah, R., and J. E. Stiglitz. 1987. The invariance of market innovation to the number of firms. *Rand Journal of Economics* 18:98–108.

Sah, R., and J. E. Stiglitz. 1988a. Committees, hierarchies and polyarchies. *Economic Journal* 98:451–470.

Sah, R., and J. E. Stiglitz. 1988b. Qualitative properties of profit-maximizing K-out-of-N systems subject to two kinds of failure. *IEEE Transactions on Reliability* 37:515–520.

Sah, R., and J. E. Stiglitz. 1991. Quality of managers in centralized versus decentralized economic systems. *Quarterly Journal of Economics* 106.289–296

Salop, S. 1976. Information and monopolistic competition. *American Economic Review* 66: 240–245.

Salop, S. 1977. The noisy monopolist: Imperfect information, price dispersion and price discrimination. *Review of Economic Studies* 44:393–406.

Salop, S. C. 1979a. Strategic entry deterrence. *American Economic Review* 69:335–338.

Salop, S. C. 1979b. Monopolistic competition with outside goods. *Bell Journal of Economics* 10:141–156.

Salop, S., and D. Scheffman. 1983. Raising rivals' costs. *American Economic Review* 73:267–271.

Salop, S., and J. E. Stiglitz. 1977. Bargains and ripoffs: A model of monopolistically competitive price dispersions. *Review of Economic Studies* 44:493–510.

Salop, S., and J. E. Stiglitz. 1982. The theory of sales: A simple model of equilibrium price dispersion with identical agents. *American Economic Review* 72:1121–1130.

Salop, S., and J. E. Stiglitz. 1987. Information, welfare and product diversity. In *Arrow and the Foundations of the Theory of Economic Policy*, G. Feiwel (ed.). Macmillan, London, pp. 328–340.

Samuelson, P. 1947. *Foundations of Economic Analysis*. Harvard. University Press, Cambridge.

Samuelson, P. 1965. A theory of induced innovation along Kennedy-Weizsaecker lines. *Review of Economics and Statistics* 47:160–173.

Samuelson, P. 1967. Indeterminacy of development in a heterogeneous capital model with constant saving propensity. In *Essays on the Theory of Optimal Economic Growth*, K. Shell (ed.). MIT Press, Cambridge.

Sappington, D., and J. E. Stiglitz. 1987a. Information and regulation. In *Public Regulation*, E. Bailey (ed.). MIT Press, Cambridge, pp. 3–43.

Sappington, D., and J. E. Stiglitz. 1987b. Privatization, information and incentives. *Journal of Policy Analysis and Management* 6:567–582.

Shavell, S. 1979. On moral hazard and insurance. *Quarterly Journal of Economics* 93:541–562.

Shleifer, A., and R. Vishny. 1986. Large shareholders and corporate control. *Journal of Political Economy* 94:461–488.

Shleifer, A., and R. Vishny. 1989. Management entrenchment: The cost of manager-specific investments. *Journal of Financial Economics* 25:123–139.

Schmalensee, R. 1982. Product differentiation advantages of pioneering brands. *American Economic Review* 72:349–365.

Schmalensee, R., and J. Willig. 1983. *Handbook of Industrial Organization*. North-Holland, Amsterdam.

Schumpeter, J. 1942. *Socialism, Capitalism, and Democracy*. Harper, New York.

Schumpeter, J. [1946] 1986. *The Dynamics of Market Economies*. McGraw-Hill, New York.

Scitovsky, T. 1950. Ignorance as a source of oligopoly power. *American Economic Review* 40:48–53.

Shapiro, C. 1983. Premiums for high quality products as returns to reputations. *Quarterly Journal of Economics* 98:659–679.

Shapiro, C., and J. E. Stiglitz. 1984. Equilibrium unemployment as a worker discipline device. *American Economic Review* 74:433–444.

Shapiro, C., and J. E. Stiglitz. 1985a. Equilibrium unemployment as a worker discipline device: Reply. *American Economic Review* 75(4):892–893.

Shapiro, C., and J. E. Stiglitz. 1985b. Can unemployment be involuntary? *American Economic Review* 75(5):1215–1217.

Shell, K., M. Sidrauski, and J. E. Stiglitz. 1969. Capital gains, income, and savings. *Review of Economic Studies* 36:15–26.

Shell, K., and J. E. Stiglitz. 1967. Allocation of investment in a dynamic economy. *Quarterly Journal of Economics* 81:592–609.

Shoven, J., and L. Bagwell. 1989. Cash distributions to shareholders. *Journal of Economic Perspectives* 3:129–140.

Simon, H. A. 1991. Organizations and markets. *Journal of Economic Perspectives* 5:25–44.

Solow, R. 1957. Technical change and the aggregate production function. *Review of Economics and Statistics* 39:312–320.

Solow, R. M., and P. A. Samuelson. 1953. Balanced growth under constant returns to scale. *Econometrica* 21:412–424.

Solow, R. M., and P. A. Samuelson. 1956. A compete capital model involving heterogeneous capital goods. *Quarterly Journal of Economics* 70:537–562.

Spence, A. M. 1976. Production selection, fixed costs, and monopolistic competition. *Review of Economic Studies* 43:217–235.

Spence, A. M. 1977. Entry, capacity, investment and oligopolistic pricing. *Bell Journal of Economics* 8:534–544.

Starrett, D. 1972. Fundamental nonconvexities in the theory of externalities. *Journal of Economic Theory* 4:180–199.

Starrett, D. 1988. *Foundations of Public Economics*. Cambridge University Press, Cambridge.

Stigler, G. 1971. Theory of regulation. *Bell Journal of Economics* 2:3–21.

Stiglitz, J. E. 1969. Theory of innovation: Discussion. *AEA Papers and Proceedings* 59:46–49.

Stiglitz, J. E. 1971. Perfect and imperfect capital markets. Presented at the Meetings of the Econometric Society, New Orleans.

Stiglitz, J. E. 1972a. Some aspects of the pure theory of corporate finance: Bankruptcies and take-overs. *Bell Journal of Economics* 3:458–482.

Stiglitz, J. E. 1972b. On the optimality of the stock market allocation of investment. *Quarterly Journal of Economics* 86:25–60. (Shortened version of a paper presented at the Far Eastern Meetings of the Econometric Society, June 1970. Tokyo.)

Stiglitz, J. E. 1973a. Recurrence of techniques in a dynamic economy. In *Models of Economic Growth*, J. Mirrlees (ed.). Macmillan, London, pp. 138–161.

Stiglitz, J. E. 1973b. Taxation, corporate financial policy and the cost of capital. *Journal of Public Economics* 2:1–34.

Stiglitz, J. E. 1974. Incentives and risk sharing in sharecropping. *Review of Economic Studies* 41:219–255.

Stiglitz, J. E. 1975a. Information and economic analysis. In *Current Economic Problems*, Parkin and Nobay (eds.). Cambridge University Press, Cambridge, pp. 27–52.

Stiglitz, J. E. 1975b. Incentives, risk and information: Notes towards a theory of hierarchy. *Bell journal of Economics* 6:552–579.

Stiglitz, J. E. 1975c. The theory of screening, education and the distribution of income. *American Economic Review* 65:283–300.

Stiglitz, J. E. 1977a. Theory of local public goods. In *The Economics of Public Services*, M. S. Feldstein and R. P. Inman (eds.). Macmillan, London, pp. 274–333.

Stiglitz, J. E. 1977b. Monopoly, nonlinear pricing and imperfect information: The insurance market. *Review of Economic Studies* 44:407–430.

Stiglitz, J. E. 1979. On search and equilibrium price distributions. In *Economics and Human Welfare: Essays in Honor of Tibor Scitovsky*, M. Boskin (ed.). Academic Press, San Diego, pp. 203–216.

Stiglitz, J. E. 1981a. Potential competition may reduce welfare. *American Economic Review* 71:184–189.

Stiglitz, J. E. 1981b. Ownership, control and efficient markets: Some paradoxes in the theory of capital markets. *In Economic Regulation: Essays in Honor of James R. Nelson*, K. D. Boyer and W. G. Shepherd (eds.). University of Michigan Press, Ann Arbor, pp. 311–341.

Stiglitz, J. E. 1982a. The inefficiency of the stock market equilibrium. *Review of Economic Studies* 49:241–261.

Stiglitz, J. E. 1982b. Self-selection and Pareto efficient taxation. *Journal of Public Economics* 17:213–240.

Stiglitz, J. E. 1982c. Utilitarianism and horizontal equity: The case for random taxation. *Journal of Public Economics* 18:1–33.

Stiglitz, J. E. 1982d. Ownership, control and efficient markets: Some paradoxes in the theory of capital markets. In *Economic Regulation: Essays in Honor of James R. Nelson*, K. D. Boyer and W. G. Shepherd (eds.), University of Michigan Press, Ann Arbor, pp. 1121–1130.

Stiglitz, J. E. 1982e. Information and capital markets. In *Financial Economics: Essays in Honor of Paul Cootner*, William F. Sharpe and Cathryn Cootner (eds.). Prentice Hall, Englewood Cliffs, NJ, pp. 118–158.

Stiglitz, J. 1983a. Public goods in open economies with heterogeneous individuals. In *Locational Analysis of Public Facilities*, J. F. Thisse and H. G. Zoller (eds.). North-Holland, Amsterdam, pp. 55–78.

Stiglitz, J. E. 1983b. The theory of local public goods twenty-five years after Tiebout: A perspective. In *Local Provision of Public Services: The Tiebout Model after Twenty-five Years*, G. R. Zodrow (ed.). Academic Press, San Diego, pp. 17–53.

Stiglitz, J. E. 1985a. Economics of information and the theory of economic development. *Revista de Econometrica* 5:5–32.

Stiglitz, J. E. 1985b. Credit markets and the control of capital. *Journal of Credit and Banking* 17:133–152.

Stiglitz, J. E. 1985c. Information and economic analysis: A perspective. *Economic Journal* Suppl., 95:21–41.

Stiglitz, J. E. 1986a. Towards a more general theory of monopolistic competition. In *Prices, Competition and Equilibrium*, M. Peston and R. Quandt (eds.). Allan, Oxford, pp. 22–69.

Stiglitz, J. E. 1986b. Theory of competition, incentives and risk. In *New Developments in the Theory of Market Structure*, J. E. Stiglitz and F. Mathewson (eds.). MIT Press, Cambridge, pp. 399–449.

Stiglitz, J. E. 1987a. Pareto efficient and optimal taxation and the new new welfare economics. In *Handbook on Public Economics*, A. Auerbach and M. Feldstein (eds.). Elsevier Science Publishers/North-Holland, Amsterdam, pp. 991–1042.

Stiglitz, J. E. 1987b. The causes and consequences of the dependence of quality on price. *Journal of Economic Literature* 25:1–48.

Stiglitz, J. E. 1987c. Competition and the number of firms in a market: Are duopolies more competitive than atomistic markets? *Journal of Political Economy* 95:1041–1061.

Stiglitz, J. E. 1987d. On the microeconomics of technical progress. In *Technology Generation in Latin American Manufacturing Industries*, Jorge M. Katz (ed.). Macmillan, London, pp. 56–77.

Stiglitz, J. E. 1987e. Design of labor contracts: Economics of incentives and risk sharing. *Incentives, Cooperation and Risk Sharing*, M. Nalbathian (ed.). Rowman and Allanheld, Totawa, NJ.

Stiglitz, J. E. 1987f. Theory of competition, incentives and risk. In *New Developments in The Theory of Market Structure*, J. E. Stiglitz and F. Mathewson (eds.). Macmillan, New York.

Stiglitz, J. E. 1987g. Technological change, sunk costs, and competition. *Brookings Papers on Economic Activity* 3.

Stiglitz, J. E. 1987h. Sharecropping. In *The New Palgrave: A Dictionary of Economics*. Macmillan, London.

Stiglitz, J. E. 1988a. Economic organization, information, and development. In *Handbook of Development Economics*, H. Chenery and T. N. Srinivasan (eds.). Elsevier Science Publishers, Amsterdam, pp. 94–160.

Stiglitz, J. E. 1988b. *Economics of the Public Sector*. 2d ed. Norton, New York.

Stiglitz, J. E. 1988c. Why financial structure matters. *Journal of Economic Perspectives* 2:121–126.

Stiglitz, J. E. 1988d. Money, credit and business fluctuations. *Economic Record* (December): 307–322.

Stiglitz, J. E. 1989a. Principal and agent. In *The New Palgrave: Allocation, Information and Markets*, J. Eatwell, M. Milgate, and P. Newman (eds.). Macmillan, London, pp. 241–253.

Stiglitz, J. E. 1989b. Imperfect information in the product market. In *Handbook of Industrial Organization*, vol. 1. Elsevier Science Publishers, Amsterdam, pp. 769–847.

Stiglitz, J. E. 1989c. Using tax policy to curb speculative short-term trading. *Journal of Financial Services Research* 3:101–115.

Stiglitz, J. E. 1989d. Incentives, information and organizational design. *Empirica* 16:3–29.

Stiglitz, J. E. 1989e. Some aspects of a general theory of economic organization. Lecture presented at the Ninth Latin American Meeting of the Econometric Society, Santiago, Chile, August.

Stiglitz, J. E. 1989f. On the economic role of the state. In *The Economic Role of the State*, A. Heertje (ed.). Basil Blackwell, Oxford, pp. 9–85.

Stiglitz, J. E. 1990a. Remarks on the occasion of the presentation of the UAP Prize. In *Journees Scientifiques & Prix UAP, 1988, 1989, 1990*, vol. 2. Conseil Scientifique de l'UAP, December, pp. 23–32.

Stiglitz, J. E. 1990b. Some retrospective views on growth theory presented on the occasion of the celebration of Robert Solow's 65th birthday. In *Growth/Productivity/Unemployment: Essays to Celebrate Bob Solow's Birthday*, Peter Diamond (ed.). MIT Press, Cambridge, pp. 50–68.

Stiglitz, J. E. 1990c. Peer monitoring and credit markets. *World Bank Editorial Review* 4:351–366.

Stiglitz, J. E. 1991a. Symposium on organizations and economics. *Journal of Economic Perspectives* 5:15–24.

Stiglitz, J. E. 1991b. Some theoretical aspects of the privatization: Applications to Eastern Europe. *Rivista di Politica Economica* (December): 179–204.

Stiglitz, J. E. 1991c. The economic role of the state: Efficiency and effectiveness. *Efficiency and Effectiveness*, T. P. Hardiman and M. Mulreany (eds.). Institute of Public Administration, Dublin, pp. 37–59.

Stiglitz, J. E. 1992a. Contract theory and macroeconomic fluctuations. *Nobel Symposium (No. 77) on Contract Economics*, L. Werin and H. Wijkander (eds.). Basil Blackwell, Oxford.

Stiglitz, J. E. 1992b. Capital markets and economic fluctuations in capitalist economies. *European Economic Review* 36:269–306.

Stiglitz, J. E. 1992c. Notes on evolutionary economics: Imperfect capital markets, organizational design, and long-run efficiency. Paper presented at Osaka University International Symposium on "Economic Analysis of Japanese Firms and Markets: A New Microeconomic Paradigm." Osaka, Japan, November 9.

Stiglitz, J. E. 1992d. The meanings of competition in economic analysis. *Rivista internazionale di Scienze sociali* 2 (April): 191–212.

Stiglitz, J. E. 1992e. The design of financial systems for the newly emerging democracies of Eastern Europe. In *The Emergence of Market Economies in Eastern Europe*, C. Clague and G. C. Rausser (eds.). Basil Blackwell, Oxford, pp. 161–184.

Stiglitz, J. E. 1993a. Incentives, organizational structures, and contractual choice in the reform of socialist agriculture. Presented at World Bank conference, "Agricultural Reform in Eastern Europe and the USSR." Budapest, August 1990, forthcoming in *Proceedings*.

Stiglitz, J. E. 1993b. *Welfare Economics with Imperfect and Asymmetric Information*. Lindahl Lectures presented at Uppsala. Oxford University Press, Oxford.

Stiglitz, J. E. 1993c. *Information and Economic Analysis*. Oxford University Press, Oxford.

Stiglitz, J. E. 1994. The role of the state in financial markets. *Proceedings of the World Bank Annual Conference on Development Economics, 1993*, pp. 19–52.

Stiglitz, J. E., and P. Dasgupta. 1971. Differential taxation, public goods, and economic efficiency. *Review of Economic Studies* 38:151–174.

Stiglitz, J. E., and A. Weiss. 1981. Credit rationing in markets with imperfect information. *American Economic Review* 71:393–410.

Stiglitz, J. E., and A. Weiss. 1983. Incentive effects of termination: Applications to the credit and labor markets. *American Economic Review* 73:912–927.

Stiglitz, J. E., and A. Weiss. 1990. Banks as social accountants and screening devices and the general theory of credit rationing. *Greek Economic Review* suppl., 12:85–118.

Summers, L., and V. Summers. 1989. When financial markets work too well: A cautious case for the securities transaction tax. *Journal of Financial Services* 3:261–286.

Taylor, F. 1948. The guidance of production in a socialist state. In *On the Economic Theory of Socialism*, O. Lange and F. Taylor (eds.). University of Minnesota Press, Minneapolis.

Tirole, J. 1982. On the possibility of speculation under rational expectations. *Econometrica* 50:1163–1181.

Wade, R. 1990. *Governing the Market: Economic Theory and the Role of Government in East Asian Industrialization*. Princeton University Press, Princeton.

Weitzman, M. 1974. Prices vs. Quantities. *Review of Economic Studies* 41:477–491.

Weitzman, M. L. 1980. The "ratchet principle" and performance incentives. *Bell Journal of Economics* 11:302–308.

Willig, R. 1992. Anti-monopoly policies and institutions. In *The Emergence of Market Economies in Eastern Europe*, C. Clague and G. Rausser (eds.). Basil Blackwell, Oxford, pp. 187–196.

Wilson, C. A. 1977. A model of insurance market with incomplete information. *Journal of Economic Theory* 16:167–207.

Wilson, R. 1977. A bidding model of "perfect" competition. *Review of Economic Studies* 44:511−518.

Wolinsky, A. 1986. True monopolistic competition as a result of imperfect information. *Quarterly Journal of Economics* 101:493−512.

Winter, S. G. 1971. Satisficing, selection, and the innovating remnant. *Quarterly Journal of Economics* 85:237−261.

Winter, S. G. 1975. Optimization and evolution in the theory of the firm. In *Adaptive Economic Models*, R. H. Day and T. Graves (eds.). Academic Press, San Diego.

Young, A. 1928. Increasing returns and economic progress. *Economic Journal* 38:527−546.

Index